Prevention and Intervention in Childhood and Adolescence 3

Special Research Unit 227 - Prevention and Intervention in Childhood and Adolescence

An interdisciplinary project of the University of Bielefeld

conducted by *Prof. Dr. Günter Albrecht, Prof. Dr. Peter-Alexis Albrecht, Prof. Dr. Otto Backes, Prof. Dr. Michael Brambring, Prof. Dr. Klaus Hurrelmann, Prof. Dr. Franz-Xaver Kaufmann, Prof. Dr. Friedrich Lösel, Prof. Dr. Hans-Uwe Otto, Prof. Dr. Helmut Skowronek*

Crime Prevention and Intervention

Legal and Ethical Problems

Edited by
Peter-Alexis Albrecht, Otto Backes

W DE G

Walter de Gruyter · Berlin · New York 1989

Peter-Alexis Albrecht
Professor of Law, University of Bielefeld

Otto Backes
Professor of Law, University of Bielefeld

Library of Congress Cataloging in Publication Data

Crime preventation and intervention.
(Prevention and intervention in childhood and adolescence ; 3)
Bibliography: p.
1. Crime prevention. 2. Juvenile delinquency--Prevention. I. Albrecht, Peter-Alexis. II. Backes, Otto, 1936– . III. Series.
HV7431.C723 1989 364.3'6 88-31093
ISBN 0-89925-497-7 (U.S.)

Deutsche Bibliothek in Cataloging in Publication Data

Crime prevention and intervention : legal and eth. problems / ed. by Peter-Alexis Albrecht ; Otto Backes. – Berlin ; New York : de Gruyter, 1988
(Preventation and intervention in childhood and adolescence ; 3)
ISBN 3-11-011741-X
NE: Albrecht, Peter-Alexis [Hrsg.]; GT

Printing: Gerike GmbH, Berlin. – Binding: Lüderitz & Bauer, Berlin. – Cover Design: Hansbernd Lindemann, Berlin.

Contents

Part III
Inquiry into the Ethical Aspects of Prevention

Contributors

Albrecht, Günter, Dr. phil., Professor of Sociology, Department of Sociology,
University of Bielefeld, Universitätsstr. 25,
4800 Bielefeld, West Germany

Albrecht, Peter–Alexis, Dr. iur., Professor of Penal Law, Department of Law,
University of Bielefeld, Universitätsstr. 25,
4800 Bielefeld, West Germany

Backes, Otto, Dr. iur., Professor of Penal Law, Department of Law,
University of Bielefeld, Universitätsstr. 25,
4800 Bielefeld, West Germany

Bettmer, Franz, Dipl. Soz., Special Research Unit 227, Prevention and Intervention,
University of Bielefeld, Universitätsstr. 25,
4800 Bielefeld, West Germany

Büllesbach, Alfred, Dr. iur., Dipl. sc. pol., Landesbeauftragter für den Datenschutz
des Bundeslandes Freie Hansestadt Bremen, Arndtstr. 1,
2850 Bremerhaven, West Germany

Böllert, Karin, Dipl. Päd., Special Research Unit 227, Prevention and Intervention,
University of Bielefeld, Universitätsstr. 25,
4800 Bielefeld, West Germany

Denninger, Erhard, Dr. iur., Professor of Constitutional and Administrative Law,
Department of Law, University of Frankfurt, Senckenberganlage 31
6000 Frankfurt 1, West Germany

Engel, Uwe, Dr. phil., Special Research Unit 227, Prevention and Intervention,
University of Bielefeld, Universitätsstr. 25,
4800 Bielefeld, West Germany

Galaway, Burt, Ph.D., Professor, School of Social Work, University of Minnesota,
400 Ford Hall, 224 Church Street S.E., Minneapolis,
Minn. 55455, USA

Grimm, Dieter, Dr. iur., L.L.M.(Harvard), Justice of the Federal Constitutional Court,
Professor of Constitutional Law, Department of Law,
University of Bielefeld, Universitätsstr. 25
4800 Bielefeld, West Germany

Grönfors, Martti, Dr., Department of General Jurisprudential Studies,
Helsinki University, Lastenkodinkatu 2 F 3,
00100 Helsinki, Finland

Josef, Norma C., M.D., Department of Psychiatry and Lafayette Clinic,
Wayne State University, Detroit,
Mich. 48202, USA

Herbort, Ursula, Dipl. Soz., Special Research Unit 227, Prevention and Intervention,
University of Bielefeld, Universitätsstr. 25,
4800 Bielefeld, West Germany

Hurrelmann, Klaus, Dr. sc. pol., Professor of Sociology and Education, Department of Education,
University of Bielefeld, Universitätsstr. 25,
4800 Bielefeld, West Germany

Karstedt–Henke, Susanne, Dr. soz. wiss., Special Research Unit 227, Prevention and Intervention
University of Bielefeld, Universitätsstr. 25,
4800 Bielefeld, West Germany

Kinkel, R.John, Ph.D., Department of Sociology and Adjunct Graduate Faculty,
Department of Management, Wayne State University,
Detroit, Mich. 48202, USA

Mathiesen, Thomas, Dr., Professor of Sociology of Law, Department of Sociology of Law,
University of Oslo, St. Olavgst. 29,
0166 Oslo 1, Norway

Messmer, Heinz, Dipl. Soz., Special Research Unit 227, Prevention and Intervention,
University of Bielefeld, Universitätsstr. 25,
4800 Bielefeld, West Germany

Otto, Hans–Uwe, Dr. soz. wiss., Professor of Social Work and Welfare Administration,
Department of Education, University of Bielefeld, Universitätsstr. 25,
4800 Bielefeld, West Germany

Polk, Kenneth, Ph.D., Professor, Department of Criminology, University of Melbourne,
Parkville Victoria 3052, Australia

Rzepka, Dorothea, Department of Law, University of Bielefeld, Universitätsstr. 25,
4800 Bielefeld, West Germany

Schumann, Karl. F., Dr. phil., Professor of Criminology, Department of Law,
University of Bremen, Bibliothekstr.
2800 Bremen 1, West Germany

Voss, Silvia, Department of Law, University of Bielefeld, Universitätsstr. 25,
4800 Bielefeld, West Germany

Introduction

The Special Research Unit 227 (Prevention and Intervention in Childhood and Adolescence, SFB 227) held its third international symposium between the 14th and 16th of October, 1987 at the University of Bielefeld (West Germany). The papers in this volume present the scientific discussion on the subject of the symposium: legal and ethical problems of prevention and intervention, with particular reference to adolescence. At this point we want to express our thanks to the German Research Association (Deutsche Forschungsgemeinschaft) which is funding the SFB 227 and thus has enabled us to go on this interdisciplinary excursion with international participation to the largely unexplored fields of prevention and intervention.

Prevention and intervention necessarily represent an intrusion into the social world of the clients. The transition from postoperative problem intervention to the preventive control of causes shifts the theoretical and practical focus from a directed control of the manifest problem case to an anticipatory control of clients who only have potential problems. Prevention has to work with assumptions about probability, whereas postoperative intervention is used to proceeding from secure basic principles for action. It thus introduces elements of uncertainty into public social activity that give rise to ethical, legal, and normative problems.
The basic problem contained in this uncertainty, which links up with any preshift of public intervention into the field of prevention, lies in the attendant danger of an uncontrolled diffusion of state control over societal processes and behavior.
The symposium addressed the various dimensions of this problem, and paid particular attention to the following aspects:

1. Can the legal system provide the means for a rational limitation of practical prevention?
2. Are the different rationalities applied by the clients, the administration, the legal system and last but not least the research community compatible when it comes to the implementation of preventive programs?
3. To what extent must research on prevention and intervention take into account ethical and normative limitations?
4. What is the relation between theoretical concepts of prevention guided by sociological and psychological concepts of social problems and their practical implementation in administrative settings?

In the present volume, these questions are dealt with in three sections: A first, theoretical section (I) discusses the legal basic elements of prevention and intervention. A second, empirical section (II) discusses various programs in West German and international practice. A third section (III) addresses the ethical problems.

Part I.
The Foundations of Prevention and Intervention in Law and Criminal Justice Policy

A legal consideration of preventive social activity must lead to a – to some extent fundamental – discussion of the structure and regulatory role of the law in the modern social welfare state.
Preventive activity is generally an expression of a much higher level of societal planning than that represented by a purely reactive intervention in a given social problem. Prevention represents and also promotes an extension of the public involvement in the living conditions of the citizen, and thereby confronts the law with the task of developing independent parameters to evaluate the changes this creates in the basic principles of the relationship between the citizen and the state.

From a constitutional perspective, *Dieter Grimm* describes the expansion and reorientation of preventive government activity, that, in trying to avoid single threats to freedom, threatens to limit the freedom of the social order in general as well as democratic and constitutional guarantees. Prevention – in this way becoming a problem of constitutional law – is viewed from the perspective of its historical development; changes in goals, and the range and intensity of preventive government activity are analyzed as a function of the change in the role of the state and scientific and technological progress. Grimm does not consider the question of whether the state is authorized to apply preventive measures as being problematic; the problem is only for what purpose, to what extent, and under what preconditions should the state be allowed to intervene. Linked to this problem, he sketches – on the basis of the existing stock of legal principles – the constitutional frameworks that permit a control of preventive government activity by applying the principle of just proportion to prevention as a protection of liberty and – correspondingly – as an interference with liberty.

Erhard Denninger also deals with the change in the substance of state activity in his article. He characterizes this as a shift in emphasis from a system of legal security to a system of security of legally protected interests (= prevention). He uses these two guiding principles to undertake an inventory of the earlier and current status of the law and the state (bourgeois-liberal constitutional state as a legal security state versus democratic social state as a "security of the objects of legal protection state" = prevention state). According to Denninger, the majority of West German doctrine of constitutional law has dogmatically paid absolutely none or not enough attention to the problems involved in the reaccentuation within the idea of law. He offers no pat solution for the problem of the conflicting goals of a "security of the objects of legal protection state" (provision for existence, legal security, risk provision, and social justice), but considers that the democratic legislator is required to overcome the lack of "universal" laws; "universal" in the sense that they apply to all persons and to all persons equally and in the sense that there is a clear allocation of responsibility for the various duties of a preventive state.

Peter-Alexis Albrecht and *Otto Backes* use an application of criminal law and the law of criminal procedure to illustrate these constitutional approaches.
Against the background of a change in the function of the state and a subsequent extension of control claimed by the criminal law to the resolution of systemic conflicts, *Albrecht* investigates the question of the function of prevention in the criminal justice system. He uses concrete preventive phenomena in three subsystems of the criminal justice system, the police, criminal courts, and the prison system, to analyze the change in the paradigm of social control.
On the system level, he notes a reversal of the legitimizing basis of the regulatory system of criminal law, namely, from an orientation toward constraint and reconciliation to a preventive and planning orientation. On the organization level of the criminal justice system this produces, according to Albrecht, a problematic increase in instrumental efficiency at the expense of guarantees of constitutional rights. On the action level, the implementation of preventive strategies leads to questionable efforts at harmonization and, as a consequence of this, a clandestine loss of autonomy for the clients.
Albrecht contrasts the noticeable trend toward a preventive optimization of control with the activation of traditional constitutional lines of defence.

Backes also sees prevention as a threat to constitutional rights in his conclusion. He clarifies this position with two examples of criminal proceedings that initially appear to indicate opposing developments but then share a covert detachment of criminal justice policy from legislative acts and apportionments of competence through the appeal for prevention: the prosecutor's practice of dismissal in preliminary proceedings and the practice of police intervention in the field of the preventive control of crime; here the procurement and processing of information. Backes notes, on the one hand, an increase in the power and competences of the police, on the other hand, a turning away from legally regulated, precise, (interventional) preconditions in favor of flexible, more easily managed alternatives. This development can be seen in both fields: in the prosecutor's office through a modification of criminal law by generalizing internal directives; in the police through the abolishment of the preconditions for intervention of "concrete danger" or "suspicion of crime" in a new police law that is being negotiated between the West German states. Like Denninger, Backes assigns the responsibility for preventive concepts – in this case, those of criminal justice policy – to the legislator.

Part II.
The Evaluation of Institutional Approaches to Crime Prevention

The concrete prevention programs reported in the second section are on the one hand linked to the theoretical approaches sketched in section I. On the other hand, they attempt to indicate ways of rationally limiting preventive state activity. The clearest characteristic of these programs is experimentation, muddling through. This appears to guarantee that the "total prevention state" has yet to become a perfected reality and is more a vision of the future – though a threatening one.

The contributions from *Burt Galaway*, *Martti Grönfors*, and *Franz Bettmer et al.* share an interest in the evaluation of victim-offender mediation programs.
Burt Galaway presents the concept and experiences of a victim-offender reconciliation or mediation project (VORP) in the USA. This has been operating in Minneapolis-St. Paul, Minnesota since 1985, and primarily serves juvenile burglars and their victims. Like other American projects, the Minneapolis-St. Paul program practices a face-to-face meeting between the victim and the offender in the presence of a mediator to discuss the victimization/offence and to prepare a mutually acceptable plan for the offender to make redress to the victim. After two years of experience, Galaway judges the concept to be feasible. He points out that the Minneapolis-St. Paul project provides a form of intervention with juvenile offenders which is logically related to the offence, provides direct accountability to victims, offers a specific and concrete way for offenders to make amends, and results in active offender participation in their own programs. According to Galaway the issues that should be addressed in future program development include decreasing rather than increasing state intrusiveness, responding to offenders who are denied an opportunity to participate because of victim decisions, specifying goals and outcome measures for the projects, and clarifying the theoretical rationale for these projects as part of juvenile and criminal rather than civil justice systems.

The mediation project reported by *Martti Grönfors* was started in 1984 as an alternative to the official system in the Finnish city of Vantaa. Grönfors presents general basic principles that work out the opportunities but also the limitations of a successful mediation and reconciliation. These are developed from the initially tentative results of a qualitative, processual analysis of interviews and documents/files during a 2-year experimental phase. He does not select the concrete result of the mediation meeting compared to the decision that could be expected from the official system as a measure for a successful mediation or – as he expresses it – a just mediation. His research interest focuses on the various cases examined as a process, looking for the significant points of interest in each case. According to this, the amount of satisfaction felt by the participants after a successful mediation session seems to make the system more "just" than the official one. At present, Grönfors considers the success of the mediation experiments still limited to individual cases, in which people's conflicts were transfered back to them. In his opinion, the idea of applying mediation as an alternative to official proceedings in criminal cases has been unjustly ignored. Realistically, he shows the dangers of an uncritical expansion of mediation, and of the co-option into the official system.

The paper from *Franz Bettmer*, *Heinz Messmer*, and *Hans-Uwe Otto* opens the series of workshop reports from the SFB 227. *Bettmer et al.* study the implementation and practical course of a model to informalize criminal social control (diversion) for 14- to 20-year-old suspects that was set up in the middle of 1986 by the youth welfare office of the city of Bielefeld in cooperation with the prosecutor's office. The present article gives an insight into the conception and practice of the informalization model and offers first – even though tentative – results for discussion. Bettmer et al.'s research addresses the mostly unexplained questions of under which conditions and with which restrictions administrative social work can contribute to the informalization of social control particularly within the framework of a victim-offender reconciliation, and which decisionmaking processes are used in this field. The experiment in the Bielefeld youth welfare office seems to be a further positive support for the success of programs like those from Galaway and Grönfors. The freedom of planning in informalized procedures at the youth welfare office mostly runs on an interaction level that is oriented at mediation. Within this interaction framework, the juvenile has enough freedom to introduce his/her information into the mediation process according to his/her own perceptions; an opportunity that is not ignored.

Subproject C1 of the SFB 227 deals with changes in the decisionmaking structure of the criminal justice system limited to juvenile criminal procedures. *Ursula Herbort*, *Dorothea Rzepka*, and *Silvia Voss* address one of two research approaches in their article: the evaluation of an administrative pilot project implemented by the Bielefeld prosecutor's office and the police. The Juvenile Court Act (JGG) allows for different forms of pretrial diversion at the level of the prosecutor. Such dismissal of cases is seen as a way of preventing disproportionate public reactions as well as negative effects of stigmatization and criminalization on the side of the juvenile clientel. On the basis of intensive interviews with juvenile prosecutors, Herbort et al. were able to determine that these legal possibilities of preventive dismissal of cases are primarily only used for certain petty crimes and are regulated with formal criteria. The area of semi-serious crime is excluded because of a lack of sufficient information. It is hoped that the Bielefeld pilot project in which the police purposefully gather prevention-related information and have a right of recommendation with regard to the prosecutor's decision will remove the current information deficits and lead to an increase in, factually correct, dismissals of cases. The present state of analysis shows that the information form introduced by the officials for this purpose appears to fulfill the prosecutor's need for improved information.

The contribution from *Uwe Engel* and *Klaus Hurrelmann* is based on a study carried out in 1987 in the SFB 227. Forms of delinquent behavior were surveyed in a sample of 7th-and 9th-grade students from the different types of secondary school. The analysis is based on the assumption that anomic and socially disintegrative behavior in adolescence should be viewed as a function of social-structural conditions and as a way of expressing insecurity. This behavior is mainly directed toward the environment, it attacks social bonds, and destroys social relationships because of its destructive and aggressive character. From their studies the authors conclude that a high risk of downward social mobility is the consequence of failure at school, feelings of injustice regarding one's own assignment of status, the anticipation of unfavorable mobility chances, status uncertainty, and status disequilibrium in everyday life at school. In addition, Engel and Hurrelmann address the question – on the basis of different individual and environment intervention programs – of the implications of strategies to prevent delinquency in schools. They start with the hypothesis that preventive and reactive interventions can only be effective if they focus on early stages in the development of delinquency and strengthen both personal and social resources.

Kenneth Polk's paper on prevention and intervention in schools is linked to the subject of the paper from Engel and Hurrelmann. The title, "School Delinquency Prevention as Management of Rabble" clearly reflects misdirected tasks that Polk sees being assigned to schools or at least special educational units in the future. He investigates the causes that he anticipates will lead to the inclusion of schools in the social control of criminality and even its prevention. He traces a development from changes in the labor market to the occurence of various forms of troubles including troubles at school. The school's response to troublesome behavior, particularly in lower-status forms of education, is that the misbehavior is fundamentally individual in character, that the forms of trouble must be classified, and that once classified students should be segregated into special units, and that they may be "helped". In Polk's opinion, the programs of these special units are potentially harmful in that they stigmatize and denigrate students, and that their removal from mainstream education further reduces their later life chances of successful adult careers. Despite his pessimistic appraisal of trends of schools, Polk sees alternatives that, however, demand a turning away from individual interpretations of youthful marginality and a reorientation of prevention programs toward structural problems.

Karin Böllert and *Hans-Uwe Otto* present a further subproject of the SFB 227 in their paper. They use an institution analysis approach to investigate the preventive orientation of the problem-solving strategies used by social workers for the example of youth services. Starting with social work's function of securing and reproducing socially constituted normality, Böllert and Otto analyze the societal framing conditions of this normalizing work from the perspective of the changes in the premises of family and employment. They use the results of this analysis to develop a concept of prevention that by actively designing life-styles, should enable the target persons to adopt a constructive, autonomous approach to their problem environments. The current goal of the research project is to study possible ways of implementing this concept of prevention in the practice of youth services. After describing the project, the authors discuss the first findings and preliminary trends of preventive youth services from the perspectives of problem definition, goal definition, etc. They stress their results with a preliminary conclusion that, on the one hand, underlines the necessity of professionalization of social workers, on the other hand, states an obvious lack of methodical procedures enabling social workers to realize their respective stores of knowledge in the interaction with addressees.

Part III.
Inquiry into the Ethical Aspects of Prevention

The intrusions into the personal integrity of a citizen in the form of preventive measures, the attendant collection of personal and psychological data, both on the state of a problem person who has been identified not only as a result of early screening but also because of their entire psychosocial environment, and random selection in treatment research raise a series of ethical problems. Already in the run-up of prevention, research on prevention and intervention has to consider ethical matters. The state of the discussion on the ethics of empirical social research can be characterized with the help of headings such as "scientification" and "intrusion in the life world". Section III. focuses on a broad range of perspectives on ethical and moral questions.

The possibilities of gaining access to the data in criminal files or police records have been recently limited for German criminological research by administrative laws in favor of the right to privacy and informational self-determination. The researcher *Karl F. Schumann* critically discusses this problem in his paper without sharing the standpoint of unlimited access preferred by his colleagues. Schumann starts with a general overview on the situation of data access in German criminological research, which, in his experience – supported by numerous examples – is characterized by a discrimination against university researchers and a preference toward researchers who are supported by the state. However, this hostility between university and state researchers appears to be vanishing, partly because all criminologists are confronted with the "ombudsmen" for the protection of individual data. Schumann then pointedly asks, "if it would be a good idea for critical criminology to join forces with the conservatives and the state researchers against the protection of private data by authorized agencies": a question that he personally dismisses on objective grounds. He contrasts the two possibilities of always or never having to obtain consent from the persons on file with a double-standard regulation by which only etiological research would have to obtain the consent from the persons whose data are held in the files but not research on control agencies.

Alfred Büllesbach, from his point of view as an "ombudsman" for the protection of individual data, also picks up the conflict between data protection and the personal right of informational self-determination. Doing so, he mainly deals with those legal questions that are connected through science with the obtaining and safeguarding of data. He discusses the basic decision of the Federal Constitutional Court, the so-called Census Decision, and its consequences for the transitional period, in which the legislator has not yet reacted to the principles that were laid down by the Federal Constitutional Court. Against the background of a permanent development of informational systems and present concepts of prevention, especially in the area of delinquency, Büllesbach draws the picture of a society in which every person is estimated as suspect and as a risk, and therefore has to underly permanent control. Considering this, to Büllesbach data protection is protection of the citizens as well as of democracy. In his point of view, the right of informational self-determination – combined with exactly defined exceptions – demands from each researcher to obtain the consent to the data survey from the person concerned, that is, in a written form after the research project and the intended application of the data have been explained.

R. John Kinkel and *Norma C. Josef* examine in their paper the ethical questions encountered when studying adolescent problems (e.g., drug abuse, suicidal tendencies, child abuse). Typically these studies deal with the prevalence of some phenomenon under consideration and subsequently assess the need and kind of prevention and intervention program to reduce the problem. Kinkel and Josef consider the ethics of informed consent for these studies to be uneven and ill-defined. The paper outlines various ways U.S. researchers have applied the ethical principles of informed consent in adolescent survey research (age 12–18). After examining the general meaning of informed consent, the authors discuss how these principles apply to research with minors; studies involving substantial risks to subjects; invasion of privacy; school related research. They point out the negative consequences for research when one follows the federal regulations literally, namely, when investigators seek to obtain parental/guardian consent when minors are subjects (e.g., serious influences by race and other factors). As a solution to the dilemma Kinkel and Josef suggest "reasonable" accomodations which under certain preconditions schedule an informed consent.

The subproject C3 of the SFB 227, within the frame of a panel study, examines the effects alternative conflict solutions and sanctioning methods have on juvenile offenders. Under the headword "colonization of life worlds" *Günter Albrecht* and *Susanne Karstedt-Henke* pick up ethical problems and questions of the validity of research in general, and relating to the interviews of their sample. First of all, the article of Albrecht and Karstedt-Henke endeavours to clarify the approach to the problem in terms, and by doing so, the concept of interaction rituals and "territories of the self" (Goffman) proves to be a suitable measure for empirical analysis of the interaction between the researcher and the subject of research. As potential problem areas of their own research the (repeated) access to juvenile offenders and embarrassing questions are problematized and checked by using various data instruments according to ethical and methodological criteria. In their paper the authors present first tentative results on the problems of stigmatization by research and the interviewers' access and contact to the juveniles. Following them, the juvenile as the person who for most parts offers the access to an interview is self-confident enough to decide whether he/she wants to allow or refuse it. Against this background negative consequences of the interview for the juvenile cannot be stated. With regard to methodical standards a systematical distortion of the sample is unlikely to occur because the decision for or against an interview seems to depend on individual family situations.

While the papers introduced up to now discussed the ethic of research, looking from the point of view of its possible limitations, the paper of *Thomas Mathiesen* deals with the theoretical scientific problem of how research results are handled by the state. As a starting point for his considerations on prevention and intervention Mathiesen chooses a true story that happened to an important research project dealing i.a. with police violence in the Norwegian city of Bergen. He attaches special importance to a detailed description of the events, i.e., steadily made topical until the publication of this volume, in order to gain an international public, as one aspect of political struggle, for a national conflict between research and state. By using the course of the conflict Mathiesen demonstrates with which strategies and tactics the state opposes the delegitimizing research results. From his observations on this case he draws the conclusion that "legalization" which means "the employment of State organized legal institutions such as the police, the courts etc.. to evaluate the conflict" transforms the conflict into something else, into a legal issue involving a different set of criteria. Relating to prevention of state crime, following Mathiesen, legalization fulfils the function of an important weapon against "preventive" measures.

The Editors

Part I
The Foundations of Prevention and Intervention in Law and Criminal Justice Policy

1.
Constitutional Observations on the Subject of Prevention

Dieter Grimm

I. The Dilemma of Prevention

Prevention has always been an indispensible part of public authority. Even the liberal state allowed its police to patrol and not merely to wait in the precinct for reports of perpetrated crimes, just as conversely no totalitarian state is able to organize the precautions against insubordination so perfectly that it could completely do without repression. Yet the rule of thumb has long held true that systems which allow individual freedom of choice only within the narrow frame of superindividually-defined material public weal resort more heavily to preventive measures than systems which see the public weal precisely in safe-guarding and enabling individual development. It is true that in such systems freedom is likewise not unlimited. It ceases in principle, however, only with the same freedom of others, and this limit, which is generally and abstractly drawn up in the law, must, according to the liberal view of the state, have been exceeded or directly threatened in a concrete situation, before the public authority could impose sanctions. Prevention was not then an independent government strategy for controlling societal development, but only repression shifted ahead in time in order to avert imminent unlawful damage. As for the rest, the preventive effect was no more than that which emanates from the mere existence of the apparatus of repression.

For some time, nevertheless, an expansion and reorientation of prevention can be observed even in states which stand in the liberal tradition. In addition to the traditional fields of application of crime prevention and protection against dangers, especially in food and drugs as well as in technological facilities and equipment, extended government precautions have come into effect against the onset of sickness and want, deviant behavior and social protest, unemployment and economic stagnation, environmental pollution and the depletion of resources. In the course of this development, prevention becomes considerably detached from its reference to legally defined injustice and is employed to avoid undesired situations of every type. This change occurs relatively smoothly, even though it fundamentally remodels the relationship of state and society. The explanation is probably to be found in the fact that almost every preventive act is able to show an evident benefit. Successfully applied, it saves the individual disadvantages which at best may be compensated for by means of repression, but for which often no reparation is possible, and it saves the entire society burdens and conflicts which are usually more expensive than timely prevention. As scientific- technological progress is always opening up new issues for prevention, it is also increasingly demanded from the state. In the end, a reversal of the liberal principle of distribution emerges, so that repression only retains its justification as a catch basin for failed prevention.

It would, of course, be an illusion to assume that the advantages of prevention are to be had for free. The costs result, however, less directly and less concretely than does the benefit. Therefore they are rarely considered in decision-making calculations. They come at the cost of the self-determination of the individual and of the possibilities of freedom of the entire system. In contrast to a state which sees itself primarily as an authority of repression and therefore can wait for the onset of a socially detrimental event in order then to react, the preventively oriented state must track down possible crises in the beginning and try to smother them before they erupt. Not only concrete dangers, but also abstract risks call the state into action under these conditions. The individual is not able to keep the state at a distance by means of legal conduct. What is more, governmental control of citizens and citizens' behavior inevitably expands. That applies in a quantitative as well as a qualitative respect. The control increases quantitatively because the sources of dangers are always considerably more numerous than the cases of damage which actually occur. It intensifies qualitatively because the roots of social risks go far into the structure of personality and the sphere of communication, so that prevention, if it is to be effective, must penetrate into the areas of personal views, life-style and social contacts.

At the same time preventive government activity eludes the traditional controls of public authority to a much greater extent than repressive acticity does. Governmental repression expresses itself in the intervention in manifest disturbances of a legally determined condition of normality with the goal of its reinstatement. It therefore acts reactively and selectively. Yet as such it is normatively relatively easily determinable by legal norms. The norm fixes abstractly what is to be considered a disturbance of order and stipulates which measures the state may resort to in order to reinstate the disturbed order.

The program of action can be formulated in a discursive public process which can be organized in such a way that the persons concerned have the opportunity to announce their interests, raise objections and suggest alternatives, so that acceptable results appear possible. The government administration is bound to this normative program. It can only examine whether the statutorily defined preconditions for its intervention exist in a given case and impose the designated legal consequence. Its decision appears then merely as an act of execution in which, however, due to the incomplete binding force of norms, elements of decision-making are always entailed. As a normatively programmed act, the administrative decision in turn is subject to the control of lawfulness by independent courts which investigate on demand of the persons concerned, whether or not the state complied with the norm.

In contrast, preventive government activity presents itself as the avoidance of undesired developments and events. Consequently, it acts prospectively and covers a broad base. Such a future-oriented and complex activity can not be completely intellectually anticipated and therefore can be partially captured in general and abstract norms. As a rule, prevention norms are limited to the assignment of goals and the listing of viewpoints which must be given precedence in the pursuit of goals. This means, however, that the program guiding administrative agencies is only to a small extent the product of the democratic process. The acting administration must complete or correct it from one situation to the next. In this way it programs itself to a large extent without applying specifically normative techniques. The possibility of court control, which depends on the existence of binding norms, is weakened to the same degree. Preventive government activity therefore leads to a dilemma. In the course of preventing individual dangers to freedom, it threatens to reduce the possibilities of freedom of the social order as a whole and at the same time partially undermines the precautions of the democratic and constitutional state which have been developed in order to limit state power in the interest of individual freedom. It is this circumstance which makes prevention a problem of constitutional law.

II. The State's Change of Function and the Role of Prevention

1. The anti-prevention liberal state

A constitutional assessment of this development can not be undertaken without knowledge of its origins and conditions. For the degree to which it can be normatively influenced and where constitutional control can begin depends on these factors. If one traces the origins, one is struck by the parallels between the growth of preventive policy and the evolution of the modern welfare state. Thus the key to prevention might also be found in the causes which brought about the welfare state. Its beginnings coincide with the failure of the reductionist liberal state model. Liberalism believed it could drastically reduce the function of the state because it assumed that societal life, not unlike nature, was ruled by laws which, if they only came into force unimpededly, would automatically result in prosperity and justice. The consequence of this premise was the uncoupling of the various social systems, first of all the economy, from politics, which up until then had claimed for itself the right to regulate the entire private and public life according to its own ideal. The right to preventive measures had always been included therein because the truth advocated by the state demanded absolute validity, and potential endangerments had to be defendend against in advance. Now each social system should be able to develop according to its criteria of rationality and precisely in this way, even more reliably achieve the public weal after which the absolute state had vainly striven. The sole prerequisite was the freedom of the individual from governmental, estate and corporative compulsion. This freedom found its limit only in the same freedom of all others. In this system reoriented from truth to freedom, prosperity should increase because the creative power of the individual was rewarded through the fruits of one's own achievement. Justice was expected to appear since equal freedom allowed no one-sided domination, but only mutual agreements which protected everybody from being overpowered and enabled a better balance of interests than centralized, authoritarian regulation had done. The construction excluded neither social differences nor poverty and want, yet in such a system which offered everyone the same chance to develop, those factors did not seem to be externally imposed, but rather individually attributable and in this respect not unjust. The self-regulating ability of society did not, however, render the state superfluous, because the atomized society of free individuals was unable to secure the prerequisites for the success of the model, freedom and equality, within itself. For this it required a further authority, located outside itself and invested with power, namely the state. But its function reduced itself to the guarantee for the presupposed, quasi-natural order, whereas it no longer needed a government provision for the general welfare in view of the public weal that automatically resulted from the free play of forces. The state fulfilled its duty by suppressing the restrictions of liberty and made use of the traditional government means of command and compulsion to do so. But in the face of the fundamental principle of societal autonomy, every repressive act of the state became "intervention", and the constructive efforts of the bourgeois society centered on the neutralization of the danger potential inherent in intervention for the autonomy of subsystems and its medium, individual freedom. The solution was found in the constitution by which the government apparatus authorized to create and enforce law was, in turn, subjected to legal commitments. Civil rights marked the area of societal autonomy in which not the reasons of state, but rather the will of the individual, was decisive. Intervention in this area could not take place at the discretion of the state, but only in the interest of society. Therefore the state needed an authorization for each intervention which the representatives of society granted in general form in the law. The purpose of the construction lay precisely in limiting government power to the combatting of disturbances. Its existence may have acted preventively, but the goal-oriented use of preventive regulation of societal developments was adverse to the system, which, of course, did not preclude that the liberal state likewise resorted to such means when it benefited the ruling class. The law laid down definitively the criteria for a disturbance as well as the admissible reaction. The government executive was bound to the law. An act that appeared as intervention without having legal backing was therefore regarded as illegal and allowed the person concerned to demand forebearance and if necessary to enforce his claim with the aid of independent courts. It was precisely this restriction of the state to exactly charaterized cases of repression which seemed to guarantee the freedom of the individual most effectively.

2. The crisis of liberalism and the expansion of state functions

It is well-known that the liberal model was not able to fulfill the expectations associated with it. It is true that freeing society from the external ties of the social order of the estates and those of the absolute state led to an unleashing of productivity and an increase of prosperity. But social justice did not appear to the same extent. The reason for that was that a just balance of interests under the conditions of private autonomy can only come into being if a balance of power prevails in society. If this is lacking, that same freedom virtually changes into the law of the strongest and the state, restricted to protection against danger, unintentionally becomes the guarantee of private oppression.

The deception of liberalism consisted in the fact that it already saw a sufficient condition for social justice in the dissolution of the barriers of the feudal system and in the abolition of privileges in favor of equality before the law, whereas in reality it only shifted the roots of injustice from legal status to the, admittedly less rigid, economic situation. Thus even before the Industrial Revolution there was mass poverty that was not caused by the individual failure taken into account by the liberal model, but rather was structurally determined. The Industrial Revolution then finally destroyed the preconditions for a societal balance of powers and created the "social question" as a consequence of the system, since the older system of social security had fallen under liberalism. With that, the liberal model was deprived of its legitimacy. The counter-movement triggered a reactivation of the state which no longer solely had to guarantee a just presupposed order, but once again had to plan the order methodically with a view to social justice. The expansion of state functions that this set off can typically be divided into three phases, without maintaining sharply divided, historical caesurae. In the first stage the state began to suppress the most evident and legitimacy-consuming abuses of freedom. As it was the civil law that had served as the vehicle of private rule by discharging the individual from the material demands for justice and completely relying on private autonomy with its two major pillars, the freedom of ownership and the freedom of contract, the reaction began with revisions of private autonomy. The powers of disposition, which were connected to property, were again restricted; certain contracts, namely those of labor law, were once again subjected to substantive requirements. This change was less effected by amendments of the civil law itself than by special commercial, labor and administrative laws which while basically leaving the civil law untouched, narrowed its area of applicability. This explains why the search for preventive elements in the German civil code (BGB) will remain fruitless. In special civil law, on the other hand, preventive attempts can already be found in this first phase, and the German attempt at solving the "social question", Bismarckian Social Security, is clearly of preventive nature. In the second stage the state proceeded to intervene in emergencies and crises and to afford compensation of relief by public means. In contrast to the measures of the first stage, however, it could no longer satisfy itself with revisions of the law, but rather had to make real contributions in the form of financial and material means. Yet its reactive use did not yet allow prevention to become a prominent part of government activity in this phase either, even if it did increase noticeably, such as in industrial safety. With the growing differentiation of social structures and functions that made society more productive but also more susceptible to disturbances, reactive crisis-management no longer seemed sufficient for securing the existence and further development of the system. Thus the state proceeded in the third stage to track down potential crises at the very beginning, to stop their emergence by preventive measures and to improve the basic conditions for growth and developement. Since then, its legitimacy has depended on successes in this field. Consequently the state no longer has a principle option. Rather it carries the global responsibility for economic, social and cultural development. Inherent limits do not exist, for the capitalist society with its inbuilt pressure for growth constantly produces new trouble spots which the democratic party state, dependent on the voters' favor, must preventively pursue if it does not want to risk a withdrawal of loyality.

3. The role of prevention

It is obvious that it took this change of the state's function to pave the way ultimately for prevention. Yet its amazing boom can not only be accounted for in this way. Rather it is the scientific-technological progress which comes into it as a driving force. That becomes immediately evident in situations where it creates security risks of unheard of scope or depletes natural resources. But scientific-technological progress also has indirect effects on the need for prevention. In economic competition its results are customarily commercially utilized or employed for purposes of rationalization and cost-saving. The resulting problems connected herewith: the progressive destruction of nature, the ever increasingly machine-adapted redesigning of the living environment, the growing strain on the human organism due to environmental irritations and chemical products, and the accelerated supplanting of interpersonal communication by machine-transmitted anonymous communication have meanwhile crossed thresholds beyond which they are no longer credited to progress but rather considered by many as an impoverishment and a threat. Indeed, the scepticism about progress could never have spread so rapidly, had not the socialization conditions of industrial society been changed by the rationalization process as well. The decreasing need for personell in the economy alongside the increasing qualification requirements for the employed is leading everywhere to a lengthening of the training and a shortening of the (weekly and life-long) work hours and for some years now to higher unemployment as well. Consequently, the proportion of the population which is subject to the imperatives of the production process and accepts its set of values is shrinking. In this way, long entrenched patterns of thinking are beginning to change. A portion of those concerned lose the will to perform, work discipline and consumer motivation and begin to turn to other values that seem irrational from the standpoint of the industrial society. Others sense a loss of meaning in life that they try to escape by means of drugs, acts of violence or diseases. The increasingly unstable families caught up in this process are not able to compensate for the deficit in socialization. Thus, in addition to the sharply registered, old disadvantages, new degradations arise which are felt to be unjust in the face of the given possibilities of relief or compensation in a prosperous society. Taken together, all these factors unfold a socially disintegrating effect. Consequently, they mount up to political problems for the state for which public solutions are expected. Thus the state becomes subjected to contradictory demands. On the one hand, in order to be able to fulfill the growing societal demands and to retain mass loyalty, it is dependent on economic growth and therefore compelled to promote it. On the other hand, it must also stem the growth in order to head off its disintegrating effects. In this connection the priority can be placed either on one side or the other according to the political view. But no political view can avoid this dilemma. The worse that can be concealed, the more frequently the state itself becomes the subject of citizen protest, as the growing civil disobedience far from criminal circles indicates. The performance and planning state's need for approval, which, due to the multifarious consternation it creates, is much greater anyway than that of the liberal state, increases in this way over and over again. Under this pressure, policy side-steps into secondary strategies. The appearance that the state has the situation under control is propagated by a symbolic policy. Lowering costs, especially in the performance systems of social security, should expand its room for action. Finally, the disintegrating potential, whose social causes did not appear rectifiable, must be neutralized in its individual effects. In this connection prevention gains new importance. For one, it offers the state the prospect of reducing social burdens, such as by the early diagnosis of diseases or dispositions to diseases, timely retraining, and so forth. Futhermore, it promises to nip deviant behavior in the bud and to hinder its actualization. Scientific-technological progress proves itself once again to be the prime mover here in that it also constantly expands and improves the preventive repertoire. The government prevention of dangers thus changes in two respects. On the one hand, it is shifted to an earlier time period. Whereas before it only acted on the acute or in any case present danger, now it already becomes effective against the sources of danger. The government focus has thus become increasingly directed to pre-delinquent, prepathological and presubversive phenomena. On the other hand, it is also being thematically reoriented. If the old prevention of danger was primarily aimed at material risks in order to protect the people, the new prevention refers primarily to human risks and favors institutions or systems.

4. The preventive set of instruments

The already classic "realprevention" in the area of technical safety could fulfill its function with the specifically governmental means of command and compulsion which the order state reduced to the protection against dangers had typically used. Facilities that from the very beginning constituted a risk for the general public were only approved with the inclusion of special safety precautions; facilities which later posed a concrete danger were shut down. Modern personal prevention can only partially reach its goal with these means. As this prevention is not so much concerned with averting immediate dangers as with tracking down potential ones, ascertaining and eliminating them preventively, it is inevitably bound up with an increased need for information. The more personal data which is accessible and may be combined, the more reliably can trouble spots be located. The compulsory census of person-related data, of course, quickly comes up against legal and actual boundaries. The state therefore resorts to other ways of gathering information. Where a data survey is virtually made very difficult, such as in the milieu of deviant behavior, it begins its own inquiries. Where it meets with legal obstacles, such as with the early diagnosis of diseases by means of detective tests or similar procedures, it creates incentives to the voluntary disclosure of data. But also the preventive measures themselves which follow the localization of danger can only be enforced to a limited extent by means of command and compulsion. In this way they resemble numerous other regulatory activities that have accrued to the state in the course of the expansion of its function. That has diverse reasons. First, the multiplication of government duties was not accompanied by a corresponding enlargement of the powers of intervention. On the contrary, regardless of the global responsibilty of the state for economic prosperity and social justice, civil rights assure the individual a continued high degree of self-determination and thus the social subsystems a relatively great autonomy. Secondly, imperative regulatory means are bound to fail, even if they were legally admissible, whenever a governmentally desired behavior depends on specific abilities, attitudes or sets of values of the citizens. Finally, there are a number of social spheres in which the use of command and compulsion is indeed admissible and actually possible, but appears to cost too much. Costs here are not only to be understood as financial, such as for example those of an extensive surveillance system, but also political, such as in the form of unified counter-pressure or the threat of loss of votes. In all these cases the state is dependent on the cooperation of autonomous decision makers in order to reach its goals and therefore must try to persuade them to show the desired behavior or dissuade them from showing the undesired one. The means of motivation are numerous. They can consist in mere information on the benefit and harm of a certain behavior, but can also be extended to the care and treatment of groups or people at risk. Here is the connection between reorientation of the police and the intensification of psychology and pedagogy in social work with which the conference deals. However, governmentally desired behavior can also be emphasized by the tightening or loosening of entrance requirements, and the expansion or reduction of capacities such as in the field of education. But the state most frequently depends on material incentives and deterents with which it rewards the desired behavior with tax concessions, premiums or the supply of goods and services and penalizes the undesired behavior with additional taxes. The intensity of the effect is extremly various yet can approach that of imperative regulation if the legally existing possibility of choice has actually been reduced to an extreme. This is not infrequently the case in the combination of public welfare with preventive control as is increasingly being applied in social policy. The allocation of government services according to need and amount is then made dependent on a legally nonenforcable equivalent performance on the part of those benefited which can consist in the disclosure of information, the consent to a treatment, or the performance of services. In this way the recourse to means of motivation which act indirectly almost always results in preventive control extending beyond the legally allowed scope of intervention and thus procuring the state entry into previously private zones.

III. The Leading Principles of the Constitution and Governmental Prevention

1. The standard of the Basic Law

According to the previous statements, the expansion and reorientation of preventive government activities can not be comprehended as a fleeting trend. It proves to be a political reaction to social change and in this respect is structurally conditioned, at least in regard to its essence, and therefore not capable of being rescinded without changing the basic structures. In the face of the unchecked scientific-technological progress from which it derives, an increase is, on the contrary, more probable than a decrease. For constitutional law the consequence is that it can neither ignore nor put an end to prevention. On the contrary, the doctrine of constitutional law must focus its attention on prevention and, guided by constitutional goals and related to the logic of prevention, develop suitable legal standards out of the given set of norms, similarly as recently occurred in the census decision of the Federal Constitutional Court for the new information technologies. With the multitude of possible subjects, forms and means of prevention on the one hand, as well as the normative points of reference on the other, that can not be done generally. Surveillance of protest groups is to be judged differently than the protection against hijacking and this in turn differently than the early diagnosis of epilepsy. That can not be expounded upon here in detail. But the constitutional framework in which the various phenomena can be dogmatically classified may well be defined. This framework is briefly sketched here. If one first makes sure of the constitutional standard values, one has to proceed from the human dignity that the Basic Law elevates to the highest principle of social order and declares to be inviolable in Art. 1, par.1, sec. 1. The state is related to human dignity in sec. 2 and assumes in relation to it a serving function with its means of power. Human dignity itself is not conceived, as the connection with human rights in par. 2 indicates and the following civil rights provisions make evident, in a submission of the individual to a given transcendentally or worldly legitimated ideal of an individual or social process of perfecting, with the result that out of human dignity the governmentally enforcable duty of the individual arises to approach this ideal to the best of his ability. The Basic Law understands dignity rather as an always existing fundamental right of man from which the right of the individual autonomously to decide on life plans and ideas of happiness follows and in those cases in which this autonomy in the early developmental stage of man has not yet or may never be realized due to serious mental or physical defects, the right to be respected as a member of the genus man. The Basic Law supports personal autonomy in the following articles in points which proved to be especially threatened in the past by concrete guarantees of freedom in the form of the free development of personality in Art. 2, par. 1, and then formulates this general freedom in individual, specifically designated freedoms. In this connection Art. 3 adds, not as an individual freedom but as a modality of the guarantees of freedom, that the dignity that expresses itself in personal autonomy and is concretely protected by civil liberties applies to everyone in the same way. Therefore autonomy can not comprise the right to destroy or curtail the autonomy of others. That results in bounds to self-determination, not, however, in the interest of a superindividual collective value, but rather in the interest of enabling the peaceful coexistence of autonomous yet socially related individuals. For the sake of this possibility is state authority necessary and authorized to the limitation of freedom. Yet the Basic Law establishes the state in Art. 20 et seq. in such a way that it remains oligated to the fundamental principle of human dignity and must legitimate the exercise of power according to it. Not the civil liberties section alone but also the organization section of the constitution is to be read as a formulation of Art. 1, par. 1, sec. 1. This is served by the principle of democracy in that it links public authority to a commission of those ruled and only issues this commission in a manner restricted in time, subject and function, since diverse opinions legitimately exist on its fulfillment under the condition of individual freedom. This is served by the principle of the constitutional state in that it does not leave the exercise of domination to the discretion of each function bearer, but rather binds it to fixed standards, that have been legally determined in advance and must serve the aim of freedom, so that the possibility of individually responsible planning and conduct of life is preserved for the individual even under the conditions of governmentally regulated freedom. This is further served by the principle of the social state in that it guarantees that the freedom which results from dignity not only exists formally but is also tangibly effective. Finally, this is served by federalism in that it enlarges the range of variations of political organization and also vertically divides state authority in order to limit its power.

2. Prevention as a protection of liberty

If one attempts to integrate government prevention into the value system of constitutional law, a question comes to the fore of how it effects the self-determination of the individual which follows from human dignity and is concretized in civil rights. From the start there is not a clearly positive or negative answer to this question. Positive and negative elements have the habit, on the contrary, of commingly, and the mixing ratio varies according to the circumstances. But the evident use, which may be put forward for almost all preventive measures, regularly shows favorably in the books on the credit side in terms of civil rights. Every prevented act of violence, every disease that did not break out, every nuclear reactor that did not burst, works out as safeguarding freedom on the side of the potential victims. If one takes that into account, prevention itself has a support based on civil rights. Today civil rights are no longer understood exclusively as a means of defense against the state. Since it has been known that the freedom protected by civil rights can not only be threatened by the state and therefore can not be sufficiently preserved by mere guarantees of private areas safe from the state, the radius of civil rights has expanded to an all around safeguarding of freedom. It is true that they still unfold their direct effect only vis-à-vis the state. But as a result of civil rights the state is not only obliged to refrain from infringements of freedom, but also actively to protect the freedoms guaranteed by civil liberties from encroachments by a third party. With regard to other individuals the protection of civil rights is put into practice mediated by state law. The state had, of course, arranged for such a protection of freedom long before the construction of a civil rights protection of freedom urged it constitutionally to do so. Practically the entire criminal law and large sections of private law serve the protection of individual freedom from illegal encroachments by third parties. A civil rights duty to protect was not needed in this respect. However, for its function it is revealing that it was adapted into the practice of the constitutional courts on the occasion of the repeal of a threat of punishment for abortion. The constitutional protection acts on the one hand, as one can see from this, as a guarantee for the existence of precautions that are essential for securing civil rights. It demands on the other hand that such precautions be made by the legislature in cases where civil rights appear either not yet or not sufficiently protected against societal threats. That can be the case essentially due to three reasons. The first lies in the formation, usually scientifically-technologically conditioned, of new types of dangers to freedom for which the old laws do not make allowance. That would apply to nuclear power or genetic engineering. The second results from the fact that the central means of protection that liberalism had foreseen for threats for freedom by third parties, the freedom of contract, was no longer able adequately to protect the individual from societal overpowering under the conditions of the industrial society. The protection of freedom then requires the increased material ties of private autonomy. The third reason has its roots in the fact that the repressive means of the protection of freedom could often only insufficiently or not at all make reparations for incurred damages. Wherever sanctions of criminal law and compensation for danger relating to civil law promise no appropriate reparation, the protection of freedom must therefore be shifted and take effect already at possible sources of damage. This case area also increases due to the scientific-technological development and the corresponding dimensions of damage appreciably. The decision in favor of the social constitutional state, whose civil rights dogmatical consequence is the duty to protection, thus comprises the decision in favor of prevention, and the question can not be whether the state is authorized to use preventive means, but only to what aim, to what extent and under which conditions the use should be allowed.

3. Prevention as an interference with liberty

The duty to protect a civil liberty is customarily fulfilled, of course, by means of the restriction of another freedom or of the freedom of another person. The protection of liberty and the interference with liberty therefore correspond to each other as, for example, the duty to protect the life of an unborn child corresponds to the interference with the right to self-determination of the mother. What is protection from the victim's point of view appears as restriction from the point of view of the one acting. Prevention makes no exceptions here. Compulsory vaccinations, use of seat belts and insurance, etc., are measures of preventive compulsion. The problem is well-known and is solved within the scope of a test of commensurability by weighing up the protected and the curtailed civil right. This solution is also applied in preventive acts, at least in as far as they employ imperative means. That is not the rule, however, as has been shown, precisely in the new forms of personal prevention. It seems either to be a simple government action or tries to employ non-imperative means. Nevertheless, it penetrates into previously private zones, exposes the law-abiding citizen as well to government controls and changes the basic conditions of the practice of liberty. Whether civil rights also protect those concerned from non-imperative prevention depends on how far this is considered as interference. The classical concept of interference did not permit that. According to this, only a government act that intentionally inflicted a directly burdensome legal consequence on the recipient by means of command and compulsion was seen as interference. This concept of interference referred to the liberal state which solely protected a presupposed social order, existing independent of the state, from disturbances. Only if a disturbance occurred was it allowed to intervene and to eliminate the problem by use of its means of power. Thus the system left it no other possibility of encountering the individual than by compulsory acts that were directed against and directly burdened him. Government activity and the protection of civil rights coincided in this way. Had the liberal concept of interference remained in the face of the enormous expansion of government activitites, this congruence would have been abandoned, and civil rights could no longer have completely fulfilled their protective function vis-à-vis the state. Such a deficit can only be avoided if one focuses on the freedom-restricting effect of government action, not on the intention thereby pursued or the chosen form of action. Therefore today any effect must be seen as interference which can be traced back to government action and which makes behavior protected by civil rights impossible for the individual. It remains then with the requirement that state action prevents behavior protected by civil rights. Not every effect of the state on the otherwise free decision of the individual is an interference with civil liberties. Neither is any observation or research an interference with civil liberties from the start, as long as the state in this connection does not penetrate into the realms or communications of civil liberties. On the other hand, behavior protected by civil liberties is not only made impossible when it is legally prohibited, but rather when it is actually made considerably more unrealizable. That could be the case where a civil right can only be exercised with the acceptance of severe drawbacks, for example, waiving public benefits, or where the execution is registered for the purpose of gathering suspicious factors. The course of this border is difficult to pinpoint depending on the circumstances. That can only be commented on in consideration of the civil right concerned and the type of prevention employed. It seems in no way to be excluded that in this connection new special personal rights similar to the right to informational self-determination proceed from the general personal rights of Art. 2, par. 1 of the Basic Law. If a non- imperative act of prevention takes on the character of interference in terms of this broad definition, it is then admissible only under those constitutional requirements that apply in general to the interference with civil liberties. It must stay within the scope of the respective interference proviso and requires a sufficiently specified legal basis. The prevailing opinion dispenses with the latter only in cases of the resultant and side effects of what in itself is an admissible state act that prove themselves in concurrence with a certain constellation of facts actually to be a restriction of civil liberties, without this having been intended or even only foreseeable. No legal basis for such unforeseeable resultant or side effects can be demanded indeed without the danger of paralyzing the state. Prevention is, of course, always a final act (which does not exclude unintended long-range effects). Thus it always requires, in so far as it takes on the quality of interference, a legal basis upon which all essential decisions must be made by parliament itself.

4. The problem of weighing up

Freedom-restricting laws, of course, always require a legitimating reason which, in view of the importance that the Basic Law accords to individual freedom, can itself ultimately only be derived from freedom itself. That is the basis of the principle of commensurability that upholds the functional dependence of government interference with the freedom of the individual and reduces the restrictions of freedom to the necessary degree. In this way it has developed to practically the most important boundary for the freedom-restricting state. As a rule it is a matter of a civil liberty being restricted because its unchecked practise would endanger the civil liberties of a third party. Endangerments that justify a restriction of civil liberties can, however, also refer to the general public or to the state as guarantor of individual freedom. The constitutionality of the restriction then depends on an appropriate balancing in which the importance of the colliding objects of legal protection, the degree of the restriction and the scope of the danger are all of weight. This constellation also occurs in numerous restrictions of civil liberties for preventive purposes. Whoever wants to be a teacher or to sell meat must have an X-ray examination so that those persons with whom he has professional contact are protected from contagious diseases. The problem of consideration here poses no additional difficulties. Yet with the modern forms of prevention new constellations arise. One of the peculiarities is that by means of preventive measures one should not combat recognized dangers but should first discover possible trouble spots. The number of the preventively examined persons can thus grow considerably, and there must already be sufficient suspicious factors and serious endangerments of a high-priority object of legal protection if the purpose of the search is to justify the restriction of civil liberties. A further peculiarity arises from the fact that prevention is often aimed at behavior that neither impairs certain persons or the general public in their freedom nor the state in its function as guarantor of freedom. On the contrary, the damages set in primarily for those who incur the damages themselves, whereas third parties at best suffer disadvantages that do not develop to encroachments on civil liberties. This is the case, with the consumption of certain drugs, with non-communicable diseases or with uncommon forms of life-style. Of course, the objects of civil liberties such as life and health suffer regardless of whether the impairment issues from a third party or from the holder of civil liberties himself. Nevertheless it can not be concluded that every danger to civil liberty that can be combatted preventively must be combatted preventively as well. Constitutional order proceeds from the dignity and self-determination of the individual. Therefore it formulates civil liberties principally as subjective liberties and leaves the practice of freedom up to the decision of those entitled to the liberties. Therein is the freedom founded for each personal combination of risk and security, hazardous enterprise and failure, even of self- destruction. The state is entitled to no judgement, so long as similar or higher-priority rights of third parties are not encroached upon. According to the Basic Law, it is appointed to enable and protect the self-development of the person. That occurs in that it safeguards the economic and cultural basic prerequisites for personality development and eliminates external dangers, but not, however in that it patronizes those elected to self-development in the choice of life objective and style of conduct. Civil liberties would otherwise secretly turn into duties. Of course, public aims can also always be put forward to justify the protection of the individual from himself: the maintenance of public order, the relieving of the general public from the resultant costs of individual venturesomeness, etc. But then one must very carefully distinguish whether in the case of maintenance of public order it is a matter precisely of the order of liberty or only of a certain status quo which is not backed by any constitutional guarantee. Similarly, a rule of consistency which follows from the principle of equality applies for the burdening of the general public with the costs of individual venturesomeness. The general public bears many resultant costs of individual venturesomeness, those of smoking tobacco and of skiing, of car driving and of speculating on the stock exchange. The fact that certain risks are taken by most people and others only by a few does not change the legal assessment. That is also a consequence of the basic decision in favor of liberty.

IV. The Unsolved Problem

It would nevertheless be rash to assume that the constitutional questions that arise with the expansion and intensification of prevention had been answered with these remarks. They form rather only the attempt to fit the phenomena into a given dogmatic framework which was not constructed with a view to the problem of prevention and thus can only cope with it incompletely. Preventive government activity has access to the control of civil liberties in as much as it, on the one hand, understands itself to be an expression of the duty to protect, and on the other, subsumes an expanded welfare state concept of interference. Its further reaching effects are very difficult to control by the constitution. That applies particularly to the change of the basic conditions of civil liberty which occurs when a society produces so many security risks, that it is only able to protect the threatened objects of basic legal protection by means of a considerable expansion of the surveillance system. Each individual precaution can then, considered alone, appear as a necessary and appropriate relatively minor burden for safeguarding a highly-valued object of legal protection, just as the bodily search at airports, and thus remove the constitutional obstacles to the interference with civil liberties and as a whole let freedom atrophy for the sake of security. The boundary is difficult to discern. Yet if it is crossed, the liberal constitution finds itself once again on the periphery of social life, without one single textual alteration having been necessary.

The weakness of constitutional law vis-à-vis prevention becomes further apparent in those problems that result from the limited legal controllability of preventive government activity. In this way dominant structural principles of constitutional order, such as the rule of law and democracy, lose their effectivity. Both depend, of course, on the medium of the law. Under democratic conditions the law first assures that all essential, collectively binding decisions take place with public participation and under public control and thus offer a certain prospect of the possibility of generalization. Secondly, it binds the state executive to the sovereign. The administration, which itself is an authority not dependent on elections, can, of course, only be incorporated into the democratic connection of legitimacy and responsibility in that it receives its program of action from the state organs which proceed from elections and are again called to account in elections. As far as it regulates itself contrarily apart from the law, the constitutional mechanisms of election, discourse and control remain without effect. The attempt of the Federal Constitutional Court to close the democratic loophole by means of an expansion of legal reservation must fail in a situation where the object of regulations resists normative, preliminary stipulations, as is the case for a number of preventive activities. The legislature, compelled to action all the same, flees then into abstract definitions of objectives and global blank authorizations which only faintly conceal that it is the administration once again that is determining its own activity.

Under constitutional aspects, the law functions first and foremost as a means to preventing governmental arbitrariness in that it binds the execution of public authority to rules which are admittedly not unchangeable, but at least fixed in advance. A protection which is not to be underestimated exists for the individual merely in this regularity of government conduct, irrespective of the content of the rule. He is not the utter mercy of a property acting state, but can calculate its actions in advance and adjust his own conduct to it accordingly. It is this certainty which makes responsible life planning and a fearless perception of his own interests possible for him. In a substantive conception of the rule of law, this protective effect is strengthened by the fact that it does not only rest on the formal requirements of legal binding arrangements of the administration, but further binds the content of the law to individual liberty. Where, on the other hand, regularity is not attainable because the program of action must first be planned, completed or changed in the face of changing situations by the acting person himself, the protection mediated by the rule of law is lost and the administration can act according to its will, which is only laboriously reined by the principle of self-obligation. Very often that seems to be the case particularly with prevention dealing with deviant or politically oppositional behavior, so that the fear is not unfounded that here the security interests of the state machinery or of powerful clients gain an ascendency over civil liberty which is not constitutionally deserved.

Yet the law not only forms the measure of conduct for the state executive but also the measure of control for the system of administrative tribunals which checks up on it. The right of the individual to have an independent court examine whether the state acted legally or not in its dealings with him and the claim to obtain redress in the case of irregular conduct first lends the constitutional binding of the state effectivity in cases of conflict, not to mention the pre-effect that the mere existence of judicial control has for the obedience of the administration. In so far the rule of law perfects itself indeed in judicial legal protection. Judicial legal protection clings, of course to the existence of justiciable norms and where these are absent, no control of lawfulness can take place. If it is exercised nevertheless, to which the administrative courts tend without consideration of the power of determination and the regulation density of norms, then justice changes from the control of lawfulness into departmental control or into a political formative agency. In this way the constitutional loophole closes in that it tears open a democratic one. That is not only a problem of government activity, but purely and simply of the regulating and planning administration which can not be conditionally programmed to the same degree as the old order administration. In the sphere of prevention, however, even the surrogate of participation of those concerned in the administrative process, which has increasingly been employed for some time now, is omitted because it would impair the effect of prevention from the start as, for example, in the broad area of security.

All these wedges which new types of state duties and sets of instruments have driven into the constitutional disciplining of state authority only indicate that the constitution is related to a problem situation that no longer corresponds to the one of today. The constitution was a bourgeois invention intended to restrict the state to the function of guaranteeing individual freedom under the premise of the ability of society to regulate itself and to bind the state, in the fulfillment of this restricted function, to the interests of an autonomous society existing separately from it. The duty hereby defined was designed in such a way that it found its solution in a higher ranking law to which the state itself was obligated. The constitution developed its specific rationality in the restriction of the state and its functionally adequate organization. The present duties of welfare prevention and developmental regulation urge the state, on the contrary, to stepped-up activities in an increasingly closer cooperation with the organized powers of society. Under these conditions, however, it is no longer a question of exclusion and restriction, but rather of performance and planning. Duties of this kind do not already find their solution in the making of norms, but first in the action that lies behind the norm, without this, however, being normatively sufficiently capable of regulation. Yet the worldwide prevalence of the constitution and its noticeable role in a system with a developed system of administrative tribunals then only conceals the creeping loss of inner formal power and closeness to the problem. Prevention is only the latest example of this.

2.
The Prevention State: The Security of the Objects of Legal Protection Versus Legal Security

Erhard Denninger

1. The track whose uncertain outcome I wish to follow here can be provisionally characterized by a double thesis: 1. The much described social or welfare state expansion of governmental duties which manifests itself among other things as the transition from the traditional protection against dangers, to the "modern" government prevention policy in the broadest sense is accompanied and supported by a fundamental reaccentuation within the complex idea of law that touches upon the foundations of the legal system. Abridged to key words this means: from *legal security* to the *security of legally protected interests* as a means of *social justice*.

And 2.: This problematical nature, which for the time being is only formulated in terms of legal theory, attains topicality and explosiveness when it is considered in a *constitutional*-theoretical way. The questions which then should be posed can be expressed in the thesis: Neither the theory of civil liberties nor the theory of the purposes of state and the theory of legislation, including the doctrine of resolved power of legislature, as the cornerstones of a substantive, democratic constitutional theory that is not only understood in a formal, organizational way, have taken sufficient notice of the transfer of emphasis from a system of legal security to a system of the security of the *objects* of a legal protection, not to mention having dealt with it conceptually in a suitable way.

Newly created definitions, such as the "civil right to security"[1], turn traditional categories upside down. They accurately describe phenomena and thus substantiate the pressure of the problem, but they offer no solutions. What is called for is a fresh attempt to determine the inner limits of the efficiency of the state, an attempt that admittedly will neither be able to reach its objective in the *Humboldtian* concept of security nor be able to find its historical truth in a new, liberal constitutionalism. Only on the basis of such a fundamental formulation of the question can, perhaps, normative standards also be attained for an answer to the question of the legal limits of government prevention policies.

The constitutional lawyer will not primarily try to get a grasp on the normatively intended question of the limits of the effectiveness of the state socio-anthropologically or individual-ethically – as *W. von Humboldt* once did[2] – but rather first and foremost constitutionally. In this connection he will see the insufficiency, as has recently been impressively demonstrated[3], of the constitution aimed at the bourgeois-liberal constitutional state for overcoming the legal problems triggered by the prevention state. But when he resignedly blames the constitution for "the creeping loss of inner formal power and closeness to the problem", that can not be the last word. A similar constitutional pessimism, all the way to almost declaring the state dead, was already manifest thirty years ago (and afterwards) in the controversy over the compatibility of the constitutional state and the modern welfare state[4]; this pessimism continued in the 60s in the conflicts on special purpose laws and planning, later in the 70s debate on democratization and participation, and on into the 80s in the controversy over the possibility of "social civil liberties". The discussions on regulation and deregulation and prevention followed: through their factual connection they confirm that classical legal forms of the "constitutional state", such as general law, become a farce indeed under completely changed social and political conditions, or even worse, their original role as instruments for safeguarding liberty can turn into its opposite. For example: The work of legislation up to now to the implementation of the reserved power of legislation on the right of privacy in the sphere of public security can serve here as a lesson of warning.

The state as security and prevention state in its function as a complement to industrial society – which *E. Forsthoff* very precisely recognized[5] – has proved itself to be extremely "alive". Should it be more tenacious of life than its constitution? Is the constitution of the industrial society, with its mass-democratic, union and party-pluralistic, yet private-egotistical reality, *structurally overtaxed* within the case of norms of a bourgeois-liberal constitutional state opened along social state lines? The overtaxing consists in the fact that society indeed unrestrainedly burdens the political system with the management of new duties, yet is unable to deliver to it any binding standards for setting priorities. Moreover, the system, as it is currently structured, is incapable of autonomously producing such standards. Thus we have no new edition of the thesis of the "Fiscal Crisis of the State"[6], and no late-bourgeois lament over the end of the intellectual self-representation of the state[7], but rather we lack qualified, positive and negative selectivity (i.e., NO and YES, BUT decisions) in the face of societal demands.

The state, or to be more exact, the political decision-making system, thereby mirrors a conflict on the macrolevel which can be recognized on the microlevel of individual-ethical demands on the individual as the basic dilemma of the liberal-social state constitutional ideology: the virtues of the development of personality, of individual responsibility, of the ethic of efficiency and domination are directly confronted by the virtues of an ethic of adaptation, adjustment to a system and subjugation. On the one hand, precision of function is demanded in a technical, economical or bureaucratic system and ideological conformity and the acceptance of heteronomous "foundations of meaning" are expected; and on the other hand, not least by the highest guardians of the law, the hymn is sung of the dynamic-creative, imaginative, innovative, self- interested and self-responsible, yet tolerant, high-performance person. The tableau of such a "*conflictual ethic*" that forces together the welfare state and the industrial, achievement-oriented society remains to be drafted in detail. The calculation of the "human" and social costs of such a long- term tension would also have to be made. Both belong to the overall picture of our constitutional reality, to the real state of our community.

2. Against this background of the problem, I return to my first thesis. Legal security, in connection to our problem, does not only mean the positivity of the legal order and the legal force of judicial or administrative decisions but rather a wealth of individual elements made positive in many individual provisions on all levels of the process of the creation and application of the law. Its ideal realization fulfills the idea of the formal constitutional state; it can, as *G. Radbruch* has so sharply illuminated[8)], come as much into conflict with the demands of pure practicality as with those of "substantive", "social" justice. On the other hand, the idea that the realization of the constitutional *state* in the sense of *legal security* is at the same time an essential prerequisite for the *societal* engendering of social justice belongs to the creed of the liberal bourgeoisie that believes in the freedom of contract, competition and the "market". A *direct* intention of the state, or of its legal system respectively, to social *justice* and corresponding interventions was not desired. This has fundamentally changed.

It should be demonstrated at this point, without pretension to novelty in details, how the direct orientation of government activity toward the guaranteeing of the security of the *objects* of legal protection modifies and dissolves the classical elements of *legal* security (or of the formal constitutional state). This goal-orientation raises the claim that one must give satisfaction to the postulates of substantive justice such as they correspond to the principle of human dignity and the objective-legal content of civil liberties. In a second step, however, one must ask whether the concept of direct, governmental protection of the objects of legal protection can really be regarded as a concept of substantive justice. One can consider legal security with respect to *four* different conditions that correspond to the functional courses in the legal direction of societal processes. They begin with the 1) creation of the law or legislation, continue on through 2) the application of the law in individual cases including judicial control and on to 3) the enforcement of the law. "Perpendicular" to these phases, 4) one has to inquire about the domination of the law in the consciousness of those subjected to it, about the anchoring of prominent legal contents in the general value convictions of the legal community. Here at the latest, the connection between formal legal security and substantive justice must become clear.

The *result* of a legal system that functions in every phase according to the guiding principle of legal security is the maximal security of the *objects* of legal protection, and indeed not only as the normative inviolability of the objects abstractly cited in the legal order; for example: "Property ... is guaranteed." (Art. 14, par. 1, Basic Law), or: "The private residence is inviolable," (Art. 13, par. 1, Basic Law) or also: "Art and science ... are free." (Art. 5, par. 3, Basic Law). The result is rather the maximal protection of *actually* existing objects of legal protection against any illegal infringement, thus, the ideal of the legal protective state, the security of the status quo. Whether the societal distribution of the actual objects is "materially" just or not does not come into the field of vision of the consideration of mere legal security. On the other hand, it is left up to the free will of the individual with which concrete contents he completes legal frameworks such as "property", "opinion", and so forth; on this side of the boundary of injuriousness, the state does not interfere.

To 1): Insecurity with the creation of law: "Secure" law and thereby "legal security" was to be expected[9] when the norms were *set* (enacted as "statues")
- in a precisely fixed and generally recognized *process*,
- with their object and circle of addressees as *general* as possible,
- for a *long time*,
- and clear in terms of the contents and *specific* and thereby *capable of enforcement*.

Each of these elements, which can only be briefly indicated here, is being questioned today in the most various (legal-) political connections. If we for once disregard the extreme position that completely denies parliamentary representation the capacity and legitimacy for "correct" decisions of general public interest, the criticism remains of the suitability of the majority principle for the deciding of problems that extend over generations, are "irreversible", or concern the continued existence or destruction of the whole people or humanity. The political concern about and provision for the objects of legal protection of the still unborn, in short, the special quality of the *content* of a decision to be made, leads to doubt about the appropriateness of the process. This could in no way be justified under the formal aspect of legal security alone. But on closer examination it is still only a matter of the special increasing gravity of the idea, long since developed by the Federal Constitutional Court, of the direct *procedural* relevance of *substantive* civil liberties.[10]

The wasting away of the personal and objective sense of the general public in modern legislation has been criticized early, often and with a wealth of nuances. The thread runs from the famous controversy over the statutory concept at the Conference of Experts on Constitutional Law (Staatsrechtslehrertagung) in 1927, through *Forsthoff's* recapitulation of the type "special purpose law" in 1955, up to *Kloepfer's* thesis in 1981 that modern legislation is characterized by the loss of "constitutional and democratic distance".[11] The fundamental problem is, of course, much older still; it dominated the Ratio-Voluntas discussion of the medieval scholasticism as well as *Rousseau's* dispute with *Hobbes*. Rousseau[12] believed he had found the philosophers' stone in his concept of law as the expression of the volonté générale, that is, the synthesis of the principles of the will and of universal reason, and thereby the ideal of *justice*, namely, the unity of objective general public interest truth and the guaranteeing of personal-individual freedom. This Rousseauism, which would like to have "objectivity", the universal applicability of natural law, along with positivism's power of enforcement and innovation, continues to be felt, mediated by the especially ethical form of the *Hegelian* concrete-universal, in the German doctrine of constitutional law up to today.

In the concept of law – in terms of natural law – as a dictatum rectae rationis[13], as the expression and order of a universal reason (and at the same time a command of God), *justice* and *legal security* are equally effective as goal- values. This also applies for general law on the basis of democratic legitimacy. Even without resorting to *C. Schmitt's* thesis of secularization[14] (which, of course, is denied no one), this becomes clear in the dual consideration that universal, equal validity also means equal treatment and equal burdens, exclusion of privileges and therefore justice, and further that with the consciousness of being universally and equally affected, not only the sense of the correctness of a regulation grows, but also that of its firm binding character. With the mutual, equally-entitled recognition as a member of a legal community, one "assures" oneself and others at the same time of the binding character of the common law.

For the people of the Renaissance and the religious wars, for the contemporaries of *Kepler*, *Galileo* and *Hobbes*, it must have been both a pleasing and an abysmally horrifying experience – an experience that we today can neither emotionally nor intellectually relive – when upon the discovery of the physical laws and thus upon finding the key to the domination of nature, they also had to experience simultaneously the collapse of the unified religious-metaphysical order. The need for a new, legitimating foundation of the social order arose out of both experiences. The extent of the inner, spiritual catastrophe into which the people had plunged can be approximately measured against the external terrors of the Parisian Blood Wedding of 1572 or those of the Thirty Years' War. Only against this background can the overwhelming attraction of the *Hobbesian* "auctoritas non veritas facit legem" be comprehended, and to a certain extent the "moral credit" as well that was conceded to absolutism as a regulatory power concentrated in *one* will. Absolutism forfeited it in less than two hundred years. Its revolutionary heir, democratic positivism[15], drew its power of persuasion neither from mere genetic legitimacy nor only from the proof in the regulatory function, but rather, as *N. Luhmann* correctly indicates[16], essentially from the ability to effect and manage technical-social *change* that rests upon the apparent optional *changeability* of the law. The voluntaristic component of order and appeasement (an elementary prerequisite of the law) which at the beginning of this development, i.e., in *Hobbes*, clearly stands in the foreground, such as legal security, becomes in the further development increasingly less important compared to the effort to do justice to the politically far-reaching, technical, ideological and societal differentiation by means of constantly "amended" standardizations. Generally the legislator is tagging along technical-social change, which is here remarked without any pejorative overtone. Quite the contrary, the legislator may be least successful when he, whether by "planning" laws or by danger prevention that plans ahead, tries to anticipate future developments. One might also recall here that the present type of legislation is a modern invention for the management of social conflicts and that the *judicial* settlement of disputes – retrospective and only cautiously abstracting and generalizing – stood at the beginning of the modern development of law.

This should not be misunderstood as a plea for the restriction of the legal function to the regulation of conflicts and damages, but rather seen as an indication that the intensification of the law's planning and social-*organizational* function, that differentiates into transitory detail, creates specific difficulties. One of them has been recognized by the Federal Constitutional Court in that the Court confers upon the legislator for the "sphere of the administering administration", that is in the sphere of administering justice, a greater discretion and more general directives than in the sphere of interference administration.[17] But another point seems more important to me here: the more that natural law forfeited its unquestioned binding character as "*just*" law in terms of content, the brighter shone positive law as an order that may not guarantee justice per se but nevertheless is safeguarded and realizable, a law that promises clear responsibilities and the ability to adapt to changing social relationships. It is precisely this shine, which at the least promised *secure* and the best also just law, that fades in the present projective-programmatical activism of countless instances involved in the process of making law. The positivity of the law – once synonymous with the concentration and strength of *one* legislative will[18] – is today in many cases merely the expression of deconcentrated weakness of will, unraveled into a multistage and polycentric process of the concretization of legal norms, whereby administrative refinement and "application" of legal norms and judicative control of legal norms and their application are interwoven in the legislative creation of legal norms.

The legal-technical individual phenomena that illuminate this development have been variously described and are well-known. It suffices to mention a few key words here:

1) The growing need to make amendments, which often in no way ensues from a change in the standards of justice or in the prominent values, but rather only from the banal change of socio-economic facts – consider inflationary compensation in salary law or similar cases – had already quickly led to a division of labor between the parliamentarian legislature and executive legislator – lawmaker and ministerial order maker. This basic scheme can be thoroughly differentiated almost arbitrarily by calling in further, more case-related, but also interest-bound authorities, for example, self-administrative-corporationally organized mixed committees as the "issuer of directives", and so forth. The problematical nature of the *dynamic blank reference to other provisions* (dynamische Blankettverweisung) that becomes important in practice especially in the law of technical security is neither dealt with finally from the point of view of the principle of the constitutional state nor from that of the principle of democracy.[19] "Public law", which is especially subject to this process of the decodification of norms and the deconcentration of the setting of norms, thus invisibly becomes a non-public law and, measured against the publication standards of *I. Kant*, practically a non-law.[20] Such a law has absolutely no chance of penetrating into the general consciousness of the law whereby, as previously mentioned, an essential factor of legal security is lost.

2) A variant arises if the legislator consciously calculates a limited period of time of his products from the very beginning, for instance, in that he limits the period of validity, or in the diluted form that a data is set for an extension of the law.[21] Such "*temporary laws*" are commonly the expression of an "uncertainty of prognosis"; we have encountered and can encounter them especially in education, but also in media law (upon the introduction of new communication technologies). As "experimental laws", even for

"pilot projects", they lay down an obligation for the enforcement agencies to report to the legislator who is still uncertain in the matter – a shy attempt at the so urgently necessary implementation control of the administration. The figure of temporary law, however, has also always been of interest to the gentlemen of the *state of emergency*; this line runs from the emergency decree practice of the President of the German Reich to the notorious "Enabling Act" of 24 March 1933, the "law for relieving the need of the people and the Reich"; the need continued, the law was twice extended by means of Reichstag law and then once again on 10 May 1943 by order of the "Führer", until it disappeared into the orcus of history with all its accoutrements: Reichstag, Reich government and Reich Chancellor of the Pan- German Reich.

3) The much criticized application of *indefinite legal conceptions* and *comprehensive clauses* can be based, which is often not clearly seen, on very different reasons that are to be assessed partly negatively and partly positively. It has become common to regard them primarily as a political weakness of articulation and decision[22], as the inability of the legislator, bowed by compromise, to bring himself to draw clear limits. Another possibility, which in the past dominated, e.g., police law, is the conscious handing over of a considerable leeway to the executive. A third perspective is gained if one understands the law as a "*strategy for optimalization*" to, for instance, the realization of civil liberties, and the legislator therefore, in addition to legal "rules", also works with legal "principles".[23] Such a dynamization of the protection of the objects of legal protection has been expressly approved and recommended by the Federal Constitutional Court in the form of the "principles of the best possible protection against dangers and risk prevention".[24] The *dynamic protection of civil liberties* by concentrating on the respectively latest state of scientific knowledge and technical feasibility is not to be achieved in the law of technical security by rigid, admittedly exact numerical limiting values, but only with the help of indefinite optimalization formulas: the direct intention of the security of the *objects* of legal protection wins out over the postulate of legal security.

To 2) through 4): Insecurity with applying and enforcing the law: The legislator has become uncertain: not only with respect to the appropriate judgement of technical and economical circumstances but also with respect to the evaluation of social developments and valuations. Thus he accepts, partly consciously, partly unconsciously, the division of labor that becomes effective in the concretization of law oriented in each individual case as a division of responsibility, as a kind of relief from the burden of his own responsibility and integrates it into his law-making program. He does this when he operates not with measure and number but with clauses of proportionality, reasonableness or hardship, and also when he states in the explanation of a draft that the legal development in this or another question must be left up to the practice, adjudication and doctrine. The adjudication, especially that of the Federal Constitutional Court, accepts and reinforces this self-moderation or self-abdication of the legislator not only when the Court bends omitted, barely precise or weak statements of the first power into shape with the help of the palliative, "interpretation of a law so that it conforms to the constitution" (="verfassungskonforme Gesetzesauslegung"), but also when it lets comprehensive clauses, among other things, apply with the remark that the individual can appeal to and obtain judicial protection at any time when he feels aggrieved by an "unjust" application of an indefinite formula. Furthermore, over many years of practice, adjudication has made comprehensive clauses sufficiently more precise with regard to the contents.[25)] The judge, who, on the one hand and particularly in his self-conception, obtains his legitimacy essentially from the strict ties to the law, enabling him to impartiality, must on the other hand recommend *his* role (what else?) and his *procedure* as a compensation for functional faults in the basis for legitimacy.

"Secure" law and thereby "legal security" is not to be obtained by qualified acts of *legislation* alone. What is additionally necessary is security in the concretization of the law in individual cases by the administration, security of the application of law in individual cases in the sense of the certainty of enforcement, i.e., the *certainty of execution* – in which the *dimension of time* plays an ever more important role for the credibility of the social constitutional state – and after that the security in the judicial control of the application of law in the sense of the *certainty of the finding* (also those that allow a *prognosis* of a decision) and the *function of pacification* of the court ruling.

Ultimately all these modalities of legal security exist in interaction, mediated by the practice, with the *security of the general consciousness of the law*: this security is produced and empowered by those modalities; the modalities are not based to the slightest extent on the confidence of the organs to feel themselves in accordance with the general consciousness of the law. Where this consciousness of the law becomes uncertain, where it is *impossible to decide* whether an ("erring") vociferous minority is moving into battle against a ("legally loyal") silent majority, or whether on the contrary the minority only announces what the majority or similar group also thinks and desires, or whether thirdly a minority articulating its wishes is not at all opposed in a specific question by a consolidated majority due to lack of interest – consider red flag key words such as the plutonium industry, abortion, squatting in or restoration of buildings, the regulation for Queen's evidences, the census, the prohibition to practice a profession, the right of election for foreigners, among many others – where in other words the administrative person and the judge can and may neither read the people's minds nor agree with everything they say, both of them have difficulty with the other elements of legal security as well.

3. If one inquires less legal-psychologically and legal-sociologically but rather constitutionally into the *reasons* for legal security deficits in the application, enforcement and control of the law, one will first be referred back to the previously described "faulty" performance of the legislator. When he produces no clear binding characters, the "subsequently arranged" powers (in terms of time and function, not hierarchically) can neither "execute" nor "control" a binding character; they can (and must under the pressure to make a decision) make an indefinite binding character to a definite one according to individually chosen standards. In so far as those involved in the process are here accorded a chance for effective codetermination of content, one can understand the

demand raised everywhere for a "proceduralization" of the law. Except for that, one should concede without illusions that the mere preservation of procedural positions instead of clear substantive powers in no way improves the situations of the persons concerned.

In the following consideration we consciously disregard the possibility that has been realized a thousand times that the legislator as a consequence of human, political or institutional failure (whatever that in detail may be) can produce "bad" laws, that is, laws which are inadequate juristic- technically as well as with respect to the object of regulation. We assume purely heuristically that he has used his opportunities in the most optimal way and continues to do so. Then, in this thought experiment, the common cause for the loss of legal security in *all* phases of the concretization of law appears that much more clearly. The often only provisional, in many cases indefinite-undecided, but on the other hand, the detailed-perfectionistic side of legislation – think of the broad sphere of technical security law, of social law or of tax law – is compelled only to a small extent by the requirements of the formal condition where a rule of law is maintained (and even that only apparently), but rather already by the circumstance that today almost all legislation is *amendment* legislation. The real reason for this legislative activism is, bluntly stated, the group-pluralistic putting through of interests, and more eloquently expressed: the striving for the optimal security of the objects of legal protection as the apparent realization of social justice. In the phases of the *application* of law and the judicative *control* of law, this striving makes itself felt in various figures of the law. They have a legal-relativizing effect in common: the law is not "unseen" but rather filtered, applied in orientation to individual cases. The best known and most effective of these correctives are the *civil rights* and their methodological pacemaker, the principle of commensurability ("prohibition of excess"). They relativize the absolute enforcement of the law not only within the scope of the police law principle of discretionary prosecution, but also, as the discussion on the regulation of "Queen's evidence" has shown, according to tendency all the way into the sphere of the criminal law principle of mandatory prosecution. They become just as effective as discretionary considerations directed by civil rights as they are in the *additional undefined discretion of denial* of the executive (in the face of all legal requirements for corresponding applications for permits).[26] That this final instrument that fundamentally destroys the classic-constitutional relationship between individual liberty and governmental restriction (liberty as a rule, restriction as exception) has already been applied only in the special matter of the use of atomic energy – see par. 7, sec. 2, Atomic Law – is no objection to, but rather a proof of, my thesis: where special situations of danger occur, the legislator passes regulations with the direct intention to the protection of the objects of legal protection. Well-tried constitutional, procedural organizations that guarantee the individual legal security as legal certainty are then sacrified to prevention as well.

The reorientation of the entire process of the concretization of the law from the primary guarantee of legal security to the direct intention to secure the *objects* of legal protection manifests itself undisguisedly in the last and most intensive phase of judicial legal control, in the control of norms by the Federal Constitutional Court. What is typical here, if one disregards for once disputes over competence and the rather helpless 'unlawfulness of arbitrary rule-legislation' to Art. 3, sec. 1, Basic Law, is the "weighing" up of two objects of civil liberty – e.g., the freedom of art against the right of personality[27)] – or of a civil right and an "objective" constitutional good such as the functional ability of the German Federal Armed Forces or the maintenance of criminal law or the collective wage system of labor partners.[28)] When a civil right stands against a civil right, the decision "can only be taken upon weighing all the circumstances of the individual case[29)]; casuistical thinking on justice prevails over generalizing thinking on legal security. The Federal Constitutional Court has developed, beginning with the doctrine of interaction[30)] and the principle of "militant democracy"[31)], a complete arsenal of concepts and principles of "constitutional key concepts", as I have so designated them[32)], with which the consequences of the direct intention to protect the objects of legal protection should be dealt with in a legal-conceptual way.

4. The expansion of preventive policy which can be observed in many fields – it extends from technical security to inner security and criminological policy and on to the prevention of diseases and to other forms of social security – is only one, admittedly important component of the presently outlined, overall development of the legal system to a system of directly intended security of the objects of legal protection. Until now the question of the causes of this development has remained unanswered; the question, posed in the introduction as thesis II, of the meaning of this development with respect to the actual productive efficiency of the modern constitutional state is also unanswered. To this point, in closing, some completely preliminary comments.

The problematical nature to which one's attention is called here expresses itself in the linking of two concepts that respectively form the titles of two books, which in turn illuminate one side of the indivisible comprehensive subject matter: the "Society of Risks", by *Ulrich Beck*, 1986, and "The Security State", 1980, by *Joachim Hirsch*. Both systems live, put in the idiom of bourgeois morals, "beyond their means". The "society of risks" lives beyond its means in that the industrial production of affluence simultaneously produces environmentally destructive and life endangering risks. The security state lives beyond its means in that it, one-sidedly bound by industrial society, forestalls social, ideological and technological conflicts, hinders their open political settlement and thereby exhausts the resources of legitimacy from which it must live as a constitutional state. The picture first becomes complete, however, when one understands the ideological key word, 'militant democracy', and at the same time the legalistic introversion of the democratic constitutional state – *Werner Süss* concisely characterized it as "bringing about peace through preventive state power" (1984) – as an attempt at an answer, a certainly misguided answer to the exaggerated expectations of security and the unreasonable demands for duties of all societal groups on the state.

To illustrate this, please allow ad hoc the use of an ideal- typical-abstracting epoch-scheme without any claim to historical accuracy in detail.

At the inception of the modern state, the function of securing peace, the external and internal appeasement of the territories of a prince that were often jumbled up together, prevailed. Standing armies of mercenaries, the development of a centralized, professional bureaucracy, the codification of the law and its application by a "learned", that is, an equally professional judiciary are the main instruments of external and internal security, the protection of the objects of legal protection by means of secured law, in short: early absolutist states that guaranteed peace. Its further development to a late absolutist, more or less enlightened welfare state ensues without a fundamental caesure. Yet a completely new form is presented by the post-revolutionary state, whether in the republican variant or whether, as in Germany until 1918, in the "constitutional", dualistic variant: decisive in both cases is the recognition and guaranteeing of the individual freedoms of civil liberties. In the thus circumscribed civil sphere, the state has no rights but also, with the exception of forebearances, and that is what is important *here, no duties*. The complete circle of governmental activities remains limited in this way. In the vision of bourgeois-liberal constitutionalism the state may be burdened first and foremost with the *securing* of *peace* and *freedom*, but not with the duty of the immediate establishment of social justice. *Bismarck's* answer to the "social question" with the social security legislation of the 80s stems from a complex political motivation but not in any case from the view that is was a central duty of the state to initiate a just distribution of goods or even only a distribution and redistribution of chances.[33)]

A completely new stage of government responsibility for duties is reached with the transition to the "sovereignty of the people", with the change from the monarchistic to the democratic principle. What this change means not only for the state formation of intent, for the state division of functions and for the legitimacy of state action, but rather most of all for the *substance* of state activity, first becomes completely apparent in the present in view of the ecological and economical limits of a fully matured social state. If one argues constitutionally, one usually considers the events of 1918/19 in Germany – in so far 1949 posed nothing fundamentally new – from the aspect of the change of the *subjects*: the form of government changes with the holders of government power and, more fundamentally, the subject of the power creating constitutional law changes as well; the sovereign people take the place of the sovereign princes. Importantly enough, herewith the foundation of legitimacy of the state also changes. In this connection less attention is usually directed to the question of continuity and change in government duties, but least of all to the question of the responsibility for duties in *terms of content*. In other words, the question which has constitutionally "been lying on the table" (of the people) since the end of the princes' reign and which, however, is certainly not to be answered with *constitutional* means is: How does a society that has democratically organized itself as a state find in terms of content the "common weal", the "interest of the general public", the "interest of the community as a whole", or "social justice"? Perhaps the question takes one by surprise because first one will object that the problem of the "correct common weal" direction of the state is no specifically democratic one; it has burdened crowned heads to an equal extent. And secondly, the answer is well-known; it results under the authority of the Basic Law at any rate from the state's determination of objectives in the constitution, from the public contest of opinion and from the democratic wrestling for power. And one refers the questioner to the formulations, that may already be characterized as classic, of the Communist Party of Germany decision of the Federal Constitutional Court in which "progress to social justice" is emphasized as a guiding principle for all state measures whose concretizations arise in the political struggle for power as a "process of clarification and change" of competing ideas of common weal.[34) Both objections miss the target, the first because the question of common weal was indeed a theoretical- philosophical one but not a constitutional-practical one for the divine right of kings: it combined the legitimacy of the subject of state power with the legitimacy for its actions; the tyrant "quoad exercitium" may occur, but seldom comes for that reason to a fall. The subjects' expectations of the achievements of the rulers remain limited.

The second objection proves itself to be "petitio principii" in that it links liberal market model thinking, the belief in the "Invisible Hand", with Rousseauean-democratic autonomy of will. Even if the most extreme prerequisite conditions for the functioning of this model could be empirically guaranteed, the theoretical problem remains of how the unity of something "correct" should be able to come to be out of almost infinitely many particular "errors". What this means in practice is that out of the multitude of individual and group interests, for everyone should be able to propose his wishes for consideration in the democratic state, through the filter of graduated majority decisions, a "resultant" of wills and interests finally emerges. Yet this is not more than a mental summary, at best a coalition paper or a government statement of policy, but hardly an objective program of action, free from contradiction and capable of holding out for a long period of time. Whoever doesn't "find himself" or insufficiently "fiends himself" therein, will continue to pursue his interests as "secondary, subordinate and anti-policy".[35) The attempt of the political system to reduce the complexity of the diversity of expectations and demands to a concept correct in itself that could earn the name, "common weal", succeeds only temporarily, incompletely and for the price of the emergence of numerous oppositional epicenters of the policy.

5. The theoretical as well as practical-political *attempts at* responses to these findings are extremely diverse, to a certain extent opposed. What appears to one as a crisis and emergency is perceived by others as a democratic virtue and as a chance to develop new values, procedures and institutions. Where one laments the loss of governability[36), and others diagnose the "new lack of clarity"[37), still others respond to the "removing of the borders" and "loss of locality" of policies with concepts of pluralizing legal order(s)[38): the place of the linear-hierarchically regulatory model is taken up by arenas of action interconnected by networks or also the interaction of partial systems which produce their own legal elements "self-referentially" and "autoproductively".[39) The use of scientific policy consultation is also variously judged; the euphoric expectations of the productive efficiency of institutionalized "Technology Assessment" (Technikenfolgen-Abschätzung) have made room for a rather more sober evaluation.[40) Yet in general the insight seems to prevail that the creation of "correct", "proper" law and thereby of "correct common weal" decisions only promises success in complex procedures with the participation of

those interested, those concerned and of experts in the matter. In so far the "proceduralization" of the law is a democratically appropriate element upon which pessimists as well as optimists, and centralists as well as pluralists can agree.

It comes as no surprise that the greater portion of the German doctrine of constitutional law, traditionally oriented to the unity of the state as the center of power, policy and law, takes either no notice at all of these new developments and their legal-theoretical and legal-sociological interpretative attempts or does so only with a secret shudder and blatant criticism. It attempts to adhere to the model of central regulation of societal processes by means of centrally created law through a number of conceptual strategies with all their practical-political consequences in order to rescue parliamentarian democracy "from the attacks of democratic utopianism" – as stated, for instance, in the fighting formula of *J. Isensee*.[41)] Some of these strategies are listed here in brief outline to afford a sufficient impression of the range of the field of discussion:

– 1. The ethical interpretation of the constitution.[42)] This was previously discussed under the aspect of "militant democracy". It is a matter of an "artificial" narrowing, that has to be put through politically, of the public weal alternatives possible within the scope of the constitution. The interpretation of latitudes of freedom as an already completed frame of social-ethical behavior in the sense of the realization of values is useful for the legitimacy of solid, political restrictions.

– 2. The citizen is seen accordingly less as the subject of civil *rights*, but more as the addressee of elementary *duties*. The old *Hobbesian* connection of protection and obedience is newly proclaimed as the "civil right to security"[43)] with the only exception that it isn't clearly stated that thereby is meant a right of the state to (unlimited) production of "security" (with corresponding restrictions of freedom) and that protection is only afforded to those who heed not only the laws but also their interpretation by those in power.

– 3. In an intensified way, this should apply to the democratic representative, the delegate. His supposedly ethically indifferent democratic basic nature must first be tamed and refined by means of a commitment to an "ethos of office" and in this way made relevant to the common weal. In so far as virtues such as incorruptibility, the greatest possible impartiality and the willingness to learn are meant here, one can accept that; yet as soon as one inquires into the objective contents of the "ethos of office" with respect to the democratic common weal, one receives no answer – of course not!

– 4. The reduction to a single center of legitimacy (in parliament) can only succeed if one maintains once and for all that the representative democracy form of rule is the only possible, sensible form of democracy at all.[44)] Then there is no longer any tension between an ideal of *self*-determination and a reality of *co*determination (as voters); direct democracy becomes non-democracy. One falls back on *Kant's* touchstone of a *hypothetical* consensus[45)] upon which, however, the enlightened monarch can rest himself just as well as the republican, weary of the people, can.

– 5. In this context the prevention strategies can finally be seen. They should already remove the germs of crystallization of future conflicts, deviations and epicenters. Where they are directly aimed at the security of threatened, universally important objects of legal protection, they indeed link the effect of appeasement with that of legitimacy. Yet "social justice" is only ostensibly achieved when a maximum of different, diverging and also contrary interests is satisfied. For unavoidably in this connection one comes up against the point of structural overtaxing of the state mentioned in the introduction.

– 6. If one characterizes as here, simplified ideal–typically, the bourgeois-liberal constitutional state, that has been historically stamped by the constitutional categories of the citizen-state relationship, as a *legal security state* and confronts it with the democratic social state as a "*security of the objects of legal protection state*", then some clarifications are appropriate at this point:

1. The (liberal) legal security state produces the security of the *objects* of legal protection as well, and that is even its ratio essendi. The decisive difference to the herein designated "security of the objects of legal protection state" = prevention state is, however, in the fact that the legal security state
   a) does not itself create the real substratum of the objects of legal protection to be safeguarded and that it
   b) leaves the actual distributional order of these objects essentially untouched up to society.

2. The "security of the objects of legal protection state" or prevention state should on the other hand perform various duties. Namely, it should
   a) produce the actual goods to a large extent itself, at any rate in the infrastructure sphere, or organize and guarantee the supply with these goods respectively – *provision for existence*;
   b) optimally protect the societally produced actual objects of legal protection and the possibilities of their production – *legal security* – but at the same time
   c) neutralize the simultaneously produced external risks and negative consequences[46)] – *risk provision* – and
   d) finally, keep open the permanent revision of the actual order of distribution at least as an actually possible alternative – *social justice*.

How strongly these settings of objectives collide with each other is shown, for example, when tax reforms, that have been recognized as politically "correct" with respect to economics and finance, demand measures for the "reduction of subsidies" and thereby interference with the "vested rights" for their realization. As it is one and the same federal state and party state organized society that must put through its technological-social concept of security (2. a, b, c above), in so far as it has one, and its social concept of justice (in so far as it has one, 2. d above) against its own thinking on demands and the protection of property (2. a and b above), immobility is essentially to be expected, incremental progress is already a lucky chance.

A way out of this situation in the sense of "pat solution" is neither in sight nor to be expected. Programs of a principally envisioned "denationalization" of the management of duties[47] or also only of an autonomizing of partial areas (whereby legal form and legal procedure are questions of secondary priority) quickly prove themselves to be bad utopias. The analysis of the ideal type of the "prevention state" shows that this is not only already a considerably conceptless reality, but also that society in the future will not be able to function without a central system of coordination. This must at least coordinate the partial systems of the social justice of distribution (collective wage system, competitive marketplace, provision for existence, social security) with the technological-ecological regulation of risks and with "classical" legal security and bring them to a functional balance.

The analysis has further shown where the institutional approach to overcoming this long-term task must be sought: first and foremost, the *democratic legislature*, with all the ties of its members to federationally organized, particular interests, must develop the consciousness and summon the effort and strength to make the necessary positive as well as negative decisions of selection.[48] The *law* must not only be a register of more or less bad, abstractly concealed group interests; it must become "universal" again, not (only) in the sense of formally equal, universal validity, but also in the sense of the classification in terms of content of the four complexes of duty of the prevention state. Otherwise we relapse into a state of the consciousness of the law that the old Romans, these legal thinkers par excellence, had already overcome: for their early images of Justice showed her not with a scale and sword, but with a scale and a *cornucopia*. We would have to attribute it to our Promethian hubris if in the third millenium the cornucopia of Justice ultimately proves itself to be Pandora's Box indeed.

Notes

1 *Josef Isensee*, Das Grundrecht auf Sicherheit, Zu den Schutzpflichten des freiheitlichen Verfassungsstaates, 1983.

2 *Wilhelm v. Humboldt*, Ideen zu einem Versuch, die Grenzen der Wirksamkeit des Staats zu bestimmen (1792).

3 *Dieter Grimm*, Verfassungsrechtliche Anmerkungen zum Thema Prävention, KritV 1986, pp. 38, 52, 54

4 Cf. the controversies between *Ernst Forsthoff*, *Wolfgang Abendroth* and *Otto Bachof*, 1954. Documented in *E. Forsthoff*, (Ed.), Rechtsstaatlichkeit und Sozialstaatlichkeit, 1968. To: "Almost declaring dead" cf. *E. Forsthoff*, Der Staat der Industriegesellschaft, 1971, p. 46.

5 *Forsthoff*, Der Staat der Industriegesellschaft, pp. 164 et seq.

6 E.g., *James O'Connor*, The Fiscal Crisis of the State, N.Y., 1973; *Rolf Richard Grauhan and Rudolf Hickel*, (Eds.), Krise des Steuerstaats? Leviathan Sonderheft 1/1978. On the "overtaxing" of the state, cf. also *Horst Dreier*, Der Ort der Souveränität, in *Horst Dreier/Jochen Hofmann*, Parlamentarische Souveränität und technische Entwicklung, 1986, pp. 11 et seq.

7 *Forsthoff*, see Note 5, pp. 51 et seq.

8 *Gustav Radbruch*, Rechtsphilosophie, 5th ed., 1956, pp. 168 et seq.

9 On the idea of the time period especially: *Helmut Coing*, Grundzüge der Rechtsphilosophie, 3rd ed., 1976, pp. 137 et seq.

10 In this connection *Erhard Denninger*, Staatliche Hilfe zur Grundrechtsausübung (Verfahren, Organisation, Finanzierung). In: *J. Isensee and P. Kirchhof*, (Eds.), Handbuch des Staatsrechts der Bundesrepublik Deutschland, par. 101, with further references, to be published in 1989

11 *Hermann Heller and Max Wenzel*, Der Begriff des Gesetzes in der Reichsverfassung, VVDStRL, No. 4, 1928, pp. 98 et seq.; *Forsthoff*, Über Massnahme-Gesetze. In: *Forsthoff*, Rechtsstaat im Wandel, 1964, pp. 78 et seq.; *Michael Kloepfer*, Gesetzgebung im Rechtsstaat, VVDStRL, No. 40, 1982, pp. 63 et seq., p. 97.

12 *Jean-Jacques Rousseau*, Du contract social, 1762, Lib. II., cap. 6.

13 E.g., *Hugo Grotius*, de iure belli ac pacis libri tres, ed. by P.C. Molhuysen, Leiden, 1919, Lib. I, cap. 1, par. 10.

14 *Carl Schmitt*, Politische Theologie, 2nd edition, 1934, 49: "All concise concepts of modern political science are secularized theological concepts".

15 On the connection of the voluntarism and the positivity of the law, cf. *Hasso Hofmann*, Legitimität und Rechtsgeltung, 1977, pp. 24 et seq.

16 *Niklas Luhmann*, Rechtssoziologie, Vol. 1, pp. 190 et seq., Vol. 2, pp. 207 et seq., pp. 294 et seq., 1972.

17 Since BVerfGE 11, 50, p. 60.

18 Cf. *G.W.F. Hegel*, Grundlinien der Philosophie des Rechts (1821), especially pars. pp. 214, 273, 279, 300, 320.

19 Cf. *Hermann Hill*, Einführung in die Gesetzgebungslehre, 1982, 114 m.w.N., further *Denninger*, Arzneimittelrichtlinien und "Verschreibungsfähigkeit", 1981, pp. 36 et seq.

20 *Immanuel Kant*, Zum ewigen Frieden, 1796, Anhang II.

21 An example: the conscientious objection reform law, KDVNG of 28.2.1983, BGBl. I S. 203, Art. 6, sec. 2.

22 Since *Carl Schmitt's* "dilatory formula compromises", cf. Verfassungslehre, 1928, pp. 31 et seq.

23 To this cf. *Robert Alexy*, Theorie der Grundrechte, 1985, pp. 71 et seq.

24 BVerfGE 49, p. 89, p. 140, p. 143

25 The guarantee of protection by means of judicial process instead of by precise laws: e.g., BVerfGE 66, 337, p. 356.

26 Cf. BVerfGE 49, 89, p. 146. On the principle of commensurability and of mandatory prosecution cf., e.g., *Manfred Schreiber*, Duldung von Rechtsbrüchen, Neue Strategie und Taktik der Polizei? In: *Schreiber, M.* (Ed.), Polizeilicher Eingriff und Grundrechte, FS für Rudolf Samper, 1982, pp. 17 et seq. Further already *Denninger*, Polizei und demokratische Politik, JZ 1970, 145, p. 151.

27 Exemplary: BVerfGE 30, 173, p. 195; 67, 213, p. 228.

28 The functional ability of the German Federal Armed Forces: since BVerfGE 28, 243, 261 ("The necessity of an undisturbed routine working of the German Armed Forces" and "The need for the maintenance of discipline"); see: The maintenance of criminal law, cf. *Wilfried Hassemer*, Die "Funktionstüchtigkeit der Strafrechtspflege" – ein neuer Rechtsbegriff? Strafverteidiger 1982, pp. 275 et seq.
On the entire problem: *Denninger*, Verfassungsrechtliche Schlüsselbegriffe, in: FS für R. Wassermann, 1985, pp. 279 et seq., p. 292, (N. 54).

29 See Note 27: E 30, p. 195.

30 BVerfGE 7, 198, p. 208.

31 Since BVerfGE 2, pp. 1 et seq.

32 See Note 28.

33 In this connection *Lothar Gall*, Bismarck. Der weisse Revolutionär, 1980, pp. 648 et seq.

34 BVerfGE 5, 85, p. 198.

35 *Ulrich Beck*, Risikogesellschaft auf dem Weg in eine andere Moderne, 1986, p. 368.

36 *Wilhelm Hennis/Peter Graf Kielmannsegg and Ulrich Matz*, (Eds.), Regierbarkeit, Vol. 1, 1977, Vol. 2, 1979; on the governability of parliamentarian democracy, Cappenberger Gespräche Vol. 15, 1979, with reports by *J. Isensee* and *Hans Meyer*.

37 *Jürgen Habermas*, Die Neue Unübersichtlichkeit, 1985, especially pp. 141 et seq.

38 Cf. *U. Beck*, Note 35, and *Karl-Heinz Ladeur*, Abwägung – Ein neues Paradigma des Verwaltungsrechts, 1984.

39 *Gunther Teubner*, (Ed.), Dilemmas of Law in the Welfare State, 1986; a good survey of the *same* is to be found in After Legal Instrumentalism?, pp. 299 et seq.; further the *same*, Hyperzyklus in Recht und Organisation. Zum Verhältnis von Selbstbeobachtung, Selbstkonstitution und Autopoiesis, in: *Michael Schmid and Hans Haferkamp*, (Eds.), Sinn, Kommunikation und soziale Differenzierung, 1987, pp. 89 et seq.

40 Cf. *Jürgen v. Kruedener and Klaus v. Schubert*, (Eds.), Technikfolgen und sozialer Wandel, 1981, there especially *Herbert Paschen/Gotthard Bechmann and Bernd Wingert*, Funktion und Leistungsfähigkeit des Technology Assessment (TA) im Rahmen der Technologiepolitik, pp. 57 et seq. Further: *Carl Böhret*, Technikfolgen und Verantwortung der Politik. In: Aus Politik und Zeitgeschichte, B 19–20/1987, pp. 3 et seq.

41 *J. Isensee*, Demokratie – verfassungsrechtlich gezähmte Utopie. In: *U. Matz*, (Ed.), Aktuelle Herausforderungen der repräsentativen Demokratie, 1985, pp. 43, 45.

42 In this connection first and foremost: *Ulrich K. Preuss*, Politische Verantwortung und Bürgerloyalität, 1984, esp. pp. 240 et seq.

43 Cf. Note 1.

44 Cf. *Ernst-Wolfgang Böckenförde*, Demokratie und Repräsentation – Zur Kritik der heutigen Demokratiediskussion, 1983, 14: "The result can be summed up in this way that democracy as a concept of state form can not be conceived in the sense of direct democracy." The necessary discussion of Böckenförde's perceptive analysis and critique can not ensue here.

45 *Kant*, Über den Gemeinspruch: ... (1793), II. Vom Verhältnis der Theorie zur Praxis im Staatsrecht (Gegen Hobbes), Folgerung.

46 Cf. *Martin Jänicke*, Staatsversagen, 2nd ed., 1987, pp. 136 et seq.

47 Approximately in the sense of the "Minimal State" by *Robert Nozick*, Anarchie/Staat/Utopia, o.J., especially pp. 143 et seq.

48 In this sense also *Peter Badura*, Parlamentarische Gesetzgebung und gesellschaftliche Autonomie, Walter-Raymond-Stiftung Kleine Reihe Heft 43, Parlamentarische Gesetzgebung und Geltungsanspruch des Rechts, 1987, pp. 9 et seq.

3.
Prevention as a Problematic Objective in the Criminal Justice System

Peter-Alexis Albrecht

I. Prevention as an Idea in Legal and Social Theory

1. Prevention as a technology of social control

"Prevention" is currently used to justify completely different measures of social policy, ranging from classical social welfare policies to classical policies of crime control. There has been a convergence of diverse sociopolitical subsystems into mechanisms of *"social control qua prevention"*. Social policy is increasingly performing functions of social control.[1] Similarly, criminal justice policy, by adopting a preventive orientation, has assumed more comprehensive powers of a traditionally sociopolitical nature than could be justified by its traditional orientation toward punishing overt, legally defined deviance.[2]
Faced with demands for a *greater preventive effectiveness* in the pursuit of empirically definable external goals, *criminal law* may soon lose most of the formal constitutional basis for its legitimacy. While the traditional model confined the social-control aspect of criminal law to the resolution of disputes and the stabilization of expectations, the current trend is for the claims of the criminal law to expand into *the use of prevention to resolve systemic conflicts.*
This *extension of the criminal law's claim to control,* which can be seen throughout the criminal justice system, is the focus of this report. The principal goal of this study is *to determine the function of what is commonly called prevention.* In this article the term "prevention" is not applied in the narrow, legal sense. Thus it means more than "special prevention"[3] or "general prevention"[4] in their usual legal meanings. What is intended is rather a comprehensive, and offensive, *strategy of social control technology* that reaches far beyond the traditional decisionmaking powers of the criminal justice system.[5]

2. On the control function of criminal law

What is usually expected from the law in general, and from criminal law in particular, is guided by its traditional objective, namely, primarily the resolution of disputes. Dispute resolution through law serves to maintain the interactional structure of a society: "The institutionalization of a body of law is the attempt to declare the normative structure of an interactional system to be 'the law' as opposed to deviant normative orientations."[6] Furthermore, the law is expected to safeguard expectations by sanctioning violations. Thus, the control aspect of law has both *symbolic* [7] and *instrumental* [8] dimensions, as we shall observe frequently below.

Law has different *bases of validity* in different types of societies. Historically these bases of validity have included early conceptions of magic, traditional views of social order, and the fiction of rational social contracts. Correspondingly, legal action (or legal practice) has been programmed to achieve various objectives. Among these are the preservation of the status quo ante by reconsiliation, the realization of the order inherent in natural law, and the pursuit of freely programmable goals, as exemplified in positive law.

In this evolutionary process it is especially the last step, the transition from natural law to positive law, which allows the external definition of aims, that is important for our study.[9] Positive law is the first type of law accompanied by an institutionalized jurisprudence. Consequently, the problem of determining the law's purpose becomes an issue only in positive law, since there are no longer any normatively binding goals, neither appeasement of the gods nor restitution of the 'natural' order. Law has, of course, always been functionally related to aims, but it is in positive law that the setting of the aims itself first becomes the object of legal discourse. Objectives of control can now, in theory, be defined arbitrarily, since they are conditional rather than absolute.[10] The law can now be understood from a functional perspective. With the 'disenchantment of the world' (Max Weber), the basis of legal validity shifted to procedural form: law was turned on its head and transformed into *formal rationality*. Its control function was defined, in the abstract, as a residual category: the securing of the boundary conditions in which societal processes can develop.[11] Criticism of the strictly formal orientation in criminal law became vocal at the turn of the century in the writings of Franz von Liszt. In his Marburger Program we find this typical comment: "The prevailing opinion determines the punishment for an offence committed by no offender; that is, its punishments correspond to the *concept* of the crime, to the *abstraction* which legislation and science have formed out of the actual offences. It asks: What does theft, rape, murder, or perjury deserve? Instead of asking: What does *this* thief, *this* murderer, *this* false witness, *this* rapist deserve?"[12] Once such questions were raised, it was only a small step to call for the differentiation of legal consequences according to the personality of the offender. Cesare Lombroso, von Liszt, and other participants in the penal reform debate at the turn of the century vehemently advocated deterrence and fines for occasional offenders, rehabilitation for those who could benefit from it, and imprisonment or at the most the death penalty for incorrigibles.[13]

This concept of treatment differentiation remains popular. We find it in the criminal law reform debate [14] and still later in the criminal justice program of the Working Group of Social Democratic Legal Practitioners (Arbeitsgemeinschaft sozialdemokratischer Juristen, ASJ). According to this program, "the measure to be taken should depend on the dangerousness of the offender. The dangerousness of the offender should be established by scientific prognosis... Only the dangerousness of the offender that has been manifested in the offence is dispositive."[15]

We have presented this brief sketch of the evolution of the validity of criminal law in order to bring out the dilemma which confronts criminal law today – the dilemma of control. If criminal law extends beyond abstract goals aimed at *differentiating a private sphere of autonomous action*, two problems arise. First, appropriate sanctions must be empirically determined. Second, criminal law thereby encroaches on the *domain of preventive societal protection*. Admittedly, this second stage has not yet been fully reached. If the formal constitutional basis of validity of the legal order becomes fragile and criminal law can no longer be justified on the basis of abstract goals of punishment (revenge, atonement, paying for one's crimes, etc.), and instead the prevention of crime becomes accepted as an additional, and later perhaps the only, duty of criminal law, we find ourselves in the midst of the prevention debate.

If we go one level deeper, we find this evolution to be rooted in a 'disenchanted' societal self-conception that attributes a produced and producible character to societal reality. The concept of legal "deviance" is expanded to become synonymous with social deviance.[16)] Consequently, the traditional claim to control is extended to the solution of systemic conflicts through prevention and to the sanctioning of societal expectations, which are now defined on the basis of realism rather than legal formalism. We shall designate this development as the transition from the liberal constitutional state to the social intervention state.

3. Changing paradigms of social control

The most significant change in the criminal law is a *change in the paradigms* under which it is conceptualized. This change has resulted in a trend away from a *repressively constraining to a preventively planning model*. The problem that results for the law in the wake of this trend can be formulated in the question, "How can one manage the creeping regulation that typifies the welfare state when law is made the tool for intervention and compensation by the welfare state?".[17)] Thus, the transition from the liberal constitutional state to the social intervention state is significant for our problem of "prevention as an objective in the criminal justice system", since linked with this transition is a *change in the role of the state for the society*, and this change in turn influences the function of the criminal law. Such changes do not take place in all spheres with the same speed and intensity; some changes lag behind others. In particular, criminal law may have been one of the last spheres to experience comprehensive functional change. Nonetheless, in this article we shall discuss the objectives of a *future* criminal law, objectives which have only begun to emerge.

Our basic assumption is that such developments as the *shift toward preventive social control*, especially in criminal law, represent a *reaction to signs of crises in areas of control*, but not necessarily in those areas in which the innovation takes place. In contrast with this perspective, the perspective which prevails within the criminal law itself prefers to treat developments within its own field as linear progress, as the way to a more humane, more rational punishment under the motto: The history of criminal law is the history of its abolition.[18)] When we adopt crises paradigms, however, then we must ask

what developments provoked the preventive turn, what societal structures the preventive turn supports, and how it does so.
Let us briefly sketch how *crises develop*? 'Modern' industrial societies live by endangering or destroying their material, ecological, social, and symbolic foundations. Emerging crises tendencies are the result of contradictory demands which the 'modern state' is expected to meet.[19] The interventionist state increasingly steps in to fill the growing functional gaps in the market. The state's administrative apparatus must increasingly assume responsibility for boosting the productivity of human labor through training, retraining, etc.; the system must further compensate for the social and material costs of private production: unemployment, poverty, environmental damage, etc.[20] Simultaneously, a *fundamental change of the social structure* is evident in this development: the social structure no longer differentiates only by class, but now also by *center and periphery*.[21] As trends in unemployment statistics unmistakably demonstrate, the proportion of the population irreversibly excluded from a productive working life is rising. Characteristic of this phenomenon is unemployment in structurally weak sectors, for example, unemployment among young people, women, and academics. This growing unproductive periphery, differing from the traditional lower class, imposes a substantial burden on the welfare state, at least if one takes this state's responsibility seriously.
The result tends to be social and cultural crises. Typically, such crises arise "when normative structures, obeying their own logic, change so as to impair the complementarity between the demands of the state machinery and the employment system, on the one hand, and the perceived needs and legitimate expectations of the members of society, on the other".[22] This societal process of erosion increasingly requires state intervention, typically through a "creeping regulation" (Teubner). Thus, the interventionist state necessarily experiences an *increased need for control*. The number of people to be controlled grows: unemployed youth, marginal groups, the elderly, etc., who must now be subjected to intensified control while they are excluded from the disciplining labor market.
This type of crisis plays a special role for conservative crises theorists. Offering slogans about the threatened "ungovernability" of the modern state, these theorists propose to strengthen social control. According to the conservative analysis, crises of ungovernability result from the fact that the gap between the volume of demands and the capacity for control creates frustrations.[23] One counterstrategy aims at "the institutions of social control, thus at those agencies that regulate the development and maintenance of social aspirations and cultural as well as political value orientations. ... What is important (in these strategies) is that interests, aspirations, and political-social orientations should be placed under control at what amounts to their point of origin."[24]
There can certainly be disagreements as to the extent and scope of preventive build up as a reaction to anticipated crises of control. Yet, what cannot be contested is the *trend* for an increasing number of sectors to come under the *sphere of influence of state-organized control*, whereby a reorientation from repressive to preventive control is promoted, mainly because purely repressive reactions, on the basis of cost alone, would hardly have a chance. Of course, control by a security apparatus was always indispensable for the order and functioning of the 'welfare state'. The new quality that now becomes visible is "that

the policy of internal security no longer comprises the use of the machinery of repressive sanctions alone, but rather transforms itself into a social policy from which rehabilitative and preventive effects are expected".[25)] At the same time the repressive repertoire of the criminal justice system significantly changes. An expansion of the criminal law's claim to control through prevention can be clearly seen. Consequently, the preventive turn is in danger of blurring or even eliminating constitutionally guaranteed preconditions for intervention.

II. The Preventive Build up of the Criminal Justice System

So far we have dealt abstractly with the question of the criminal law's control capability, the expanding function that prevention plays in securing this capability, and the impact of the prevention bandwagon on social theory. Let us now turn to the *concrete preventive phenomena* that appear within the institutions of the criminal justice system, including the police, the criminal courts, and the prisons. We shall concentrate on a discussion of *selected preventive elements* which indicate the change in the social control paradigm. We shall demonstrate how far this paradigmatic change has already progressed and which dangers for the rule of law thereby emerge. Consequently, it is unavoidable that we shall primarily deal with the *negative aspects* of prevention strategies within the criminal justice system.[26)] The risk of exaggerating the negative side may be acceptable, since up to now the supposed utility of preventive strategies has been overstressed and their dangers have been virtually ignored.
In the analysis of the three subsystems (police, criminal courts, prisons) of the criminal justice system, the well-known categories of system, organization, and action are a useful heuristic.[27)] Thus, we want to ask what systemic functions prevention performs for the police, for the criminal courts, and for the prisons (*system level*). Next, we shall sketch how and with what intentions the preventive orientation is transformed into organizational practice in the police, in the criminal courts, and in the prisons (*organization level*). Finally, we shall examine each subsystem to discover the central preventive elements which influence the interactions of controllers and clients (*action level*). Throughout our discussion we shall pay particular attention to the control functions performed by prevention on each of the three levels and to the implications for our framework of social theory.

1. Police and prevention

When we begin with the analysis of preventive orientations in the police subsystem, it quickly becomes clear that prevention on the *system level*, mainly as a validator of social order and a legitimizer of state action, serves as a *'rhetorical Elmer's Glue-All'*.
Increasingly, public debate about the police focuses on preventive strategies. The phrase, "prevention is the noblest duty of the police", has already become a cliché.[28)] As early as 1976 the German Federal Bureau of Investigation (Bundeskriminalamt) organized a

conference titled "Police and Prevention". In his concluding summary, the then president of the Bureau, Horst Herold, reported a unanimous opinion that the first preventive duty of the police is not to avert *concrete* danger. Rather, the preventive duty is pushed forward into a realm where the police do not even have a right to interfere, but where *abstract* dangers threaten to become concrete. Herold saw in this a "breakthrough and a revolution of not yet assessable significance", namely, a new direction in the conceptualization of "police", opening the concept up to socio-planning content as well.[29)]
Alfred Stümper immediately expanded this approach. In an article titled "The Changing Concept and Changing Duties of the Police", he summarized, "What is required is not only an interagency strategy of crime control, but one that also incorporates the entirety of human and social conditions".[30)] Stümper further emphasized that isolated police prevention must begin in the broader human, societal, and state realms. Even very specific preventive measures are often possible only with interagency cooperation, such as with health, welfare, education, tax, and other nonpolice agencies.[31)] According to Stümper, the police should "take increasing initiative in interagency affairs and support the activities of other agencies".[32)]

The *symbolic* and possibly socially integrative *utility* of such a preventive orientation of the police is obvious: It strengthens the population's feeling of security and, largely, for this reason, permits a normatively secured, institutionalized, pre-active *reaction* to a putative *threat to the state and the society*. Prevention of the officially presented type initially encounters no public political resistance. The mechanisms are pointed out by Albrecht Funk et al.: "Isn't it better to let oneself be preventively searched at airports than to circle in the air as a hostage? Isn't it more advisable to help young people caught in a criminal milieu, using police prevention and social assistance, than to leave each individual in a classical liberal's freedom, letting him fail and then locking him up? At first blush, every citizen answers such a question with an unqualified 'Yes'." But just as pertinently Funk et al. add that "citing easy cases obscures the problems which lurk behind the general model of a prevention police. ... What we need is an explicit analysis of competing values. Even airport security checks lose their innocence when one remembers that they serve more general state purposes of surveillance and searches by permitting the photocopying of visas and the recording of border crossings."[33)]

The ultimate goal is to *expand the grounds for, and to advance the timing of, police intervention*. The *practical effects* of this preventive orientation, which may include social disintegration, are usually lost in the public discussion. Wolf-Dieter Narr warns with unusual clarity against early intervention: "Organizing the police preventively ... would mean enabling them to be active where nothing has yet happened, where no suspicion yet exists."[34)] Narr sees the danger of the police being equipped with preventive tools which allow them to work in a socially prevasive manner and to overact.[35)] For Narr, the consequences of such a conception of preventive-police are apparent: If one wants to provide people and places with total protection at all times, one must violate the integrity of these same people and places. Thus, Narr sees in this idea of prevention "the end of all civil liberties for the sake of guaranteed security, despite the obvious fact that security cannot even begin to be guaranteed in this way".[36)]

There is a *tension* between these beliefs in a socially planning police force (Herold) or even in a multi-agency preventive strategy (Schwind, Stümper), on the one hand, and the fear that absolute police authority and Orwellian total control will destroy civil liberties (Narr), on the other. Clearly, then, everyone has the same *target*: the *legitimating of expanded police authorization to intervene* – it is only that some desire it, while others warn against it.[37)]

As we move from the system level to the *organization level*, the practical effects of this preventive orientation become more clear. The effective implementation of strategies for a preventive police force requires *modernizing the police* in several ways. Here the watchwords are professionalization, differentiation, and rationalization.

Within the police,[38)] professionalization of the police machinery is seen as a necessary *prerequisite for effective crime prevention*. Along with professionalization and differentiation of areas of police activity, a "forensic science"[39)] develops. It adheres to the principle that "a rational orientation to, and penetration of police work by, an efficient, forensic science is ... not only useful, but in the long run also unavoidable in the interest of internal security".[40)] *A preventive reorientation* of police activities on the organizational level *requires, and is expressed in*, 1) the development of areas of police activity going beyond the classical duties of administration and crime-fighting into explicitly preventive aims (e.g., juvenile police officers, police social workers) or analysis and planning functions,[41)] and 2) the creation of a police science that develops, systematizes, and prepares for implementation new scientific disciplines. As police skills of observation become sharper, more causes of delinquency come into police view, and more criminogenic areas that were hitherto unmonitored become the subject of police work.

Consider some examples. One product of the expansion of police activity is the "youth" or "juvenile police officer", who in many large cities already belongs to the standard repertoire of preventive police work.[42)] When the juvenile officer is called in, the officer tries, especially in the no-man's-land between parents and school, on the one hand, and recreational facilities, on the other, to restrain endangered and delinquent minors from criminal acts and to reduce the opportunities for crime. The juvenile officer uses appropriate influence to achieve these goals at a stage where the police are not yet authorized to intervene with force.[43)] An extreme variant, first tested in the United States, assigns a police officer as a "school resource officer" for the express purpose of maintaining contacts with endangered juveniles in the *schools* themselves and then keeping an eye on these juveniles.[44)]

These and similar early and profound interventions into the social and cultural affairs of private persons are the components of prevention strategies that are already being implemented under the label "interagency preventive crime control policy". In a publication series of the Lower Saxony Ministry of Justice, subject headings range from "Socialization and Crime Prevention Activities of Kindergartens and Schools" and "Recreational Activities Instruction as an Essential Extension of a Crime Prevention Policy" to the by now firmly institutionalized police prevention program itself: "Social Work as a Preventive Tool in Police Work".[45)] *Cooperation* between social service agencies and the police may be beneficial. Nevertheless, the constitutionally dubious

information gained by the police has unintended *secondary consequences*, and the image of the police profession suffers deterioration. These two effects make this cooperation problematic and counteract the successes of social work activities by the police such as psychological and social counseling.[46)]
Even more apparent is the unrestrained acceleration of police information gathering through specific and organizationally well-established strategies of investigation. Merely mentioning such frightening labels as "organized crime", "drug crime", and "terrorism" moves even the highest courts [47)] to legitimize a basically unproven and unverifiable claim by the executive that it needs to employ undercover officers, or "confidential agents". Under the slogan "let's take the offensive against crime", the police emphasize a "new component" in their procedure: Information gathering must begin before the crime takes place.[48)] This will be obvious if one merely imagines an undercover officer occupying the space that was formerly unmonitored. To put it more plainly: "'Action, not reaction.' One cannot wait until an incident provides an excuse for action." Wolfgang Sielaff further advocates the expansion of the approach to fighting crime from an offence-oriented approach to one that is person-and group-rather than offence- specific.[49)] Finally, Sielaff calls for offensive and systematic information gathering (preemptive investigation) as a source of data and in-depth analysis. *"The period of suspicion is to be shifted ahead."*[50)]
The trouble with these new preventive forms of police organization is not only the way in which they *operate*, but also, and even more, the obvious resulting violation of due process when 'evidence' procured by undercover officers and confidential agents is introduced at trial and the Federal Court of Justice refrains from recognizing applicable exclusionary rules.[51)] The 'ghost of prevention' that the Court conjures up by allowing dubious evidence certainly will not be exorcised from the trial courts for the sake of scrupulous observation of due process when these courts rule on the admissibility of evidence gathered by undercover officers. The result can only be to promote the ideology of prevention as legitimizing forms of police organization which, as they become entrenched, will reduce the principle of a criminal procedure governed by constitutional rules and serving as a role model of civil- liberities-oriented special prevention to an absurdity.[52)]
On the *action level*, i.e., where police and clients interact, a preventive orientation leads to a *displacement of police attention*.
On the one hand, new categories of persons and of behaviors arise which were not provided for in the classic criminal-law repertoire: *"pre-delinquents"* and *"the potentially dangerous"* are examples. These are necessarily accompanied by a *change in ideas of legal rights*. Once social science has armed the police with new tools, the classical and constitutionally safeguarded presumption of innocence, which on paper continues until conviction, is transformed into a factor interfering with preventive strategies. This is obviously true for the confidential agent, since he occupies the previously control-free space. But even for police social workers, formal guarantees of legal rights are an obstacle to activating social-worker competence and resources. The silent suspect can neither converse nor cooperate with the social service specialist who wants to employ scientized and professional helping methods. Therefore, the client's silence must be broken and his/her readiness to cooperate must be secured at the point when the police

first intervene.[53)] In the process, the ambivalent relationship between "help" and "control" threatens to become a lopsided domination by control. The risk that social workers will be co-opted into serving the crime-solving interests of the police will remain serious as long as the structural causes of role conflicts, such as those arising from strict application of the principle of mandatory prosecution, are not removed.

The use of prevention further leads to a displacement of police attention to *victim-relevant structures*. Just as the preventive perspective tends to deny the status of a responsible citizen to the offender, likewise, the victim is not so much a subject as an object, the focus of police interest. The (potential) victim is an *object of prevention technology*.

The negative consequences of preventive strategies are too easily overlooked on the action level, as we have already seen on the system and organization levels. Rudolf Rengier has systematically examined the consequences of *technical prevention* in the case of bank robbery.[54)] Although he assesses positively a "certain *suppressive effect*" (i.e., the lack of a disproportionate increase in this kind of crime), there may be *neutralizing effects* (i.e., an increase in the rate of other crimes) and these cannot be empirically determined. However, Rengier labels the negative consequences of the concept of technical prevention "clearly visible". These consequences are the so-called *"escalation effect"* and the *"escalating suppression" or "escalating displacement effect"*. Bank robbery, for example, can escalate to hostage taking or can be shifted to robbery of money carriers, which pose greater dangers to the potential victims.[55)] Rengier finds confirmation, at least in the case of bank robbery,[56)] for the thesis, emphatically advocated by Gunther Arzt, that "the prevention of crime by prophylactic measures is to a large extent the displacement of crime onto the weak".[57)] The insights gained from the analysis of this type of crime persuaded Rengier that it is advisable "to proceed more carefully in the future with the strategy of technical prevention and to consider the drawbacks more carefully".[58)]

An increase in suppression effects and in displacement effects as a result of technological prevention can be seen in many types of crime. In the United States widespread geographical displacement effects have arisen with the introduction of community or neighborhood watch programs.[59)] The American experience substantiates the proposition that *technological prevention* by nature is not prevention, but only *diversion or displacement*. Therefore, if certain objects and residential areas are technologically transformed into hermetically secured fortresses, criminals will shift their activities to less protected, but also less rewarding, goals. Criminal activity is thereby merely displaced, both geographically and by type. In other words, when opportunities for burglary are substantially reduced, robbery becomes more attractive – a displacement by type that is verified today in all official crime statistics.[60)]

Provisionally assessing the elements of police prevention on the system, organization, and action levels, we find that the growth of preventive aspects of police activity goes hand in hand with the expansion of the police. The important preventive aspects are the increasing emphasis on the planning of police strategies and the accompanying reorientation of the police that is entrenched by organizational support. This new orientation focuses on cases of deviance which, although feared, have yet to materialize. Simultaneously, police

attention is slowly displaced onto pre-delinquent modes of behavior and potentionally dangerous situations, particularly under the encouragement of technological prevention.
This expansion of the police, which includes an expansion of their claim to control, is desired by some and feared by others. It can best be interpreted in the context of a *developing interventionist security state* [61], whose administrative system is increasingly becoming a substitute for natural structures of social control. The elements of prevention described above contribute to the preventive arsenal of a repressive police force. At the same time, new powers of social design are assigned to, or arrogated by, the police.
The scenario of a comprehensive social security state is still a futuristic one. But this may be due to the fact that the societal and state crises of control are, for the present, only anticipated rather than real. It takes little imagination or anxiety, however, to predict that the eruption of control crises would activate the still mostly latent preventive elements on all levels. This would happen in two ways. First, new preventive weapons would be added to the traditional crime-fighting arsenal. Second, the preventive tasks of the police would be redefined as societal reformation. This latter threat is an especially likely consequence of the welfare state's tendency to legislate in new areas. *Traditional aspects of life* fall more and more under the influence of state agencies and thereby lose their socially integrative importance, while natural structures of control fall into ruin.

2. Criminal courts and prevention

When we seek the aid of social theory in understanding the preventively oriented control function of the criminal courts, a promising framework is that of functional change. The function of adjudication has changed from a deviance-limiting and dispute-settling one to a more actively planning one. Given the existence of social and governmental crises of control, the *expanding preventive arsenal* of the court system, and particularly of substantive and procedural law helps to *reverse the bases of legitimacy of the system of criminal law.*
When the court system is overburdened – as it necessarily is – with demands for achieving concrete goals, a *dilemma of legitimacy* arises, just as inevitably, starting on the *system level.* The strictly context-free application of legal rules collides with demands for an efficiency- and effectiveness-oriented justice. The reconciliation of these two principles in practice is difficult. By using the *concept of prevention* to create a *new basis of legitimacy,* one can, however, justify both the traditional criminalization of deviant behavior and at the same time goal-oriented policies. Decisions by the criminal courts can increasingly – when desired – be justified on the basis of alleged preventive effectiveness.
Going hand-in-hand with this is the growing *offender orientation* of substantive and procedural law. In this respect, juvenile criminal law plays a pioneering role. Nevertheless, the reference to personality characteristics and environmental factors in the judgments that even juvenile courts render is often only formalistic. This illustrates the room for maneuvering that judges enjoy when giving reasons which supposedly take the facts of the case and information about the offender into account.[62] Formal judicial

reasoning stands or falls by its independence from context. In contrast, 'empirically' based reasoning refers to causes and effects. It deals, at least nominally, with the person of the offender, his/her biography and his/her environment, as possible causes of criminality, and thereby also refers to empirically verifiable outcomes, such as the prevention of deviance through resocialization and education. Such reasoning is accompanied by an *extension of the court's interest*: the abstract perpetrator of the offence is assigned a past and a future. At the same time, the court attempts to extend its competence [63] into domanis previously outside its purview. Thus the courts claim to classify a milieu, a way of life, a family, etc. as criminogenic (in the sense of a relevant cause of the behavior being judged), just as they try to determine what detailed steps should be taken to prevent further criminal offences. The *classical notion of "infliction of harm"* thereby gains an *empirical, rational, and preventive guise*, despite the well-known failure of evaluation research to substantiate the socializing and resocializing claims of the preventive approach. The only 'success' is usually in legitimizing the system. Thus, prevention serves as a *strategy for modernizing traditional forms* of social control *in a way that is superficially compatible with the welfare state.*

On the *organization level* of the criminal courts, the corresponding points of contact in social theory can be found in a *crisis of instrumental performance suffered by the administrative system*. In dealing with this crisis, prevention expands its function and serves as a tool for adding *pragmatic flexibility* to *conditions of intervention* laid down by the constitution. The crisis of performance shows up primarily in overburdened courts and overcrowded prisons. These problems often serve as a central argument for a preventive reorientation of social control.[64]

The criminal courts are evidently suffering from a steadily increasing caseload, but this, in turn, is certainly due to a massive increase in so-called petty crime. Since the legislature is currently showing a great reluctance to promote decriminalization by statute, the courts and other criminal justice institutions cannot avoid developing their own strategies for relieving their burdens. Under the watchword *"diversion"*, cases are increasingly being dismissed, without the courts even being involved, through action at the prosecutorial level. Sections 153 and 153a of the Code of Criminal Procedure (StPO) and sections 45 and 47 of the Juvenile Court Act (JGG) constitute the entering wedge for strategies of diversion.[65]

The central problem posed here for the criminal justice system can be formulated as a dual demand. On the one hand, the system must react so flexibly that it can keep functioning despite steadily increasing demands unaccompanied by any resources for the expansion of its own machinery. That is, the time between police in-take and court decision, and the time between court decision and sentence execution, must not be too long, and the prisons must not be filled beyond capacity. On the other hand, in dealing with this task the system must effectively preserve the public impression that illegal behavior will be punished, regardless of any other considerations, in accordance with the principle of mandatory prosecution. In other words, the *instrumental and symbolic demands on the system* of state-organized social control must be brought into harmony. Too strong an orientation to the instrumental problems would shake the symbolic foundation; too great an emphasis on the symbolic aspects would allow the criminal justice system to break down.

In theory, two strategies are possible here: *decriminalization or preventive reorientation.* Movement toward legislative decriminalization is not yet in sight, although it is precisely in the growth area of petty crime (shop-lifting, nonpayment of transit fares, etc.) that decriminalization is long overdue. Were the legislature to decriminalize these areas and to place such offences into the civil law, then the criminal justice system would experience some real relief. A serious defect in the existing strategies for decriminalization can be seen in the symbolic realm: fears are expressed that decriminalization of certain modes of behavior would reduce the attribution of wrongfulness to these modes of behavior. An alternative interpretation of preventive reorientation would be that it reduces these secondary consequences by filtering cases through various forms of discretion provided for in the substantive and procedural law, while at the same time providing relief to the criminal justice system.

Yet, the ideological nature of the concept of prevention requires caution. To be specific, prevention hides a strategy for creating new forms of sanctions beyond the traditional repertoire of the criminal law.[66)] The flood of clients that threatens to engulf the criminal justice system is redirected into this preventively landscaped overflow basin. The *increased control* that is thus intended is obvious. The prevention of further criminal offences serves as a legitimatizing cloak to excuse all kinds of measures impacting the clients of caregiving, counseling, and other extramural programs, but the real effect is to gain *flexibility* in controlling the number of people to be sanctioned. Further, since prevention is a legally vague concept and thus eludes close examination, it can be implemented relatively arbitrarily.

The increase in pragmatism and flexibility that prevention makes possible does not necessarily lead to a linear increase in repression. It can also take the form of a linkage between predelinquency monitoring and the dismantling of traditional forms of repression and, in practice, this amounts to a differentiation in the repertoire of legal sanctions. This differentiation, however, receives its justification from outside rather than inside the law, e.g., by reference to claimed or assumed preventive effects.[67)]

Any claim to achieving the desired prevention of further criminal offences is, of course, unprovable. Apart from this empirical problem, the functional displacement that accompanies the increased pragmatism and flexibility must raise numerous constitutional problems in a state system based on separation of powers and checks and balances. Among these problems are supervision of the police, discretion of the prosecutor, and adjudication by non-judges.[68)] Several commentators on criminal justice policy have urgently warned that the apparent advantage of an increased ability to control is largely counteracted by the multitude of constitutional problems, especially those related to inequality, due process, and the rule of law itself.[69)]

Despite these dangers, the new preventive arsenal at the organizational level of the court system brings so many advantages to its users (e.g., caseload management, flexibility, and vagueness) that considerable time will probably pass before the legislature responds with any attempts to reform the substantive criminal law and portions of the criminal procedural law.[70)] The criminal courts are not only using the idea of prevention to expand their claim to control, but at the same time they are less than perfectly replacing the legislature and thereby short-circuiting the reforms in the substantive and procedural criminal law that should be developed through the democratic process of legislative debate.

The dilemma of legitimacy facing the criminal courts that first appears on the system level could have been resolved on the organization level through increased pragmatism and flexibility. Instead, it breaks through to the *action level*, where it affects concrete courtroom interaction. As an example, we now turn to a currently debated reform proposal that aims to mobilize the potential of prevention by separating the issues of guilt and punishment into *two criminal trial phases*.

Those who seek to preventively reinforce the criminal courts and their instruments of control are at least consistent when they label their proposal to divide the trial into two phases along with other such preventive reforms as efforts to humanize the administration of justice.[71)] The idea of the division of the trial into two parts is currently presented most clearly by the authors of the so-called alternative draft of the trial reform proposal.[72)] Central to a structural reorganization of the criminal process is the *division* of the trial into a *guilt determination phase and a punishment phase*. The impetus is the observation that: "The fundamental change in the focus of substantive criminal law from the offence to the offender, combined with a sentencing system that has been reoriented toward special prevention, primarily as a result of the criminal law reform statutes of 1969, requires that the trial be conducted in a manner that permits a better examination of the offender's personality and a closer consideration of the expected effects of sanctions."[73)]

According to these conceptions, then, the court first decides the issue of the defendant's guilt (the guilt phase) and in a second, formally separated and independent trial determines the legal consequences for the defendant (the punishment phase). One must concede to the advocates of this viewpoint that there are some reasonable, pragmatic arguments that make such a procedural course of action appear sensible.[74)] Nevertheless, we interpret these 'reform' efforts largely as an attempt to harmonize the symbolic and the instrumental expectations of the system of social control, but at the expense of those whom the system is expected to serve.

Instrumental jurisprudence in criminal law aims principally at achieveing a *"quick justice"*. The idea is not to help the statutorily relevant facts of the case or specific categories of criminal law achieve psychological prominence, but rather to attach an ethical or normative label to the defendant.[75)] This "psychologically naive rationalism" in criminal law is, in the view of Detlef Krauss and other commentators, completely deliberate. The idea of *"getting quickly to the facts"*, which of course has great relevance to economizing on resources, is elevated to a dogmatic principle.[76)] Selective perceptions are already a serious problem in criminal trials. The further "reduction of complexity", to borrow a metaphor from Luhmann, such as would occur in the proposed "guilt phase" of a bifurcated trial, would only exacerbate this problem.

As a complementary (but up to now largely tacit) plank in its platform, the reform movement intends to *balance* the shortened guilt phase of the trial with a punishment phase that focuses on *resocialization*. In the alternative draft, bifurcation of the trial "synthesizes the legal and the social-welfare aspects of the criminal process" making possible a more intense effort to uncover the defendant's personality and to seek an appropriate and just sanction, with resocialization as the principal aim.[77] The judge should be given the ability to prescribe a "just, individualized, and resocialization-oriented sanction".[78] Such a "criminologically well-founded and individualized sentence is also a prerequisite for the resocializing effects of imprisonment that are required by the law of prison administration".[79] The reformers are willing to accept the fact that the defendant relinquishes self-determination; he/she is 'put under a microscope', surrendering "more personal data than in normal life, more even than before an inquisitorial court".[80] The discussion of the necessary and appropriate sanctions should be as open and free as possible,[81] for this facilitates the search for a fully persuasive sanction which, in turn, renders an appeal superfluous.(!)[82] At this point the "round table" model of the criminal trial is cited: "The defendant participates more actively and spontaneously in the trial proceedings, he assesses his influence on the trial and his chances of resocialization more favorably", and "a more relaxed atmosphere with better mutual understanding" prevails.[83] Thus, the welfare state in its drive to expand the sphere of regulation has already encroached, in the intentions of the 'reformers', on the formal law of criminal procedure. "The welfare state principle in modern criminal law stands or falls with the trusting cooperation of its clientele."[84] Rolf-Peter Calliess calls this a "right of participation in a dialogically structured sanctioning process".[85]

In all this, however, there is a great deal of wishful thinking. It is a fallacy to believe that deterrence-oriented severity (and this is all that the proposed "reduction of complexity" really is) could be compensated for by subsequent measures of special prevention aimed at individual needs. Heinz Giehring aptly describes the problem as follows: "At least as long as the promising concept of socialization is compromised in the competing goals of criminal law and in the reality of life in prison, it would be illusory and dangerous to trivialize the serious divergence of interests under the banner of a common search for suitable measures to solve the life problems of the accused."[86] According to Klaus Volk there is a "fatal correspondence between the reform model of a bifurcated trial and the old common-law division of the inquisitorial trial into the general and special inquisition".[87] Moreover, an accused person who keeps silent, "withdrawing from the evolving therapeutic community and enduring rather than gladly accepting the care offered by the welfare state, thwarts all attempts at individual prevention and resocialization",[88] despite the fact that he/she is claiming nothing more than a fundamental constitutional guarantee.

Should this 'reform' approach also be coupled with the dubious proposal that the trial be *closed to the public*,[89] then one would have to agree with Dieter Engels and Helmut Frister, who do not accept such a fundamentally "artificial readiness to cooperate" as genuine and, moreover, regard it as unnecessary to resocialization. "It is really an expression of the defendant's resignation and not of his active cooperation in his own (re)socicalization." To this extent the dismantling of the adversarial process unfairly masquerades as an instrument of resocialization and as an effort to find 'a shared path toward restitution'. "In reality, the way is paved to a quick and easy verdict – by overlooking the defendant's (opposing) interests in making those facts that are favorable to him completely clear. Here, therefore, the principle of the welfare state, and the defendant's right to resocialization that is derived from this principle, are being misused to resolve the conflict of interests between the state and the defendant, to the dertiment of the defendant."[90)]

As we saw for the police on the action level, the idea of prevention here tends to transform the suspect or defendant into an *object of state care*, especially when the 'interests of the welfare state' come into play. Thus, concepts of prevention in the judicial process can impose serious burdens on citizens and bring with them a considerable diminution of constitutional safeguards.[91)]

3. Prison and prevention

In the realm of incarceration, the so-called tertiary prevention level, the concept of prevention is synonymous with the concept of resocialization. Prevention or resocialization is the officially declared aim of the law of prison administration (section 2 StVollzG). Thus, the idea of prevention serves as a complex focus for legitimizing claims of control on the *system level* of prison administration. In addition, with the aid of the concept of resocialization, social-structural problems can be superficially defused or disguised in several ways. These include the individualization of social problem situations, their depoliticization, the apparent dismantling of repressive structures, and the demand for conformity. We shall designate this phenomenon as the *ideological function* of the idea of prevention or resocialization.

By locating the causes of deviant behavior within the individual, the *idea of treatment* tends to obscure the societal relevance of criminality and to neutralize as *individual personality problems* social conflicts which manifest themselves in criminality.[92)] Thus the idea of treatment, which assumes that prisons can, in principle, resocialize, prevents the societal causes of criminality from coming into view and prevents the preconditions for their removal, ranging from public consciousness all the way to the political implementation of social change.[93)] The preference for therapy over punishment is seen as a modern approach to channeling the societal potential for conflict and as an answer to the present form and dynamics of this potential.[94)] By being individualized social problems appear to be administratively soluble through assumptions about individual aspirations, and at the same time these social trouble spots are split up into "social atoms".[95)] The societal context fades into a fairly insignificant marginal attribute of the case.[96)] As a result it seems as though the welfare state cares about the psychic needs of its citizens. The *societal* crisis of legitimacy is converted into *individual* crises of meaning and identity.[97)] Michel Foucault has impressively described this process by observing that the criminal system has succeeded in "producing the criminal as a pathologized subject".[98)] Thus, it was possible to erect a barrier between criminals and the social classes from which they emerge.[99)]

Once social problem situations have been individualized, they are also *depoliticized*. Thus it is no surprise that broad strata of the educated elites of western societies have reacted to the failure or decline of social reform movements by retreating from a political orientation to individualized, therapeutic objectives. The strategy of individualization also offers to law-and-order politicians the bonus of neutralizing potentially destabilizing criticism of the system.[100)]

The normative anchoring of the concept of resocialization has been acknowledged as a remarkable achievement of reform,[101)] but this normative anchoring can also be used to show how reform policy can serve to neutralize protests against the inhumanity of prisons. Thomas Mathiesen calls this a system of "silent disciplining". Old and new goals are often put into parallel operation. In other words, what exists is partly reorganized so that both types of goals have a place next to each other – but with the old ones predominating.[102)] Furthermore, evaluative studies [103)] show that despite the reform hoopla, only a slight material improvement for inmates has yet emerged. As everybody knows, rhetoric races far ahead of practice in this realm. While the talk is of incarceration as treatment, the reality of incarceration is still largely dictated by custodial routines.

The *dismantling of repressive structures* in prisons, which has been proclaimed under the banner of resocialization, also proves upon closer examination to be more apparent than real. Franco Basaglia even places the concept of prevention close to traditional methods of torture: "Today a new-fangled version of torture seems to be coming into fashion: preventive torture. It operates with much more polished tools than its crude precursors; it doesn't exhort confessions, but rather assent – agreement with reasons of state, and power no longer fears being unmasked as such."[104)] At the same time, the concept of resocialization relieves the bourgeois conscience. The growing public consciousness of crime-related problems assumes an orientation that allows the public to exculpate itself of its criminogenic roles through the delusion that the criminal is a sick individual who must be isolated and entrusted to the responsibility of 'experts'. This 'humane' resocializing imprisonment has an intrinsic byproduct: society absolves itself.[105)]

When the social conditions of criminality and criminalization have been individualized, pathologized, and depoliticized, and when the state's response is an apparently liberal one, the demand for conformity appears eminently just and fair. Public legal education is given the hard task of leading the people to a life of obedience to the law and loyalty to the state. "In this way education and resocialization during imprisonment use ethical-legal appeals to the prisoner's sense of justice in order to pursue the goal of imparting basic value concepts to the prisoner that will enable him in the future to lead the life of a legally loyal citizen."[106)] If one crosses out the lofty language, one arrives – with Hildur von Schweinitz – at the following insight: "The intended result of imprisonment, resocialization, is more or less predefined as the desire to improve, the ability to work, and the fulfillment of legal bourgeois norms. As successful steps along the road to resocialization, the prison system values cleanliness, willingness to work, good behavior, and conformity to the regulations." It follows therefrom that the step-by-step resocialization of prisoners "in the sense of bourgeois norms can be measured by their increasingly frictionless functioning within the institution".[107)] Consequently, the system of criminal law as a whole tends to be integrated as a special subsystem into the entire processes of socialization and education that the state is institutionalizing into an ever more closely-meshed network. "The whole point of this network is to impart to each

individual behavior models and competences that accord with his societal status, and thus to reproduce the status structure itself."[108] The theory of resocialization, which, rather than rendering real economic assistance, one-sidedly aims at exercising moral-pedagogical influence over marginal groups, thus easily turns out to be ideology.[109]
Ultimately the concept of resocialization outstandingly performs the function of *rationalizing and scientizing state punishment and therewith the state's crime policy.* State punishment is thus made practically unassailable. We shall designate this as the *"defensive function"* of the prevention concept. In Günther Kaiser's view, only the "postulate of the scientism and rationality of criminal sanctioning processes" supports the concept of resocialization in criminal law.[110] However, it is not easy for the social scientist to find scientifically credible evidence for any kind of success in the resocialization of prisoners. Empirical evaluation research in prisons, at least if initiated and conducted by the authorities of social control, is under pressure to demonstrate that the burdensome interventions ultimately produce positive results, and that they also serve the well-recognized interests of the inmates.[111] The administratively doctored results coalesce "into a synonym for 'practical relevance', which, in turn, is called upon to furnish legitimacy and meaning".[112] Franziska Lamott summarizes her observations of social-therapeutic treatment of prisoners as follows: "The scientization of the reform, which follows the logic of applied science, ultimately conserves, with its quasi-objective methods, the status quo of the prison system." At the same time it creates the illusion that the criminal justice authorities are willing to accept reform, because it encourages policymakers to do what they intend to do anyway – procure additional legitimacy.[113]
In the process the production of criminological knowledge is increasingly withdrawn from the autonomous arena of scientific research and becomes determined by the heteronomous agenda of policy and practice; "other issues are 'suppressed', consciously excluded, or disqualified as 'mistaken'".[114] Along with scientific results of this kind, "generalized claims to the objectivity and neutrality that are attributed to science get thrown onto the argumentational scale" during political discussions.[115] Without reviewing the evaluation-research literature on therapeutic programs in prisons, it should be mentioned that even the enlightened layperson still has little chance, in the jungle of social scientific methods of evaluation, to make critical use of such administratively dressed-up results. Thus, faith in the changeability of the world through expert intervention remains largely unbroken, so that the rapidly spreading prevention euphoria can entrench itself relatively uncontestedly behind the rationalization and scientific formulation that it itself promotes.
The relationship between imprisonment and prevention, when seen from a control perspective, is a dual one. On the one hand, preventive measures "outside the walls" are expected to reduce the need for imprisonment, thereby making prison an object of prevention. On the other hand, within the prisons the label "prevention" can be attached to anything that can be connected with the so-called crime-free life of social responsibility after release from prison. An essential aspect of this preventive orientation on the *organization level* of prison practice is the undisguised possibility of weakening legally guaranteed rights and misusing them to apply pressure under the guise of treatment. We shall designate this as the *"abuse function"* of the concept of resocialization.[116]
Another aim of the preventive orientation is a reweighting within the separation of

powers. This shift, which can be described as "professionalization", leads to an *upgrading of the executive.* Social workers, psychologists, prison officers, etc., using (questionable) diagnostic criteria, gain considerable unchecked influence over decisions on the granting of privileges, reassignments to low-security facilities, and paroles. These and other tendencies can be related to the emerging paradigm shift in the sphere of justice which accompanies the introduction of supposedly objective penal goals. New professions and professional roles have come into existence, new courses of training have been created, and a network of specialists now spans prison society, schooled to "prevent conflicts, avert unrest, and ease dissent – in short, to speed up the 'normalization' of conditions".[117] The scientization of the helping professions promotes, at the same time, public and professional support for the expansion of resocializing and therapeutic institutions. The support of reform by professionals hoping for job opportunities is spreading appreciably.[118] The interplay of expanding social work and "therapy" also promises "fulfillment of the social worker's old dream of finally having a tool in hand to provide individual and need-based help to the helpless, the desperate, and even the 'stubborn' client. For social service and counseling agencies, which are often regarded by the public with scepticism and abhorrence, 'therapy' promises an increase in prestige; for the individual social worker, 'therapy' promises a possible improvement in status and therewith an improved position on the job market."[119]

A further development that is fraught with consequences for the organization level of the prison system can be described as a change in the *requirements of 'work discipline'.* Whereas prisons traditionally considered only raw labor important, preventively oriented incarceration aims additionally to influence the *'social abilities'* of its clientele.[120] One consequence is that the personality of the prisoner becomes an object of 'helping' intervention, 'treating' intervention, and – as it is a matter of preventing recidivism – 'preventive' intervention. The training of prisoners in 'social competence' thus comes more to the fore in practice. But the term "social competence", at least when applied to real prisoners, i.e., members of the lower class who, as a rule, have no power and no promising future, hides a specific *moral model of conditioning.*

The 'attitudes' that this training is intended to instill reflect the image of the 'docile malefactor'. The entire approach is based on the *assumption,* typical for prevention in the sense used here, that the clients of the criminal justice system are *'socially incompetent'.* This thesis only begins to be plausible when one defines certain behavioral standards as absolute – namely those of the orderly member of the middle class in his/her own context. It should be clear to many who have contact with the world of the clients of the criminal justice system, and a critical eye, that the 'social competence' of the average prison inmate is higher than the apologists of incarcerational prevention would admit.

A dialectic of reform and control is built into the debate about "treatment as a tool of prevention in prisons" and can be analyzed in the logic of this debate. From preventively based ideas about prison reform follow, at least by suggestion, demands for an even greater *expansion of control beyond the walls* as well. On the one hand, the demand grows for keeping prisoners in contact with their normal social environments. This demand has two plausible justifications. One is the minimization of damage caused by detention (a restrictive argument); the other is training in appropriate social behavior

within a natural environment (a preventive argument). On the other hand, this trend threatens to bring with it an expansion of social control into this same environment. In the words of one of those involved in the continuing debate about structural changes in probation and parole services, it appears that "the immediate local environment is not entirely unsuitable for organizing effective care".[121)] No constitutional considerations will be a match for this trend toward making use of the local environments, if it is supported by the logic of prevention. This trend will prevail especially when it is defended as a combination of "more effectiveness and more economy", that is, when privately organized forms of control are increasingly incorporated so as to relieve the public budget.
The preventive orientation in prisons has crucial negative effects on the *action level*, i.e., on the level of concrete interaction of 'controllers and clients'. The reduction of prisoners to indicators of externally defined success (with criteria such as the capacity for resocialization) lead to *processes of self-pathologizing*. A questionable classification of prisoners by probability of resocialization, coordinated with differentiated forms of sentence serving, (probation, low-security incarceration, high-security incarceration) provides the administrative foundation for an inhumane selection system.
In this system, the inmate is assigned the task of coping with a *major institutional contradiction*. The idea of prevention stylizes prison as a place of help, but this interpretation expresses more a longing for the reconciliation of conflicting duties (i.e., help versus security) than an appropriate description of the reality of prison life.[122)] This construction facilitates 'therapeutic work' in prisons. It is the prerequisite for social service personnel perceiving themselves as clearly focused on their clients and their disturbances. This happens in therapeutically organized prisons first and foremost through processes of psychologizing, in which the behavior of a prisoner is separated from its original context, objectified as an expression of his/her inner psychological deformation, and mirrored back to him/her as a trait of his/her personality.[123)] We see in preventively/therapeutically organized prisons increasingly the tendency for social and normative conflicts to be individualized and pathologized. The burden of failure is almost exclusively placed on the 'disturbed personality' and hardly ever on the situation in which the inmate was undone. Thus, in the majority of cases apparently 'humane treatment' necessarily becomes, in the compulsory situation of a prison, a mechanism for inducing conformity. "The attempt to evade it is interpreted – immanent in the logic of psychological interpretation – only as further evidence of the disturbed state" of the prisoner.[124)] When the adaptive strategies of the inmates are attributed to them as fixed individual personality traits, the fact that the inmates are forced to adapt to the repressive structure of the prison (and despite all contrary suggestions it is repressive) is overlooked. It would be more correct to understand their behavior as an attempt to react to the restrictive and repressive structural conditions of the institution in such a way as to survive within the system. The issue on the interactional level in preventively/therapeutically organized prisons is summed up by Lutz Gero Leky as follows: "Whoever senses that he is identified by his handicaps and has the impression that the therapist, in cooperation with the administration, classifies him this way, prescribing certain measures for him and opening and closing his file at regular intervals, can only fend off, over adapt, blend in, or escape. The therapist may see such behavior as a worsening of the symptoms of the client and, when nothing else

helps, finally commit him to those who know how to deal with prison troublemakers the old-fashioned way."[125)]
Even if in everyday life the concept of resocialization (or prevention) is more a normative ideal than a constantly applied strategy, this glance at the action level shows that the idea of prevention can easily be an *obstacle to the protection of human and civil liberties* in prison.

III. Summary and Outlook

We have treated several central aspects of the problem of "prevention as an objective in the criminal justice system". Our point of departure was the consideration that the preventive orientation makes the criminal justice system assert claims to control on which it can make good only with great difficulty under the constraints of formal constitutional guarantees. We showed that the expansion of the claim to control is related to the control crises of state and society and to an accompanying change in the functions of the state, subjecting the administrative and legitimizing system to increasing burdens. Prevention was interpreted as a strategy to master the concomitant problems.
From this perspective we have analyzed the preventive build-up of the criminal justice system in three central sectors. It was demonstrated that in the subsystems of the police, criminal courts, and prisons manifest or latent attempts at prevention are emerging on all levels.
On the *system level*, a reversal of the legitimizing basis of the system of criminal law is beginning to appear. A constraining and reconciliating legitimacy is giving way to a prevention- and planning-oriented legitimacy. The main function of the idea of prevention on the system level is to serve as a comprehensive *basis of legitimacy for the expansion of the claim to control of criminal law*. Meanwhile, in the police sector, the attempt is made to obtain much earlier authorization to intervene. In the courts, this process expresses itself in an increased orientation toward the offender and in an expansion of the – mainly rhetorical – competency to judge. Finally, in the prisons, prevention or resocialization serves as a basis of legitimacy for a concept of help that functions according to the patterns of the welfare state. However, upon closer examination, it proves to be an ideologically buttressed modernization strategy of traditional repressive control and is only superficially compatible with the welfare state.
On the *organization level*, the *augmentation of instrumental efficiency* of the criminal justice system was identified as the main function of prevention. In the police sector, the increase of efficiency through preventive organizational forms takes place under the banner of professionalization, differentiation, and rationalization. In the courts, the state tries to head off the crisis of instrumental efficiency through pragmatic strategies of flexibility (e.g., diversion). In the prisons, 'hard' forms of control are coming to be replaced by 'soft' ones. Creeping regulation in the welfare state has thus already reached the organizational level and is heading toward 'soft' maximization of control. Consequently, the price of the instrumental augmentation of efficiency is high throughout

the criminal justice system; too high, in fact: basic constitutional guarantees fall more and more victim to preventive intervention.

On the *action level*, as preventive strategies are implemented, a *dubious attempt at harmony* takes place, and in its wake the clientele suffers a *gradual loss of autonomy*. The preventive-welfare state's colonization of new realms of life leads in the police sector to a disregard of the personal quality of legal subjects: the citizen becomes the object of police prevention strategies. In the courts as well – starting with the reform model – the modernization strategy, superficially compatible with the welfare state, takes its toll: the surrender of autonomy for the sake of an uncertain welfare state 'goodwill' bonus. How this coerced cooperation pays off in the reality of prison life seems clear: the result is over-adaptation to the "total institution" and compulsion to self-pathologizing. Here we also register a loss of autonomy as the price of 'privileges' that are not won by legal action but rather bought by apparent success in conformity.

In our introduction we observed that the extreme paradigm of prevention is still futuristic. The aspects of prevention treated in this article merely show the way into the future – some more so, others less so. The way to the prevention state takes one through state and societal crises of control. To prevent crises of control that will inevitably bring with them totally preventive strategies of control that destroy the constitutional state, it is crucial to practice socio-economic and socio-cultural prevention, in other words, *structural prevention*. The tendency to a preventive optimization of control can still be counteracted, but only with a *legal action approach emphasizing the defence of traditionally constitutional rights*.

Notes

1 See Piven, F.F., and Cloward, R.A. (1977): Regulierung der Armut. Die Politik der öffentlichen Wohlfahrt. Frankfurt a.M.; Rödel, U., and Guldimann, T. (1978): Sozialpolitik als soziale Kontrolle. In: Starnberger Studien 2. Frankfurt a.M., pp. 11 et seq.; Mutz, G. (1983): Sozialpolitik als soziale Kontrolle am Beispiel der psychosozialen Versorgung. Munich

2 See exemplarily to this the first volume of the series of publications of the Lower Saxony Ministry of Justice: 'Criminological Research': Schwind, H.-D., Berckhauer, F., and Steinhilper, G. (Eds.) (1980): Präventive Kriminalpolitik – Beiträge zur ressortübergreifenden Kriminalprävention aus Forschung, Praxis und Politik. Heidelberg

3 See Albrecht, P.-A. (1985): Spezialprävention angesichts neuer Tätergruppen. In: ZStW 1985, pp. 831 et seq.

4 See Wolff, E.A. (1985): Das neuere Verständnis von Generalprävention und seine Tauglichkeit für eine Antwort auf Kriminalität. In: ZStW 1985, pp. 786 et seq.

5 On the contextual dependence of the concept of prevention in criminological theory, see Albrecht, P.-A. (1983): Perspektiven und Grenzen polizeilicher Kriminalprävention. Ebelsbach, pp. 7 et seq.

6 Eder, K. (1980): Die Entstehung staatlich organisierter Gesellschaften. Frankfurt a.M.

7 Symbolic: the meaning that the concrete acts take on, e.g., that society must be protected, crime must be punished, wrongs must be made right again. On this level, problems with so-called social integration occur, i.e., law loses credibility and predictability; sanctions are no longer taken seriously; the state is denied the right to sanction certain modes of behavior.

8 Instrumental: e.g., the commitment of a convicted defendant to prison as a physical act of incarceration. On this (organization) level, so-called system crises then arise: the prison cells become

scarce, the costs for carrying out sanctions under criminal law rise, the number of convicts increases disproportionately, etc.

9 See for a survey Luhmann, N. (1983): Rechtssoziologie. Opladen, pp. 10 et seq.; more specifically pp. 190 et seq.

10 Luhmann defines contingency "practically" as a "danger of disappointment and the necessity of letting oneself in for risks" (note 9, p. 31).

11 See Eder, note 6, p. 165

12 von Liszt, F. (1905): Der Zweckgedanke im Strafrecht. In: Strafrechtliche Aufsätze und Vorträge. Berlin, Vol. 1, p. 175

13 See von Liszt in the Marburger Program, note 12, pp. 126 et seq.

14 Exemplary is Nedelmann, C. (Ed.) (1968): Kritik der Strafrechtsreform. Frankfurt a.M.

15 In: Recht und Politik 1976, pp. 252/253

16 See in this connection the analysis of texts of judgments from juvenile court proceedings in Kreissl, R. (1983): Soziale versus juristische Realität. In: Albrecht, P.-A., and Schüler-Springorum, H. (Eds.): Jugendstrafe an Vierzehn- und Fünfzehnjährigen. Munich, pp. 111 et seq.

17 Teubner, G. (1985): Verrechtlichung – Begriffe, Merkmale, Grenzen, Auswege. In: Kübler, F. (Ed.): Verrechtlichung von Wirtschaft, Arbeit und sozialer Solidarität. Frankfurt a.M., p. 303. The metaphor of creeping regulation in the welfare state stems from the debate on the societal evolution of the law and stands next to other escalations that led to the constituting of the bourgeois state. Constitutional, democratic, and social escalation may be distinguished (cf. Teubner *ibid.*). The concept of creeping regulation in the welfare state was applied to economic and social law (cf. the contributions in Kübler *ibid.*); yet it may be likewise applied to criminal law.

18 For a criticism of this traditional type of observation see Foucault, M. (1976): Überwachen und Strafen. Frankfurt a.M.

19 O'Connor, J. (1974): Die Finanzkrise des Staates. Frankfurt a.M., which deals with the financial crisis of the state, observes "that the capitalistic state must try to fulfill two fundamental and often contradictory functions – accumulation and legitimation. This means that the state must try to preserve or to create those conditions in which a profitable accumulation of capital is possible. The state must also, however, try to maintain or to create the conditions for social harmony" (O'Connor *ibid.*, p. 16).

20 Habermas, J. (1973): Legitimationsprobleme im Spätkapitalismus. Frankfurt a.M., pp. 51/52

21 Hirsch, F. (1980): Die sozialen Grenzen des Wachstums. Reinbek

22 Habermas, note 20, p. 71

23 Offe, C. (1979): Unregierbarkeit. Zur Renaissance konservativer Krisentheorien. In: Habermas, J. (Ed.): Stichworte zur 'geistigen Situation der Zeit'. Frankfurt a.M., p. 297

24 Offe, note 23, pp. 300/301

25 Schulz, and Wambach (1983): Das gesellschaftssanitäre Projekt. Sozialpolizeiliche Erkenntnisnahme als letzte Etappe der Aufklärung?. In: Wambach, M.M. (Ed.): Der Mensch als Risiko. Frankfurt a.M., pp. 76/77

26 The author has discussed several positive elements of preventive strategies elsewhere (cf. note 3).

27 This three-level classification is not always precise. I shall base my categories on the *central* preventive purpose. Nevertheless, levels can overlap just as easily as they can retain exclusivity.

28 Gemmer, K.-H. (1976): Zur Problematik polizeilicher Prävention. In: Arbeitskreis des Bundeskriminalamtes Wiesbaden from 3. to 7.11.1975: Polizei und Prävention. Wiesbaden, p. 11

29 Herold, H., note 28, p. 187

30 Stümper, A. (1980): Die Wandlung der Polizei in Begriff und Aufgaben. In: Kriminalistik 1980, p. 242

31 Stümper, note 30, p. 244

32 Stümper, note 30, p. 244; Schäfer, H. (1986): Die Prädominanz der Prävention. In: GA 1986, pp. 49/50: Schäfer states a claim to police omnipotence that could hardly be surpassed.

33 Funk, A., Kauss, U., and von Zabern, T. (1980): Die Ansätze zu einer neuen Polizei. In: Blankenburg, E. (Ed.): Politik der inneren Sicherheit. Frankfurt a.M., p. 78

34 Narr, W.-D. (1979): Hin zu einer Gesellschaft bedingter Reflexe. In: Habermas, J. (Ed.): Stichworte zur 'geistigen Situation der Zeit'. Frankfurt a.M., p. 512
35 Narr, note 34
36 Narr, note 34
37 See finally the comprehensive analysis of Busch, H., Funk, A., Kauss, U., Narr, W.-D., and Werkentin, F. (1985): Die Polizei in der Bundesrepublik. Frankfurt a.M./New York
38 Steffen, W. (1983): Professionalisierung und Prävention. Antworten der Polizei auf die Kriminalitätsentwicklung. In: Kerner, H.-J., Kury, H., and Sessar, K. (Eds.): Deutsche Forschungen zur Kriminalitätsentstehung und Kriminalitätskontrolle. Cologne et al., pp. 823 et seq.
39 For a good example see Kube, E., Störzer, H.U., and Brugger, S. (Eds.) (1983): Wissenschaftliche Kriminalistik. Grundlagen und Perspektiven. Vol. 1: Systematik und Bestandsaufnahme. Wiesbaden; idem (1984): Wissenschaftliche Kriminalistik. Grundlagen und Perspektiven. Vol. 2: Theorie, Lehre und Weiterentwicklung. Wiesbaden
40 Kube, E. (1984): Wissenschaftliche Kriminalistik – Ziele und Aufgaben. In: Kube, E., Störzer, H.U., and Brugger, S. (Eds.): Wissenschaftliche Kriminalistik. Grundlagen und Perspektiven. Vol. 2: Theorie, Lehre und Weiterentwicklung. Wiesbaden, p. 432
41 The multitude of recently established scientific research divisions in German state criminal investigation departments serve as proof.
42 For a good example see Philipp, P. (1981): Das Modell der polizeilichen Jugendarbeit beim Polizeipräsidium München. In: Kreuzer, A., and Plate, M. (Eds.): Polizei und Sozialarbeit. Wiesbaden, pp. 87 et seq.
43 Philipp, note 42, p. 91
44 Albrecht, note 5, pp. 39 et seq.
45 Schwind et al., note 2. On the prevention program of the police and social workers (PPS) see Wilhelm-Reiss, M.: In: Schwind et al., pp. 405 et seq.
46 On the topic of misgivings on principle see Albrecht, note 5, pp. 266 et seq.
47 See especially BGHSt (GS) 32, 115, pp. 120 et seq.; BGH NStZ 1982, p. 40; 1983, pp. 325/326; see also BGH StrV 1985, pp. 309/310; BVerfGE 57, 250, p. 284; but see the verdict of the criminal court of the City of Basel of 30.11.1983, StrV 1985, p. 318
48 Sielaff, W. (1983): Bis zur Bestechung leitender Polizeibeamter?. In: Kriminalistik 1983, p. 419
49 Sielaff, note 48, p. 421
50 Sielaff, note 48, p. 422
51 See also the decisions cited supra note 47
52 For more detail see Albrecht, note 3, pp. 866 et seq.
53 On this subject see the sample cases cited in Albrecht, note 5, p. 273, in which with the help of social worker 'competency' the due process rights of the accused are violated.
54 Rengier, R. (1985): Kriminologische Folgen der Bekämpfung des Bankraubs durch technische Prävention. In: MschrKrim 1985, pp. 104 et seq.
55 Rengier, note 54, p. 115
56 Rengier, note 54, p. 115
57 Arzt, G. (1976): Der Ruf nach Recht und Ordnung. Tübingen, pp. 38 et seq.
58 Rengier, note 54, p. 115
59 Albrecht, P.-A. (1982): Der Weg in die Sackgasse? Zur Einschätzung von Präventions- Programmen der amerikanischen Polizei. In: Schüler-Springorum, H. (Ed.): Mehrfach auffällig. Munich, pp. 215 et seq.
60 See also Meyer, M., and Ventzke, K.-U. (1980): Opfererfahrung, Selbstschutz, Prävention. In: KrimJ 1980, pp. 179 et seq.
61 See Hirsch, J. (1980): Der Sicherheitsstaat. Frankfurt a.M.
62 See for additional details Kreissl, note 16, pp. 116/117
63 Kreissl, note 16, pp. 116/117
64 See in particular Steinhilper, G. (1984): Möglichkeiten für eine bessere Kriminalitätsvorbeugung. In: Schäuble, W. (Ed.): Kriminalitätsbekämpfung – Eine Herausforderung für Staat und Gesellschaft. Public Hearing of the CDU/CSU-"Bundestag" parliamentary group on 15.5.1984 in Bonn. Bonn

65 On criminal law relating to young offenders see Heinz, W., and Spiess, G. (1983): Alternativen zu formellen Reaktionen im deutschen Jugendstrafrecht. In: Kerner, H.-J., Kury, H., and Sessar, K. (Eds.): Deutsche Forschungen zur Kriminalitätsentstehung und Kriminalitätskontrolle. Cologne et al., pp. 896/897; see also Kunz, K.-L. (1984): Das strafrechtliche Bagatellprinzip. Berlin; Kausch, E. (1980): Der Staatsanwalt. Ein Richter vor dem Richter?. Berlin; Kotz, P. (1983): Die Wahl der Verfahrensart durch den Staatsanwalt. Frankfurt a.M.

66 E.g., Pfeiffer, C. (1983): Kriminalprävention im Jugendgerichtsverfahren. Cologne et al.

67 An impressive example is the privately organized "bridge"-projects (registered societies) which have recently appeared in the juvenile court system. They are effectively organized for bureaucratic influence, and their effect is to reduce the caseload of criminal justice agencies. As a result, compulsory labor in community service, a form of *educational discipline* authorized by section 10 of the Juvenile Court Act but which for good reasons had been applied sparingly, was upgraded in some jurisdiction far beyond statutory limits and applied across-the-board. The alleged but by no means substantiated social and educational effectiveness served to legitimate reform. In some places, the whole structure of (low-level) criminal sanctions was displaced, see Pfeiffer supra note 66, admittedly at the cost of far less intervention-intensive means of correction provided for by law, such as warnings (section 14 of the Juvenile Court Act) and apologies (section 15 of the Juvenile Court Act).

68 See the article of Otto Backes in this volume

69 On this subject see supra notes 65 and 68

70 This is best seen currently in the dismantling of avenues of legal redress; see Albrecht, note 3, pp. 866 et seq.; Volk, K. (1982): Strafrecht und Wirtschaftskriminalität. In: JZ 1982, p. 90

71 Wassermann, R. (1970): Zur Soziologie des Gerichtsverfahrens. In: Naucke, W., and Trappe, P. (Eds.): Rechtssoziologie und Rechtspraxis. Neuwied/Berlin, p. 146

72 Alternativ-Entwurf/Novelle zur Strafprozeßordnung und Reform der Hauptverhandlung (AE-StPO-HV) (1985), published by a working group of German and Swiss experts on criminal law (Arbeitskreis AE). Tübingen

73 AE-StPO-HV, note 72, p. 3

74 E.g., the protection of the defendant who has not yet been found guilty from the public discussion of his/her personal circumstances and the elimination of the so-called dilemma of the defense attorney (alternative pleading), AE-StPO-HV, note 72, pp. 53 et seq.

75 For background see Bockelmann, P. (1980): Bemerkungen über das Verhältnis des Strafrechts zur Moral und zur Psychologie. In: Jäger, H. (Ed.): Kriminologie im Strafprozeß. Frankfurt a.M., pp. 11 et seq.; Krauss, D. (1980): Das Prinzip der materiellen Wahrheit im Strafprozeß. In: Jäger, H. (Ed.): Kriminologie im Strafprozeß. Frankfurt a.M., pp. 65 et seq.

76 Krauss, D. (1980): Der psychologische Gehalt subjektiver Elemente im Strafrecht. In: Jäger, H. (Ed.): Kriminologie im Strafprozeß. Frankfurt a.M., pp. 110 et seq.; for a survey see Albrecht, P.-A. (1983): Unsicherheitszonen des Schuldstrafrechts. In: GA 1983, pp. 195 et seq.

77 AE-StPO-HV, note 72, p. 5

78 AE-StPO-HV, note 72, p. 54

79 AE-StPO-HV, note 72, p. 55

80 AE-StPO-HV, note 72, pp. 58/59

81 AE-StPO-HV, note 72, p. 73

82 AE-StPO-HV, note 72, p. 4

83 AE-StPO-HV, note 72, p. 51

84 Wolter, J. (1980): Schuldinterlokut und Strafzumessung. Rechts- und Sozialstaat, Rechts- und Sozialwissenschaften im Strafprozeß. In: GA 1980, p. 105

85 Calliess, R.-P. (1973): Theorie der Strafe im demokratischen und sozialen Rechtsstaat. Frankfurt a.M., p. 204

86 Giehring, H. (1978): Rechte des Beschuldigten, Handlungskompetenz und kompensatorische Strafverfolgung. In: Hassemer, W., and Lüderssen, K. (Eds.): Sozialwissenschaften im Studium des Rechts. Vol. 3, Munich, p. 188

87 Volk, K. (1980): Wahrheit und materielles Recht im Strafprozeß. Koblenz, p. 22

88 Volk, note 87, p. 23

89 Arbeitskreis AE (Ed.) (1980): Alternativ-Entwurf, Novelle zur StPO, Strafverfahren mit nichtöffentlicher Hauptverhandlung. Tübingen
90 Engels, D., and Frister, H. (1981): Nichtöffentliches Verfahren vor dem Strafrichter?. In: ZRP 1981, p. 116
91 Similarly see Engels, and Frister, note 90, p. 117
92 Von Hofer, H. (1974): Behandlung und Strafe. In: ZRP 1974, p. 83
93 Walter, J. (1982): Abschied vom Behandlungsvollzug?. In: Pies, E. (Ed.): Strafvollzug an Jugendlichen. Contributions and material of a conference from 12. to 14.3.1981 in the Katholische Akademie Trier. Trier, p. 130
94 Reinke-Köberer, E. (1984): Therapeutisierung oder Kriminalisierung – die Scheinalternativen der Rehabilitation. In: KrimJ 1984, p. 181
95 Von Kardorff, E. (1982): Die Strategie der Therapeutisierung – Zum veränderten Handlungstyp in der Sozialarbeit. In: Neue Praxis 1982, p. 7
96 Kargl, W. (1982): Die Kritik des Schuldprinzips. Frankfurt a.M./New York, p. 266
97 Gröschke, D. (1982): Kritik der Therapeutik in der Sozialarbeit – Wiederaufnahme eines unerledigten Themas. In: Neue Praxis 1982, p. 164
98 Foucault, M. (1976): Überwachen und Strafen. Frankfurt a.M., p. 375
99 Foucault, note 98, p. 368
100 Gröschke, note 97, p. 166
101 On this see Albrecht, note 3, p. 834 with further citations, pp. 845 et seq.
102 Mathiesen, T. (1985): Die lautlose Disziplinierung. Bielefeld, p. 69
103 Kersten, J., and von Wolffersdorff-Ehlert, C. (1980): Jugendstrafe. Frankfurt a.M.; Kersten, J., Kreissl, R., and von Wolffersdorff-Ehlert, C. (1983): Die sozialisatorsische Wirkung totaler Institutionen. In: Albrecht, P.-A., and Schüler-Springorum, H. (Eds.): Jugendstrafe an Vierzehn- und Fünfzehnjährigen. Munich, pp. 186 et seq.
104 Basaglia, F., and Basaglia-Ongaro, F. (1980): Befriedungsverbrechen. In: Basaglia, F., and Basaglia-Ongaro, F. (Eds.): Befriedungsverbrechen. Frankfurt a.M., p. 21
105 Hilbers, M., and Lange, W. (1973): Abkehr von der Behandlungsideologie?. In: KrimJ 1973, pp. 57/58; Wetter, R., and Böckelmann, F. (1972): Knast-Report. Frankfurt a.M., p. 214
106 Würtenberger, T. (1983): Erziehung, Kommunikation, Begegnung im Strafvollzug. In: Festschrift für H. Leferenz. Heidelberg, p. 199
107 Von Schweinitz, H. (1980): Grenzen interner Therapiemodelle im "Erziehungsvollzug". In: KrimJ 1980, p. 125
108 Baratta, A. (1977): Strafvollzugssystem und soziale Marginalisierung. In: Festschrift für T. Würtenberger. Berlin, p. 375
109 Kargl, W.(1982): Die Kritik des Schuldprinzips. Frankfurt a.M./New York, p. 327
110 Kaiser, G. (1981): Differenzierte Behandlungsmethoden im Vollzug. In: Loccumer Protokolle 20/1980: Gibt es ein Recht auf Strafe?. Conference from 30.5.1980 to 1.6.1980. Rehburg- Loccum, p. 99
111 Hassemer, W. (1982): Resozialisierung und Rechtsstaat. In: KrimJ 1982, p. 162
112 Lamott, F. (1984): Die erzwungene Beichte. Tübingen, pp. 33/34
113 Lamott, note 112, p. 42
114 Brusten, M. (1984): Forschung für wen, für was und mit welchen Konsequenzen?. In: Petersohn, F. et al. (Eds.): Problematik des Strafvollzugs und Jugendkriminalität. Heidelberg, p. 67
115 Kreissl, R., and Ludwig, W. (1986): Rationalisierung des Strafrechts durch Kriminologen?. In: Brusten, M., Häussling, J.M., and Malinowski, P. (Eds.): Kriminologie im Spannungsfeld von Kriminalpolitik und Kriminalpraxis. Stuttgart, pp. 73 et seq.
116 For more on this point see Albrecht, note 3, pp. 834 et seq.
117 Basaglia, and Basaglia-Ongaro, note 104, pp. 21/22
118 Lamott, note 112, pp. 73/74
119 Von Kardorff, note 95, p. 2
120 See, for example, the "primer": Justizministerium Baden-Württemberg (1982): Das soziale Training im Strafvollzug. Stuttgart

121 Best, P. (1984): Ambulante soziale Dienste der Justiz. In: Steinhilper, G. (Ed.): Soziale Dienste in der Strafrechtspflege. Heidelberg, p. 14

122 Lamott, F. (1983): Zur Sicht der Fachdienste. In: Albrecht, P.-A., and Schüler-Springorum, H. (Eds.): Jugendstrafe an Vierzehn- und Fünfzehnjährigen. Munich, p. 167

123 Lamott, note 122

124 Lamott, note 122

125 Leky, L.G. (1980): Zwang im Verhältnis Therapeut-Klient in geschlossenen Institutionen. In: Schulz, W., and Hautzinger, M. (Eds.): Klinische Psychologie und Psychotherapie. Kongreßbericht Berlin. Vol. 5, Tübingen/Cologne, p. 125

4.
Criminal Justice Policy without Legitimacy

Otto Backes

Criminal justice complains that its resources in personnel, which could no longer be expanded in recent years, are tied up too much by the prosecution of petty criminality; to its mind that therefore the possibilities of dismissals in the area of petty criminality are to be used more than in the past in order to be able to employ the freed-up capacities for the prosecution of semi-serious and serious criminality.

The police complain that they are not able to counter the modern forms of criminality effectively with outdated methods of criminal investigation; they take the view that a preventive combatting of criminal offences must take effect before the fact and react already to situations tending toward crisis.

The complaints may be justified. Nevertheless, one can ask whether the desired changes can be answered for in terms of criminal justice policy. For criminal justice policy as well, understood as legal policy in the area of criminal law,[1)] remains bound to the principles of criminal law and the givens of the constitutional law. Hence it follows that a criminal justice policy that disregarded such principles and givens would lack legitimacy even if it could be based on a legal foundation or achieve a parliamentary majority for such a law.[2)]
The following contribution inquires into the legitimacy (in terms of criminal justice policy) of the practice of the dismissal of cases in preliminary investigations (A) as well as of the police practice of intervention in the area of preventive combatting of criminal offences (B) and attempts in closing to point out the conflict between prevention and constitutional rights that is emerging in both areas (C).

A. The Practice of the Dismissal of Cases in Preliminary Investigations

According to the order formulated in section 152, paragraph 2, of the Code of Criminal Procedure (StPO), the prosecutor's office is fundamentally obligated to intervene in the case of all actionable criminal offences in so far as sufficient, actual points of suspicion exist. Exceptions from this principle of mandatory prosecution are admissible unter certain conditions in sections 153 et seq. StPO.

I. The Scope of the Dismissals of Cases

The ratio of the exception to the norm formulated in the statute presents itself differently, however, if one considers the scope of the dismissals of cases in the prosecutor's practice of execution.
Out of the 2,178,000 proceedings in the year 1984[3], the prosecutor's office settled about 33 % with indictments (17.3 %) and petitions for release of an order of summary punishment (16.5 %). It dismissed 4.5 % of the cases with no obligations attached on the basis of triviality according to section 153, paragraph 1 StPO and 5.5 % of the cases subject to a condition (usually to a financial contribution to a non-profit institution) according to section 153a, paragraph 1 StPO. To these dismissals of altogether 10 % of the settlements of proceedings, one must also calculate a portion of the dismissals based on factual or legal grounds (28.5 %) according to section 170, paragraph 2 StPO. Of course, the decision of the prosecutor to dismiss the case according to section 170, paragraph 2 StPO or to prefer charges is, according to current opinion, not a discretionary decision. Nevertheless, the real reason why the prosecutor dismisses these cases does not always lie in the fact that no sufficient suspicion of a criminal offence could be established. On the contrary, as the empirical judicial research of recent years has been able to show,[4] the interest of the prosecutor in further clearing up the still unproven facts of a case by his own or by police follow-up investigations differs extremely. If it is a matter of criminal offences to which the prosecutor gives no great importance (slight damage, no prior charge), he will dismiss the case according to section 170, paragraph 2 StPO even when further clarification would be entirely possible. The negation of the interest to prosecute in these cases represents in reality a decision in terms of criminal justice policy that "effects a decision on the case without resorting to the court".[5] If one adds these discretionary decisions, which admittedly are unknown and disguised in their order of magnitude, to the openly displayed discretionary decisions,[6] then the decisions in which the principle of mandatory prosecution is diverged from can hardly still be only exceptions to the rule.

II. The Change in Criminal Theory

The increasing restriction of the duty to prosecute, which is made imperative by the principle of mandatory prosecution, it is claimed, is in the meantime less a means for relieving criminal justice than a procedural expression of a change in criminal theory as it has long since taken place in substantive law.[7] The prosecutor must already *take prevention purposes into consideration in the preliminary investigation* and must express this in his decision.

What this means is as follows: The compulsory prosecution of criminal offences and the compulsory public prosecution of crimes corresponded as a procedural correlate to the criminal law that aimed at retaliation; with the overcoming of retaliatory criminal law and its supplanting by a preventive criminal law, general-preventive and special-preventive views have entered into substantive criminal law which make it possible that a sanction needs not be imposed or could be mitigated despite the unlawful and reproachable constitution of an offence. This basic decision in criminal justice policy has also had an effect on the administration of the principle of mandatory prosecution. The decision on indictment or dismissal is related to the social organizing act of the assessments of sanctions by the judge. Since, despite the commission of an offence, he is permitted to waive sanctions, it is argued "that the prosecution's closing order is comparable to the judicial social organizing acts in connection with the assessment of sanctions". Consequently, the prosecutor in no way merely prepares the actual criminal proceedings in the preliminary investigation and closing orders but rather "in as far as he is functionally comparable to the judge", makes "decisions of practical criminal justice policy oriented in the broadest sense to the rules of meting out punishment".[7]

This new legitimation of decision-making behavior on the part of the prosecutor proceeds from two premises:

1. that the prosecutor himself, as a judge, actually investigates the case he has dismissed, and
2. that the prosecutor, as a judge, reflects upon the preconditions for and consequences of his social organizing act with regard to all incriminating and exonerating circumstances.

As pertains to the first premise, it was proved in the previously mentioned investigations of empirical judicial research that the prosecutor's office, even if varying in terms of specific crimes, actually takes over the results of the police criminal investigations in the area of petty and semi-serious criminality and orders possible follow-up investigations less for the purpose of amplification than to reinforce the previous result of police investigations. The criminal investigations of the prosecutor himself are hardly worth being mentioned. As emerges from the statistics of the prosecutor's offices of 1984,[8] an average of 5.3 % of the working hours included for hearings and individual investigative activity are used for the interrogations of witnesses, 4.6 % for the interrogations of suspects and 2.1 % for visits to the scene. As Feltes has more exactly calculated with the example of Hamburg,[9] this means, in absolute numbers, approximately 1 day of hearings and 1 hour of individual investigations per week. If one considers that these individual investigations also occur primarily in the area of serious criminality, then that means that the individual criminal investigations of the prosecutor are practically nil for the area of petty and semi-serious criminality that is of interest here. As far as it is a matter of clearing up the facts of the case, the prosecutor's office is virtually excluded and, to borrow a coinage of Hartung, degraded to a "file-churning machine".[10] "The chief criminal investigator" is the police.[11]

Yet a prosecutor who accepts the criminal investigations of the police as fact and launches no further investigations of his own may avoid the difficulties of being the inquirer, investigator and judge of a case in one person and in so far, for psychological reasons, can only fulfill his obligation to objectivity with great difficulty.[12] Meanwhile he runs the danger of judging a case to be ready for dismissal or indictment without having established objectively and sufficiently – as in the above-mentioned second premise – the circumstances that speak for and against the defendant.

In reality the prosecutor adds only two pieces of information to the result of the police investigation before he decides between dismissal or indictment: the information of the Federal Central Register on previous convictions as well as possible entries in the prosecutor's office's own index file on dismissals of cases. With this information, all the important data for the prosecutor's decision have been gathered. The assessment of this data and thereby the decision for dismissal or indictment is essentially determined by three factors: a prior charge against the defendant, his reaction to the charge as well as the extent of damage. In proceedings against someone previously convicted for the same offence, charges will be preferred rather than dropped. Whoever confesses has a better chance of dismissal than someone who refuses to give evidence or denies the charges. A damage of less than 20.00 German marks usually meets with a dismissal with no further consequences; greater damage (up to about 100.00 German marks) meets with an informal, sanctioning dismissal or with an order of summary punishment. Of course, there are differences according to the type of offence here as well.[13)]

Such a generalizing assessment of the facts of the case, however, has little to do with the prescribed investigation of incriminating and exonerating circumstances or with the observance of the principles that apply to the meting out of punishment. Neither general-preventive nor special-preventive deliberations are carried out with respect to the concrete case. The imputation of responsibility is neither individually examined nor concretized. It is much more a matter of presumptions, generalizations and everyday theories about personal liability. This is the deeper reason why the prosecutor's decisions on dismissal are not functionally comparable to those of the judge. The judge examines in an *individual case* the guilt of the *offender* and comes to his decision upon consideration of aspects of special and general prevention.[14)] The prosecutor does not need such investigations because he already has a relatively clear picture of dismissable and indictable *offences* in his mind before his decision to dismiss and only investigates the actual case to see if it corresponds to this preconceived image.

This is also confirmed by the *Directives and Orders of the Prosecutor's Office* , issued to render the provisions for dismissal more precise (sections 153, 153a StPO). They are consistently occupied with the formation of case groups for which the application of the provisions for dismissal is (still or no longer) possible. If, for example, it is ruled that only by the third offence should a passenger without a ticket be dealt with by criminal law, or that no informal, sanctioning dismissal may ensue in the case of drunk driving, then these typifications contained in the orders determine the prosecutor's decision and not the objectively established incriminating and exonerating circumstances of the individual case. The "context of criminal justice policy" claimed for the prosecutor's decision to dismiss is merely the result of an examination of the necessity of punishment of such offences, but not of the offender's need for punishment. If the prosecutor, in spite of the commission of an offence, rejects the laying down of a public indictment, then he replaces the assessment of the offence in criminal justice policy (as it had been defined by the legislator) with a political evaluation of the offence as it is reflected in the directives, orders and everyday routine of the prosecutor's practice. The picture in which the prosecutor is "a judge before the judge"[15] must therefore be corrected. In so far as the prosecutor's office sets up generalized standards for the application of the penal statutes by means of directives and orders, it acts also as a *"legislator before the legislator"*.

III. The Advantages of a "Practical Criminal Justice Policy"

If the development of the practice has been outlined correctly, then – seen from the perspective of the Code of Criminal Procedure – the function of decision–making and to a certain extent of sanctioning has been shifted among judge, prosecutor and police. In a state based on the separation of powers and divided up into multifarious dependencies and checks, such a functional displacement must throw up numerous constitutional problems, e.g., legal control of the police, decision-making control of the prosecutor, adjudication by non- judges, and so forth. These and similar constitutional problems that arise out of the functional displacement shall, however, not be considered here. Rather one must inquire what makes the current practice of the prosecutor so attractive that one tries to legitimate its preservation and if possible also its further expansion with the intention of criminal justice policy. Behind the practice of the prosecutor, can one possibly distinguish a concept of criminal justice policy, even if only recognizable in the early stages, which is not developing purely accidently?

The so-called *"practical criminal justice policy"*, as it is practiced by the prosecutor's office and approved of by the ministers of justice, has considerable *advantages* from the point of view of its users in comparison with legislative criminal justice policy:

1. The avoidance of criticism

Criminal Law Amendment Acts usually go back to ministerial bills that originate in the Ministry of Justice. Such bills are not only, as most statutes, closely scrutinized by an interested lobby but rather become, as Maihofer has described in detail,[16] "mere instruments of politics ..., of the gaining of prestige or of the search for confrontation, even a tool for striking out against the political opponent and campaign publicity among the political constituents in a moved-up election campaign". Reform plans that are treated parliamentarily are discussed and not infrequently talked about too much and watered down. If in the mean time one would like to push through his priorities in criminal justice policy in a more intact way, then a much quieter,"more decent" way presents itself in criminal law via the prosecutor's office. Removed from a parliamentary and public discussion, one can set targets which must be attended to in everyday practice, whereby directives and other guiding principles in the interest of the desired equal treatment provide the necessary pressure. Section 153a StPO is an example of this. By means of this provision, the decriminalization of substantive criminal law in the lower sector is virtually practiced on a wide front; this would run up against great resistance in the parliamentary and public discussion were it not completely rejected.[17] A directive for the application of the provisions for dismissal in the case of resisting executory officers reads, e.g., as follows[18]:

"Section 153 StPO, or at least section 153a StPO, can be applied if the offence remains without considerable consequences and special circumstances exist, such as if the offender were considerably intoxicated or if the cause for the officer's intervention was slight when considered in hindsight."

Similar provisions are found in the directives of application for sections 153, 153a StPO for offences involving property, physical injury and traffic, unauthorized departure from the scene of an accident, insults, etc. Were one to append these provisions as supplementary sections to the respective penal provisions of substantive law, it would become apparent that the penal code of the prosecutors is, to a certain extent, different from the published Penal Code (StGB).

2. The avoidance of general-preventive risks

The quoted directive for dismissal in the case of resisting executory officers also makes clear the risk that would be connected with a corresponding restriction of this criminal offence in the case of publication: intoxicated offenders would feel themselves all too easily encouraged to resist police officers. If one wants both to avoid the weakening of the (real or supposed) general-preventive power of penal statutes and yet not to punish, then the chosen, secret way via the directive is superbly qualified indeed. This new type of legal structuring – to advertise externally more regulatory content than is deemed necessary internally – publicly demonstrates the unswerving quality of the statutes, whereas the practice of application has already brought out its own typology of statutory definitions of offences. "For a pragmatic policy of reform that recognizes the need for the drastic relief of the judiciary and enforcement agencies but fears the supposed social-psychological effects of an express weakening of the severity of sanctions, the detour via the prosecutor is the path of least resistance."[19]

3. The avoidance of commitments

As the Penal Code remains intact in this form of so-called "practical criminal justice policy" and thus can be applied again at any time, it does not need to be fixed to a specific program of criminal justice policy[20] if "only" directives or orders are issued. For the intention in terms of criminal justice policy that perhaps can be found behind a legislative act that is to be restricted or the ideological content of a statute are not open to discussion. The corrections which are undertaken to the statutory definitions of offences by means of directives and orders appear much more to be the expression of pragmatic considerations and thus plausible to a great extent: restrictions on the constraint to prosecute due to problems of capacity, the necessity of generalizing directives because of equal treatment, and so forth. On the basis of such "material constraints", even prosecutors of greatly different origin in terms of criminal justice policy can agree very quickly. Thus, on the other hand, the retraction or change of directives, when it is deemed opportune, need not be justified in terms of criminal justice policy. This course of action has the advantage of allowing a quick, flexible reaction from the top without having to disclose the prominent reason if assessments in criminal justice policy make this seem expedient.[21)]

IV. Misgivings about the "Practical Criminal Justice Policy"

In the face of these and other advantages, it can not be expected that the practice of application can be altered to sections 153 et seq. StPO and that the tendency to the neutralization of criminal law "on the fringes" by means of directives, orders, etc., can be countermanded. As a partial decriminalization certainly seems sensible and justifiable, it is particularly difficult to argue against the practical criminal justice policy of the prosecutor's office. Yet misgivings exist about the chosen direction.

The first misgiving is that the application of criminal law has become *unpredictable* in a broad sphere due to the decision-making practice of the prosecutor's office. Thus, for example, when a shoplifter is caught for the first time, no criminal lawyer can predict anymore whether the case will be dismissed without any consequences or subject to a condition or whether even charges will be preferred. The knowledge of sections 242, 248a StGB, 153 et seq. StPO will not help him as long as he is not familiar with the directives, orders, etc., that were issued to them (the "soft law" of the practice). The application of section 153 StPO is recommended to the prosecutor's office (without the judge's consent) in the case of shoplifting if the damage is not greater than 30.00 German marks (Bremen), 50.00 German marks (Baden-Württemberg) or 100.00 German marks (North Rhine-Westphalia). The application of section 153a StPO is also permitted unrestrictedly for more extensive damage in Bremen and North Rhine-Westphalia and for damage as great as 250.00 Germans marks in Baden-Württemberg. These directives apply only "in principle" and for the "normal case"; in individual cases it can be quite advisable to deviate from them. Such a regionalization of the law may at least be able to make equal treatment in the realm of the respective Ministry of Justice possible, or perhaps only in the realm of the office of the chief prosecutor or of the prosecutor's office; but the clear predictability and scrutiny of the decision-making practice of the prosecutors is just as scarcely possible as it is with the ultimately noncommital generalization for the individual case.[22)] The necessary "formalizations" of the social control of criminal law may only be achieved by precise statutory regulations.

Since the prosecutor's office takes over the facts of the case as investigated by the police without carrying out their own inquiries, at least in the more minor spheres of criminality, and basically judges them in a generalized way according to directives, this leads to a schematized form of settlement. To a large extent, the written form takes the place of the verdict; the substantive decision that is to be justified argumentatively is replaced by a routine program. But this method of settlement hardly requires any juridical competence. Therefore it seems likely – and this is the second misgiving – that the prosecutor's office leaves these cases up to the discretion of the investigating *police* to a great extent in order for them to come to an independent *final judgment*.

Thus, for example, the decree of the Minister of the Interior of the Land Schleswig-Holstein of 7 December 1984[23)] provides that in order to accelerate the processing of minor juvenile offences (e.g., shoplifting, obtaining services under false pretenses, damage to property, traffic offences), the police can issue the juvenile a warning and recommend the dismissal of the case to the prosecutor's office if it is a first offence, the juvenile has confessed and is reasonably self-critical, the consequences of the offence are insignificant and the police are convinced that a warning suffices as an educational measure. In suitable cases the police can also propose a restitution, an apology or similar measure toward the reinstatement of public peace between the offender and the victim. The police then check whether and how far a proposed or introduced measure has been carried out. According to the Minister of the Interior,[24)] the prosecutor's office as a rule follows the suggestions of the police; it diverges from them in only 5 % of the cases.

The criticism is not directed against the quality of the police decisions but rather against the possibility (that arises here) of having the inquirer and judge of the facts of a case once again united in one person. Thus it can not be ruled out that, e.g., the police officer's reference to his competence in being able to make a suggestion of dismissal to the prosecutor promotes in an extraordinary way the offender's willingness to confess as well as his readiness to make the efforts toward restitution recommended to him by the police. Such a development cancels the well-founded separation of state powers between the police and the prosecutor's office and leads to a dangerous lack of differentiation, whereby this danger can certainly not now be proved by observed abuses yet has always been latent in the inquisitorial situation of investigation and decision.[25)]

B. The Police Practice of Intervening before the Fact in Order to Combat Criminal Offences

Preventive thinking in criminal justice does not only lead to the described change in the decision-making behavior of the prosecutors or to the shifting of competences among legislator, prosecutor's office and police that result therefrom. Within the scope of the preliminary investigation, preventive thinking also leads to the legally established limits of intervention being suspended and moved up.[26)] Preventive measures – restricted to prevention in cases of crises – should help here to prevent worse things from happening.

Thus, for example, in its decision on the severing of contact to the defence counsel in terrorist proceedings,[27] the Federal High Court of Justice (BGH) expressly declared solitary confinement (provided contrary to the wording of section 148 StPO) to be lawful because the severing of any communication with the defence counsel would alone prevent the danger of the prisoners granting the kidnappers help by way of information or of their being able to influence the commission of flanking terror attacks. In the "Traube case" the argumentation was similar; the findings in the cases of the so-called "use of a stool pigeon" read similarly.[28] What, of course, can not fail to be heard in these decisions is the note of regret at having to interpret so extensively or even to disregard the wording of the statute. Thus one can explain the attempt to restrict such justifications to the existence of "extraordinary circumstances" or to the combatting of "especially dangerous criminal offences or ones that are difficult to clear up" and to make them contingent on the presence of a "strong suspicion of a criminal offence".

With the police it is completely different. For a long time they have demanded and advocated modern methods of investigation for a more efficient combatting of "modern" criminality. Therefore they aggressively declare the development and use of preventive methods to be a necessary *modern criminological strategy* that has already led to a sweeping change in the area of security in the past 15 years and marks the "way into the year 2000".[29]

In the following I will go into more detail about which reasons have led to this change within the police department (that to a great extent has already taken place) (I) Further I will deal with which legal foundation it is based on in the currently applicable (II) and potentially future (III) law and, in closing, which effects on legal policy result therefrom (IV).

I. The New Designation of Functions

The functions of the police have been traditionally described as the averting of dangers and the prosecution of criminal offences. This description contains restrictions: the police should not go into action purely to preserve public security and order but only to ward off concrete dangers; the police should also not prosecute criminal offences preventively, but rather investigate only if there is the suspicion of a criminal offence ("right of first seizure"). Therefore, in principle, the individual case triggers the police intervention, which, of course, does not exclude the police from developing "noninterventionist" activities (which are independent of an individual case, such as patrolling) for the averting of dangers or the preventive combatting of criminal offences.

To the extent that the criminological recognition grew up that criminal offences are not monadistic isolated phenomena that originate exclusively in the evil will of an individual but rather arise in a social context that must also be considered, the traditional designation of functions of the police was felt to be too narrow. According to Stümper, the "modern" combatting of criminality "can no longer be operated from the somewhat petty-bourgeois aspect of criminal justice policy that sees each individual offence as isolated... It is no longer a matter of the offender and his offence but rather – as far as possible – of the elimination of criminality in general... For our enemy is not the individual, but criminality itself."[30)]

The demand for a new criminological strategy thus arises necessarily. What is decisive here is no longer primarily the clearing up and prosecution of individual criminal offences, but rather "the very fundamental neutralization, isolation and elimination of the original basis, structure and logistics"[31)] that are the preconditions for the genesis of criminal offences. It is no longer a matter of individual, but of "societal prevention".[32)]

This expansion of the functional area (practiced under the keyword "operative criminological strategy") in which the police claim for themselves the "general mission" of providing for the permanent compilation of the "big picture of 'internal security'" as a basis of political decisions[33)] assumes that the police obtain a comprehensive picture of those societal groups and situations which they wish to effect in terms of their criminological strategy. A proven way to do this is by *obtaining information* especially with electronic data storage and data alteration.[34)] The consequence is that the computer becomes an "instument for diagnosing the entire society"; "a new style of prevention that shifts and redesigns this state"[35)] arises.

For the execution of their new and broadly designated functional position, in the past years the police have set up a substantial arsenal of means for obtaining, storing and altering information that is growing in step with technological progress. Currently in use are thus, e.g., as follows:

- observation
- hidden use of technological means (bugging devices, infra-red devices, selectively aimed microphones, hidden cameras, etc.)
- use of undercover agents
- use of confidence persons
- investigation of public assemblies
- person-related files of the detective force
- police observation
- compilation of personality profiles
- systems for documentation of traces
- data adjustment
- search for wanted persons by scanning devices.

Thanks to the new police functional position, the comprehensive, systematic and often covert use of these modern means of gathering information takes place primarily in the areas of the "prevention of dangers" and the "preventive combatting of criminal offences", which have been moved up before the traditional areas of the averting of dangers and the prosecution of offences. Without going into the substance of the meaning of these concepts here, it must be stated that they do without the previous linking to the facts of a concrete danger or to the suspicion of a criminal offence in the sense of section 152 StPO. Whoever practices the "prevention of dangers" and the "preventive combatting of criminal offences" does not wait for the dangerous situation to get worse, but rather acts preventively by storing knowledge from the field of potential risk development for a later intervention. In so far the classic distinction between preventive and repressive police activity is made practically invalid because everything seems to be used for prevention.

II. The Legal Foundations De Lege Lata

But neither the expansion of the functional position nor the use of modern means of predominantly "electronic knowledge" (Herold) can change the fact that the new criminological strategy also needs a legal foundation in valid law.

Certainly since the decision of the Federal Constitutional Court of 15 December 1983 on the census law[36)], there has been no more doubt that police data collecting and data processing also needs a statutory foundation. For when fundamentally every citizen has the right to decide himself on the disclosure and use of his personal data, then the restrictions of this right require the express statutory foundation out of which three things must arise:

- the precondition and scope of the restriction must be clear and recognizable for the citizen (order of the clarity and certainty of statutes),
- they must observe the principle of commensurability, and
- in the face of the dangers to personal rights that emerge with the use of EDP, increased organizational and procedural precautions must be taken (order of the procedural protection of civil rights).

1. Within the scope of the preventive combatting of criminal offences, the Code of Criminal Procedure is of first consideration as a sedes materiae of a statutory foundation for police interference with the right to informational self-determination. Even if the police activity in this area is consistently oriented toward prevention, its regulation in the Code of Criminal Procedure remains absolutely possible and sensible because of the obvious material connection with the prosecution of criminal offences.

Due to the lack of special statutory regulations in the Code of Criminal Procedure for the individual methods of modern information acquisition, the provision of section 163 StPO could be taken as a statutory foundation. According to this, "agencies and officers of the police force" are to "investigate criminal offences". But disregarding the fact that, according to prevailing opinion,[37)] section 163 StPO only lays down the function of the police to prosecute criminal offences and can not, however, be taken in itself as an authorizing norm to prosecute criminal offences, then the opposing opinion[38)] – assuming for once its correctness – must be difficult to reconcile with the criteria of the clarity of statutes, the commensurability and the procedural protection of civil rights established by the Federal Constitutional Court. Furthermore a comprehensive clause included in the Code of Criminal Procedure that invested the police with powers would be a curiosity beyond compare: it would grant the "helping organs" of the prosecutor's office more powers than the prosecutor's office itself. This contradiction can not be done away with by the remark that the police – in contrast to the prosecutor's office – act preventively. For if, despite the presence of a concrete suspicion of a criminal offence, the Code of Criminal Procedure clings (for constitutional reasons) to a thoroughly differentiated system of individual authorizations which more precisely determine the preconditions of and the competence to use the respective measures of information gathering, then without such a suspicion, the police can certainly not claim for themselves authorizations to gather information that are going beyond and, in terms of content, organized at will[39] – unless one would like to dissolve the historically founded relationship between the police and the prosecutor's office that controls them in connection with the prosecution of criminal offences. And unless one would like to help the police to a virtually uncontrollable pre-investigating realm for conducting their own observations whose legal foundation (section 163 StPO) would find itself an enclave, completely contrary to the system, in the preliminary investigation controlled by the prosecutor's office.

2. The attempt to play down police interference with the right to informational self-determination as a pure sovereign activity[40] or as *"interference with no compulsory nature"* in order to deny its need for regulation as an infringement of civil rights is also bound to fail. This is based on the view that within the Code of Criminal Procedure one can distinguish between "typical compulsory interference" that requires a special authorization and those measures which could still be founded on section 163 StPO as "interference with no compulsory nature" ("Threshold Theory"). But since the decision of the Federal Constitutional Court on the census law, this view can no longer be held. In this decision it isn't calculated whether the interference has a compulsory nature or takes places as the result of a specific legal act[41]; actual infringements of civil rights which are undertaken without the consent of the person concerned by way of data collection and data processing are also subject to the requirement of legislative reservation.[42] For data interference that must be regulated occurs whenever the individual "can no longer see with sufficient security the whole extent of which information pertaining to him is known in certain spheres of his social environment and (he) is not relatively able to estimate the knowledge of potential partners in communication"[43]. According to this, the well-aimed, systematic and usually secret data gathering of the police in the area of the preventive combatting of criminality is to be characterized fundamentally as data interference in need of regulation.[44]

3. These types of interference will also not find a statutory support outside the Code of Criminal Procedure in the *rule of averting dangers of the State Police Code* because both a "concrete" danger and a "disturber" are usually missing in the data collections in the realm before the fact.

This lack can not be redressed in that comprehensive rules in police law and in criminal procedure (in their unproductiveness for police data-oriented prevention) are simply added and presented as a fundamentally sufficient basis for police data collection and data processing.[45)]

But when no authorizations laid down in a special legal way are available for the systematic data interference of the police in the area of danger prevention and the preventive combatting of criminal offences,[46)] and the manifold attempts to claim comprehensive statutes of police law or criminal procedure as a basis of legitimation also fail, then the current police practice of data gathering and data processing dispenses with the required legal foundation in the circumscribed areas before the fact – disregarding only a few exceptions – and violates the civil right to informational self-determination.[47)]

III. The Legal Basis de Lege Ferenda

The correction of this unlawful practice is promised, de lege ferenda, by the "Rough Draft (RD) to alter the Model Draft (MD) of a unified Police Code of the Federal Republic and the states in accordance with the resolution of the Conference of the Ministers of the Interior of 25 November 1977 (as of 8 February 1985)".[48)] It tries to put the new and expanded functional position of the police on a legally acceptable basis; it has the chance of being accepted by the state parliaments also in a more or less altered form.[49)]

In the interest of our thematic context, the following observations refer only to those regulations of the RD that deal with the collection of person-related data for the preventive combatting of criminal offences.

1. On legislative competence

The decision of the Federal Constitutional Court on the census law not only gave the authors of the RD on the Police Code of 1985 the opportunity to examine the legal consequences of this decision on police data gathering and data processing, but also, first and foremost, finally to "legalize" the long-claimed, expanded functional position. Thus section 7a RD provides for data gathering independent of the presence of a concrete danger in so far as this is required by the "preventive averting of dangers"; and section 1a RD allows the police the "preventive combatting of criminal offences" – as a subcategory of the averting of danger – without suspicion of a criminal offence. To fulfill the latter function the police may not only collect person-related data from everyone (section 8a RD) and in certain cases practice "special forms of data gathering" (section 8c RD) – these are invasive methods such as long–term observation, hidden use of technological means, etc.; they can also store, alter and use all these data (section 10a, paragraph 1 and 4 RD).

The comprehensive authorizations are also made expressly available for the "preventive combatting of criminal offences". At first glance it seems that only a preventive police function of averting danger is herewith described. However, in reality, here it is also a matter of prosecution. That especially results from section 10a RD, which permits the expansion of systems for the documentation of traces and grants the police the power to store and use person-related data within the scope of the preventive combatting of criminal offences not only when this is necessary for prevention but also for the "future clarification of criminal offences". Persons are also stored in these data files for whom no indication exists that they will commit criminal offences; but the files are kept so that *after* the commission of a criminal offence, suspects can be filtered out of them. But whoever gathers, stores and uses information in order to be able to clear up criminal offences after the fact more effectively does not want to prevent these offences but rather to prosecute them. "The producing of effects which ... should occur after the commission of a criminal offence can never be the averting of danger but always only prosecution."[50)]

However, the states do not have the competence to regulate the prosecution of criminal offences. In so far the rough draft violates the legislative competence of the Federal Government (Articles 74, 31 Constitution) by numerous provisions in which reference is made to the "preventive combatting of criminal offences" and prosecution is substantively regulated.

Of course it can not be ruled out that, within the scope of the preventive combatting of criminality, purely preventive measures for the prevention of criminal offences may also be developed for whose legal anchoring the states would be responsible. Yet the RD does not specify with a single word where the line between preventive and repressive police activity is and how the data which are fed in and flow together out of both areas can be distinguished. Yet as long as this is still unsolved and regulations in the Code of Criminal Procedure are lacking for repressive police activity, then a new regulation of the Police Code, as the grounds for the rough draft expressly state (2.3.3), is not "sensible" due to the manifold borderline problems. But the hope that the federal legislation will adopt "corresponding" provisions into the Code of Criminal Procedure is probably unfounded so long as one does not completely surrender the safeguarding rules of the Code of Criminal Procedure – as it will be attempted to show in the following.

Furthermore, the state legislator should also not subject the entire preventive combatting of criminal offences to his regulatory competence because otherwise the labelling of police measures as prevention could lead to a repeal of the criminal law and of the law of criminal procedure. This applies exemplarily to Herold's vision of criminal justice policy as he would like to locate police investigations so prematurely in the realm "before the commission" of crime, that criminal offences can no longer even occur. The repeal of criminal law, however, would only result in the creation of a police law with no bounds.

The disregard of the legislative competence of the Federal Government is moreover not only a formal violation. On the contrary, a "question of power" of central importance is being decided here. The police are uncoupling themselves not only from the Code of Criminal Procedure but also from the control by the prosecutor's office at the same time; for beyond the Code of Criminal Procedure, the prosecutor's office can claim no controlling powers over the police.[51)] It is to be feared that this process results in constitutional losses not only in general, but also in individual cases.

2. "Straightforward" data collection

According to the regulation provided for in section 8a RD (data collection), the police can collect person-related data if this is, e.g., "necessary on the basis of actual indications for the preventive combatting of criminal offences".[52)] These "actual indications", however, need not thicken to the point of a concrete danger of the commission of a criminal offence. On the contrary, the risk of criminal offences being committed suffices.[53)] Experiences in crime detection, prognoses and everyday theories about which milieus, populations and actions could have a latent criminogenic potential suffice to determine the risk. This early access to data allows the police to procure preventively person-related material for the time when it is needed. As the grounds for the RD show, the prognosis that in the future – once again – criminal offences will be committed needs "not be so timely that one can already talk about a danger for public security ...".[54)] The growth in power of the police that lies in this *data stockpiling*[55)] certainly does not manifest itself in the behavior of the individual police officer in the street. However, it can be seen in the large-scale police operations that are planned on the basis of the big pictures of "internal security", strategically prepared and run by electronic data processing, such as in demonstrations.

It is obvious that with such police strategies that are so risk-oriented, the more information is available, the more effective they will be. The limiting of data collection to "disturber" or even "suspects" would therefore be extremely hindering. Logically, the RD also does without such restrictions and permits the collection, storage and use of data also "on other persons" if this is "necessary" on the basis of actual indications for the preventive combatting of criminal offences. As this decision is the duty of the police alone, the prosecutor's office is hindered from having a controlling effect or even only from having knowledge of it.

3. "Special forms" of data collection

Section 8c RD, under which the police in the future should be provided with the disposing power over instruments of investigation which up to now have only been granted to the secret services (referred to with the euphemistic title "special forms of data collection") is especially to be criticized. This regulation must be described more closely on the basis of the criteria of the clarity of statutes and of commensurability set up by the

Federal Constitutional Court for the restriction of the right to informational self-determination.

a. At first glance the provision gives the impression that secret investigation is only permitted for the preventive combatting of the most serious criminal offences (paragraph 1, number 2). That is induced especially by the reference and linking to section 100a StPO, which allows the monitoring of telephone communications during the preliminary investigation for particularly serious criminal offences that are definitively listed in a catalogue. But section 8c RD continues: it provides for secret investigation also for certain criminal offences against sexual self-determination, against property and assets as well as against the environment. Of course, the entire enumeration of statutory definitions of crimes regarding the clause in paragraph 1, number 3 would never have been necessary for this clause had but allows the "special forms" for preventive combatting also for "other criminal offences". The qualification that the "other criminal offences" are committed "professionally, habitually or by gangs" is practically meaningless. For in order to suppose the existence of a "gang" it suffices that several (according to adjudication, two suffice) persons have bound together on the basis of an express or a tacit agreement, for a certain period of time, in order to commit several independent, yet individually not yet specific, offences. However, as according to section 8c RD the criteria for a "gang" must neither have been proved nor have thickened to suspicion, then mere suppositions in this direction suffice in order to practice secret investigation for practically every criminal offence – even for pocket picking[56]. If one further considers that section 8c RD, just as section 8a RD, permits the collection of person-related data on "other persons", the "non- disturbers", as well, then on the basis of this legal situation, no one can assume any longer that even his most private sphere is safe from a private investigation by the police – not even someone who has never even considered committing a criminal offence. This regulation is absolutely irreconcilable with the constitutional order of the clarity of statutes whereby the restrictions of the right to informational self-determination must arise clearly and recognizably for the citizen.

b. The secret investigation with the means mentioned in section 8c RD is also irreconcilable with the principle of commensurability, which will be shown with the example of two of the cited possibilities of interference.

The RD wants to legalize the "long-term, planned *use of confidence persons*". As the adjudication has long since recognized the *use of confidence persons* for the combatting of (serious) criminality, mentioning this method seems to mean nothing special at first. If one visualizes, however, the preconditions for the use of a confidence person according to section 8c RD, the picture changes. Typically, the confidence person tries to investigate (by way of observing but occasionally also by provoking an offence) whether presumed but already suspected persons commit criminal offences. The provocation of the offence serves in this case to "concretize" a decision to commit the deed that was already present in the suspect (latent decision) in order to prove his guilt. Yet as section 8c RD is provided as an empowering rule for precisely those cases in which the concrete danger of the violation of a statute does not yet exist, it is here a matter of the provocation of "non-disturbers" into action, of the effect of stool pigeons (agent provocateur) on persons who previously were merely classified as "potential risks".

"Suspicion" as well as "danger" is linked to the individual person's modes of behavior that indicate which actions have been or could be committed by him. But it is characteristic for "risk"[57] that it is determined by various "social features and living situations which are separable from the individual", such as nationality, profession, place of residence, etc., and which are related to one another as factors and give rise to the suspicion that the commission of criminal offences could be likely. As the grounds for the draft illustrate unmistakably, it is solely a matter of the prognosis that "in the future – once again – criminal offences will be committed".[58] Therefore it is not necessary that the observed, actual persons must have given rise to this speculation by their behavior. On the contrary, already determined – depersonalized – risk factors could represent sufficient "actual indications" that justify the assumption "that in the future – once again – criminal offences will be committed". Thereupon the bearer of such risk factors, the so-called "risk person", can be subjected to detailed investigation. It is no longer the behavior of an actual person but rather the diagnostic product of the "risk person" that triggers police action. So the individual, actual person can "move completely within the framework of legality"[59] and nevertheless becomes a preferred object of the control of criminality as the bearer of certain risk factors, as a "risk person". Riehle justly concludes: "If such a development could be put through, then living a lawful life would no longer guarantee that one would not become the addressee of a confidence person – and thereby of the agencies of the control of crime."[59]

If, however, the confidence person does not only investigate offences and the preparation of and the decision to commit them, but may also arrange for them to be committed, then his activity is finally aimed at testing the firmness or the susceptibility of the object of his investigations; legal loyality is not being investigated but rather the man's character. The stool pigeon "tests the degree of the law abiding ... and has the best chance with those victims who can not counter *this* temptation with sufficient resistance".[60] When one considers out of which milieu confidence persons are often recruited, that they are under pressure to succeed for various reasons and yet could never really be held responsible for their actions, then it appears questionable if the "hardness test" to which they subject their victims – the RD speaks of "long-term, planned use" – is appropriate and necessary for the clearing up of criminal *offences* at all. The activity of a stool pigeon, who not only controls the future commission of criminal offences but also produces them, represents a very high price which can hardly still be justified as an appropriate measure for the combatting of criminality and as a loss to be borne by the citizens. The stool pigeon's success may prove that the victim actually was a risk and capable of committing criminal offences; but this only confirms that the use of the stool pigeon brought to light what this victim was willing to do "in reality", but not what he would have done had the stood pigeon never been used. In criminal law, however, it is a matter of what you do, not what you have in mind.[61] Whoever denies this and takes the view that a preventive combatting of criminal offences could not otherwise be successful proceeds from a different criminal and criminal procedure law from the one that applies.

What further must be objected to legally is the method of the *"hidden use of technological means"* for data collection mentioned in section 8c paragraph 1. Herewith the police should now be granted investigative means which up to now have been reserved for the secret services. The police could thus secretly use bugging devices, hidden cameras and whatever technology develops in the line of new spying devices for the investigation of almost every criminal offence. Where this development is leading to and how far it leaves the applicable legal state behind it should be demonstrated with an example of a case decided by the Federal High Court of Justice (BGH).[62]

Because of the suspicion of professional drug dealing, the telephone line of the husband Sch. was monitored in accordance with section 100a StPO. Since one of the residents had had a telephone conversation and afterwards had not replaced the receiver properly, it was possible to eavesdrop on and record the ensuing conversation conducted by the married couple in the room ("room conversation") in which the husband took stock of his previous heroin deals.
On the unusability of the "room conversation" recording, the BGH states among other things:
"In the senate's opinion, the recording of the 'room conversation' touched upon the inviolable realm of private lifestyle which is under the absolute protection of the civil right in article 2, paragraph 1 in connection with article 1, paragraph 1 Constitution and upon which public power may therefore not exert influence...
The discussion between married persons in the marital residence is to be classed with this inviolable area. If the state could claim for itself the right to control conversations held in the most intimate family circle, this could not be reconciled with the principle of human dignity. If one wanted to recognize the admissibility of such an extensive surveillance, then it wouldn't be clear why it should be restricted to the tapping of telephone lines and weren't also admissible for the use of typical bugging devices. But then no space within the most private sphere of life would remain in which marriage partners could be certain that their conversations were not being monitored. The possibility of expressing emotions, feelings, opinions or impressions of experiences without the fear of state authorities' monitoring the conversation would then be unbearably hampered. This also would be true for any confidential communication between married couples. This would mean a serious impairment of human dignity. Further, such a measure would considerably deny the persons concerned the 'inner space' which must be left to them for the free and self-responsible development of their personalities ..."[63]

Nevertheless, section 8c RD wants to permit such measures and not only for the serious offences named in section 100 StPO but rather for almost all criminal offences. This is not altered by section 8c, paragraph 2 RD which provides that data collection out of residences may only take place if this is necessary for the averting of a "current, considerable danger"[64]; for the draft does not disclose when, from the police's point of view, "considerable" danger exists. Even the stipulated judicial competence to issue an order for eavesdropping in residences is practically devalued by the fact that in situations of danger any police officer may decide and, for instance, may assign a confidence person with a camera and bugging device to the home of a person, even if no indications exist that this person will commit criminal offences.

IV. The Effects on Legal Policy

The preceding observations hopefully suffice to demonstrate now some questionable effects on legal policy that result from the "new criminological strategy" of the police.[65)]

1. The police as the dominant prosecuting authority

The plentitude of the data material gathered and processed by the police within the scope of their preventive activity lends them enormous decision-making power. They not only decide autonomously which areas of criminality they want to examine preventively, which priorities they want to set and how many of their personnel and material resources they want to use for this.[66)] But they also decide first and foremost from the aspect of opportunity whether, when and how much of their knowledge they will convey to the prosecutor's office. For the police, the investigation of structural connections of certain scenes and groups is often more important than the prosecution of a criminal offence committed in this area. Therefore, they will not reveal their inside information prematurely in repressive prosecuting activity.[67)] On the other hand, the prosecutor's office is expressly denied direct access to the knowledge discovered by the police on the basis of their preventive combatting of criminal offences and stored in data files.[68)] In so far it is restricted to the material selected out and delivered by the police; the prosecutor's office becomes a marginal recipient of information next to – or more precisely – before which the police establish themselves as the dominant prosecuting authority.

2. The unnerving of the citizens

The new Police Code wants to allow the police extensive interference with the right to informational self-determination as well as with other civil rights. Even if the police only made cautious use of the powers conceded to them in the RD, a serious unnerving and paralyzing of the citizens would proceed from the mere fact that they were also entitled to more extensive observation.[69)]

The Federal Constitutional Court observes, for example, as follows[70)]:

"Whoever is uncertain of whether deviating modes of behavior are at any time being noted and permanently stored, used and transmitted as data will try not to become conspicious by such behavior. Whoever assumes that the attendance of a meeting or the participation in a citizen's action group is being officially registered and that consequently risks could arise for him will perhaps dispense with practicing his corresponding civil rights (Articles 8, 9 Constitution) ... Thus it follows that the free development of the personality under the modern conditions of data processing assumes the protection of the individual against the unlimited collection, storage, use and transmission of his personal data."

In comparison to this, section 8b RD provides that the police can gather person- related data also by means of video and tape recordings "at or in connection with" (therefore also removed from the scene of) public events, gatherings or meetings if actual indications justify the assumption that dangers for public security or order exist. Since such actual indications can easily be discerned for large-scale demonstrations, and the draft doesn't prescribe that the actual indications must be present in the person of the participant who is being observed, it is entirely up to the police to what extent they record person-related data on demonstrators (and transmit them to the German intelligence services).

Herewith, however, the principle confirmed by the Federal Constitutional Court, according to which each person must decide himself on the disclosure and use of personal data and that this self-determination may only be partially interfered with, is completely inverted by the new Police Code.

3. "Security before data protection"

Yet still another development appears questionable. The opinion that "security goes before data protection"[71] is advocated not only by the police in connection with the preventive combatting of criminal offences and for its justification. A not unproblematic priority is herewith fixed. In what is to be considered as security, which areas it comprises, which precautions it requires and who determines its substance – all that is completely open. "Security" is no juridically contoured concept that can be dealt with easily. Whoever demands that "security" must go "before data protection" actually demands that the law has to yield to a policy of security.
In his study "On the Constitutionality of Nuclear Energy"[72], Rossnagel impressively pointed out the legal changes that can be forced in order to protect nuclear plants from the oversized potential of damage that can result from human misbehavior – criminal behavior in particular. The futurologic legal investigation of technological material compulsions and their effects on the law drafts a future "legal system of nuclear security" and asks pointedly how much freedom this future law still guarantees, measured against today's standards, and how much resistance the civil rights could still oppose to individual security measures.

A part of what Rossnagel had prognosticated in his 1984 work on the freedom-restricting legal changes in the sphere of "societal prevention of dangers" for the security of nuclear technological plants had already gained form in the RD of 1985. Here it is not meant that the RD of 1985 was formulated with the aim of having early control over risks which could possibly emerge from the resistance of the population to the nuclear energy policy being put into effect. What is more important is that the RD makes a differentiated set of instruments available to prepare the ground for every policy (also nuclear energy policy) whose realization would afford individuals the chance to endanger or injure "vital security interests" by criminal behavior even if in this way the positions of the civil rights of a multitude of completely unsuspicious citizens are massively impaired. The justification for this may be that the "policy of security has become a policy of existence ..."[73], especially with reference to the threat of international criminality, drug traffic, terrorism and violent conflicts with militant groups. Nevertheless, the reference to these dangers can not justify a police law that is neither restricted to combatting these dangers nor attempts to prevent the misuse of the granted power of intervention by procedural safeguarding or sufficient legal control.

4. The problems of legitimation

A police service that believes itself to be "called to the ... general mission" of having to prepare political decisions expertly by permanently compiling big pictures for "internal security" and a policy that, by referring to this "internal security", can always be assured of police help in getting it put through represent a dangerous alliance for the positions of civil rights guaranteed up to now. A police department that wants to practice a policy of security by means of the far-reaching, preventive combatting of criminal offences does not only extend itself to a foreign task; it especially runs the risk of increasingly losing sight of its own duty, i.e., protecting the rights to freedom of the citizens. Claiming the police for a policy of security as well as the fact that more and more people would begin to identify police activity with both the collection and registration of person-related data on 'Everyman' and with secret investigation would also lead to a considerable loss of trust in the police on the part of the population. The police themselves would find themselves in a difficult crisis of legitimation were they to embark on a criminal justice policy without legitimacy.

C. Prevention and Constitutional Rights

What is most striking about the above-sketched developments in the divisions of the prosecution and the police seems to be their contrarity: the withdrawal of control through decriminalization in sections 153, 153a StPO and the expansion of control for the preventive combatting of criminal offences in the RD for a new State Police Code. Upon closer study, however, similarities appear: The quiet detaching of criminal justice policy from legislative acts and assignments of competence with the claiming of prevention as an apparent basis of legitimation for the desired or already executed change. With a reference to the fact that the prosecutor also has to take general-preventive and special-preventive purposes into consideration in the preliminary investigation, the statutory definitions of crimes of the Penal Code are "corrected" and rewritten in generalizing directives on the lower margin. Thus not only the Penal Code is altered, but the constitutionally established competence of the legislator is set aside at the same time, and a new "division of business" is taken up: the prosecutor's office crowns itself as legislator and leaves the investigation *and* punishment of petty criminality more and more up to the police (or to diversion agencies) and retires from the role of the "chief criminal investigator" without a sound.

The process is similar in the area of the preventive combatting of criminal offences by the police. By referring to the fact that offences must be combatted preventively, the police detach themselves both from the concrete danger and from the suspicion of a criminal offence as a precondition for intervention and allow the risk of disturbance to be sufficient for intervening in a supposedly preventive police fashion. By the incorporation of this function in police laws, not only the prudently graduated interventionary authorization of the Code of Criminal Procedure are undermined and the prosecutors' powers of direction and control excluded, but the civil rights of even non-suspicious persons are massively interfered with.[74)] The police's growth of power, however, does not only lead to an expansion of the possibilities of control, but also to an increase in the potential for direction and herewith to a further "over-policing" of societal spheres of life.

The diminishing regard of constitutional rights with the reference to prevention is, however, in no way accidental but actually pre-existent in the statutes. Riess, for instance, concedes frankly[75)] "that the public interest required in sections 153, 153a StPO" was "an empty form that could be filled out at will", but that perhaps precisely fulfilled the function of transforming the "changing value decisions in criminal justice policy and substantive law in the law of procedure". In other words, interest determines what prevention is; the norms themselves only serve the function of lending an apparently constitutional covering to these changing interests.[76)] In reality, however, they must be soft, flexible, fuzzy and without contour in order to be able to be functionalized for respective utilitarian purposes.

Even the RD of a new state police law only vaguely mentions the preconditions under which the police may intervene preventively: the interventions are no longer made actually dependent on legally normed and precisely regulated statutory definitions of offences, but rather on the police estimations of risk oriented toward the interests of internal security and made from situation to situation. But the preventive measures themselves are just as indefinite as the preconditions. Neither the type nor the duration, nor the intensity of the hidden use of technological means is regulated, for example; the interests of prevention know no bounds.

Suggestions on how the problems of petty criminality or the preventive combatting of criminal offences may be solved in detail can not be made here. But the preceding observations should have demonstrated two points. First, criminal justice policy may be practiced neither by the offices of the chief prosecutor or by ministries via directives and orders nor by the police by the means of situational pictures for internal security but rather must be practiced by the legislator. And secondly, the legislator must examine very carefully whether and to what extent he leaves room for preventive approaches in the statutes. For prevention opens the door wide to the personal expedience of each respective user of the law and thus allows a deflection of legislative set targets and in so far represents a permanent threat to constitutional rights.

Notes

1 Zipf, H. (1980): Kriminalpolitik. 2nd ed., Heidelberg, p. 6

2 Cf. also Hassemer, W. (1981): Einführung in die Grundlagen des Strafrechts. Munich, p. 182, pp. 301/302

3 The figures have been taken from the statistics in Statistisches Bundesamt Wiesbaden (Ed.) (1985): Staatsanwaltschaften 1984, pp. 10 et seq.

4 In this connection, see Blankenburg, E., Sessar, K., and Steffen, W. (1978): Die Staatsanwaltschaft im Prozeß strafrechtlicher Sozialkontrolle. Berlin; Steffen, W. (1976): Analyse polizeilicher Ermittlungstätigkeit aus der Sicht des späteren Strafverfahrens. BKA-Forschungsreihe, Vol. 4, Wiesbaden; Blankenburg, E. (1973): Die Staatsanwaltschaft im Prozeß sozialer Kontrolle. In: KrimJ 1973, pp. 188 et seq.; Kunz, K.-L. (1980): Die Einstellung wegen Geringfügigkeit durch die Staatsanwaltschaft. Königstein

5 As in Wagner, W. (1972): Die Exmittierung der Staatsanwaltschaft. In: DRiZ 1972, p. 167; see also Riess, P. (1981): Die Zukunft des Legalitätsprinzips. In: NStZ 1981, pp. 2 et seq.

6 Considered in this connection are, in particular, dismissals with no obligations attached according to section 154, paragraph 1 StPO (insignificant incidental offence) as well as section 45, paragraph 2, of the Juvenile Court Act (refraining from prosecution), which together accounted for 5.1 % of the settlements in 1984. – The types of settlements mentioned here make up a total of ca. 77 %; the remaining types of settlements – such as, e.g., transfers of cases – are not of interest in this connection.

7 Riess, note 5, pp. 6/7

8 Staatsanwaltschaften 1984, note 3, p. 24

9 Feltes, T. (1984): Die Erledigung von Ermittlungsverfahren durch die Staatsanwaltschaft. In: KrimJ 1984, pp. 50 et seq., pp. 57/58

10 Quoted in Henkel, H. (1953): Strafverfahrensrecht. 1. ed., Stuttgart, p. 198

11 Feltes, note 9, p. 59; Rüping, H. (1983): Das Verhältnis von Staatsanwaltschaft und Polizei. In: ZStW 1983, pp. 894 et seq., p. 912

12 Cf. Roxin, C. (1969): Rechtsstellung und Zukunftsaufgaben der Staatsanwaltschaft. In: DRiZ 1969, pp. 385 et seq.

13 Kotz, P. (1983): Die Wahl der Verfahrensart durch den Staatsanwalt. Frankfurt a.M., pp. 102 et seq., pp. 192 et seq.

14 Whereas the prosecutor usually only has the record at his disposal for the basis of his decision, the judge has the accused in person before him and thus at least the possibility to come to individualized conclusions. That he does not always make use of this to the extent desired does not change the fact that he has fundamentally a better point to decide from than the prosecutor.
Kunz goes into detail about the disadvantages of a decision, based on the record as it stands, on petty offences; see Kunz, K.-L. (1984): Das strafrechtliche Bagatellprinzip. Berlin, pp. 331 et seq.: "An authentic, individual impression of the nature of the offence and the offender's personality can only be achieved over the medium term by an *oral hearing* that must be localized on the level of the court." – Similarly: *Alternativ–Entwurf*, Novelle zur StPO (Tübingen 1980), published by a working group of German and Swiss experts on criminal law, which for constitutional reasons demands the replacement of section 153a StPO by a judicial hearing with the trial process in camera.

15 This is the title of a study by Kausch, E. (1980): Der Staatsanwalt. Ein Richter vor dem Richter?. Berlin

16 Maihofer, W. (1981): Gesetzgebungswissenschaft. In: Winkler, G., and Schilcher, B. (Eds.): Gesetzgebung. Kritische Überlegungen zur Gesetzgebungslehre und zur Gesetzgebungstechnik. Vienna, pp. 3 et seq., p. 23

17 The "creeping legalism" of section 153a StPO by means of directives, decrees, etc. on the one hand and the thus effected undermining of substantive criminal law on the other illustrate graphically the stylistic main characteristics of current law worked out by Naucke: a continuous positivity and – in contradiction to this – a continuous disintegration of this positivity; see Naucke, W. (1986): Versuch

über den aktuellen Stil des Rechts. In: KritV 1986, pp. 189 et seq. Critical also of a partial annulment of criminal law by the law of criminal procedure is: Riess, note 5, p. 5

18 General Directive of the Chief Prosecutor of Bremen from 4 June 1986

19 Kunz, K.-L. (1984): Die Verdrängung des Richters durch den Staatsanwalt: eine zwangsläufige Entwicklung effizienzorientierter Strafrechtspflege?. In: KrimJ 1984, pp. 39 et seq., p. 44

20 Kunz, note 19, pp. 44/45: "The prosecutor's minimizing ... instead of a statutory definition for granting privileges for petty offences ... means both the anticipation and the renunciation of more consistent, but also more rigorous changes of substantive law." Similar is Naucke, who rightfully accords sections 153 and 153a StPO only an apparent decriminalizing function; see Naucke, W. (1984):
Über deklaratorische, scheinbare und wirkliche Entkriminalisierung. In: GA 1984, pp. 199 et seq., pp. 205 et seq.,

21 A further advantage for the proponents of the practical criminal justice policy lies in the fact that the prosecutor's office can simply shift the responsibility for the non-application of criminal laws to the police, thanks to the transfer of the investigatory function to them, or can reject the responsibility with a reference to the insufficient resources of personnel and equipment as, for instance, occurs in the area of environmental criminal law.
Furthermore, section 153a StPO is in no way restricted to substantive criminal law. Thus it reads, for example, in an order of the Chief Prosecutor of Bremen dated 23 September 1976: "The growing overcrowding of the prisons ... that is further increased .... by the closing of the outer camps in winter makes the following measures mandatory: 1. Increased use is to be made of sections 153 and 153a StPO in the prosecution of petty offences..." What is astonishing about this order is the view expressed therein that the prosecution of petty offences can lead to the (over-) crowding of prisons at all.

22 The federally uniform minimizing directives which were to be taken up in the RiStBV would be able to solve the problem of regional differences but not, however, the problem of the schematic application according to the record as it stands; see in this connection Kunz, note 14, pp. 327/328. – Misgivings also expressed in Weigend, T. (1984): Strafzumessung durch den Staatsanwalt? Lösbare und unlösbare Probleme bei der Verfahrenseinstellung unter Auflagen (§ 153a StPO). In: KrimJ 1984, pp. 4 et seq. Weigend's suggestions on legal policy with regard to section 153a StPO would, however, find little resonance in practice since they propose the restriction of precisely those possibilities in the practice of the application of section 153a StPO that the prosecutor's office values most.

23 Decree of the Minister of the Interior of the Land Schleswig-Holstein – IV 410b – 32.11 – of 7 December 1984 pertaining to the procedure for accelerating the processing of minor juvenile offences ("diversion").

24 Response of the Minister of the Interior of Schleswig-Holstein to a question raised in Parliament concerning preliminary investigations of juveniles according to the so-called Kieler Model, printed in Information der Polizei Schleswig-Holstein (1986), No. 2, p. 6

25 The numerous 'diversion models' that are currently being carried out in the Federal Republic of Germany also aim at a legal upgrading of police activity. There are no misgivings about this nor about the shift of competence connected with it as long as the legal protection of the defendant is not curtailed and police activity does not remain in a zone of virtual uncontrollability. But it is not a sufficient safeguard against this, however, to require that the defendant has to "confess", be "reasonably self-critical" or be "in accordance" with the measure. Such requirements can be very readily met for extremely different reasons. The result may then be an early end of the case by mutual consent but, burdened with the odium of plea-bargaining, it remains a result "in the shadow of the law".

26 See the contribution of Peter-Alexis Albrecht in this volume that treats this subject in detail.

27 BGH NJW 1977, p. 2172; in comparison to this, the BVerfG NJW 1977, p. 2157 based itself in its decision severing any communication from the inmates on a legal regulation that was made in a rapid-fire decision and went into effect two days before the decision, cf. sections 31 et seq. EGGVG.

28 Cf., e.g., BGHSt 32, 115, pp. 121/122 – On the legal assessment of the use of a stool pigeon in an unconstitutional way, see Roxin, C. (1985): Strafverfahrensrecht. 19. ed., Munich, section 21 B

29 Stümper, A. (1979): Die Polizei auf dem Weg in das Jahr 2000. In: Kriminalistik 1979, pp. 254 et seq.
30 Stümper, A. (1975): Prävention und Repression als überholte Unterscheidung?. In: Kriminalistik 1975, pp. 49 et seq., p. 52
31 Stümper, A. (1980): Die Wandlung der Polizei in Begriff und Aufgaben. In: Kriminalistik 1980, pp. 242 et seq., p. 243
32 In the words of the former president of the German Federal Bureau of Investigation (Bundeskriminalamt), Horst Herold, in an interview. In: TransAtlantik 1980, No. 11, pp. 29 et seq., p. 37
33 Stümper, note 29, as well as note 31, p. 245, in which it is considered necessary to found a "General Administration for Internal Security" and also to compile permanently "pictures of the world situation" with possible effects and possible countermeasures.
34 See also Herold, H. (1985): Information und Staat. In: Festschrift für R. Wassermann. Neuwied, pp. 359 et seq.
35 Herold, note 32, p. 40
36 BVerfGE 65, 1, pp. 41 et seq.
37 Roxin, note 28, section 10 B; Rainer Müller in Karlsruher Kommentar. Munich, No. 1 to section 163 StPO; Riegel, R. (1980): Probleme der polizeilichen Beobachtung und Observation. In: JZ 1980, pp. 224 et seq., pp. 225/226; Vahle, J. (1983): Polizeiliche Aufklärungs- und Observationsmaßnahmen. Diss. Bielefeld, pp. 49/50
38 Schwan, E. (1979): Die Abgrenzung des Anwendungsbereiches der Regeln des Straf- und Ordnungswidrigkeitenverfahrensrechtes von dem des Rechts auf Gefahrenabwehr. In: Verw.Arch 1979, pp. 109 et seq., pp. 111/112, pp. 116 et seq.; Kubica, J., and Leineweber, H. (1984): Grundfragen zu den Zentralaufgaben des Bundeskriminalamtes. In: NJW 1984, pp. 2068 et seq., pp. 2071/2072
39 Similarly, Riegel, note 37, p. 225
40 Thus Kubica and Leineweber, note 38, p. 2072
41 Götz, V. (1985): Allgemeines Polizei- und Ordnungsrecht. 8. ed., Göttingen, section 8 II. Götz distinguishes between "interference by a specific legal act" and "the actual infringement of civil rights" that do not need to be assigned to the more narrow province of authorizations to intervention. He attributes data interference to the latter category. The reason for this division is apparent. For "if it were proper that data gathering and data processing were only admissible when they were based on the statutes that authorize intervention, then they would be only restrictedly possible, indeed". Since this result is not desired, the necessity of an area-specific regulation is also negated.
42 Thus aptly, Vahle, note 37, pp. 10 et seq., p. 12, p. 25
43 BVerfGE 65, p. 43
44 For a closer legal evaluation of the individual police measures in this area, cf. Denninger, E. (1985): Das Recht auf informationelle Selbstbestimmung und innere Sicherheit. In: KJ 1985, pp. 215 et seq., pp. 232 et seq.; Vahle, note 37, pp. 26 et seq., pp. 44 et seq.
45 Such is the thesis of Scholz, R., and Pitschas, R. (1984): Informationelle Selbstbestimmung und staatliche Informationsverantwortung. Berlin, pp. 170 et seq., who not only understand section 163 StPO to be an empowering statute but also consider the comprehensive rule in police law to be applicable before concrete situations of danger occur. The observations of Scholz and Pitschas are not even initially convincing. In their view, the right to informational self-determination ends in "reasons of public weal legitimated by the constitution". The task of taking precautions for the protection of the security of civil rights assumes a multitude of accessible information for its fulfillment. "The security of civil rights ... therefore also means state data-oriented prevention at the same time." This "genuine government function" receives its constitutional legitimation from the principle of due process and the principle of social justice and the welfare state. Data-oriented prevention anchored in a "civil right to security" consequently limits the right to informational self-determination. A scrutiny of the modern police methods of obtaining information therefore leads to the predictable result that the currently practiced police data-oriented prevention can essentially rely on the existing legal foundations. In correct opposition to this, Denninger (note 44, p. 216) states: The "civil right to security" is an invention of the author which, in its vagueness and generality, does not exist in the Constitution. It is the attempt to neutralize the new civil right to informational self-determination "in the confrontation

with a newly invented, constitutional figure of 'state data-oriented prevention' and 'data responsibility'" and to let it fade out again.

46 The Bremen Police Code of 21 March 1983, that contains a data protection regulation for a specific area, is an exception.

47 Schoreit, A. (1985): Verwaltungsstreit um Kriminalakten. In: NJW 1985, pp. 169 et seq.; Schoreit, A. (1986): Die Führung sogenannter polizeilicher Kriminalakten und das Verfassungsrecht. In: Computer und Recht 1986, pp. 87 et seq.; opposed to this: Honnacker, H. (1986): Rechtsgrundlagen für die Führung kriminalpolizeilicher personenbezogener Sammlungen (Kps). In: Computer und Recht 1986, pp. 287 et seq.

48 In the justification of the RD, however, the view is expressed (3.1) that the draft affords "only a clarification of the legal situation" for individual questions in order to eliminate uncertainties. For: "all planned regulations amount ... in principle to a more precise legal fixing of the *'situation as is'*" (my emphasis).

49 Critical views on the RD can be found in Schoreit, A. (1986): Weiterer Ausbau der zentralistischen polizeilichen EDV-Systeme zum Nachteil der Justiz. In: DRiZ 1986, pp. 54 et seq.; the reaction of the German Association of Judges (Deutscher Richterbund) is printed in DRiZ 1986, pp. 234 et seq.; especially: Bürgerrechte und Polizei (Cilip), No. 21 (2/1985), pp. 21 et seq.

50 Thus aptly Schwan, note 38, p. 121; cf. also Sydow, F. (1977): Verbrechensbekämpfung nach neuem Recht. In: ZRP 1977, pp. 119 et seq., pp. 124/125; Schoreit, A. (1986): Keine Rechtsgrundlagen der zentralen Datenverarbeitung des Bundeskriminalamtes. In: Computer und Recht 1986, pp. 224 et seq., pp. 229/230. Schoreit aptly refers to the actual goals of police data processing: "By means of electronic data processing, concrete suspects are to be screened out" of the data banks, "as far as criminal offences have occurred; it is absolutely no longer a matter of deterring already registered persons or others". Just as decisively critical is the reaction of the German Association of Judges, note 49, pp. 234 et seq.: The concept is "misleading and dangerous because it blurs the competences between the prosecutor's office and the police and leaves room in the future for the interpretation that next to the judiciary prosecution there is now an original police prosecution".

51 Therefore the German Association of Judges (note 49) justly demands that it first be determined in the Code of Criminal Procedure which interferences by means of data gathering and data processing are admissible with concrete suspects and third parties. Only when this has been regulated in detail in a uniform, national way will there be room in police codes for additional regulations on preventive police data interference.

52 See also the grounds for section 8a RD

53 Cf. Funk, A., Kauss, U., and von Zabern, T. (1980): Die Ansätze zu einer neuen Polizei. In: Blankenburg, E. (Ed.): Politik der inneren Sicherheit. Frankfurt a.M., pp. 16 et seq., pp. 59/60, p. 80: The transition from suspicion to risk is a transition "from a security concept fixed by statutes to a global security concept determined by the situation".

54 The grounds for RD in 3.7

55 According to Schoreit, note 49, p. 55, it is, e.g., in the so-called police crime records that are filed on all criminal offences, really a matter of having "sufficient material available for the founding of the police process of suspicion in future cases" when it is needed. Consequently, a "storage of data stocks to an almost unlimited extent" is made possible "for purposes which have yet to be determined individually".

56 Cf. BGHSt 23, pp. 239/240: A gang in the sense of section 244, paragraph 1, number 3 StGB can consist of two members and: "Experience teaches that such mutual bonding exists precisely in the pairing of specialists (pickpockets, larcenists using tricks, safecrackers)...." (p. 240).

57 On the following cf. especially the thorough analysis by Riehle, E. (1985): Verdacht, Gefahr und Risiko. Der V-Mann: ein weiterer Schritt auf dem Weg zu einer anderen Polizei?. In: KrimJ 1985, pp. 44 et seq., pp. 52 et seq.

58 The grounds for RD under 3.7

59 Riehle, note 57, p. 53

60 Riehle, note 57, p. 55

61 Jakobs, G. (1985): Kriminalisierung im Vorfeld einer Rechtsgutsverletzung. In: ZStW 1985, pp. 751 et seq., p. 761: In the criminal law of a free country it is not a matter of controlling the internal situation but rather of controlling the external one. "The inquiry into the internal situation is only allowed for the interpretation of disturbing external factors that already exist."

62 BGHSt 31, pp. 296 et seq.

63 BGHSt 31, pp. 296 et seq., pp. 299/300

64 Cf. now also BGH NJW 1986, p. 2261 on inadmissible tape recordings: "Outside the statutory monitoring of telephone communications, it is fundamentally inadmissible, even in cases of serious criminality, to tape-record the accused's non-publicly spoken word by means of a bugging device kept hidden from him in order to be able to use the manner of his conversation as evidence against his will."

65 On the legal problematical nature of other interventionary measures for specifically preventive police purposes, cf. an exhaustive treatment by Denninger, note 44, pp. 232 et seq.

66 Illustrative of this is Schäfer, H. (1986): Die Prädominanz der Prävention. In: GA 1986, pp. 49 et seq., pp. 53 et seq.

67 Cf. also Seelmann, K. (1983): Zur materiell-rechtlichen Problematik des V-Mannes. In: ZStW 1983, pp. 797 et seq., p. 816, as well as Preuss, U.K. (1981): Prozeßsteuerung durch die Exekutive. In: StrV 1981, pp. 312 et seq.

68 Section 10b, paragraph 9 RD

69 The fear that those who are hindered in or prevented from demonstrating could resort to sabotage is also not to be dismissed out of hand: cf. this with the Spiegel series: Schlacht um die Kernkraft, in No. 31 of 28 July 1986 and No. 32 of 4 August 1986, p. 77 (Neues Konzept: Sabotieren statt Demonstrieren).

70 BVerfGE 65, 1, p. 43

71 Critical of this is Lisken, H. (1986): "Mißtrauen" als Verfassungsprinzip. In: Kriminalist 1986, p. 323. Lisken pleads for a precise and moderate assignment of competences and authorization, speaks out against the application of "Wallraff" methods and cooperation with the secret services. "We do not want to protect the 'State', but rather the people in the constitutional state."

72 Rossnagel, A. (1984): Radioaktiver Zerfall der Grundrechte? Zur Verfassungsverträglichkeit der Kernenergie. Munich

73 Stümper, note 29, p. 254

74 Jakobs, note 61, 753, has justly indicated the danger of an approach that tries to justify the shift ahead of criminal law with the principle of the protection of the legally acknowledged interests alone. For whoever "only" wants to protect the legally acknowledged interests soon finds himself faced with endless possibilities because the logical continuation of this thought means that he must "combat with criminal law even the dangerous thoughts of potential offenders and further still the sources of these dangerous thoughts". Whoever defines the offender solely as the enemy of the legally acknowledged interests no longer sees him as the citizen who "is defined from the very beginning also by his right to a sphere free from control". This constitutive meaning of the rights to freedom is also lost in an approach which only makes the preventive combatting of criminal offences the measure of all things. In this way, not only the individual chances of development of each person would be impaired, but also the public weal itself because self-determination, as the BVerfG in the decision E 65, 1, p. 43 resolved, is an elementary functional condition of a free, democratic community founded on the cooperative ability of its citizens.

75 Riess, note 5, p. 7

76 In detail on this point, Naucke, W. (1985): Die Wechselwirkung zwischen Strafziel und Verbrechensbegriff. In Sitzungsberichte der Wiss. Gesellschaft an der J.W. Goethe-Universität Frankfurt. Vol. XXI., No. 5, Frankfurt a.M., pp. 161 et seq., pp. 184/185. Also critical is Hassemer, W. (1982): Über die Berücksichtigung von Folgen bei der Auslegung der Strafgesetze. In: Festschrift für H. Coing. Munich, pp. 493 et seq., pp. 522 et seq.

Part II
The Evaluation of Institutional Approaches to Crime Prevention

5.
Informal Justice: Mediation between Offenders and Victims

Burt Galaway

Informal Justice: Mediation between Offenders and Victims

*They had taught me about power and the abuse of power. Evil would always come to me disguised in systems and dignified by law. There would always be cadres and shower rooms, and they would always have dominion over me. They had taught me to hate them, but more significantly, they taught me that I was probably just like them, that I would abuse power whenever I had it, that I was the enemy of anyone who found himself beneath my boot.**

A sharp distinction cannot be made between the concepts of prevention and intervention; preventive actives are interventions which may be directed either toward individuals or toward a general improvement of social conditions which are thought to relate to delinquency or other social problems. Preventive interventions when carried out by government always involve a degree of coercion. The coercion is obvious when the preventive activities are directed toward individuals such as when parents are required to have their children vaccinated against disease or are required to send their children to state licensed or operated schools. But preventive interventions such as provision of public housing, day care centers, child health clinics, and so forth which provide opportunities for citizens rather than mandatory requirements for participation are also coercive in as much as the power of government is utilized to reallocate resources in a way which might not occur through voluntary association.

Interventions which occur in response to a specific behavior, such as a delinquent act, are also often defined as preventive. The American juvenile justice system rests upon assumptions that the state can intervene benevolently in the lives of youth who have committed a delinquent act in order to prevent subsequent delinquency or adult criminal behavior; further the vast discretion extended to governmental officials regarding choice of interventions is justified on the grounds that the interventions are benevolent and will have preventive effects. While these assumptions are often challenged (Allen, 1964, 1981; Tannenbaum, 1951; Becker, 1963; Platt, 1977; Fox, 1974; Wolfgang, Figlio and Sellin, 1972, p. 252; Hamparian, Schuster, Dinitz and Conrad, 1978) and recent authors have

* Conroy, P. (1986): The Lords of Discipline. Boston: Houghton Mifflin, p. 184

even suggested that the juvenile justice system may actually be criminogenic (Shireman and Reamer 1986, pp. 67-68) the assumptions nonetheless provide the guiding ideology for juvenile justice interventions. Most juvenile justice interventions have no direct relationship to the offense or harm done, treat the youthful offender as a passive recipient of services rather than an active participant, provide no direct accountability of the youth to the persons harmed by the delinquent act, often carry out treatment in isolation from youths' communities and support systems, and do not involve efforts to develop support systems which might include victims and key elements of the youths' communities. Further, interventions carried out by large state bureaucracies are often impersonal and mechanical despite the benevolent intent.

Contrasted with this are the programs of the victim/offender reconciliation or mediation projects (VORP) which have been emerging in the last fifteen years (Gehm, 1986; McKnight, 1981; PACT Institute of Justice, 1984; Peachey, Snyder and Teichroeb, 1983; Peachey, in press; Umbreit, 1986; Zehr and Umbreit, 1982; Zehr, n.d., Chupp, in press). These projects are based on principles of holding the young person directly accountable to his/her victim, accountability to victim takes preference over accountability to the state, both victim and offender are to be provided with an opportunity to participate in key decision making, peacemaking between victim and offender is the objective of intervention, and there should be a reduction in state intrusiveness. A 1986 survey (Gehm, 1986a) identified 47 American VORPs as well as an additional twelve Canadian and nineteen English projects. One of these projects, designed primarily for juvenile burglars and their victims, has been operating in the Minneapolis-St. Paul, Minnesota, since 1985. This paper will report on the first two years experience of the project.

Victim-Offender Mediation in Minneapolis-St. Paul

The Minneapolis-St. Paul project is sponsored by the Minnesota Citizens Council on Crime and Justice, a nonprofit, non-governmental agency which engages in both criminal justice and victim policy development as well as provision of direct services including crisis intervention for crime victims. The program was designed to serve primarily juvenile burglars and their victims. Burglaries were selected to deal with a relatively serious property offense and to rationally limit the number of referrals to guard against the danger of being overwhelmed wiht referrals. The project has received a few adult referrals and has also received some juvenile referrals for offenses other then burglary including one armed robbery and one sexual assault case. The first referrals were made in February 1985; 183 offenders including eight adults, had been referred to the project by the end of 1986. The project accepts all referrals although 18 of the offenders did not participate in the program for these reasons: six of the referrals were withdrawn by probation officers and two by judges, four youth had approached victims on their own and made restitution, two were incarcerated outside the area as a result of new offenses, two youth were missing, and treatment professionals working with two youth declined to permit participation in the program.

Referrals to the program are made by probation office staff involved in completing presentence investigations or intake staff as a pretrial diversion program. Referrals are made by telephoning the Citizen's Council office where an intake worker secures required information. A VORP case manager arranges to meet with the young person and his/her parents before telephoning or visiting the victim. During the visit with the offender and parents, the case manager secures perceptions of losses, discusses VORP procedures, and prepares the young person for participation in the victim-offender mediation meeting. Parents are not encouraged to participate in the victim-offender mediation meeting although they are not prohibited from doing so. The meeting with the offender and parents usually occurs between mailing an introductory letter and telephoning the victim.

The case manager telephones the victim to schedule a visit at the victim's home or business to discuss the VORP program. The preference is to explain the program and invite victim participation during a visit although sometimes the case manager must provide information regarding the program in the telephone conversation. During the visit the case manager will ask the victim to review the victimization including perceptions of losses and will provide the victim with an opportunity to discuss reactions to both the victimization and experiences with the criminal justice system. The VORP program will be explained and the victim will be invited to participate.

Meeting the offender prior to meeting the victim creates inconvenience in those situations where a victim declines to participate as this decision must then be discussed with the offender. An understanding of the offender, however, is helpful to respond to victim questions and to provide information to use for a decision about participating. The case manager, having first met the offender, is better prepared to meet with the victim.

If the victim agrees to participate, the VORP case manager arranges a meeting and serves as a neutral facilitator. The location for the meeting is discussed during the preliminary visit with the victim and is held at a location convenient for the victim. One hundred twenty-eight victim-offender mediation agreements have been negotiated; meetings for 23 percent (29) were held in victims' homes, 40 percent (51) at victims' places of business or work, 11 percent (14) at institutions where offenders were incarcerated, 15 percent (19) at neutral locations in victims' communities, six percent (8) at the VORP office, and five percent (7) at other locations. The meeting has two distinct phases. First, victim and offender are given an opportunity to share reactions regarding the victimization, subsequent experiences with the criminal justice system, and to ask questions of each other. A second phase of the meeting focuses on the damage that was done and the development of an agreement by which the offender can make amends to the victim. Apologies are extended by the offender and accepted by the victim in the course of most meetings. When negotiations are completed an agreement is placed in written form, signed by all participants, and is presented to the probation officer for approval.

The 165 youth who participated had a total of 162 victims; some youth had more than one victim and in other situations more than one youth had the same victim. Fifty-four percent (87) of the victims agreed to participate, 46 percent (75) declined to participate. The victims who declined to participate have usually indicated that they did not want to go to the trouble of attending a meeting with the offender, usually because the losses were small or they didnt't think it was worth the bother, and didn't think a meeting would serve any useful purpose. Table 1 shows type of victim for both participating and nonparticipating victims. Sixty-seven percent (109) of the victims were individuals or households and an additional 13 percent (21) were owner operated business. Only 20 percent (32) of the victims were organizations. The organization victims were more likely to participate in VORP than the individual victims; forty-three percent of the individual victims participated compared to 76 percent of the owner operated business and 75 percent of the other organizations.

Table 1: Victim Participation by Victim Type

Victim Participation

	YES	NO	TOTAL
Individuals/Households	(47) 43%	(62) 57%	(109) 100%
Owner-Operated Business	(16) 76%	(5) 24%	(21) 100%
Managed Business	(10) 77%	(3) 23%	(13) 100%
Schools	(4) 67%	(2) 33%	(6) 100%
Other Gov't Organizations	(4) 67%	(2) 33%	(6) 100%
Charitable, Religious, or Social Agencies	(6) 86%	(1) 14%	(7) 100%
TOTAL	(87) 54%	(75) 46%	(162) 100%

Ninety-five percent (128) of the 135 victims and offenders meetings have resulted in negotiation of a victim-offender agreement acceptable to both victim and offender. Only one of the agreements has been altered by a probation officer and none has been altered or rejected by judges. The agreements have provided for monetary restitution where the offender makes a money payment to the victim, personal service restitution where the offender makes payment by providing services or labor directly to the victim, community service restitution where the offender and victim agree that the offender will make repayment through contribution of labor to a community organization, apology only, and an occasional miscellaneous requirement.

Table 2 shows the distribution of agreements by the type of restitution to which the victim and offender agreed.

The two other agreements provided for behavioral commitments; for one the victim was the father of the offender who had run away from home and returned to burglarize his home. Another victim, representative of a small business, suggested to the offender the choice of 30 hours community service or 30 hours doing school work at home; the offender agreed to the homework.

Table 2: Agreements by Type of Restitution

Monetary Restitution	(56)	44%
Personal Service Restitution	(22)	17%
Both Personal Service and Monetary Restitution	(8)	6%
Community Service Restitution	(13)	10%
Both Community Service and Monetary Restitution	(2)	2%
Apology Only	(25)	20%
Other	(2)	2%
TOTAL:	(128)	100%

Table 3 summarizes victim losses and terms of the restitution agreements. Seventy-one of the 84 victims experienced after insurance settlement financial losses averaging $349; in addition insurance companies for fifteen victims experienced losses averaging $1964. From the offender perspective, 85 percent (84) of the offenders were involved in acts resulting in losses to direct victims and/or insurance companies averaging $631 per offender; eighty-five percent (84) of the offenders caused victim damages not covered by insurance averaging $295 per offender. Although 82 percent of the victims (or their insurance companies) experienced loss, only 57 percent negotiated monetary restitution with offenders; victims negotiating monetary restitution negotiated for a mean of $313 compared to mean losses of $743. Fifty-nine percent (58) of the offenders agreed to monetary restitution averaging $252 per offender. Twenty-seven percent (27) of the offenders agreed to personal service restitution averaging 36 hours and fifteen percent (15) agreed to do community service averaging 39 hours. Responsibility for monitoring compliance with the agreements is shared by VORP case managers and probation officers. VORP case managers maintain contact with victims and probation officers maintain contact with offenders. VORP follow-up with victims is done by telephone. When failure to comply with the terms of an agreement occurs, the VORP case manager contacts the probation officer and a joint decision is made as to what action might be required. If necessary, an attempt will be made to get the parties back together to re-negotiate the terms of the agreement. All agreements include a date by which the restitution obligation is to be completed.

All of the agreements had been closed; of the closed agreements, 52 percent (66) have been closed as fully completed by the deadline, 19 percent (24) as fully completed but beyond the deadline, nine percent (11) as renegotiated and completed, and 21 percent (27) as not completed. The first three types of closures are considered successful closures for an overall successful completion rate of 79 percent. The completed agreements have resulted in monetary restitution to direct victims of $8,280, (72 percent of the negotiated amount) monetary restitution to insurance companies of $3,096, (100 percent of the negotiated amount) community service restitution of 489 hours, (84 percent of the negotiated amount) personal service restitution of 127 hours, (13 percent of the negotiated amount) $90 contributed to charity, and 28 completed other requirements (usually apologies).

Table 3: Victim Losses and Terms of the Restitution Agreement

	TOTAL	Agreement (n=128) Number	Percent	Mean	Offenders (n=99) Number	Percent	Mean	Victims (n=84) Number	Percent	Mean
Losses:										
To Direct Victims	$24,801	(105)	82 %	$236	(84)	85 %	$295	(71)	80 %	$349
To Insurance Co	$29,457	(19)	15 %	$1550	(19)	17 %	$1550	(15)	15 %	$1964
Total	$54,258	(110)	86 %	$493	(86)	87 %	$631	(73)	82 %	$743
Restitution Plans:										
Monetary										
To Direct Victim	$11,505	(64)	50 %	$180	(58)	59 %	$198	(47)	56 %	$266
To Insurance Co.	$03,096	(6)	3 %	$516	(6)	6 %	$516	(3)	4 %	$810
Total	$14,601	(66)	52 %	$221	(58)	59 %	$252	(48)	57 %	$313
Personal Service Restitution	969 hr.	(30)	23 %	32 hr.	(27)	27 %	36 hr.	(18)	21 %	54 hr.
Community Service Restitution	585 hr.	(15)	12 %	39 hr.	(15)	15 %	39 hr.	(10)	12 %	59 hr.

Is Crime Victim Offender Mediation feasible?

Determining the feasibility of crime victim offender mediation involves answering questions such as are victims willing to participate, are victims and offenders able to reach mutually acceptable agreements, and are offenders able to comply with the terms of the agreements? The two year experience of the Minneapolis-St. Paul program suggests that the concept is feasible; fifty-four percent of the victims chose to participate in meetings with their offender, 95 percent of the meetings resulted in agreements, and 79 percent of the agreements have been satisfactorily completed. Monetary restitution was negotiated in 52 percent of the total agreements; offenders responsible for monetary restitution had a mean obligation of $252. Other agreements called for community service, personal service restitution, or apologies only. This experience suggests that victims are reasonable in their requests, take into consideration the youth and resources of offenders, and negotiate agreements which offenders are not able to complete.

The Minneapolis-St. Paul experiences mirrors information available from the national VORP management information system maintained by the PACT Institute of Justice (Gehm, 1986b). During the first year of operation (July 1, 1985 through June 30, 1986) data on 311 cases were reported by nine different American VORP programs (the Minneapolis and St. Paul programs were two of the nine). Sixty percent (183) of the cases resulted in a victim offender meeting, 27 percent (81) did not result in a meeting because of victim unwillingness, six percent (17) did not result in a meeting because of offender unwillingness, for two percent (5) of the cases the victim could not be found, in two percent (7) the offender could not be found, and in four percent (13) of the cases the matter was resolved without a meeting (data was missing for five cases). Ninety-four percent of the meetings resulted in a signed agreement. Sixty-one percent (105) of the agreements called for monetary restitution; the mean amount of monetary restitution negotiated was $175.00 (the highest amount was $3100).

These experiences are further confirmed by a growing body of research. In the first year the Minnesota Restitution Center found that 31 of 44 victims were willing to travel to the state prison to meet their offender and negotiate a restitution agreement (Galaway and Hudson, 1975, p. 359). A study of victims from 19 American restitution programs found that 46 percent would want to meet with their offender to develop a restitution contract in future victimizations, thirty-six percent would not want to meet, and eighteen percent did not respond (Novack, Galaway, and Hudson, 1980). A study in the Tulsa juvenile court found 71 percent of the victims willing to meet their offenders (Galaway, Henzel, Ramsey and Wanyama, 1980, pp. 42-48). Cannady (1980) found that 17 of 19 victims of juvenile offenders placed on probation in Charleston, South Carolina, reported a willingness to meet their offenders, Kigin and Novack (1980) reported that 74 percent of 176 victims of juvenile offenders in St. Cloud, Minnesota thought that they should be involved with the offender in determining a restitution obligation. Shapland, Willmore and Duff in a study of victims of violent crime (assault, sexual assault, and robbery) in Great Britain found that 17 percent of the Coventry victims and 19 percent of the Northampton victims would have liked to have met with the offender and judge to work out a sentence. Thirty-two percent of the victims in the Florida plea bargaining research attended plea bargaining conferences (Hines and Kersletter, 1979). A survey of a random sample of the public of Columbia, South Carolina found half of the respondents reported willingness to be involved in personal service restitution if they were victimized for malicious damage to their home (Gandy and Galaway, 1978).

There is also a growing body of research evidence to support the experiences of the Minneapolis St. Paul program and other VORPs that victims will not be vindictive in their negotiations with offenders. The Florida plea bargaining research found that, "contrary to the expectations of some observers the victims did not demand the maximum authorized punishment" (Heinz and Kerstetter, 1979). Victims in the Minnesota Restitution Center program agreed to participate in negotiating restitution contracts fully understanding that the outcome of the process would be a much shorter period in prison for their offenders (Hudson and Galaway, 1974). Directors of five juvenile restitution programs argued for victim involvement as an essential ingredient for juvenile restitution programs and note, "the stereotype of the outrage, vindictive victim has been used as an excuse to exclude victim involvement for the sake of protecting the child from retaliation. The stereotype has not been born out by experience" (Maloney, Gilbeau, Hofford, Remington and Steensen, 1982, p. 5). Henderson and Gitchoff (1981) report from their clinical work with crime victims that victims were willing to accept noncustodial sentences and restitution. Shapland's study (1981, p. 6) of victims of violent crime in England found that "both in their wishes at the beginning of the case as to what sentence should be passed and in their reactions to the actual sentence, victims were not punitive". Mcguire's study (1982) of burglary victims in England found victims were not the punitive "hang 'em, fog 'em, lock 'em up forever" people that popular myth suggest. The 1982 British crime survey inquired of respondents identified as victims about the treatment they thought their perpetrators deserved to receive; only half thought their offenders should be brought before the courts and only ten percent said they should be imprisoned for their offenses (Hough and Mayhew, 1983, p. 28). Hagan interprets his Canadian findings as "...full exposure of the victims to the criminal justice process involves fewer risks than agents of the system may have previously assumed" (1983, p. 217). Forty-eight percent of the victims in a St. Cloud, Minnesota study of juvenile offenders and their victims reported that no punishment other than restitution should be imposed (Kigin and Novack, 1980).

Finally, emerging evidence indicates that restitution obligations will be completed. Eighty-six percent of the 14,012 youth discharged from restitution programs during the first two years of the national (U.S.) juvenile restitution initiative funded by the Office of Juvenile Justice and Delinquency Prevention were discharged as successful meaning that the youth had completed restitution obligations and had not re-offended while in the program (Schneider, Schneider, Griffith, and Wilson, 1982). The National (U.S.) Assessment of Adult Restitution Programs examined eleven adult restitution programs in the United States and found program completion rates ranging from 62 percent to 91 percent (Hudson, Galaway, and Novack, 1980). McEwen and Maiman's study in Maine found that terms of small claims orders which had been negotiated between victim and offender were more likely to be completed than those that had been judicially ordered (1981). Schneider and Schneider (1985) found that a specific, programmatic focus on restitution substantially increased the probability of the obligation being completed.

The experience of the Minneapolis-St. Paul program, the collective experience of other VORP projects, and the available research indicates that mediation between crime victims and offenders is feasible. Concerns that victims do not want to participate, the mediation session might become explosive, or victims will make unreasonable demands given the limited means of offenders are exaggerated and are not supported by experience or research. Most of the documented crime victim offender mediation to date has involved juvenile property offenders and their victims. A few reports, of the use of victim-offender mediation with adult offender and with offenders who have committed violent crimes are beginning to emerge. Twenty-five percent of the cases reported to the national VORP management information system involved adult offenders and five percent of the cases involved person offenses (Gehm, 1986b). Case studies of the use of victim offender mediation with offenders who committed crimes of violence are being reported (Umbreit, 1986, in press).

Conclusions and Challenges

The experience of the Minneapolis–St. Paul project is supported by other experiences and research evidence to indicate that implementing victim offender mediation in relation to juvenile offenders and their victims is feasible. Over half of the victims agreed to participate, practically all meetings resulted in agreements, the agreements are reasonable given the youth and means of the offender, and over 80 percent of the agreements are completed. There are, however, some nagging questions which require attention. Is intrusiveness reduced? What is the appropriate response to youth unable to participate in victim offender mediation because their victims decline to participate? What are appropriate outcome measures for victim offender mediation? Does victim offender mediation result in a private settlement which may be inconsistent with public interest?

Reduction of State Intrusiveness. Reduction of state intrusiveness, usually stated as a reduction in use of incarceration, is a goal for most VORP's. Two research studies on this question have reported differing results. Dittenhoffer and Ericson (1983), from an analysis of cases referred to a single Ontario VORP, concluded that the types of offenders coming into the program were unlikely to be at risk of a prison or jail sentence. Coates and Gehm (1985) compared a group of adult offenders who came into three Idiana VORP's with a matched group of offenders who are not referred to VORP; while they found no difference in the probability that the two groups would receive a sentence of incarceration, the VORP group was significantly less likely to go to a state prison (they were more likely to be sent to a county jail) than the non VORP group, and the VORP group were incarcerated for a significantly shorter period of time than the non VORP group. There has been no such comparison in the Minneapolis–St. Paul program although there is no indication that the presence of a VORP agreement has any impact on the disposition decision. Restitution is routinely ordered as a probation condition in these jurisdictions; the Hennepin Juvenile Probation Division has a restitution unit which systematically secures victim restitution requests and presents these to the court for consideration at the disposition. Restitution agreements negotiated through a victim offender mediation process may be more reasonable, given the age and means of the offender, than those imposed by court order; further, the young person who has been involved in the process of negotiating an agreement is more likely to have a sense of commitment to the agreement than to an imposed requirement. This avoids the question, however, of whether the VORP process is operationalized in Minneapolis and St. Paul results in a reduction of state intrusiveness. Intrusiveness is unlikely to be reduced unless the VORP process is used as a replacement for other juvenile justice responses to the offender. The Minneapolis–St. Paul VORP is attempting to move in this direction by accepting referrals of young persons who have committed felony level offenses but who can be diverted to VORP instead of juvenile justice processing. A proposal has been made to the county prosecutor to undertake a field experiment in which randomly selected youth from a defined population pool could be referred to VORP with outcomes of this group and a control group compared.

Youth Whose Victims Decline to Participate. Thirty-seven percent of the youth were unable to participate in a victim offender meeting because their victims declined to participate. If VORP is to replace other juvenile justice responses, what is a reasonable response for these young people? Are they denied the opportunity for the replacement? This issue has not been explicitly considered by the Minneapolis-St. Paul programs although I have dwelt with it in previous papers (Galaway, 1983, 1985) and have proposed a response along two lines. Additional victims will be willing to participate if the mediation is conducted through the mediator as a third party and does not necessitate a face to face meeting. Other victims will want no involvement in the project at all; offenders of these victims could be involved in developing a plan to make a charitable contribution, either in money or service, comparable to the value to the damages done.

Outcome Objectives. Reconciliation is an objective often espoused by VORPs. There are serious problems however with attempting to operationize this concept although the matter is being given considerable thought and attention by VORP advocates. Reconciliation when it occurs, may well result from by factors beyond the immediate control and the influence of VORP staff. Reconciliation in the sense of a meaningful personal encounter between an offender and victim is more likely to relate to personal characteristics of offenders and victims than program activities, which, at most, may only be able to provide an opportunity for reconciliation to occur. If program activities can not logically lead to the accomplishment of an objective, the program should not be evaluated in terms of whether or not something occured which can not be attributable to program activities.

Some VORPs also pursue an objective of rehabilitating the offender. Advocates of this position argue that the process of being accountable, owning up to errors, and making amends to victims may have education and rehabilitation functions. While changing from law breaking to law abiding behavior is certainly a desirable outcome, credibility is challenged to believe that the rather cursory involvement of VORP in the life of an offender (probably at most no more than two or three hours of contact time with the VORP staff and victim) can reasonably be expected to make a major impact upon the life style of the offender. Recidivism, the usual measure rehabilitation, is more likely to be a function of the total societal reaction to offenders than the effects of a single program with a very limited involvement in the life of the offender. The global goals of reconciliation and rehabilitation should be respected as VORP goals (although both are desirable); VORPs can reasonably be evaluated in relation to three more limited goals.

First, VORP's might be held accountable for increasing citizen participation in the justice system. Increased citizen participation will occur in two ways. Citizen victims will participate directly with their offenders in negotiating restitution agreements. In addition, citizens may be involved as VORP volunteer case managers to facilitate the negotiating sessions. In a society with values emphasizing citizen participation in the affairs of state, increasing citizen participation does not require further justifications; it is a goal sufficient in its own right and does not need to be defended as leading to some more long term benefit. The specific measures of citizen participation will be the proportion of victims who agree to participate as citizen victims in the VORP process, the number of citizen negotiators, and the proportion of the total victim offender agreements which are negotiated by citizen volunteers. The Minneapolis-St. Paul program regularly reports information regarding the number of citizen victims who participate; unfortunately the VORP has not been able to focus specifically on the process of recruiting citizen volunteer case managers and is currently emphasizing this aspect of the program.

A second goal for VORP's is to hold wrongdoers directly accountable for their wrongdoing. Directly accountable means accountable to the persons they haved harmed. Accomplishing personal accountability in this way inherently makes sense and does not require further justification to any society which values the concepts of individual freedom and individual responsibility. The measures of personal accountability will be the proportion of offenders who are able to negotiate agreements with their victims and the extent to which the negotiated agreements are completed. The Minneapolis-St. Paul VORP's are reporting information on both these measures; 97 percent of the offenders who met with their victims successfully negotiated agreements; 83 percent of the closed agreements have been satisfactorily completed.

A final goal will be to conduct the VORP process in such a manner that the key participants – victims and offenders – report that they have been treated fairly. Citizen perceptions of fairness on the part of governmental agencies (including private agencies cooperating with government) is also a goal which is acceptable and does not require any further justification in a democratic society. In January 1987 the Minneapolis-St. Paul projects began using a simple, self report instrument to get feedback from participating victims and offenders regarding satisfaction with the VORP process and views as to whether the outcome of the process was fair to both victims and offenders. The three outcome goals of citizen participation, offender accountability, and fairness are all related to VORP programing activities, are relatively easily measured, and are more appropriate goals for VORP projects than abstract concepts such as reconciliation and rehabilitation.

Victim offender mediation and crime as a public wrong. Two objections are often encountered toward the idea victim offender mediation is a part of the criminal or juvenile justice process and toward use of mediation as a replacement for other juvenile justice responses to offenders. One objection is that mediation permits the victim an opportunity to use the criminal or juvenile justice system as a means to secure private gain which is inappropriate because these systems respond to public, not private, harms. A criticism of replacing other juvenile justice responses to the offender with victim offender mediation is that this will not be a sufficiently severe sanction to accomplish public goals.

The essence of the first objection is that crime is a wrong against society thus public officials act on behalf of society to further socially desired goals. The penalty imposed, therefore, should meet social goals and should not benefit individual victims. The individual who has been harmed is to seek redress through civil law procedures. This argument fails to recognize the symbolic nature of the victim's participation in the penal process. The victim participates as a representative of society, as every person, rather than as a private individual (Thorvoldson, 1984). The victim stands in the place of all of us in bearing the brunt of the harm from the criminal offense. Thus, victims should have the opportunities to stand as representatives of all of us in the penal process and to receive benefits, in the form of restitution, in their role as every person. The Minneapolis-St. Paul project views the participating victim as a representative of all of society and considers VORP a public, not private, response to the offense. VORP agreements, once negotiated, are subject to approval by the court and, ideally, are presented at the disposition hearing at which any party may object to the agreement and have the objection considered by the court before arriving at a final decision.

The second objection, that the VORP procedures may not be a sufficient penalty to accomplish social objectives, creates a dilemma. On the one hand a major challenge is to reduce the intrusiveness and harshness of the juvenile justice system, to recognize the dangers of intrusion, and to recognize the possibility that the intrusiveness of the system may be criminogenic itself (Shireman and Reamer, 1986). On the other hand, a dogmatic insistance on VORP as the sole requirement for juvenile offenders may result in VORP being used for a narrowly defined group of youth who have committed relatively minor offenses. This matter requires careful thought and policy development to begin defining the group of offenses for which VORP might be the only response as well as a group of more serious offenses for which VORP might be combined with other sanctions such as community service sentencing.

References

Allen, F. (1964): Borderline of Criminal Justice. Chicago: University of Chicago Press.

Allen, F. (1981): The Decline of the Rehabilitative Ideal: Penal Policy and Social Purpose. New Haven: Yale University Press.

Becker, H. (1963): The Outsiders: Studies in the Sociology of Deviance. New York: Freee Press.

Coates, R., and Gehm, J. (1988): Victim offender mediation: An empirical assessment. In: Wright, M., and Galaway, B. (Eds.): Putting it Right: Victim Offender Mediation in Theory and Practice. London: Sage.

Coates, R., and Gehm, J. (1985): Victim Meets Offender: An Evaluation of Victim Offender Reconciliation Programs. Valparaiso, Indiana: PACT Institute of Justice.

Cannady, L. (1980): Evaluation of the Charleston Juvenile Restitution Project Final Report. Washington: Metametrics, Inc.

Chupp, M. (1988): The practice of victim offender reconciliation: programme procedures and rationale. In: Wright, M., and Galaway, B. (Eds.): Putting it Right: Victim Offender Mediation in Theory and Practice. London: Sage.

Dittenhoffer, T., and Ericson, R. (1983): The victim offender reconciliation program: A message to correctional reformers. University of Toronto Law Journal 33(3), 316-347.

Fox, S. (1974): The reform of juvenile justice: The childs right to punishment. In: Juvenile Justice 25, 2-9.

Galaway, B. (1985): Victim participation in the penal-corrective process. In: Victimology: An International Journal 10(1-4), 617-630.

Galaway, B. (1983): Probation as a reparative sentence. In: Federal Probation 46(3), 9-18.

Galaway, B., Henzel, M., Ramsey, G., and Wanyand, B. (1980): Victims and delinquents in the Tulsa Juvenile Court. In: Federal Probation 44(2), 42-48.

Galaway, B., and Hudson, J. (1975): Issues in the correctional implementation of restitution to victims of crime. In: Galaway, B., and Hudson, J. (Eds.): Considering the Victim: Readings in Restitution and Victim Compensation. Springfield, IL: Charles Thomas, 351-360

Gandy, J., and Galaway, B. (1980): Restitution as a sanction for offenders: A public's view. In: Hudson, J., and Galaway, B. (Eds.): Victims, Offenders, and Alternative Sanctions. Lexington: MA D.C. Heath Lexington Books, 89-100

Gehm, J. (1986a): National VORP Directory. Michigan City, Indiana: PACT, Inc. (2nd Edition)

Gehm, J. (1986b): Reports from the National VORP Management Information System. Valparaiso, Indiana: PACT Institute of Justice

Hagan, J. (1983): Victims Before the Law: The Organizational Domination of Criminal Law. Toronto: Butterworths

Hamparian, D., Schuster, R., Dinitz, S., and Conrad, J. (1978): The Violent Few: A Study of Dangerous Juvenile Offenders. Lexington Massuchetts: D.C. Heath Lexington Books

Heinz, A., and Kerstetter, W. (1979): Pretrial settlement conference: Evaluation of a reform in plea bargaining. In: Law and Society Review 13, 349-366

Henderson, J., and Gitchoff, T. (1981): Victims perceptions of Alternatives to Incarceration: An exploratory study. Paper presented at the First World Congress of Victimology, Washington, D.C.

Hofford, M. (1981): Juvenile Restitution Program Final Report. Trident United Way, Charleston, South Carolina

Hough, M., and Mayhew, P. (1983): The British Crime Survey: First Report (Home Office Research Study No. 76). London: Her Majesty's Stationery Office

Hough, M., and Mayhew, P. (1985): Taking Account of Crime: Key Findings From the 1984 British Crime Survey (Home Office Research Study No. 85). London: Her Majesty's Stationery Office

Hudson, J., and Galaway, B. (1974): Undoing the wrong: The Minnesota restitution center. In: Social Work 19(3), 313-318

Hudson, J., Galaway, B., and Novack, S. (1980): National Assessment of Adult Restitution Programs Final Report. Duluth, Minnesota: University of Minnesota School of Social Development

Kigin, R., and Novack, S. (1980): A rural restitution program for juvenile offenders and victims. In: Hudson, J., and Galaway, B. (Eds.): Victims, Offenders, and Alternative Sanctions. Lexington, Massachusetts: D.C. Heath Lexington Books, 131-136

Malony, D., Gilbeau, D., Hofford, M., Remington, C., and Steenson, D. (1982): Juvenile restitution: Combining common sense and solid research to build an effective program. New Designs for Youth Development. May-June, 3-8; July-August, 1-6

Mcguire, M. (1982): Burglary in a Dwelling. London: Heineman

McEwen, C., and Maiman, R. (1981): Small claims mediations in Maine: An empirical assessment. In: Maine Law Review 33, 237-268

McKnight (Edmonds), D. (1981): The victim-offender reconciliation project. In: Galaway, B., and Hudson, J. (Eds.): Perspectives on Crime Victims. St. Louis: C. V. Mosby, 292-298

Novack, S., Galaway, B., and Hudson, J. (1980): Victim offender perceptions of the fairness of restitution and community service sanctions. In: Hudson, J., and Galaway, B. (Eds.): Victims, Offenders, and Alternative Sanctions. Lexington, Massachusetts: D.C. Heath Lexington Books, 63-69

PACT Institute of Justice (1984): The VORP Book. Valparaiso, In: PACT Institute of Justice

Peachey, D., Snyder, B., and Teichroeb, A. (1983): Mediation Primer: A Training Guide for Mediators in the Criminal Justice System. Kitchner, Ontario: Community Justice Initiatives of Waterloo Region

Peachey, D. (1988): Victim offender reconciliation: Fruition and frustration in Kitchner. In: Wright, M., and Galaway, B. (Eds.): Putting it Right: Victim Offender Mediation in Theory and Practice. London: Sage

Platt, A. (1977): The Child Savers: The Invention of Delinquency.

Schneider, A. (1986): Restitution and recidivism rates of juvenile offenders: Four experimental studies. In: Criminology 24(3), 533-552

Schneider, A., and Schneider, P. (1985): A comparison of programmatic and ad hoc restitution in juvenile courts. In: Justice Quarterly 1(4), 529–547

Schneider, P., Schneider, A., Griffith, W., and Wilson, M. (1982): Two Year Report on the National Evaluation of the Juvenile Restitution Initiative: An Overview of Program Performance. Eugene: Institute of Policy Analysis

Shapland, J., Willmore, J., and Duff, P. (1985): Victims in the Criminal Justice System. London: Gowen Publishing

Shireman, C., and Reamer, F. (1986): Rehabilitating Juvenile Justice. New York: Columbia University Press

Tannenbaum, F. (1951): Crime and the Community. New York: Columbia University Press (2nd Edition)

Thorvaldson, Hb (1984, November): Restitution by offenders in Canada: An analysis of proposed federal legislation. Paper presented at the American Society of Criminology 36th Annual meeting, Cincinnati, Ohio

Umbreit, M. (1986): Victim/offender mediation: A national survey. In: Federal Probation L(4), 53–56

Umbreit, M. (1988): Violent offenders and their victims. In: Wright, M., and Galaway, B. (Eds.): Putting it Right: Victim Offender Mediation in Theory and Practice. London: Sage

Wolfgang, M., Figlio, R., and Sellin, T. (1972): Delinquency in a Birth Cohort. Chicago: University of Chicago Press

Zehr, H., and Umbreit, M. (1982): Victim offender reconciliation: An incarceration substitute? In: Federal Probation 46(4), 63–68

Zehr, H. (n.d.): Mediating the Victim-Offender Conflict. Atron, PA: Mennonite Central Committee

6.
Mediation-Experiment in Finland

Martti Grönfors

General

A locally-modified version of community mediation was started in the City of Vantaa, Finland, in 1984. Alongside mediation, research was carried out as well, with the years 1984-1985 being the actual experimental years. Since that time thorough research has been conducted on various aspects of mediation, and the comments here are based mainly on the empirical research. The final analyses are still continuing, so in some instances the results are tentative. The empirical work consisted of interviews with the participants in mediation – conducted as focused personal interviews – interviews with the mediators, shifting through masses of various documents which were kept during the two year period, going through the prosecution files, police files and court records. In addition, the personal experiences of the two researchers, who had been with the project right from the beginning, were utilized as additional material.

Conflict and its Resolution

Conflicts differ in their nature, and it is important to recognize what kind of a conflict is being dealt with before its resolution can be attempted. Also conflict is not always negative as it contains energy for change either at the level of individual human interaction, community or the whole society. Conflict is also something different from a mere problem. To make a somewhat simple distinction between the two, conflict refers to communication and interaction, while a problem relates primarily to an individual person. While a conflict cannot be satisfactorily resolved unilaterally, the solution to a problem lies mainly within the person having a problem. The consequences of ignoring conflicts can be more destructive, at least in the long run, than attempts at handling or resolving them (cf. Sarat, A.D. "The Emergence of Disputes" in a Study of Barriers to the Use of Alternative Methods of Dispute Resolution. Vermont Law School Dispute Resolution Project, Sth Royalton, VT, 1984: pp. 29-36).

Dispute Processing Options:

I. Unilateral actions on the part of a disputant
   a) Inaction
   b) Active avoidance
   c) Self-help
      1. Redefinition of problem
      2. Elimination of the deficit
      3. Use of social work and other agencies

II. Dyadic options – contacts between disputing parties
   a) Coercion (threats & use of force)
   b) Negotiation

III. Third party resolution techniques
   a) Conciliation (bringing parties together for negotiation)
   b) Mediation (structured communication, recommendations)
      1. General mediational projects
      2. Projects mediating limited disputes for the general public
      3. Projects mediating general disputes for a limited segment of the public
   c) Arbitration
      1. General arbitration projects
      2. Arbitration of small claim matters
      3. Consumer arbitration
      4. Contractually based arbitration
   d) Fact-finding
      1. Media action lines
      2. Trade association projects
      3. Government projects
   e) Administrative procedures
      1. Court oriented processing
      2. Informal court operated processing
      3. Routine administrative processing
      4. Measures reducing or eliminating the need for adjudication
      5. Measures simplifying adjudication
   f) Adjudication

(McGillis, D & H. Mullen, Neighborhood Justice Centers; an Analysis of Potential Models. US. Dept. of Justice, Oct. 1977: p. 5)

In attempting to resolve the conflict there are various characteristics which influence the birth of the conflict, its nature and progress. Firstly, there are the personal characteristics of the participants, their values, motivations, aims, their physical, psychological and social resources, their beliefs about the conflict and their thoughts how the matter should proceed. Secondly, the relationship between the participants, their attitudes, beliefs and expectations from each other. Thirdly, the kinds of matters disputed about, matters relating to its birth, its extent, the degree of seriousness, the motivation for continuing or resolving the conflict, how the conflict is seen and whether it is thought to be a unique event or a continuation of events. Fourthly, the social setting which influences the continuation or resolution of the conflict, and the chances of a resolution. Fiftly, the progress of conflict is influenced by the existence of other interested parties who have their own outside reasons for continuing or resolving the conflict. Sixthly, various strategies and tactics used in disputing; positive or negative factors, such as promises, threats and punishments; openness or the lack of it; what is attempted to be influenced and by what means. And at last, what are the consequences of keeping up conflict or resolving it? What is gained or lost, and how is the participants reputation affected by it? (Deutsch, M., The Resolution of Conflict; Constructive and Destructive Processes. New Haven, Yale Univ. Press, 1973: pp. 5-7)

Style of Mediation

There are two main, opposing ways of handling disputes: namely, cooperative and competitive styles. The former is characterized by open and honest exchange of information, while the competitive style is marked by secrecy and wrong information. If positive solutions are attempted, at least the following are important. The attitude of both parties should be positive towards the resolution of their conflict. Information supplied for the resolution should be open and accurate. There should be an active search for common aims and advantages. Parties should develop a trust in each other and behave honestly and with friendliness towards each other. The matters under dispute should be clearly defined and a non-accusatory attitude should be employed. The matters should be the focus, not the personalities involved.

Vantaa-Project, Aims and Framework

Either at the outset of the project or as a result of the early mediation experiences, certain broad and general aims were established for the project. Among the more important ones were the following:

1. An attempt to hand back some power to the community and individuals.
2. An assumption that conflicts (also criminal ones) are a part of the normal communication processes.
3. Solutions to conflicts should be attempted as quickly as possible and as close to the place of their occurrence as possible.
4. Acceptance of differences is positive and enriching. Handling conflicts develops communal life positively and can unite community members.
5. It is desirable that the horizons of all people are widened. Open-minded people are a positive community resource.

6. Instead of treatment or punishment, it is important to develop the communicative skills of the people, and shift attention to compensation.
7. Non-judgmental interaction is encouraged.

For the practical day-to-day operations certain general operating principles were considered important. The mediators should work together with the participants not for them. Mediators are not solving problems, they are not experts, but are helping the participants to develop their own communicative skills. It is of paramount importance that mediators recognize what is under dispute as often the dispute which participants bring forth is not the real dispute between them. In mediation negotiations the actual process of mediation is more important than the practical and/or concrete end results. Mediators' overall aim is to provide the participants with survival skills, and to provide a model by which the disputants can in future resolve their conflicts without the aid of a professional mediator.

Structure and Organisation of Vantaa-Project

The project was established as an "open system", with no clear decisions made in advance as to where the cases come from, what kinds of cases were handled and so on, as these were considered being part of the experimentation. One purpose of the project was to provide guidelines to other possible similar mediation schemes in future. It was emphasized right from the beginning that the scheme should operate as an alternative to the official system, not as a supplement to it.

Finance for the initial project came from a variety of sources: state finance for the research, municipal and church finance for the practical operations of the project. During the experimental years the main control of the project was in the hands of the researchers and voluntary mediators, also the advisory panel of the local authorities exercised considerable power, as they partly controlled the case input.

Mediators, who were voluntary and unpaid, were trained for their task in three different ways: Firstly, by an initial 30 hour theoretical course organized by the local adult education college. In that course they were given some rudimentary knowledge of the workings of the justice system, some theoretical knowledge about mediation and related matters. Secondly, mediation skills were primarily learned in weekend live-in seminars, where role-play was used extensively in the learning to become mediators. Thirdly, in-job individual and group supervision was provided throughout the experimental period.

Cases

Cases for mediation came directly from the participants, either from the aggrieved party or from the party against whom certain accusations or claims were made. These could, in principle, be of any kind, either civil matters or matters which would be defined as criminal if they were brought to the notice of the authorities. The parties contacted the mediation office which was staffed during office hours, or left a message on an answer phone to be contacted by the office personnel if contact was made outside the office hours.

Authorities, especially the police, the prosecutor and the child welfare officers were encouraged to refer suitable cases to mediation. The guidelines for the suitability of cases was roughly the following: the cases should be clear*cut, where there is no dispute about the guilt of the person, as it is not a proper use of mediation if it is expected to act as an investigatory service. These cases should be relatively minor ones, and of the kind where there is room for negotiation and compromise. Particularly suitable were thought to be the cases where the victim of a crime has the onus whether to proceed further with the prosecution. For example a common assault, when there are no injuries, is one offence of this type. Rape, although a crime of this type, was ruled out because rape is considered a very serious offence and because of its nature it was not thought suitable for mediation.

Roughly 140 cases were handled by the service in the two experimental years. Towards the end of 1985, the number of civil cases had declined to almost nothing. The criminal cases were primarily minor violent offences, minor property offences, including vandalism. In 52 cases a written agreement involving compensation was prepared, and in further 12 cases a promise was given that the disputed matter was resolved. Of the 29 agreements in 1984, 25 were fulfilled. The information for 1985 is not adequate enough for the similar figures be given for that year.

Evaluative Comments

Quantitative analysis becomes very difficult, as the total number of cases handled by mediation was relatively low, and the breaking down of the initially small figures into various categories would make them so small that there would not be more than a few cases in each, hence making any conclusions drawn from the operation of mediation meaningless. For that reason only a qualitative, processual analysis seems possible. This form of analysis has examined the various cases as a process looking for the significant points of interest in each case. Viewed from this angle it is then not important, for example, that an agreement was reached. It is more important to see what is the nature of the case, the characteristics of the participants, and the way in which the agreement either was or was not attained.

From this examination it appears that the mediation seems to operate at its best when there is a true conflict, discernible between the participants. Therefore, it is important to recognize in mediation the different types of conflicts. A conflict also has to be kept separate from a mere problem, which can be either a psychological or a practical problem. The techniques of solving problems require different expertise from the technique of resolving conflicts. Problems in general need expert advice and not mediation skills. Therefore, it is questionable if mediation is an answer for problems, the answer for which seems to lie in individuals, not in the relationship, as is the case with conflicts. As the mediators are trained in communicative skills, they cannot be expected to act as experts in a multitude of personal problems people have. Or even more emphasized, when for example the mediator is expected to act as a lay lawyer, the use of mediation in this way actually could jeopardise the rights of the people using mediation, as mediators cannot be aware of the legal complexities which people encounter. Similar comments apply to cases where people suffer from personal problems which would require extensive counselling. Again mediation is not a service which is intended for that purpose. At best mediation could act as a referral service when cases identified as problems are brought to them.

An objective conflict is given if the true conflict is perceived by the parties as such. A symptomatic conflict is one where the issue which brought the parties to mediation differs from the true underlying conflict. A situational conflict is one where the circumstances of the participants bring them into conflict with one another. A wrong conflict can occur when the participants are fighting over issues which are not the real issues between them. A false conflict can occur when there is absolutely no reason for the parties to be in conflict with each other. There could also be wrong conflict parties locked into a battle with each other. The task of the mediator is to find out what kind of conflict it is before it can be dealt with appropriately.

It appears that when mediators are dealing with problems, rather than with interpersonal conflicts, they are stepping into an expert role (psychologist, lawyer) and enter an area for which they are neither trained nor competent to deal with. In the negotiated settlements in cases which could be classed as problems, the mediators have negotiated compensations in cases in which no Finnish court would order compensation, and it seems that in some cases the compensation agreement is bigger than a competent court would have settled. In cases where there are personal problems involved, mediators who take the role of a counselor, undertake tasks which can exceed their competence, and also can create dependency relationships which the mediators are unable to realize as such, or bring to a satisfactory halt. In cases where the mediators attempt to deal with the problem as if it were a true conflict situation, the solution cannot be at the best interests of both parties, as it should be in mediation. There are also some indications that a relatively higher failure rate in reaching satisfactory conclusion to a case could be related to confusing a problem with a conflict.

When mediators concentrated on inter-personal matters, it usually resulted in the mutual satisfaction of the participants. When the mediators acted as experts by concentrating primarily on fixing compensations, especially monetary compensations, the level of satisfaction was somewhat lower. The recipient of the compensation often felt that the compensation was not enough and the person required to pay it thought it was too much. Serious problems were encountered with the quality of justice, when for example unemployed young people agreed to relatively large amounts of compensation, although no such compensation probably would have been ordered against them had the case gone directly to the court. Also, the needs of justice probably were not served in cases which were dealt with in court as well, after a successful mediation. Although the court may reduce the sentence of conditional imprisonment from say 6 months to 3 months, the effect felt by the offender is not the same as intended by the court. Before mediation can operate effectively in conjunction with the official criminal justice system in the case of crime, the prosecution must make more use of the provision of non-prosecution and the court should have more power and willingness to suspend sentencing in successfully mediated cases.

From the interviews with participants to mediation, it becomes overwhelmingly clear that the participants have welcomed this opportunity to communicate with each other. This seems to be the case particularly with juvenile offenders, who were almost without exception positively surprised that they were able to have a voice in their own matters. Although it is not possible to ascertain from the material available if this method of handling disputes has been carried through to other dealings by the participants, at least it could be said that they have been shown other ways of handling their conflicts than those which they thought possible.

It appears that while the participants are in general impressed by the informality of mediation, it is apparent that with the service becoming more established (in 1985), the formality, routine and bureaucratic way of handling also tended to increase. Evidence for this is given by the kinds of solutions to conflicts which were negotiated. While in the early days of the service a true effort seems to have been spent in finding the kinds of solutions which suited the particular case best, towards the end of the experimental period more and more cases included a purely financial settlement. When in 1984 ca. 20 % of the cases included either an exclusive or partial reparation by work, only one agreement in 1985 involved compensation by work. This seems to point to the dangers of these types of innovations, as it seems that without continued attention to the aims and procedures there is a tendency to resort to those solutions which people are familiar with.

The issue of how "voluntary" mediation is, proves a difficult one. It is particularly difficult in the case of crime offenders. With those cases which come directly from the public, the offender usually agrees to mediation from the fear of prosecution. In cases which come from authorities (police, prosecutor, and child welfare officers), the issue of voluntariness must be weighed against the expectations of the offenders – i.e., whether or not the case should go to court – and usually they expect that mediation is better in terms of the outcome than prosecution or court appearance. In interviewing the young offenders it became quite apparent that most of them did not even realize that their participation in mediation was voluntary, nor did they realize very often that mediation was operating outside the official system, but believed it to be a part of the official system. Even in spite of the fact that it was explained to them when the suggestion to go to mediation was made.

Reasons for agreeing to come to mediation vary from one case to another. In the case of juvenile offenders, the victims are motivated by the desire to deal with their case in a more humane way than does the official system. Sometimes the fact that participants knew each other prompted its being brought to mediation. As far as the police is concerned, the motivation for diverting cases to mediation varies from the genuine feeling that a particular case is more suitable for mediation than for official system, to diverting "messy", but not particularly serious cases to mediation. Prosecution cases seem to be diverted for similar reasons, although there seem to be some indications that prosecution could be motivated, with the tacit co-operation from the mediation service, by the desire to catch offenders of gang-offending when some have escaped the official notice. From the analysis of successfully mediated cases, it is possible to see that in the cases which come directly from the offenders themselves, the chances of a successful outcome have increased, as the level of motivation of both parties usually is high.

The level of participation in the process of mediation by the participants depends a great deal on the role which the mediators take in the negotiations. Some participants felt that the mediator was on the side of one party or another, and this usually did not aid mutual communication. Some mediators experienced problems in communication when the relative power positions of the participants were very different (young versus older persons, articulate versus inarticulate, and so on). Some mediators felt that their role as facilitators of communication was hampered by the (self)righteous attitude of some victims of crimes, also by the sullen attitude of some young offenders.

The choice to use lay-mediators seems to have been the right one, in that they are able to adopt the principles of mediation quicker than people trained in helping professions, who in general find it quite difficult to adjust from their role as a problem-solver to that of a communication facilitator.

The mediators themselves, when their motivations for joining the service were examined, showed that they had higher than average awareness of community problems, and also higher than average interest in dealing with the particular kinds of problems they had encountered in their community. They were not a really truly representative sample of the community sentiment. Many had personal experience of some of the problems which are involved in the workings of the official criminal justice system. They had, for example, a family member who had been, in their opinion, roughly treated by the official system, or they had observed in their neighborhood that the way in which the official system operates, especially in the case of younger people, is not to their liking. There were also some law students who wanted to see how community alternatives to justice worked out in practice. Surprisingly few mediators joined the service from the conventional "do-gooding" need, and those who did, quite quickly had to abandon their ideas in facing the majority opinion of the mediators, who operated from a certain critical and ideological standpoint.

On the whole, it appears that the mediators have proved to be a truly positive community resource. Mediation work has been experienced as a meaningful way of participating in community life. Most mediators think that they are doing a worthwhile job and are answering a clear community need. One of the most difficult issues for the mediators to comprehend is that they are primarily only facilitators of communication, and not a problem-solving service. Those mediators who in their everyday work deal with people's problems have found it particularly difficult to shift their thinking.

The Place of Mediation in Modern Community

The area covered by this experimental service was very large, i.e., of some 50000 inhabitants. Therefore, it can be said that its effect on reducing community tensions at the level of general community would be negligible. So far the effect is felt mainly by direct participants, by mediators themselves, and maybe also by certain local authorities, who have had a chance to think differently about conflicts in the community they are serving.

Mediation is suitable primarily in cases of conflicts where the participants know each other, and where there is a chance that they will also have to meet each other in future. It is best suited to handle inter-personal conflicts, and least suited to handle cases where the participants are unwillingly tied to contracts (especially financial ones) over a long period of time.

The cost of mediation has not been calculated, as the experimental years would give somewhat misleading figures. However, it is felt on the basis of evaluating the various aspects of mediation, that the value of mediation rests on factors other than financial costs.

The issue of how "just" mediation is could be looked at in a number of different ways. It is possible to look at it in the "objective" way by comparing, for example, the amounts of compensation fixed for equivalent cases dealt with by mediation and the official system. Also it would be possible to look at what could have happened, for example, to offenders had they been dealt with at courts for similar offences. Both these comparisons are important only to the extent that they give some quantitative measure of mediation. And in this respect it appears that mediation could be little or not at all more "just" than the official justice system. In relation to compensations, it appears that the level of compensations agreed in mediation could be actually higher than would have been the case had they been fixed by the courts. With the lack of established possibilities of waiving prosecutions in all cases of successful mediation, most offenders who came to mediation through the official system had to face both mediation and a court appearance. In so far as the majority of cases were relatively minor ones, where either a fine or a conditional sentence of imprisonment was imposed, a slight reduction in those does not compensate for the dual procedure.

It is more important, however, to look at the way in which the participants felt about mediation. Looked at in a qualitative way, the amount of satisfaction felt by the participants after a successful mediation session seems to make the system more "just" than the official system. People generally felt that they were getting justice, although objectively they actually could have been worse off than without the intermediate step of mediation.

In the Finnish system, mediation cannot be said to reduce the work of the official justice system to any significant degree, as those cases which came from the authorities were usually also dealt with by the official court system. An exception to this was the small category of crimes where the complainant had the power to stop further proceedings after a successful mediation. Such crimes are crimes involving minor violence, where there were no injuries to the complainant, minor cases of wilful damage, etc.

In the individual cases, which were successfully mediated, it can be said that peoples' conflicts were transferred back to them. An active participation in the disposal on one's case must be a small way towards giving power back to people over their own matters. The larger issue of community empowerment cannot really be ascertained from this experiment, as the mediation service could not at all be said to have touched the general life of the community very much. However, should mediation spread to many other spheres of community life, and become an established way of dealing with various community problems, it could then be said to have transferred power back to the community in a real and concrete way, but that time is still quite a long way off.

Similar comments apply to the effect of mediation on the general society. However, there has been a marked increase in mediation schemes in Finland since the beginning of this experimental project, and at the moment there are schemes either underway or being planned in over 20 cities throughout Finland. So even if mediation cannot be said to have (yet) had any significant role in a general critique of society, it can be said to have provided a well-wanted service in the community. What can be stated is that an uncritical expansion of mediation may not serve the ends of the well-thought-out development of mediation. It appears that enthusiasm about mediation has overtaken a considered ideologically-grounded establishment of this service to the community. The basis of mediation, even now, is mainly a populist one rather than that of a political or ideological one.

As with many other new innovations, a lot of people are convinced that mediation is working, even though there is little concrete evidence for these claims. The Finnish word for mediation (which translates "let us make up") sounds so positive that "it must work". Hence not enough attention seems to be paid to the question of how mediation could provide a truly positive alternative for dealing with crimes and other conflicts. Above all, mediation as an idea seems to attract people of very varied political and ideological backgrounds, from the far left to the far right, all arriving at the same conclusion that mediation must work, but approaching it from very different and sometimes totally contradictory points of view.

The idea that people should generally – within limits of their reason and ability – be given a chance to deal with their own conflicts, must be supported on the basis of this evaluation. However, as is evident from the examination of the cases in this research, the victims of crimes and offenders, as well as those who are involved in civil conflicts, often start negotiations from a quite imbalanced position of power. This imbalance could be used for gaining an advantageous position in negotiations, hence the mediators have been trained to balance the power differentials. Should mediation extend widely into many different walks of life, the possibility of extortion and naked use of power could actually increase. Therefore, it appears that there should be a check on those cases where this kind of usage is possible, and this seems to be against the total abolishment of the due process model.

Mediation, in the case of criminal matters, seems to be a true alternative to the criminal justice system only in cases when a successfully mediated case does not have to be dealt with by the official system. At the moment, both the legal restrictions for waiving prosecutions and the judicial practice seem to work in such a way that in criminal matters mediation is an addition to any other procedure rather than an alternative to it. When public funds are being used for running the mediation, it is much more difficult to institute a totally new way of handling criminal conflicts. The old bureaucratic thinking, which contains elements of judgement and punishment, is so deeply entrenched in the minds of the bureaucrats that it seems very difficult to introduce non-judgmental and non*punishing ideas into dealing with criminal matters. When mediation is closely linked to the existing bureaucracy, there are also power-games involved. This project has not escaped these, and any bureaucratic power-game, when it is connected to mediation, makes mediation less of an alternative than it could ideally be.

The issue of co-option is connected to the previous point, and it is evident from this experiment that the danger of co-option into the official system is quite real. In the climate which views mediation very favorably, there are plenty of those who consider mediation instrumentally only, either pushing their own careers, or the prestige of a particular office, or the prestige of an organization, hence there is much competition over the control of mediation. The more the instrumental concerns dominate mediation the less are the chances of considering mediation as an independent system of handling conflicts for the benefit of the people whose conflicts are being handled by the service.

7.

Informal Justice and Conflict Solution – A Research Report on New Interventive Strategies of Administrative Social Work in the Field of Juvenile Delinquency

Franz Bettmer / Heinz Messmer / Hans-Uwe Otto

Especially in the USA, there is a great number of programmes which try to surmount the obvious deficits of the criminal justice system that have been known for a long time, by means of alternative forms of dealing with criminal offences (cf. Alper/ Nichols, 1981). Programmes of that kind are mainly characterized by the fact that the processes of proceeding and deciding are carried out by extra-judicial institutions and organizations. In this respect, they belong to the field of informal justice. Being handled within these programmes, criminal offences are not cut down to the aspect of the violation of a norm as it is the case in judicial proceedings. Instead, the issues on hand are primarily taken as conflicts or problems which – as "property" of the participants (Christie, 1977) – are better left and also solved in their social context of origin. A mediation procedure like that, however, has to meet certain requirements. It must necessarily be openly designed in order to guarantee a stronger participation of the parties involved and a consideration of each of the individual perspectives. As far as the concept is concerned, the result of the procedure is not achieved by means of referring to objectively given criteria of decision, but is, first of all, legitimized instead by the agreement of the participants in the procedure. Thus, principles of judicial adjudication must be abandoned to a large extent.

Previous experiences with programmes of informal justice have shown, however, that alternative possibilities of coping with conflicts and criminal offences are not easily to be realized. The transmission of prototypes of informal justice to the field of social control in modern capitalist societies (as to be recognized in the American Neighborhood Justice Centers; cf. Merry, 1982) causes some problems. Under the aspects of a relief of formal justice, of lower costs and more durable solutions, and of a positive effect on local value structures, for example, rather disappointing results have been noticed in the NJCs (cf. ibid.; Cain, 1985). Moreover, it has been suspected that – instead of a resocialization of conflicts – thresholds of the access to formal institutions of justice will be built up (cf. e.g., Hofrichter, 1982) and that social inequalities of power will not be levelled in informal procedures because of the waiving of the guarantees of due process (cf. e.g., Abel, 1981). The practice of informal justice is frequently interpreted as an integrated element of the justice system which supports an expansion of state control (cf. e.g., Abel, 1982).

Against this view of informal justice, however, it must be objected that it is based on a curtailed view of the state as a monolithic unity. In order to understand the institutions of informal justice, it is however necessary to take into account the contradictions of the respective social fields tey are embedded in (cf. O'Malley, 1987). Otherwise, specific chances of concrete figures of informal justice will get out of view (cf. Cain, 1985).

The reality of courses of proceedings and decision-making in alternatives to the criminal justice system have not as yet been examined to a large extent. The programmes, however, find themselves exposed to the accusation that they often miss their aims already in the practical realization of conceptions (cf. Merry, 1982). This is where the research project begins to examine the empirical field of a corresponding programme which is carried out by the Bielefeld youth authority in co-operation with the public prosecutors. This programme is an attempt to take advantage of the greater possibilities informal procedures provide to achieve special preventive effectiveness (cf. Bettmer, 1986) and, at the same time, to take into account especially the interests of the victims. The investigation on hand deals with the scope and possibilities of a specific youth aid orientation of actions within the framework of informal procedures, and aims at gaining basic knowledge on a possible dispersal of social control as well. Here, the main interest lies especially in institutionalized strategies of settlement in administrative social work,and in its control-paradigmatic conventions.

1. Uncertainties in the Informal Procedure and Influences of the Criminal Justice System

Subsequently, not only the concrete feasibilities of the specific organization of procedures at the Bielefeld youth authority are taken into view, but also the restrictions towards a realization of the objectives. What has to be considered is that the caseload of the Bielefeld programme consists of referrals by the public prosecutors and that the proposals of the social workers of how to settle the cases are checked by the judicial authority. On the one hand, this reduces problems concerning the legitimacy of proceedings; on the other hand, however, this gives a chance to the criminal justice system to influence directly the results of the informal procedure. Therefore, one has to take into account especially the diverging alignments in settling cases of the different institutions (public prosecutors and youth authority) since the influences of criminal law – that is what the hypothesis says – can assert themselves in the concrete courses of proceedings in different ways and intensities[1].

The informal dealing with juvenile delinquency by the youth authority claims not only to have the function of relieving the courts but also to bring about a performance that is more adequate to the problems and thus to get better results in the field of special prevention than the criminal justice system does. This is, first of all, to be achieved by basing decisions on considerations of the individual perspectives of the parties involved and their particular social contexts where motives of conflicts and offences can be located. Thus, decision-making in informal procedures means that the social facts of the offence are not reduced to those aspects which are relevant to judicial norms, but other criteria are called in which are rather unimportant in judicial proceedings. These could, for example, be built of:

- situative circumstances or peculiarities of conflicts or criminal offences,
- current or socio-structural backgrounds of problems and causes of conflicts or offences,
- interests of victims in compensation.

The main interest of the informal procedure moves from the clarification of norms to the genesis of the offence or conflict, to the context of causes and to social or material consequences. That means that starting-points are given not only for the idea of a resocialization of conflicts, but also for patterns of handling cases that are genuinely specific for youth welfare institutions.

Informal procedures, thus, are becoming very complex. The points of reference for concrete decisions can only be determined during the course of the procedure. The conception of the procedure must therefore be limited to the conditions that build the framework for the interaction between the participants. First of all, there are no regulations about which topics and contributions are relevant and which are not. As informal procedures are essentially characterized by the missing of an objective system of reference for the adjudication, participation and agreement of the participants (delinquent and victim) become the prerequisites of decisions.

Here, the question to be answered is if (and under which conditions) an acceptable consensus can really be found on the basis that the integration of the participants in their social coontexts is considered and that differences between the individual perspectives can be overcome. There are no adequate theoretical foundations for informal procedures yet that considerations about the scheme of the programme could be linked to (cf. Cain, 1985). Hence, it is also empirically relevant to ask which are the essential criteria of decisions in informal procedures, and whether the agreement of the participants on a decision actually takes place on a voluntary basis.

The indefiniteness of the procedure is connected to a great uncertainty of performance on the part of the responsible social workers of the youth authority. The existence of the programme mainly depends on whether results can be presented to the public prosecutors; for a high rate of unsuccessful informal procedures would endanger their function of relieving the criminal justice. That is why the process of deciding can only partly be left over to the parties which are directly involved in the offence. The social workers have to control and intervene in order to secure that a result is achieved. In this process, however, they are dependent on agreement since they cannot push through a decision against the definite will of one of the participants in the process of negotiation. On the other hand, the final settlement of the procedure also needs the agreement to the decision of the informal procedure by the public prosecutors who – as a higher authority of decision – can also revise such results of the informal procedure that are based on a consensus between all parties involved. That means that, in the process of negotiation and decision, the social workers have to keep in mind that the outcome should meet the expectations of the public prosecutors.

Thus, the social workers are given an actual potential of power as well which is, so to speak, "borrowed" from the justice system. For to the juvenile delinquents it might seem reasonable to accept an agreement or the proposals of the social workers since the only alternative is to start a new judicial proceeding with an unknown outcome. An investigation will have to show to what extent the social workers try to overcome their uncertainties by reverting to judicial norm codifications under these cicumstances. Elements of the formal procedure do have some effect anyway since preceeding legal clarifications of the facts, explicit definitions of delinquent and victim and the existence of a confession are required for carrying through an informal procedure. In this respect, an interpretation of the incidents along judicial norm codifications has already been performed providing distributions of roles and interpretations of the facts that can be made topical by the social workers if necessary. The judicial norm may become the smallest common denominator to all participants in order to overcome problems of communication and decision. Moreover, the reference to judicial patterns of interpretation provides a better chance of the achieved results being accepted by the public prosecutor. If uncertainties are reduced in this way, a re-formalization of the informal procedure might occur since the premises of formal proceedings become decisive for the handling of the cases.

An analysis of processes of negotiation and reactions is meant to clear up how potential influences of judicial norm codifications and conditional programming are manifested in the decisions of the informal procedures and, most of all, in the structuring of the procedures, and also if indications for a net-widening emerge. Such indications are given if the consensus strived for turns out to be a merely rhethorical fact, if decisions bear the character of sanctions and their level of repressivity is higher than that of judicial sanctions, if measures are frequently taken in cases that would otherwise have been dismissed by the public prosecutors – or if a greater scope of the participants' lives is submitted to social control by the informal procedure than by judicial proceedings. What remains to be investigated is to what extent the framework of administrative social work increases the problems; although we back up here the thesis that a privately managed programme would, in principle, be faced with the same basic dilemma of uncertainties and influences of judicial orientations in the informal procedure.

2. Practice of the Programme and Analysis of Processes

The practice of the programme at the Bielefeld youth authority is based on a co-operation of public prosecutors and juvenile court assistance. The public prosecutors select cases that, from their point of view, seem to be appropriate for being further dealt with in the context of informal procedures by the youth authority. The relevant records are passed on to the juvenile court assistance for this purpose. The staff of the youth authority now try to find a conjointly solution of the respective problems by means of a specific procedure of negotiations and reactions that the persons involved in and, if need be, their parents agree with. The results are communicated to the responsible public prosecutors who cancel the judicial proceedings if they also agree to the solution. This procedure is judicially based on Section 45 Paragraph 2 No 1 of the JGG (juvenile criminal justice act) which says that an abandonment by the public prosecutors is possible if educational measures have been initiated or taken place. This marks out the scope of competence that is given to the social workers in informal procedures. In this context, it should be noted that, in contrast to other programmes in the FRG, the Bielefeld form of procedure is not based on offering the judicial authorities to carry out certain measures for certain types of offences. That means that the public prosecutors cannot select cases to be dealt with in the programme with regard to certain sanctions which, then, would only have to be carried out by the juvenile court assistance. The design of the procedure and the decisions on proposals that are submitted to the public prosecutors for the abandonment of the proceeding are both in the hands of the youth authority alone. Thus, the youth authority can also propose a settlement without consequences and without taking interventive actions itself, e.g., by referring to the effects on the juvenile delinquents of being questioned by the police or to previously carried out measures by the parents. On the other hand, the scope of the social workers' activities depends on the preparedness for co-operation of the juvenile delinquents and the victims. They have to agree to both taking part in the informal procedure and accepting the decisions made in it. Hence, there is no previously formulated offer for special cases, but the possibilities of dealing with the case are only limited by the agreement of the parties involved. This represents an essential expansion of the field of work of the juvenile court assistance as it is stated in Section 38 of the JGG. Following that, the juvenile court assistance acts as an institution to help the public prosecutors with inquiries, primarily investigating individualities of juvenile delinquents, introducing social aspects into the proceedings and proposing sanctions in the trials. In the programme under investigation, however, practically all the dealing with a case – after the facts of the offence have been legally estimated according to penal code by the public prosecutors – up to the selection and realization (provided the public prosecutors agree) of reactions falls on the juvenile court assistance. The far-reaching independence in the design of procedures that is open to the juvenile court assistance in the model under examination, is the essential requirement for creating possibilities to overcome the judicial way of thinking which concentrates on the violation of a norm in order to achieve a better consideration of the interests of the people concerned, especially those of the victims, and thus to favor special preventive aspects.

Decisions and structures of procedures are recorded, on the one hand, by means of a documentation of all steps of the procedures for all the cases in the programme, on the other hand, by selected observations and taperecordings of the negotiation processes between social workers and delinquent juveniles or victims. That covers the different segments of the social workers' role as mediators: they have to weigh up the demands of the victims and the delinquent juveniles' abilities to take burdens, and justify the participants' perspectives towards the expectancies of criminal justice. Conversely, the following negotiation processes with the public prosecutors must be prospectively integrated into the negotiation process with the participants. The topic of the criminal justice perspective ought to be the more important in the informal procedure the poorer the chances can be expected of achieving an agreement of the public prosecutor to a purely informal solution as an equivalent for a penalty through the public prosecutors. Hardly ever in the course of the programme in practice have the public prosecutors yet announced reservations about the procedure. Therefore, the social workers face the problem of having to anticipate the expectations of the public prosecutors in order to avoid later revisions of their results. In the individual cases, however, it is very difficult to estimate which aspects of the offence will be decisive for the current expectations of the public prosecutors and what weight they should be given.

On the whole, the allocated cases in the programme in practice are relatively homogenous with regard to the seriousness of offences according to the Criminal Code. About 120 cases were dealt with in 1987. For 67 of these cases, the documentation of the courses of procedure has been finished as well. This is done by means of questionnaires which are answered by the social workers themselves. The largest proportion of these 67 cases can be classified to the category of single or repeated shoplifting, followed by larceny, damage to property, physical injury, assault, and traffic offences. Other offences, such as burglary, fraud, trespass, aiding and abetting, are only recorded in a small number. The decisions that were suggested in the practice of the informal procedures primarily concentrated on obligations (these are orders to work in the field of local social services for the most part) and on dismissing cases without further measures. In 11 cases, a redress was realized; in 5 of these cases, a delinquent-victim- reconciliation was carried out.

A first survey on the processes of deciding in the practice of the programme shows that the social workers first of all check with the records or in an interview with the juvenile concerned whether a further intervention is reasonable at all, or whether sufficient reactions have already taken place in the social surroundings of the juvenile. Should further measures be considered necessary, the main concern at first and of prime importance is the regulation of material and immaterial damage caused by the offence. A redress or reconciliation procedure always takes obligations by the delinquent juvenile that can be attributed an educational value to and that can be represented as an appropriate equivalent to penalties towards the public prosecutors. Such forms of settlement, however, are relatively suspectible to interferences of the procedural organization, e.g., if the damage cannot be assessed definitly, or if one of the participants does not agree to a settlement in the informal procedure. If, however, an agreement is reached, there are scarcely any problems as far as a realization is concered.

On the other hand, the possibilities to refer to situative structures of problems that can be noticed in the offence are strictly limited from the start. Against the background of the shown dependency on the system of criminal justice, it seems plausible that, for example, socio-structurally orientated measures of support by the youth aid can hardly be pushed through as sufficient measures as soon as they leave the context of individualizing interventions that can be done without delay and that are connected with a burden for the juvenile concerned. Therefore, when redress obligations or reconciliation procedures cannot be employed and a measure seems to be necessary at the same time, work orders are reverted to in most cases, since they can be employed like a penalty. The decision on whether a dismissing of a case without consequences or a work order is suggested, is clearly orientated to the judicial criteria of the extent of damage and the amount of value at issue in the respective case. The extent of damage and the amount of value in cases that the social workers suggest work orders in, usually is twice as high as in cases that are proposed to be dismissed without further consequences.

The developments in the practice of the programme, however, seem to confirm that these tendencies are primarily due to uncertainties (caused by the lack of routine) towards the public prosecutors' expectations. Thus, a definite increase in the extent of damage can be recorded in the course of time for cases that were suggested to be dismised without taking further measures. This gives some reason to believe that the practice of deciding with an orientation to anticipated public prosecutors' expectations is gradually balanced, but what still has to be empirically clarified is to what extent the conditions of acceptance by the public prosecutors themselves change in the course of the programme in practice.

These are first impressions gained from the documentation of the courses and decisions of procedures. The aggregated data allow some conclusions to be drawn on the influencing of results in the informal procedures by the criminal justice system. However, they do not give any information about the contributions of the juveniles concerned and possibly of the victims to the making of decisions. For this, the observations of the direct interactions in the informal procedures must be consulted.

3. On the Analysis of Informalization of Social Control as an Interactive Process

Alternative methods of sanctioning and solving conflicts in the field of juvenile jurisdiction aim at procedural results that are meant to help avoiding unnecessary interventions. This concerns both the penal and the educative aspect of a measure to be taken. Thus, under the headword "Informalization of Social Control", methods of intervention of the youth authority are to be examined with a view to whether they allow the juvenile delinquents to take over the whole or part of the responsibility for forms of coping with the consequences of their deviant behavior. The main question asks about the juveniles' chances of participation in procedures of solving problems, working from the assumption that their integration in the bringing about of consensus on the procedural decisions also supports their preparedness to accept the consequences of these decisions because of their own shares of the responsibility. Therefore, an essential aim of this investigation is the question how one can describe the distribution of chances of influence by those who take part in informalized procedures, and which weight can be attributed to their contributions in respect to the procedural decisions[2)].

The core of interventive methods of the youth authority mainly consists in the direct contact between social workers and juvenile delinquents and, in case, also victims. A discussion is supposed to help the social workers to get an idea of the juveniles' situations and primarily to look into the question where further interventions as educational measures are required in addition to the talk. Thus, the offence itself is not meant to be the center of interest in the procedure but rather a peg on which the situative background of delinquency can be reconstructed according to the prerequisites. This contacting talks also offer the chance to the juveniles to introduce their own perspectives concerning the facts of the offence, possible explanations of causes, and alternatives of solution, so that their definitions of situation can become both integral elements and the basis of procedural decisions. Such criteria serve as references for the evaluation of informalized procedural steps on the level of interactive processes between social workers and clients.

4. A Quantitative Analysis of Informalized Processes of Intervention

In order to investigate adequately the complexity of the communicative processes of interactions in the context of negotiating decisions, we apply various methods of analysis parallel to each other. First of all, the non-verbal or pragmatic elements of the communicative event are measured with the help of rating scales at several times during the talk and for each speaker, e.g., confidence of behavior, grade of participation of juvenile and victim, dominance of the social workers, mutual receptiveness of the speakers etc. Furthermore, the talks are completely recorded on tape (provided all participants agree to that). On the basis of these recordings, selected discussions are transcribed for further case analyses.

In addition, these recordings are the basis of another procedure by means of which the separate sequences of sentences of the talk can be completely categorized. This procedure was developed on the basis of theoretical considerations by Th. Scheff (1968), who started from the assumption that the attribution of responsibility in conflictuous interactive processes is, at least in parts, a product of social constructions produced in negotiating processes. According to Scheff, processes of negotiation consist in a series of suggestions and reactions to these suggestions which are continued until one offer has achieved the status of a situative definition. H.B. Schmitz (1978; cf. also Ungeheuer/ Schmitz, 1982) subsequently designed a method of analysis with the aid of which a negotiation process can be operationalized into single negotiating moves. A single negotiating move combines each type of move with a level of negotiation and assigns it to one of the speakers. Types of moves express a speaker's kind of relation towards the contents of the discussion, that is whether information is given or wanted, or whether it is understood or questioned or doubted. Levels of negotiation describe the topic of discussion about which information is exchanged, e.g., whether it is rather the factual aspect of the offence that is talked about (What happened?) or rather normative aspects (How could it happen? Why did you do it?); whether judicial codifications of formal procedures are brought up or whether possible solutions of problems are searched for apart from judicial codes. For the analysis of conversational situations, a total of 70 negotiating moves have been differentiated as a basis of classification[3)].

At present, we are still collecting data with this procedure and thus we are just beginning with a systematical analysis. However, it is possible to sketch out some trends which have appeared in outline so far.
The majority of talks between juveniles and social workers are highly cooperative and achieve a consensus on the different negotiating levels of the discussion. The analysis of the talks with regard to types of moves shows that the quantitative distribution of contributions is almost equal between juveniles and social workers. This seems to indicate that there is enough freedom for the juveniles to develop chances of participation. Moreover, it can be observed that the juveniles have enough scope not only to answer the social workers' questions but also to intervene independently in the course of the talk so that they can define situations according to their own perspectives. From this point of view, there are fair chances for the juveniles to influence the negotiations of far-reaching definitions of problems. In addition, it was noted that the manner of the participants mutually reacting to each other's contributions obviously hardly ever raises any communicative problems between juveniles and social workers. Thus, it might well be concluded that a mutual adoption of perspectives on problems may succeed and an agreement on the interpretation of problematic situations can be achieved between the participants.

The distribution of the conversational sequences on the different levels of negotiation in the cases analyzed so far shows that the juveniles' conditions of negotiation come quite close to the given criteria of informalization on the level of interactions. As a rule, the juvenile is first of all explained the meaning and aims of the talk. This is important as it enables the juveniles to evaluate and control for themselves the relevance of their statements and contributions. According to Scheff (1968), this is an essential condition for being able to direct the processes of negotiation with regard to the ascription of responsibility. It also becomes clear that the core of such talks not so much serves to investigate the facts of the offence but rather to talk about the conditions and situative circumstances that led to the violation of a norm. Private and subjective consequences for the juveniles which have already been caused by an offence (feelings of guilt, punishment by the parents, future or already carried out reparations) also build a main interest of the discussion. In contrast to these features suggesting satisfying conditions of negotiation for the juveniles, it is remarkable that only little is said on the topic of the solution of problems. Since, however, the procedure operationalizing the separate negotiating moves does not allow to make conclusions about basic causes, we have to rely on individual case analyses for further considerations. In this way, we realized that in several cases it was in fact not necessary to negotiate decisions on the settling of the case because the offence was to be considered a less serious case or a passing phenomenon which made no further measures necessary. This was also a matter of consensus between social workers and juveniles. In several cases, however, it became obvious that the responsible social workers anticipated the expectations of the public prosecutors on a procedural decision and suggested additional educational measures which – because of the seriousness of the offences – were considered to be decisive for a dismissing of the proceedings by the public prosecutors though they turned out to be irrelevant in the course of the discussions. (Educational measures, as a rule, is work of benefit to the public the juvenile has to do for a certain number of hours). Hence, the results imply that the prerequisites on part of the youth authority are given so that informal procedural processes can be implemented. At the same time, it is a fact that the implementation of informalized processes can also be controlled by the public prosecutors by means of reserving for themselves the final decisions of whether or not to take the juveniles to court regardless of educational measures that have already been carried out or suggested. This reservation of decisions by the public prosecutors will have to be examined further in the course of the investigation asking to what degree it limits educational initiatives.

5. A Qualitative Analysis of Delinquent-Victim-Reconciliation Procedures

In this programme, some special attention is directed to violations of norms that can potentially be settled by conflict reconciliation[4)]. It is a fact, however, that appropriate cases have only reluctantly been passed on to the youth authority by the public prosecutors. But available possibilities of conflict reconciliation do not only fail because of the referral methods of the public prosecutors. It has also happened several times that social workers preferred other procedures to a direct confrontation between delinquent and victim. Since there are no systematic results available yet, we can only make some preliminary assumptions. Apparently, social work has not yet been able to free itself from the traditional procedural method of a fixation on the juvenile delinquent. Its routine procedures have so far been restricted to acting in the interest of the juvenile in court. The fact that in the context of conflict reconciliation the interests of the victims are to be taken into account as well, demands additional and innovative qualities of the role of social workers. They do not only deal with the matter of the juvenile delinquents any longer, but may also find themselves to be an agent of representing the interests of the victims. As a "third party", they now have to neutrally balance the different positions against each other. To be a mediator, however, it takes a certain competence of activities which is not automatically available to the social workers. This may be one of the reasons why social workers resort to routine procedures marked by an orientation to the delinquent and by individual case attendance.

Empirically more relevant, though, is another aspect which explains why the direct confrontation between delinquent and victim in procedures of conflict reconciliation has often come to naught already in the run-up: that is the consultation of a lawyer to represent the interests of the victim[5]. In these cases, the social workers are frequently faced with the fact that an informal settling of the conflict fails because of the resistance of the lawyer, who must not necessarily be interested in a quick and uncomplicated end of proceedings. Also, if claims for redress have been raised to such a height by the lawyer that an informal compensation is no longer possible, it might be better for the juvenile under these circumstances to go through the proceedings of criminal and civil law where adequate reparations can be negotiated. Against this problematic background, there have been several cases where the social workers acted as mediators between delinquents and victims and tried to reduce the influence of the lawyer by giving well-directed information and making offers to the victim. Although this procedure is usually successful, it both takes a lot of time and is a strain on all participants so that a direct contact between juvenile delinquent and victim does not come about anymore.

On the other hand, previous experiences with conflict negotiating talks have shown that the effects of such methods of intervention are predominantly positive. Above all, there is the observation that techniques of neutralization as described by Sykes and Matza (1957) can no longer be fully maintained by a juvenile delinquent when directly facing the victim. Basically, those techniques of neutralization are made use of which play down the consequences of the offence for the victim or which ascribe part of the responsibility for the coming about of the conflict to the victim.
In one of our documented cases, for example, a discussion took place with three juveniles who had brutally beaten up a class-mate who was by far inferior physically. In this conversation, where the victim was not present, the juveniles compensated the consequences of their offence by denying their responsibility and describing the victim's suffering as exaggerated at the same time. In a second talk in the presence of the victim, their system of justifying strategies largely broke down and ended in an apology and a symbolic gesture in the form of a present as well. As far as the delinquents were concerned, other cases took a quite similar course, though not as strikingly.

For the victims, the effect of these procedures is that they are able to address their demands for compensation of the material or emotional damage they have suffered, directly to the persons who caused it. Usually, the victim is better off here than in traditional court proceedings since settlement and reconciliation take place more quickly (for incidental action and private action as well as adhesive proceeedings are not possible in trial at the juvenile court)[6]. What seems to be even more important, however, is the emotional effect of such talks. While at the juvenile court an examination of the victim as witness in the trial is often refrained from, in conflict mediation procedures the victim is given the chance to articulate the emotional strain caused by the offence. Therefore, both the material and the immaterial interests of the victims can obviously be better considered in conflict mediation procedures than in traditional proceedings, although it must not be overlooked that this also means the great risk to the juvenile delinquents of having to face exaggerated expectation of redress they cannot evaluate correctly for lack of experience.

In the context of reconciliation procedures between delinquent and victim, what can be realized is that the social workers as an intervening third party must be ascribed to a greater importance than has been generally presumed on the basis of previous experiences[7]. An important circumstance is that different interventive forms of social work action disclose themselves to the social workers in the field of juvenile jurisdiction as soon as they deal with conflict mediation betweeen delinquent and victim. First of all, one has to stress that efforts of reconciliation between delinquents and victims can limit unnecessary educational measures and sanctionings. When the damage is put right and delinquent and victim have agreed on a compensation, there is no reason to see why additional interventions should be necessary on top of it. The reconciliation concept is thus based on a principle that implicitly limits sanctioning interventions (cf. also Galaway/ Hudson, 1975; Galaway, 1985). By means of including the victim into procedures of reparations, the basis and justification of social work with juvenile delinquents is changing as well.

Especially during the direct confrontation between delinquent and victim, it turns out that demands are made on social work which cannot be brought into accord with its traditional routines of practice and which lead to new requirements of social workers' competences of action. With regard to the juvenile delinquent, the task of giving information falls to the social workers, who often have to clear up false ideas of a procedural kind, especially about the strict separation of criminal and civil law aspects of proceedings. The social workers, in their role as passers of information, must also prepare the basis of a reconciliation procedure. One of their essential tasks is to inform the victim of an offence about the juvenile delinquent's attitude of being prepared to make reparations and thus to motivate the victim to take part in a reconciliation procedure.

This means, that the social workers must try and build up the organizational framework for a compensation of the damage. Once delinquent and victim have been brought together, the contact runs through several stages making demands on the social workers. As a rule, the discussion starts off with the reconstruction of the facts of the offence which is the obvious common denominator between delinquent and victim. The delinquents are asked to describe the basic motives of the offence and the background of their problems, while the victims mainly stress the material and emotional consequences of the offence towards the delinquent. In this phase of the talk, the social workers surely can try to be unbiased, often however, they face a situation where they must counteract a polarization of positions. Doing translating work between the participants in the procedure, the social worker has to see that a possible imbalance of influence between delinquent and victim in the interactive situation is avoided. Concerning the aspect of neutrality in reconciliation procedures, the social workers are mediators between two parties in a precarious situation. This, however, cannot be avoided since the social workers can only succeed in reducing ineffective communication and in levelling out mutual distrust between the parties when they start to prepare the way for mutual communicative chances where one party tries to push through its individual interests regardless of the aims of the procedure.

Only when the different perceptions and relevant systems of delinquent and victim have come closer, the negotiation of compensations can be tackled. Now, the task of the social workers is to reveal the interests of the parties involved. What has been observed is that the delinquents frequently have a sceptical attitude towards the demands of the victims conjecturing that the victims try to gain a financial advantage from the past offences. This is an indirect effect of neutralization strategies of denying or at least playing down the consequences of an offence to the victims. In this context, the social workers' main role is that of a mediator when they have to criticize subjective justification systems. As regards the victims, it is first of all a matter of clearing up the material or symbolic dimension of redress. What could be observed was that the victims did not ask for punishment in every sense of the word but were satisfied with the compensation of all damage done or with an apology by the delinquents[8)]. To the victims, the social workers as partners in conversation are primarily in demand in their function as mediators. Previous analyses have shown that, at this point, the social workers are also confronted with procedural problems when certain contents are involved. When the damage has reached a certain extent, an informal settlement of the conflict faces immanent limits since the material dimension of compensating the damage is based on legally complicated prerequisites the social workers cannot master on the grounds of their training. With regard to an informal agreement before the courts come in, the question must be asked whether such a deficiency can be put right by arranging special offers of further qualification to the social workers.

In summary, the previous results give the impression that extra-judicial strategies of coping with problems on the level of interaction, in contrast to legally formal procedures, are much more suitable to specify a need for interventions and to realize it in a way that is comprehensible to all parties involved in the procedure. Even though there is still a lot of stress between the criminal justice system and social work which restricts the youth authority's actions of developing and continuing its professional competence, the given results do point to implications that educationally significant expansions of the spectrum of reactions in juvenile legal aid are possible. On the whole, informalized alternatives of procedure start off closer to the concerned juveniles' views of the problems and relevant systems giving them the chance to share the responsibility for influencing the working off of legal consequences. Interventive forms that are orientated towards communication reach their highest value in a reconciliation procedure between delinquents and victims, that is where a practicized communication of social responsibility is given (cf. also Frehsee, 1987). In this way, stigmatizing biographies of delinquents can be avoided as well as legal consequences that are favorable for the victims can be promoted. Social work in a field close to justice faces a new scope of design that does not cancel the clients' ability of action and helps to cut back irrational wishes for punishment as well.

Notes

1 That is why we start from the assumption that an "informalization" of social control is not yet realized through an appropriate conception of a programme, but has to be repeatedly put through in every single case.
2 The theoretical background of these considerations can only be negatively determined for the time being. For legal and procedural sociological analyses have shown that social facts are reduced to their judicial relevance by means of the conditional programming of law (cf. Luhmann, 1969). That means that natural rules of everyday life are cancelled aggravating the comprehensibility of the procedural processes in court for the lay public (for a closer look see the investigations by Leodolter, 1975, Schütze, 1978, Muth, 1984, and also Soeffner, 1984, for basic facts).
3 On the functioning of this analyzing procedure see Messmer, (1988).
4 For a number of years, delinquent-victim-reconciliation procedures have been tested as programmes in some cities of the FRG. Part of these have also been investigated at the same time. There are no systematic results available on this practical complex yet.
5 This result corresponds to experiences made in other projects of delinquent-victim-reconciliation, just see Kuhn, (1987) and Viet, (1988).
6 A closer integration of the victims into the judicial course of proceedings is generally considered to be desirable because of a minor position of the victim in court proceedings (Berckhauer/ Steinhilper, 1985; Frehsee, 1985; Hilse, 1985).
7 This circumstance deserves some special attention. Reports from the different programmes in the FRG ascribe the effects of their results completely to the direct confrontation between delinquent and victim. But this is too brief. The available literature on "Dispute Settlement" or "Third-Party-Intervention" shows that the importance and function of an intervening party must not be underestimated in the context of conflict mediation. Although some links to this are given in the FRG (cf. the summarizing work by Holtwick-Mainzer, 1985 and Nothdurft/ Spranz-Fogasy, 1986), the practical movement of delinquent-victim- reconciliation procedures has not yet manifested itself in this tradition of ideas.
8 It can be proved that the demands for an infliction of punishment are fewer than preferences for restitutive and informal kinds of reaction also within those groups of the population who have once before been victims of offences; on this, see the representative interviews by Sessar/ Beurskens/ Boers, 1986.

References

Abel, R.L. (1981): Conservative conflict and the reproduction of capitalism: The role of informal justice. International journal of the sociology of law 9, 245-267

Abel, R.L. (1982): The contradictions of informal justice. In: Abel, R.L: The politics of informal justice, Vol. 1, New York et al., 267-320

Alper, B.S., and Nichols, L.T. (1981): Beyond the courtroom. Programs in community justice and conflict resolution, Lexington

Berckhauer, F., and Steinhilper, G. (1985): Opferschutz durch Strafrecht und Strafverfahren? In: Janssen, H./ Kerner, H.-J. (Eds.): Verbrechensopfer, Sozialarbeit und Justiz. Bonn-Bad Godesberg, 81pp.

Bettmer, F. (1986): Probleme der Informalisierung sozialer Kontrolle im Bereich abweichenden Verhaltens. In: Müller, S., and Otto, H.-U. (Eds.): Damit Erziehung nicht zur Strafe wird. Sozialarbeit als Konfliktschlichtung. Bielefeld.

Cain, M. (1985): Beyond informal justice. Contemporary crises 9, 335-373

Christie, N. (1977): Conflicts as property. The British journal of criminology 17, 1-15

Frehsee, D. (1985): Die Idee der Schadenswiedergutmachung durch den Täter. In: Janssen, H., and Kerner, H.-J. (Eds.): Verbrechensopfer, Sozialarbeit und Justiz. Bonn-Bad Godesberg, 117pp.

Frehsee, D. (1987): Schadenswiedergutmachung als Instrument strafrechtlicher Sozialkontrolle. Berlin

Galaway, B., and Hudson, J. (1975): Sin, Sickness, Restitution. In: Galaway, B., Hudson, J. (Eds.): Considering the Victim. Springfield, 59pp.

Galaway, B. (1985): Restitutive Justiz. In: Janssen, H., and Kerner, H.-J. (Eds.): Verbrechensopfer, Sozialarbeit und Justiz. Bonn-Bad Godesberg, 471pp.

Hilse, J. (1985): Hilfen für die Opfer von Straftaten. In: Janssen, H., and Kerner, H.-J. (Eds.): Verbrechensopfer, Sozialarbeit und Justiz. Bonn-Bad Godesberg, 345pp.

Hofrichter, R. (1982): Justice centers raise basic questions. In: Tomasic, R., and Feeley, M.M. (Eds.): Neighborhood justice. Assessment of an emerging idea. New York, London, 193-202

Holtwick-Mainzer, A. (1985): Der übermächtige Dritte. Eine rechtsvergleichende Untersuchung über den streitschlichtenden und streitentscheidenden Dritten. Berlin.

Kuhn, A. (1987): Körperverletzung als Konflikt. Zwischenbericht 1987 zum Projekt Handschlag, hrsg. vom Trägerverein "Hilfe zur Selbsthilfe" e.v., o.O.

Leodolter, R. (1975): Das Sprachverhalten von Angeklagten bei Gericht. Kronberg/Ts.

Luhmann, N. (1969): Legitimation durch Verfahren. Neuwied, Berlin

Merry, S.E. (1982): Defining "success" in the neighborhood justice movement. In: Tomasic, R., and Feeley, M.M. (Eds.): Neighborhood justice. Assessment of an emerging idea. New York, London, 172-192

Messmer, H. (1988): Zur Quantifizierung qualitativer Daten. Probleme der methodischen Fixierung von Interaktionsprozessen im Rahmen einer Aushandlung außergerichtlicher Verfahrenserledigungen. Kriminologisches Journal 20 forthcoming

Muth, J. (1984): Die Jugendgerichtsverhandlung aus der Perspektive des Angeklagten. In: Reichertz, J. (Ed.): Sozialwissenschaftliche Analysen jugendgerichtlicher Interaktion. Tübingen, 58-110

Nothdurft, W., and Spranz-Fogasy, Th. (1986): Der kulturelle Kontext von Schlichtung. Zum Stand der Schlichtungsforschung in der Rechts-Anthropologie. Zeitschrift für Rechtssoziologie 7, 31pp.

O'Malley, P. (1987): Regulating contradictions: The Australian press council and the "dispersal of social control". Law and society review 21, 83-108

Scheff, Th.J. (1968): Negotiating reality: Notes on power in the assessment of responsibility. Social problems 16, 3-17

Schmitz, H.W. (1987): Tatgeschehen, Zeugen und Polizei (BKA- Forschungsreihe, Bd.9). Wiesbaden

Schütze, F. (1978): Strategische Interaktion im Verwaltungsgericht – eine soziologische Analyse zum Kommunikationsverlauf in Verfahren zur Anerkennung als Wehrdienstverweigerer. In: W. Hoffmann-Riehm et al. (Eds.): Interaktion vor Gericht. Baden-Baden, 21-100

Sessar, K., Beurskens, A., and Boers, K. (1986): Wiedergutmachung als Konfliktregelungsparadigma? KrimJ 18, 86pp.

Soeffner, H.-G. (1984): Strukturanalytische Überlegungen zur gerichtlichen Interaktion. in: Reichertz, J. (Ed.): Sozialwissenschaftliche Analysen jugendgerichtlicher Interaktion. Tübingen, 189-225

Sykes, G.M., and Matza, D. (1957): Techniques of Neutralization: A Theory of Delinquency. American Sociological Review 22, 664pp.

Ungeheuer, G., and Schmitz, H.W. (1978): Problemstellung und Methoden der Untersuchung: Kommunikative Probleme von Polizeibediensteten als Zeugen und Sachverständige vor Gericht. In: Knuf, J.: Polizeibeamten als Zeugen vor Gericht. (Sonderband der BKA-Forschungsreihe) Wiesbaden, 12pp.

Viet, F. (1988): Der "Täter-Opfer-Ausgleich" als eine Aufgabe der Jugendgerichtshilfe. Fünf Jahre Erfahrungen aus Braunschweig. ZfJ 75, 17pp.

8.

Police and Prevention. A Research Report on Cooperation in the Criminal Justice System

Ursula Herbort, Dorothea Rzepka, Silvia Voss[*]

A. Prevention as a Goal of Prosecutorial Disposition Strategies

I. Types of Disposition Compared for the Years 1983–1986

1. Prevention and Intervention in the Juvenile Court Act

The Juvenile Court Act of the Federal Republic of Germany (Jugendgerichtsgesetz, JGG) gives prosecutors several options for discontinuing prosecution before the beginning of the principal court hearing (pretrial diversion). One purpose of such dismissals is to unburden the criminal justice system (Heinz, 1984, pp. 291 et seq.; Sonnen, 1981, p. 180; Kunz, 1980, p. 29). Another is to protect juvenile suspects from disproportionate sanctions by the state, as well as from the damage that ensues from stigmatization and criminalization (Lundman, 1976, pp. 430 et seq.; Morris, 1978, p. 46; Voss, 1986, p. 79). In these ways, prosecutorial dismissals are expected to have the further effect of preventing criminal behavior (Ostendorf, 1987, No. 3 before sections 45, 47 JGG; Heinz and Spiess, 1983, p. 903 for further proof).

The concept of "prevention" can be characterized in various ways according to various criminological approaches. *On the one hand,* when the state declines to intervene and impose sanctions it avoids repressive measures that would otherwise threaten to stigmatize suspects and to exacerbate their subsequent criminal behavior. This concept ascribes the positive effects of such self-restraint principally to the fact that state inaction tends to preserve the suspect's social context, especially in so far as it consists of parents and educators. The social context is held to be a more successful force for the stabilization of norms and the correction of behavior than state action. "Prevention" thus also refers to the use of forces for guidance that are inherent in society (Eisenberg, 1985, No. 19 et seq. to section 45 JGG). This notion of prevention in criminal justice can be called a *judicial* concept of '*diversion without intervention*'. These assumptions underlying the principle of public-sector deference are anchored in section 45 of the Juvenile Court Act.

* Subproject C1 of the Special Research Unit 227, Director P.-A. Albrecht.

On the other hand, however, section 45 of the Juvenile Court Act also offers an *interventionist* concept of prevention that authorizes quasi-sanctioning state activities. These mainly include imposition of obligations (such as restitution, compensation, and fines), work requirements, required safe-driving courses, etc. Such activities can be referred to as '*diversion with intervention*' or 'diversion with treatment' as long as the state continues to refrain from imposing formal sanctions.

In German criminal law, the decision to implement one or the other of these strategies of diversion in juvenile cases belongs mainly to the prosecutor. Contrary to the situation in the United States, the German police do not have the right to close a case for lack of evidence. Every criminal case, even one without any suspects, must be referred to the prosecutor. Only the prosecutor has the authority to decide on a summary dismissal, thereby preventing a court trial.

Three basic kinds of disposition are available to the prosecutor:

- (1) *"Formal reactions"* are charges brought before a juvenile court, as well as charges brought according to the simplified juvenile procedures provided for in section 76 of the Juvenile Court Act.
- (2) *"Informal reactions"* include measures that rely on parental correction, as mentioned above, as well as quasi-sanctioning state activities, in both cases fitting the requirements of section 45 of the Juvenile Court Act. Additionally, informal sanctions include dismissals undertaken according to adult criminal law (sections 153 and 153a of the Code of Criminal Procedure) (Strafprozeßordnung), which have the further advantage that they do not become part of the suspect's educational records (Erziehungsregister).
- (3) *Cases* which are dismissed because legal or factual grounds exist for discarding the original suspicions against the suspect. In such cases we say that the prosecutor acts on the *presumption of innocence* which requires the dismissal according to section 170, paragraph 2, of the Code of Criminal Procedure.

The relationship among *all* kinds of reactions permits us to make various predictions about how prosecutors will choose among preventive strategies in the process of managing their caseloads.

The administrative institutions of criminal justice, in particular the justice ministries and the offices of chief prosecutors (Generalstaatsanwaltschaften), have appealed in recent years to the juvenile prosecutors to make more use of prosecutorial authority to dismiss cases. It is not clear whether these recommendations are attributable to an increased understanding of the role of prevention in a criminologically sophisticated legal order. An alternative explanation is the desire to reduce the overload on scarce resources of the justice system through procedural streamlining (cf. Feltes et al., 1983, p. 890). It is, in either case, a clear official policy of the justice system to work toward an increased use of the possibilities of the options afforded by section 45 of the Juvenile Court Act. In addition to criminal justice policy, specialists in juvenile criminology overwhelmingly agree that the preventive potential of case dismissals should be used more systematically (Heinz, 1983a, pp. 20 et seq.). There are even euphoric calls for a "reform from below" (Pfeiffer, 1983, p. 128).

2. The dilemma of official statistics

In the Special Research Unit of Bielefeld our project has been attempting to observe the process whereby this trend toward prevention in criminal justice policy is translated into prosecutorial practice. The research question is then whether the officially announced standards are actually reflected in an increase in the informal and a decrease in the formal disposition of cases. The official statistics of the prosecutor's office (Zählkartenstatistik) give the impression that the originally overwhelming share of formal case dispositions is slowly declining and that the two kinds of disposition are approaching a one-to-one relationship (the data are taken from unpublished statistics of the statistical office for data processing and statistics in North Rhine-Westphalia, Landesamt für Datenverarbeitung und Statistik; cf. also Heinz and Spiess, 1983, p. 928). The official statistics, however, have a crucial defect: they register only the most severe reaction in a criminal case. If several persons are involved in the case, the reactions toward the other participants, whether equally severe or more mild, are not reflected in the statistics. For example, if there are four suspects whose cases are heard together and all four are charged, only *one* charge is included in the statistics. Even when one of these four persons' cases is dismissed, the only information recorded is still the charge. Since there are 1,3 subjects in the average juvenile criminal case (Feltes, 1983, p. 70), we estimate that in the official criminal justice statistics about 30 % of all case dispositions go unrecorded.

Consequently, the imprecisions in the official statistics have persuaded us to resort to a study of *files* in which *subjects* rather than *cases* are the units of record in order to discover how different suspects are differently treated.

With an analysis for the years 1983–1986 in the prosecutor's offices of two cities in North Rhine-Westphalia (Muenster and Bielefeld), each of which reflects the average trend of case dismissals in all 19 prosecutor's offices in North Rhine-Westphalia, we intend to study how concepts of prevention were put into practice over the course of four years. At the same time, the analysis will serve as a comparative and impact study of an administrative model which has been implemented in Bielefeld in 1987 to improve communication between participants in judicial proceedings (cf. B and C below). The survey will be continued until late in 1988. Results for the year 1987 are not yet available.

3. Changes in the types of disposition in the office of the Bielefeld juvenile prosecutors

The following graph allows us to draw initial *tentative* conclusions for the office of the Bielefeld prosecutors. This graph presents the change over time in various kinds of case disposition for 1983–1986.

The analysis of changes over time is based on samples taken from the subpopulations of the individual years. Each cohort provides a sample of approximately 230 persons, drawn from a population of 2.000 to 2500 suspects in the group aged 14–20. The 10 % random sample yields unmistakable and statistically significant trends.

Fig. 1: Types of disposition for the years 1983-1986, fourteen-to-twenty-year old group suspected of theft, battery and/or vandalism
(Office of the Bielefeld Juvenile Prosecutors)

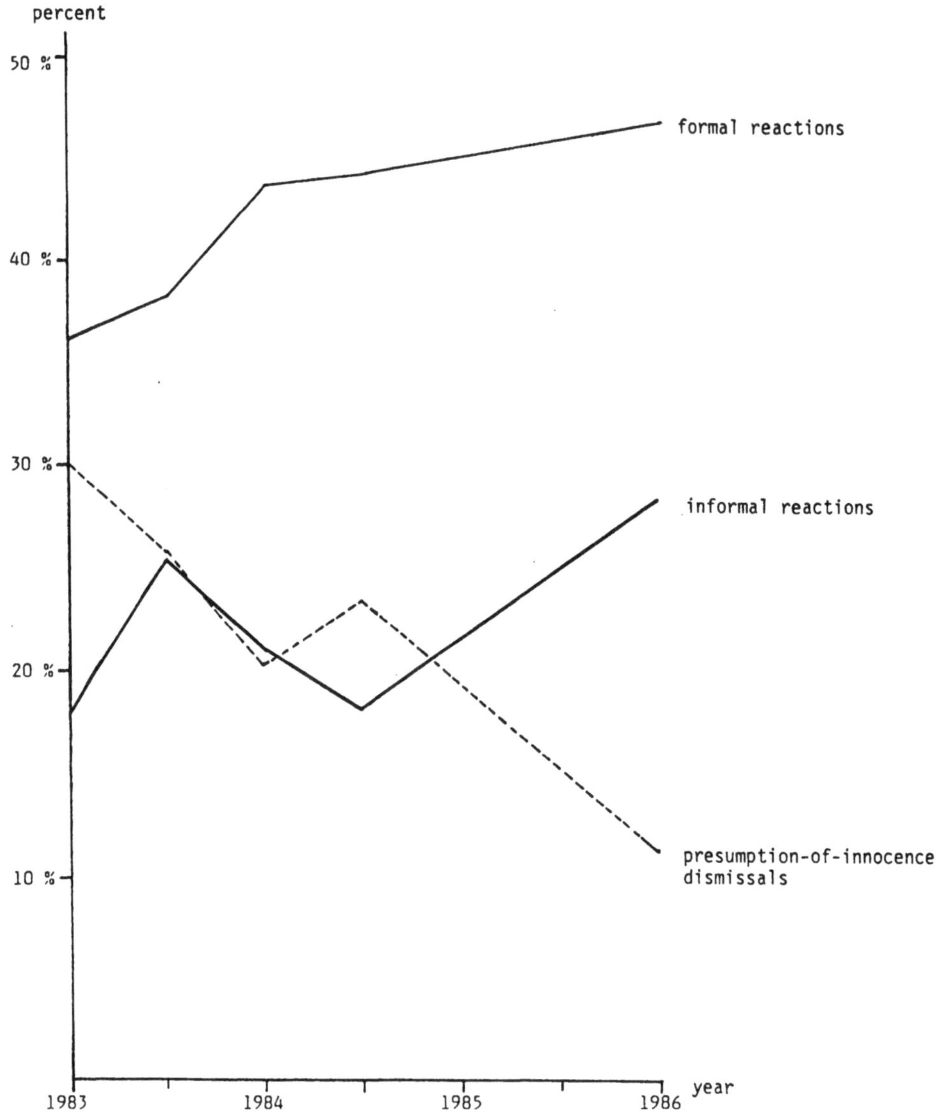

Our results show that, contrary to the conclusions drawn from official statistics, *no reduction in the proportion of formal decisions* has been achieved. In fact, the proportion of formal decisions has increased from 36 % in 1983 to 47 % in 1986. *The proportion of informal sanctions* has also *increased* during the same time period, but on a lower level: it rose from 18 % to 29 %.

While the rates of formal and informal sanctions were increasing, there was a corresponding *decrease in the frequency of dismissals according to the presumption-of-innocence procedure laid down in section 170, paragraph 2, of the Code of Criminal Procedure*. Such dismissals dropped from 30 % in 1983 to 12 % in 1986. The connections among all these changes become clear when we consider all of the available options for the reaction of the prosecutor.

We can, then, state the following:

(1) Contrary to the officially announced trend toward decriminalization in juvenile justice, *the proportion of formal reactions* by the state has been *increasing*.

(2) There has also been an *increase in the proportion of informal reactions*, although this result *cannot be interpreted as a rise in the rate of decriminalization* since alternative interpretations of this increase are reasonable.

One possible explanation for the contrary development of informal reactions and presumption-of-innocence dismissals could be that prosecutors have been counter-acting the officially promoted decriminalization program by *substituting one dismissal procedure for another*. To be specific, according to this hypothesis prosecutors do not accept the demands of their superiors to respond to juvenile criminality with de-criminalization, so the increasing number of cases they have agreed to dismiss under section 45 of the Juvenile Court Act could have been selected from the cases that they formerly would have dismissed anyway for lack of evidence (to this hypothesis see Ostendorf, 1987, No. 5 before sections 45, 47 JGG).
Such processes of substitution among the legally permitted kinds of dismissal are certainly not a contribution to decriminalization. If this thesis can be confirmed, then one must conclude that the current practice shows some *signs of increasing criminalization*.

The *counter-hypothesis* is, namely that the reduction in presumption-of-innocence dismissals results from a *substantial increase in the effectiveness of criminal investigations* or from *structural changes in inputs into the prosecutor's office* (for example, changes in selection practices by the police). Such increased effectiveness or changes would show the consequence that less dismissals based on the presumption of innocence *can* be undertaken and the alternatives of informal and formal case dispositions *must* be chosen.
Concerning the prosecutor's office of Bielefeld the last hypothesis seems to be confirmed. In Bielefeld the decrease in dismissals following section 170, paragraph 2, of the Code of Criminal Procedure is going in line with a decrease in non-confessive suspects. A reason

for the increasing willingness to confess cannot be gathered from the data. *Therefore, concerning the Bielefeld data, the hypothesis of substitution cannot be confirmed.* The statewide survey will have to examine in detail the link between a confession and the dismissal of cases following section 170, paragraph 2, of the Code of Criminal Procedure.

II. Analysis of Narrative Interviews with Prosecutors (Pretest for Statewide Interviews with Prosecutors)

The statistical time-series analysis of the decisionmaking behavior of prosecutors is a first step in our study of preventive and interventionist strategies of social control. A second step is now taking place in the form of a statewide study of files in nineteen offices of prosecutors and in the form of interviews with approximately 160 juvenile prosecutors in North Rhine-Westphalia. In this second stage we are investigating the individual and organizational factors that influence decisionmaking among prosecutors. We seek the determinants of prosecutorial behavior in attitudes and beliefs, organizational conditions, bureaucratic influences and environmental relations.

In order to develop a standardized questionnaire, we conducted intensive interviews with twenty juvenile prosecutors from all three Superior State Court Districts (Oberlandesgerichtsbezirk) in the State of North Rhine-Westphalia. The standardized survey of all prosecutors in North Rhine-Westphalia, which is currently underway, is based on this pilot study. The interviews concentrate on the following questions:

- What information is available to the prosecutor for use in criminal cases?
- What factors are used as the basis for decisions about dismissals under section 45 of the Juvenile Court Act?
- Is there a need for changes in criminal procedure that would favor the use of section 45 of the Juvenile Court Act?

1. Factual criteria for the use of section 45 of the Juvenile Court Act

a) In all our interviews we heard repeatedly that the information on which the juvenile prosecutors act is usually restricted to the investigation files kept and furnished by the *police*. The major part of these files is the statement of the suspect to the police about the circumstances of the crime, sometimes including information about one or several motives, as well as statements of the witnesses and other evidence about the circumstances of the crime. In rare cases the attitude of the suspect toward the crime is also described. The prosecutors also have access to data about previous investigations of the suspect in the same court district (Landgerichtsbezirk). It was consistently reported that the behavior of the suspect during interrogation and the situation in the parental home as well as the reactions of the parents and his/her social milieu are generally *not included in the files*, and that prosecutors do not receive information about these matters in any other way. Furthermore, it is quite unusual for the police to include in these files their own evaluations of the suspect or of the appropriateness of further prosecution.

This *meager supply of information* is surprizing, since section 45 of the Juvenile Court Act deviates strongly in its assumptions from other criminal procedures. The application of the procedures in section 45 is to be based on the so-called "educational principle" which dominates the entire Juvenile Court Act (to the problematical relationship between punishment and education see Bohnert, 1983). These dismissals are not conditioned on the seriousness or the type of the crime (cf. Eisenberg, 1985, No. 17 to section 45 JGG). The bulk of the factors relevant for the decision are *unrelated to the crime itself.* If the prosecutor does not know anything about these factors, however, then a broadened application of the law appears to be clearly frustrated by inadequate information.

b) Thus, in the office of the Bielefeld prosecutors in 1986, there was documentation about the consequences of the crime for the suspect or about educational measures that had been or were to be taken in only 7.5 % of all cases. In their ignorance of differentiated background information, the prosecutors resort to a global action plan. The interviewed prosecutors told us that, in practice, the following factors are decisive in determining their application of the law: *the type of crime, the amount of damages, the prior record of the suspect and the willingness of the suspect to confess.* When the suspect was not willing to confess, prosecutors refused on principle to apply any of the options in section 45 of the Juvenile Court Act, although only paragraph 1 of this section requires a confession as a prerequisite for dismissal.

In the prosecution offices throughout almost all of North Rhine-Westphalia, an understanding has been reached that section 45 of the Juvenile Court Act will be used only in cases of theft, nonpayment of transit fares, driving without a license, sometimes battery and vandalism, and in rare cases fraud. With rare exceptions, prosecutors refuse on principle to use this law in felony cases.

Prosecutors are careful to dismiss cases of property crime only when the damage does not exceed a *specific value.* This value is set by either the individual prosecutor or the customary guidelines of the prosecutor's office. Without exception the maximum was fixed at between fifty and one-hundred German marks. Section 45 of the Juvenile Court Act is applied overwhelmingly to first offenders, and rarely to second offenders. The cases of repeat offenders (two or more prior cases), if at all dismissed, are dismissed almost always in connection with educational measures taken according to section 45, paragraph 2, number 1 of the Juvenile Court Act, or else the dismissal occurs according to section 45, paragraph 1.

c) On the basis of the interviews we can recognize a *trend* that we shall seek to determine in further research whether it obtains throughout North Rhine-Westphalia: The generalization is that cases are dismissed whenever the four formal criteria, mentioned before, permit a dismissal. When at least one criterion is not met, then supplementary information which might justify a dismissal is generally *not* sought out by the prosecutor; a charge follows. The legal possibilities of section 45 of the Juvenile Court Act are thereby severely constrained by the prosecutors' *formalistic application of the law.* In the vast majority of cases, only a few characteristics of the crime and of the suspect are taken into account so as to affect the prosecutorial decision. Consequently, educationally relevant factors distinguishing one suspect from another are, we have found, unknown to the prosecutor and thus play no role in his/her decisionmaking.

2. Expansion of juvenile prosecutors' information

a) There are *many reasons for the prosecutors' deficit of information*. It is well known that prosecutors are no longer unreservedly characterized as chief criminal investigators (cf. Steffen, 1976; Uhlig, 1986, pp. 247 et seq.). The police have to a large extent assumed the exclusive responsibility for gathering and aggregating information, especially in the area of petty crime, in which juveniles are typically involved. The superior access of the police to information that is relevant to prosecutorial decisions makes this division of labor understandable. From the initial arrest at the scene of the crime, through police interrogation of the suspect, all the way to conversations with parents and interrogations of witnesses, the police have direct and comprehensive contact with the crime and the suspect. Only in major, complex cases do prosecutors themselves get involved to conduct personal interrogations and to order specific kinds of additional investigation. In other cases the prosecutor relies on the written information in the files received from the police. Of course, this information is prepared, filtered, and perhaps also consciously or unconsciously evaluated. This is part of the job of the police which means to give the prosecutor what he/she wants to make prosecutorial decisions. Nevertheless, the police are actually the central actor in determining how much information is available to the prosecutor. The power of the police to include information in or to exclude information from the files gives the police a controlling influence over the application of preventive legal norms.

b) If prosecutors refuse to conduct their own investigations despite their knowledge of how little information they receive, perhaps they regard their current, objectively inadequate level of information as neither a hindrance to their work nor a reason for systematic reform. To a limited extent, our evidence supports this explanation, at least for the very large class of petty crime. This attitude of the prosecutors was *not* based, however, on a *conscious rejection* of the concept of legal prevention. Rather, prosecutors were *ignorant* of the rationale and preventive value of a case dismissal through which the state would refrain from imposing sanctions and thereby consider the educational reactions of the social milieu. This idea from criminology was practically unknown to those making the decision to prosecute or dismiss. Instead, they saw the many atypical demands placed on them by a decision under section 45 of the Juvenile Court Act as nothing but a *gratuitous addition to their workload*. We have here, then, a procedure mandating dismissals, but ignorence of its purpose and effects appears to lead its underuse.

Despite their admitted lack of information, the prosecutors tended to perceive no difficulty reaching a *proper decision*. About half the interviewees expressed some lack of confidence in their decisions, but usually when they had dismissed a case solely on the basis of information about the offence. These prosecutors thought that additional information about the social circumstances leading to the crime, if unfavorable toward the suspect, could have led them to press charges. Conversely, almost all the prosecutors reported having charged a suspect solely because of missing supplementary information. At trial, they said, they had often told themselves that they would not have even charged the suspect if they had had more information about the case.

c) If prosecutors lack of information only because they do not receive it from the police, then a *reform* of the current dismissal practice could be brought about through *improved communication* between police and prosecutors. But perhaps prosecutors would not use information about the "environment" of the crime and the personality of the suspect even if they had such information. So we were interested in the meaning that juvenile prosecutors attached to such information. When asked what effect better access to information would have on their behavior in disposing of cases, the interviewees were reticent. Many were fairly certain that they would continue their current decisionmaking practices. The interviewees described their practices as "working", "trouble-free", and not forcing them to do "extra work". They did, however, see supplementary information as useful in *legitimating* their decisions. Another large proportion of the interviewees expressed the belief that improved access to information could change their decisionmaking behavior. The anticipated changes included not only an increase in "educationally" based dismissals but also an increase in the number of criminal charges supported by educational considerations.

d) Our initial tentative conclusion, to be tested further with the statewide sample, is therefore to suggest that it is not preventive considerations as much as administrative and bureaucratic problems that determine how section 45, paragraph 2, of the Juvenile Court Act is used. As a result, the area of semi- serious crime is practically untouched by preventively aimed dismissals. Only certain petty crimes, selected according to formal criteria, get dismissed. The need of changes in dismissal strategies is not particularly great in the area of petty crime, since *formal standards consistently* applied may be fully adequate here and realize equality. Where decriminalizing prosecutorial strategies can benefit most from criminological expertise is in the areas of semi- serious and serious crime. This will require, however, new judgmental procedures and tools.

B. Prevention-Related Sources of Information Available to the Police

I. A Study of the Bielefeld Police

At the prosecutorial level, we have discovered a particularly acute lack of information about the *characteristics* referred to in sections 43 and 45 of the Juvenile Court Act: Motive for the crime, attitude toward the crime, provocations by the victim, restitution, behavior upon arrest or during interrogation, and harm suffered by the suspect

Fig. 2: Program of § 45 JCA

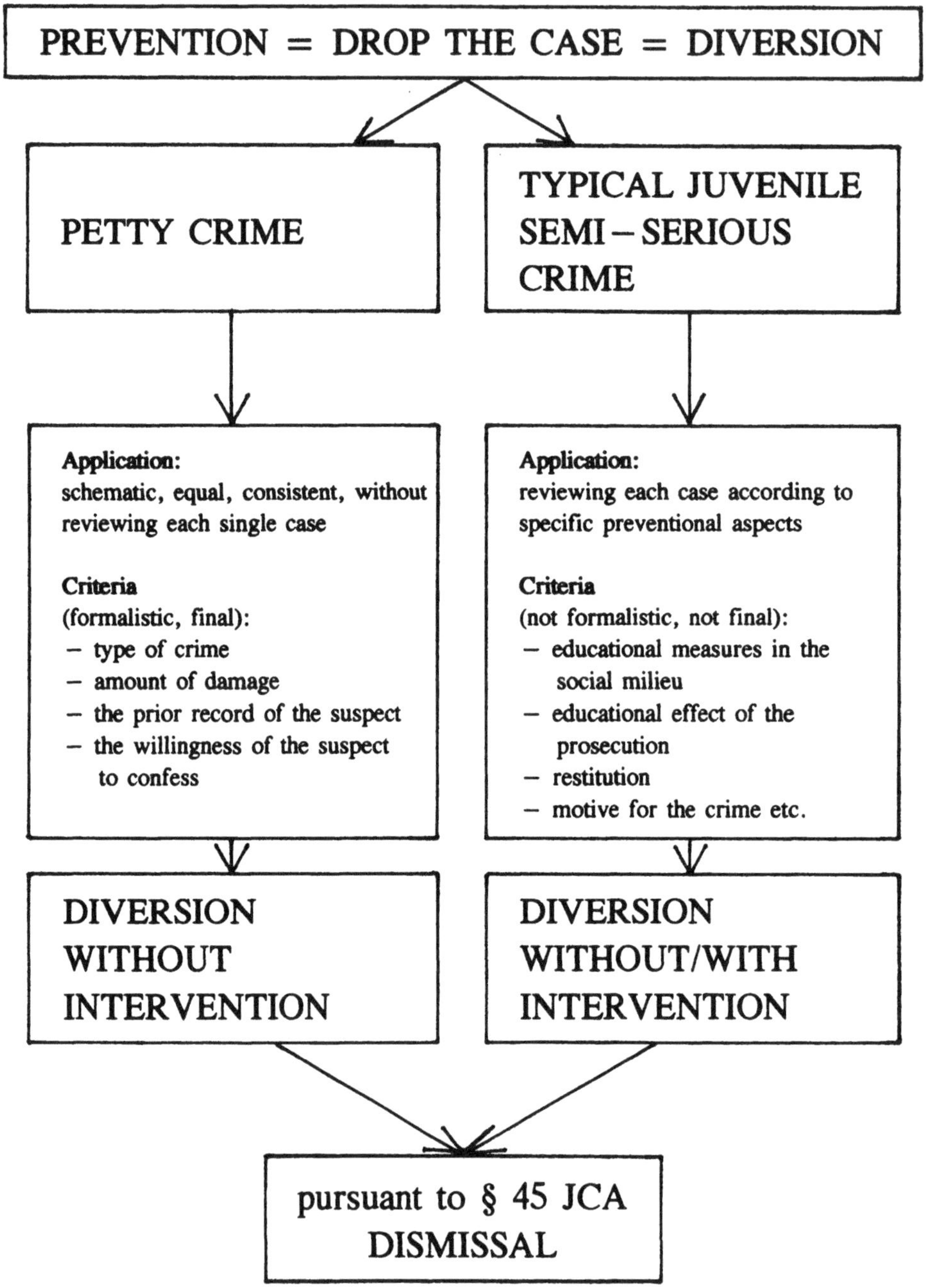

are among the characteristics that shall, according to these sections, be used to assess the place of the crime in the total life of the juvenile suspect (cf. Eisenberg, 1985, No. 10, 12 to section 43 JGG). According to section 45, educational measures taken by those responsible for the suspect's education and the educational impact of the investigation are particularly significant in determining whether to dismiss a case or not. The paucity of prosecutorial information about these prevention-related facts leads us to ask, during the police-related part of the project, whether prosecutors lack this information because of *inadequacies in the investigation, in the transmission of the information by the police to the prosecutor, or both*. Consequently, three specific questions are pertinent here:

(1) Do the police currently discover any such prevention-related facts in their investigations?
(2) If they do, do they recognize these facts as decisionally relevant and transmit them to the prosecutor?
(3) If the police do not currently obtain such information, could they get it from their existing sources without additional investigation?

To answer these questions, we needed to study the police at work. This study focused on an important part of the police investigation, the *interrogation of the suspect*.

As a research method, we chose *non-participant observation* combined with a *semistandardized data-collection instrument*. In our first set of observations, from August 1986 until February 1987, we attended 136 interrogations of fourteen-to twenty-year-old suspects in three kinds of cases typifying juvenile crime: theft, battery, and vandalism. The observers were three lawyers with social-scientific training. About 60 % of the interrogations were conducted by the detective force (Kriminalpolizei) and 40 % by the regular police (Schutzpolizei) (neighborhood investigation units; Bezirksermittlungsdienste). One purpose of the observations was to determine as completely as possible the nature of information gathering during an interrogation.

To determine which data from an interrogation find their way into the files (as part of the transcript, in a "note" by the police officer, or otherwise), *we analyzed additionally the files in the office of the prosecutor*. After the police investigation, nearly all files related to the observed cases were collected. The decisionally relevant information from the records of our police observations as well as information about final notes, data about previous investigations of the suspect, and decisions by the prosecutor were recorded on our instrument.

II. Traditional Prevention-Related Police Knowledge and its Transmission to the Prosecutor

The main themes in the police interrogations were determined by having the observers rate the importance of each theme in a list of standardized themes on a rating scale. Among the themes, *the solution of the crime* and *the proof of guilt* were *clearly dominant*. This finding fits with the characterization of police work in literature (cf. Girtler, 1980, pp. 40 et seq.) as well as with the findings from our own survey of prosecutors (see A II).

The main personal questions are directed at filling out a personal information form for each interrogation of a suspect. In the 136 interrogations that we observed, the police almost always collected *complete data* about sex, nationality, education, occupation, etc..., and by recording these data on the form they were transmitted to the prosecutors. By contrast, the officers learned little about the social status of the suspect's parents, since questions were almost never asked about the parents' education or occupation. Whether an individual interrogator collected and transmitted additional personal information was a matter of his/her individual preference.

To anticipate the final *result*: *Only to an extremly limited extent do the police gather explicitly prevention-related facts in a case, and the extent to which these facts are brought to the attention of the prosecutor is even more limited.*

1. For the application of section 45 of the Juvenile Court Act, a central question is whether the *educational authorities* have reacted with *educational measures* to the crime. In *70 %* of the 136 observed interrogations, the interrogating police officers failed to ask even one question about such reactions. In those few cases in which such information was sought almost exclusively reactions by parents could be discovered ranging from 'moral sermons' about deletion of pocketmoney to corporal punishment. And even these morsels of information were seldom transmitted to the prosecutor.

2. The police were similarly reluctant to let the prosecutor know whether the *discovery of the crime* and *the police investigations of the suspect* had had *"educational effects" in the sense of section 45 of the Juvenile Court Act*. Although the officers in 13 interrogations told the observers that the procedure was having an educational effect on the suspect, in only two of these cases did they then notify the prosecutor of their belief.

3. The issue of the *"attitude of the suspect toward the crime"* (traditionally categorized as "remorse" versus "indifference") is also defined as relevant to prevention. It was discussed in 30 % of the cases, and when the officers perceived "remorse" they communicated this to the prosecutor. When they did not perceive remorse, they generally remained silent about this issue.

4. In an insignificant number of instances information about provocations by the victim, bodily harm suffered by the suspect, and restitution was recorded. When such information was recorded, it was also transmitted to the prosecutor.

5. In addition to the information contained in the interrogation transcript, *"notes"* also played a role in communications between the police and the prosecutor. It is often said in police circles that notes are the vehicle used for any prevention-related observations that police officers have reason to make. In only half of all the interrogations, however, were any notes written, and half of these were mere summaries of the facts in the case. So only a quarter of the interrogations resulted in notes that provided evaluations and/or additional information. Concrete recommendations by the police about the further conduct of the case were transmitted in only five instances.

We see, then, that the police only rarely make explicit statements about prevention-related issues. Is this due to a lack of insight or observation by the police? We think not. The clear impression of our observers was that *the police were simply unaware of the importance of this kind of information for the further conduct of the case.* No wonder, then, that the officers rarely asked about educational reactions by the parents, pay no attention to such information when it does crop up in the interrogation, and fail to transmit such information to the prosecutor. Since the police are not held accountable by the prosecutor for performing the duty to seek and relay the additional information defined as decisionally relevant by section 45, paragraph 2, number 1 of the Juvenile Court Act, the officers see no need to alter their investigatory practices.

III. Possible Neglected Information Sources for Prevention-Related Assessments by the Police

We now wish to clarify another of our principal theses *concerning semi-serious crime typical for young people*. It is that the police, in the course of their routine investigations aimed at solving crimes, make use of sources of information that could also permit them to discover additional, prevention-related factors without substantial additional effort or expenditure and without sacrificing the achievement of their traditional goals.

1. Initial arrest

The initial arrest at the scene of the crime (in minor cases, sometimes a mere stop) is almost always performed by officers of the regular police. Their reports are used by the interrogating and investigating police officers, and later by the prosecutor. It has often been found that official documents simplify reality in ways that serve the purposes of their writers, and these initial investigative reports are no exception. The constant need to give the police officer in charge of a case the fastest possible written basis for his/her interrogation leads those writing up the initial report to become fixated on statements by the suspect that help solve the crime, such as a confession, as well as on facts that tend to legitimate police behavior, such as attempts to evade or resist arrest. Additional information about the person and his/her behavior, initial indicators of his/her attitude toward the crime, and visible effects of his/her being discovered and taken away are normally not recorded. Nor do most initial reports record accusations and other reactions by the parents, although these can be observed when the suspect is released into parental custody or when the parents and the police converse by telephone. *Consequently, an opportunity to pass on unfalsified, spontaneous, and clear impressions about the suspect and his/her parents gets lost.*

2. Background knowledge of police officers

Police officers have a body of background knowledge about a suspect in addition to what they learn from the current case, and in addition to information about the suspect's prior criminal record and prior police contact. The extent and the nature of this background knowledge varies according to whether the regular police (neighborhood investigation units) or the detective force are handling the case.

The neighborhood investigation units, based in local police stations, are distributed across the city. The responsibility of individual police officers is restricted to specific neighborhoods and includes the processing of cases of minor crimes, including minor theft, vandalism, battery, but also, for example, traffic offences. The work of these officers is organized in such a way as to give them a close, face-to-face relationship with the population.

One consequence is that youthful repeat offenders will encounter the same officers or their colleagues at the police station. An officer will have exposure to and knowledge of an offender's lifestyle and social environment which reaches beyond what is gathered during police investigations.

By contrast, the work of an individual officer in the detective force is essentially restricted to a single kind of case, and such an officer deals with suspects from all neighborhoods. Although an extensive understanding of the situation of the suspect is therefore harder to gain, this disadvantage is remedied to a certain extent through exchanges of information inside the organization, such as in conversations and meetings.

3. Statements by the suspect

a) Before a suspected juvenile is formally interrogated, there are many opportunities for an initial conversation with him/her. These include the search, the pick-up before the interrogation, and visits to the home by officers of the neighborhood investigation units.

b) The actual interrogation of the suspect furnishes three kinds of crucial information: *statements by the suspect, behavior of the suspect,* and *educational comments by the police officers* that qualify as "educational measures" under section 45 of the Juvenile Court Act.

Our observations have revealed no incompatibility between solving the crime and discussing the personal relationships and other aspects of the situation of the suspect. These objectives can be served simultaneously in an interrogation without substantial friction. We found, however, that *the posing of questions relevant to sections 43 and 45 of the Juvenile Court Act depended on the initiative of the interrogating officer.* Suspected juveniles varied in their willingness to speak in detail about themselves and their families.

Despite the limited social competence of young people, there have been claims that juvenile offenders will use the interrogation to their tactical advantage. Arguing against this claim is the fact that *sources of information* outlined in this paper are available to the *police for checking statements* made by the suspect. We have indeed observed that police officers, when suspicious of the credibility of statements about the personal life of the suspect, check these statements.

In many interrogations we were able to record appeals by police officers to the conscience of the suspect. The talks ranged from urgent warnings not to enter into a criminal career, through appeals to the good sense of the suspect, all the way to stern, fistbanging lectures. In such 'moral sermons', the suspect was generally told what consequences his/her crime was going to have for him/her and also for the parents. By such lectures the officer is, without realizing it, taking an educational measure, in the sense of section 45 of the Juvenile Court Act, which can justify a dismissal.

4. Information from the parents

Information comes from parents both during and outside the interrogation, and in both the presence and the absence of the suspected juvenile.

a) Before the interrogation, as mentioned above, there are contacts during searches and visits to the home. The most frequent contact with parents takes place over the telephone. Our observers learned from the officers whether such conversations had taken place in any particular case and, if so, what had been said. The information acquired in this way is concentrated on personal relationships, such as between parents and child, the family's financial situation, and the parental reaction to the accusation of a crime. One reaction we have also observed is for parents to ask the officer to give the youth a tough enough lecture to "scare him/her straight".

b) During our observations some of the suspects were accompanied to the interrogation by one or both of their parents. In addition to participating in the interrogation, parents also sometimes conversed with the police before or after the interrogation.

The presence of the parents, however, provides the officers an opportunity to ask questions relevant to a possible dismissal, particularly about actual and expected reactions. Whenever parents took part in the discussion, questions relevant to a dismissal decision were raised. For example, parents sometimes offered information about the suspect's motive or described how the suspect had already been punished. Extensive conversations about individual living conditions, both with and without the presence of the suspect, were numerous.

Statements made by parents who accompany the suspect to the interrogation can be a *rich source of information relevant to prevention.* Such statements can give police officers a first impression of the parents' character and, in many cases, educational behavior.

5. Statements by other persons

a) In some cases the suspect is accompanied to the interrogation by other family members (such as siblings or grandparents), friends, teachers, social workers, or neighbors. The police then come into contact with these other persons, who also tend to be significant reference persons for the suspect. To that extent, what we have just asserted about the value of statements by accompanying parents is true also for these persons.

b) In addition to statements by the suspect and by persons accompanying the suspect, the police can also use statements by other participants, by witnesses, and by victims as sources of information. When the suspect does not confess, the police value statements by other participants as tools to influence the suspect to give up his/her denial or, if that fails, to win a conviction in court.

Let us *sum* up. The police already use, even if not uniformly, a network of comprehensive information sources, although primarily from the *perspective of crime solution.* The investigation is centered on the offence itself, although some of the information that emerges from the investigation is relevant to the decision about "dismissal versus prosecution". Yet, such relevant information is not categorized in this way. Instead, the information is perceived as a "by-product" of the investigation and used, to the extent possible, to solve the crime (for example, as raw material for ice-breaking questions and threats). The contents of the criminal files of the police provide further evidence *that routine police investigation does raise issues relevant to prevention but fails, for lack of demand from the prosecutors, to make the resulting information available for use outside of the police organizations itself.* When we suggest expanding the notion of an "investigation" *to take into account all facts relevant to prevention,* we do not imply that investigational activity should be expanded. We particularly do not suggest that additional interrogations of reference persons of the suspect are conducted; this would not only be more work but would raise issues of individual rights. Instead, such an expanded investigation could rely on more conscious use of the informational value of the contacts that the police now routinely make as they are solving the crime. A reasonable *limit* to such expansion is provided by the principle of *proportionality,* which would prohibit making a legal mountain out of a criminal mole-hill. If, for example, a first apprehension for shoplifting were used as an excuse for a detailed expose of the individual living conditions of the suspect and a finding that he/she is particularly endangered and in acute need of corrective education, this would be going too far.

C. Innovative Informational and Communicational Structures for Exploiting the Preventive Potential in Section 45 of the Juvenile Court Act

I. The Bielefeld Inter-Agency Pilot Project

1. Purpose of the project

Since the beginning of 1987 the office of the Bielefeld prosecutor and the Bielefeld police have been conducting a pilot project in which they make use of the above-described information sources to comply with the intent of section 45 of the Juvenile Court Act. After a long and ultimately stale-mated discussion about preventive opportunities offered by the informal disposition of cases under the Juvenile Court Act and about how to improve the distribution of decisionmaking powers (Kunz, 1984; Kausch, 1980; Riess, 1981), the idea emerged of trying out innovative informational and communicational structures linking prosecutors and police in Bielefeld. This idea was encouraged by the Ministry of Justice and eventually caught on in the prosecutorial and police organizations. Considering the independence of their investigational activities and their collective consciousness, the police outgrew some time ago their traditional characterization as the "assistent to the prosecutor" ("Hilfsbeamter der Staatsanwaltschaft"). Attempts of individual police officers to pass on to the prosecutor their impressions from direct contacts with suspected persons and their families are now transformed through a pilot project into a *uniform and consistent* practice.

The pilot project offers the prosecutor's office an opportunity to change its method of deciding whether to dismiss or prosecute. This decision has until now been based on *formal and global criteria.* The pilot project seeks to make the decisionmaking both *proportinate and case-specific.* This change is to be based on information that the police will deliberately furnish about prevention-related facts. The intended mechanism is the prosecutor's use, when appropriate, of *previously unused sources of information* in deciding how to deal with a case. Subproject C1 of the Special Research Unit 227 has taken responsibility for the evaluation of this pilot project.

2. The information form

To deal appropriately with each individual juvenile offender and thus to expand the supply of information available to prosecutors, a two-paged *information form* was developed. Police officers fill out this form after their investigation and forward it to the prosecutor's office. During this experiment the form is being used in the minor and semi-serious cases most typical of young offenders, namely theft, vandalism, battery.

a) The content of the information form is guided by the legal requirements of sections 43 and 45 of the Juvenile Court Act. Prevention-related information in this context is information that helps determine the importance of the crime in the total life of the juvenile offender. Especially important are questions about educational measures taken by third parties and the educational effects of the investigation. The prosecutor is interested in any *factually supportable impressions of the investigating police officer.* The police officer, in summarizing his/her impressions, may *"recommend considering"* the prosecutorial *options* offered by the Juvenile Court Act. This formulation embodies the compromise that the two agencies have worked out to protect the legal monopoly over decisionmaking power enjoyed by the office of the prosecutor.

b) The choice of a *standardized form* has several benefits. It serves to direct the *attention* and, consequently, the *investigational activity of the police officers toward prevention-related issues.* When the information form was under development, the two agencies both wanted to avoid an aimless "fishing expedition" into the individual living conditions of the suspected juvenile, although it might interfere with a more detailed collection of basic information. A standardized form tends to restrain overbroad inquiries into the suspect's social life. Furthermore, the alternative procedure of requiring more detailed written conclusions in an open-ended format would have led to extensive additional investigatory effort by the police. Since there is no possibility of obtaining more personnel resources, it was necessary to find a procedure that would encourage the police to rely on their existing sources of information. Again, a standardized form was believed to be effective in achieving this effect.

A standardized form is not a panacea, however. The traditional decisionmaking practice was faulted for being so standardized that prosecution decisions hardly took into consideration individual differences among suspects. The designers of the pilot project did not want merely to replace one standardized measure with another. Consequently, specifics that do not fit any of the pre-set categories on the standardized form can still be described briefly in words. At the end of the information form there is a blank column which provides (limited) space for additional information, such as observations about the individual living conditions of the suspect or additional grounds for the action recommended by the police.

3. The implementation

The purpose and content of the new information form were explained in detail to all of the approximately one-hundred affected investigating officers. With the cooperation of the prosecutor's office, a short introduction was given to juvenile justice policy in general as well as to the purposes of section 45 of the Juvenile Court Act in particular. This action, unusual for a hierarchical organization, aroused a substantial interest in this model among the police officers. Some officers concluded that their previous conduct of investigations had been vindicated, while other officers thought that they had got some new ideas for dealing with young suspects from these discussions.

Contemporaneously with the introduction of the pilot project, we observed further interrogations of suspected juveniles in the same three kinds of cases: theft, battery, vandalism. This second set of 166 observations took place between February and July 1987. The purpose was to answer the following questions:

(1) Are the police discovering more prevention-related facts than they did before, namely during the first set of observations?

(2) If so, is this increase in information due to the improved use of existing information sources, or to additional investigatory activities? If the police have expanded their investigations, did this expansion have the effect of subjecting the social life of the suspect to disproportinate scrutiny?

(3) If new kinds of information are being collected, do the police perceive them as relevant and pass them to the prosecutor?

4. The evaluation

The police were instructed by an official memorandum from the Bielefeld district chief of police to fill out the newly introduced form after the police interrogation in all cases of theft, vandalism, and battery with suspects from fourteen to twenty years old. The interrogating officer was further instructed to make an action recommendation about the case. The officer may, however, explicitly state that he/she declines to express an opinion. The completed form is then made part of the files and sent to the prosecutor's office, with our research in the Special Research Unit receiving a copy. The staff of the prosecutor's office notes on each form whether any investigations of the suspect have ever been conducted in the court district (Landgerichtsbezirk) of Bielefeld and what decisions the prosecutor makes. In addition, for each case a file search form is filled out. This procedure makes certain that our project is informed of all information forwarded by the police to the prosecutor's office. In this way, we can include in our analysis all information that the prosecutor has available when he/she makes a decision, including information that becomes available only after the conclusion of the police investigation.

Since the evaluation of these data is complicated and time-consuming, especially because it can take six months or more for a case to be decided, we do not yet have any results from this part of our study to report.

II. Initial Conclusions

1. Findings during observations

We initially restrict ourselves to the core categories: "educational measures" in the social milieu and the "educational effect of the prosecution". While in the first set of observations the suspect was asked about educational sanctions in only about 30 % of the cases and there was information in the files about this issue in only 20 % of all cases, these proportions rose to the point that *the question was posed in 60 % of all cases* in the second set of observations. Correspondingly, in an increasing number of cases the authorities were aware of an actual or expected reaction to the crime in the suspect's social environment. In *35 %* of the cases, *the parents had already reacted or were expected to do so.* In most instances, such expectations were based on clear and specific reasons.

In *27 %* of the cases there was information about a *reaction of the victim.* This consisted primarily of forbidding the suspect from entering the victimized premises again or demanding a reward for information leading to arrest and conviction. In *16 %* of the cases, steps had been taken by miscellaneous persons or institutions. Various such reactions were reported, including termination of the suspect from his/her job, imposition of a curfew making the suspect stay home between certain hours, expulsion from school, and corporal punishment. Multiple responses were possible by our observers.

No increase was registered in information about the "educational" effect of the prosecution. That does not mean, however, that the police officers were unaware of any such effect, since the analysis of the use of the information form makes it clear that they were. The reason is rather that our observers tended to use this coding category only when there was a clear statement by an officer pointing directly toward it.

2. Initial analysis of the information forms

Through September 1987, we tabulated *263* information forms. In *57 %* of the cases, *educational reactions by other persons or institutions* were known about. The parents had reacted in 30 % of the cases, and in an additional 11 % a reaction was expected. A sanction was imposed by additional persons or institutions (such as juvenile home director or youth welfare office) 37 times; 30 times the officer expected to see a sanction imposed by someone from this group.

If we now turn to the *"educational" effect of the prosecution* itself, in one-third of the cases the police officers did not consider themselves capable of estimating this effect, and in *two-thirds of the cases the officers concluded that such an effect had taken place.* An educational effect was ascribed to the interrogation in 34 % of the cases, to police warnings in 32 %.

3. Preliminary conclusion: substantial increase in prevention-related information

The introduction of the information form resulted in an substantial increase in prevention-related information. The officers were apparently sensitized to certain problem areas by the training they had received and by the introduction of the form itself, which they were required to fill out after each interrogation. In addition, the presence of the observers led to the frequent repetition of questions such as "What did your parents say about this?". And this was an intended effect. We noticed that the police officers did not record only the obvious kinds of parental reactions in response to the form's question about "educational measures taken by other persons and institutions". Specific reactions of various other persons and institutions, varying from one case to another, were noted. When the police recorded their belief that their investigation had had preventive effects, they may have been entirely realistic. In many cases of punishable offences by juveniles, the censuring effect of being discovered and being informally identified as the guilty party is enough to arouse the offender's guilty conscience and revive his/her latent appreciation for social norms. Making these norms even clearer by enforcing them with formal sanctions is often superfluous, especially since the threat of such sanctions is always present in any case.

In a survey of a representative sample of fourteen- to seventeen-year-olds in Muenster, conducted by subproject C3 of the Special Research Unit 227, the respondents were asked what the worst consequences would be of committing a crime. While 70 % regarded the police interrogation as "very bad" or "fairly bad", only half the respondents classified the judge's admonition, the fine, the performance of public service, or restitution of the damage as this bad. It is of interest that the only consequences perceived as even worse than contact with the police are time in a juvenile prison (internal working paper, project C3, p. 4).

To summarize, the collection of information has been improved, and this has generally been accomplished *without extending* the scope of criminal investigations, the investigatory effort of the police, the danger to the suspect's individual rights, or the harm to the other interests of the suspect.
The net result has been a broadened basis for the prosecutor's decisions on the disposition of juvenile cases without engaging additional institutions as, for example, the juvenile court aide or the youth welfare office.

III. Prospect for the Future

Research to date tends to support the belief that formalistic decisionmaking based on a few simple criteria set by applicable statutes can be satisfactory for disposing of cases of petty crime. More attention must be paid, however, to applying these criteria *equally and consistently*. According to our preliminary findings, when the criteria are applied consistently the current rate of charges can be substantially reduced.

In prosecuting the semi-serious crimes that are typical of juveniles, prosecutors have taken practically no cognizance of those prevention-related elements of the case that section 45 of the Juvenile Court Act defines as prerequisites for a dismissal. The Bielefeld Inter-Agency Pilot Project may be able to close this perceptual gap by exploiting existing sources of police information. If so, a reasonable concept of "prevention" may be promoted and the rate of charges may be consistently diminished for the semi-serious crimes typically committed by juveniles.

The Bielefeld Inter-Agency Pilot Project harbors not only hopes but also dangers (cf. Voss, 1986, p. 80).

One danger lies in the possibility that prosecutors will exploit the individualized, prevention-related information that becomes newly available purely to *legitimize* formalistic case dispositions in the area of petty crime. Such a prosecutorial strategy could lead to an increasing substitution of "preventional" dismissals for presumption-of-innocence dismissals, and this trend would be an instance of criminalization rather than prevention.

If the sources of information on which prosecutors rely are expanded without limit, social control could be intensified and sanctions could be imposed on juveniles for behaviors that had not been sanctioned before ("net-widening effect") (Brusten, 1987, p. 207; comprehensive to the criticism of diversion cf. Heinz, 1987b, p. 131). There could even be reason to fear that the enrichment of prosecutorial information will lead to an increase in the absolute number of cases going to trial, not to an increase in the rate of dismissals. The research project will endeavour to discover how prosecutors use the prevention-related information they receive. Meanwhile, initial indications lead us to believe that *both the information and the recommendation* that prosecutors obtain from the *police* could justify a much greater rate of preventive dismissals than we have observed so far.

References

Bohnert, J. (1983): Strafe und Erziehung im Jugendstrafrecht. In: JZ 1983, 517

Brusten, M. (1987): Die polizeiliche Vernehmung und ihre Bedeutung für das spätere Strafverfahren. In: 10. Strafverteidigertag. Landsberg, 207

Eisenberg, U. (1985): Jugendgerichtsgesetz mit Erläuterungen. 2nd ed., Munich

Feltes, T. (1983): Der Staatsanwalt als Sanktions- und Selektionsinstanz. In: Kerner, H.-J. (Ed.): Diversion statt Strafe?. Heidelberg, 55

Feltes, T., Janssen, H., and Voss, M. (1983): Die Erledigung von Strafverfahren durch Staatsanwaltschaft und Gericht – Brauchen wir die sogenannten Diversionsmodelle in der Bundesrepublik. In: Kerner, H.-J., Kury, H., and Sessar, K. (Eds.): Deutsche Forschungen zur Kriminalitätsentstehung und Kriminalitätskontrolle. Vol. 2, Cologne et al., 858

Girtler, R. (1980): Polizei-Alltag. Opladen

Heinz, W. (1984): Strategien der Diversion in der Jugendgerichtsbarkeit der Bundesrepublik Deutschland. In: RdJB 1984, 291

Heinz, W. (1987a): "Schneid abkaufen" oder "weiche Welle" – die Alternativen?. Materialien zum Referat bei den bayerischen Jugendamtsleitertagungen 1987. Unpublished manuscript

Heinz, W. (1987b): Neue ambulante Maßnahmen nach dem Jugendgerichtsgesetz. In: MschrKrim 1987, 129

Heinz, W., and Spiess, G. (1983): Alternativen zu formellen Reaktionen im deutschen Jugendstrafrecht. In: Kerner, H.-J., Kury, H., and Sessar, K. (Eds.): Deutsche Forschungen zur Kriminalitätsentstehung und Kriminalitätskontrolle. Vol. 2, Cologne et al., 896

Kausch, E. (1980): Der Staatsanwalt. Ein Richter vor dem Richter?. Berlin

Kunz, K.-L. (1980): Die Einstellung wegen Geringfügigkeit durch die Staatsanwaltschaft (§§ 153 Abs. 1, 153a Abs. 1 StPO). Königstein

Kunz, K.-L. (1984): Das strafrechtliche Bagatellprinzip. Berlin

Lundman, R.J. (1976): Will Diversion Reduce Recidivism?. In: Crime and Delinquency 1976, 428

Morris, A. (1978): Diversion of Juvenile Offenders from the Criminal Justice System. In: Tutt, N. (Ed.): Alternative Strategies for Coping with Crime. Oxford/London, 45

Ostendorf, H. (1987): Kommentar zum Jugendgerichtsgesetz. Neuwied/Darmstadt

Pfeiffer, Ch. (1983): Justiz und Kriminalprävention. In: Schüler-Springorum, H. (Ed.): Jugend und Kriminalität. Frankfurt a.M., 128

Riess, P. (1981): Die Zukunft des Legalitätsprinzips. In: NStZ 1981, 2

Sonnen, B.-R. (1981): Die §§ 45 und 47 JGG – Eine Betrachtung der Anwendungspraxis und der Möglichkeiten. In: DVJJ (Ed.): Die jugendrichterlichen Entscheidungen – Anspruch und Wirklichkeit. Munich, 177

Steffen, W. (1976): Analyse polizeilicher Ermittlungstätigkeit aus der Sicht des späteren Strafverfahrens. Wiesbaden

Uhlig, S. (1986): Die Polizei – Herrin des Strafverfahrens?. In: DRiZ 1986, 247

Voss, M. (1986): Diversion: Eine neue Form der sozialen Kontrolle. In: Müller, S., and Otto, H.-U. (Eds.): Damit Erziehung nicht zur Strafe wird. Bielefeld, 79

9.
Delinquent Behavior in Adolescence: Potential and Constraints of Preventive Strategies in School Settings

Uwe Engel and Klaus Hurrelmann

We consider delinquent and desintegrative behavior in adolescence as a function of social structure and as an expression of status insecurity. Anomic behavior mainly is outwardly directed behavior that attacks social bonds and makes social relationships dissociative because of its 'aggressive' character.

In the first part of the paper we present the results of an empirical analysis that is based on a self-administered standardized questionaire. The probability sample is made up of 1,717 students in seventh and ninth grades in all main types of secondary schools in Northrhine-Westfalia. We use a self-report technique covering several forms of delinquent behavior. The empirical analysis strongly confirms the hypotheses, according to which the anticipation of unfavourable mobility chances, feelings of injustice regarding the basic status allocation process, school failure and achievement-related status dynamics as well as structural characteristics are expected to be major sources of delinquent behavior in adolescence.

In the second part of the paper we discuss the implications for preventive strategies in school settings with the aim to prevent delinquent behavior. We start from the central thesis that preventive and corrective interventions can only be effective when they are focused on early steps in the genesis of delinquency and when they strenghten both personal as well as social resources. We give an overview of some school based individual and environmental intervention programs.

1. Some Social Antecedents of Delinquent Behavior: The Importance of School-Related Variables

The empirical analysis that we are going to present will be taken as an exemplary analysis that points to both the *possibilities and limits of social intervention*. Every strategy designed for this purpose must necessarily take into account the *nature of the conditions* that give rise to, or that at least contribute to the occurrence of the respective target-behavior. First, we have to consider conditions closely associated with the individuals, even though these conditions are, in turn, mostly founded in social background and living conditions as well as in features of the social environment, into which the individuals are settled. Scholastic or academic achievement and self-esteem, for instance, can be taken as examples of this kind of conditions. Furthermore, stress is to be laid on social conditions referring to the value system as institutionalized in the respective social setting, as well as on conditions referring to the opportunity structure (e.g., 'unfavourable mobility chances', below). But we have also to acknowledge conditions that are genuinely social in nature, as for instance, the strength of the social bond that ties together the individuals of a community, a characteristic which to a high degree is a clear function of the social structure underlying this community (Engel 1988).

Taken together, the potential sources of delinquent behavior , the target variable with which we are dealing here, cover a wide range of conditions, and it is one aim of the following analysis to give an idea of the span of heterogeneity introduced in this respect:

On the one hand, we have properties of individuals, on the other hand properties of the social structure. To introduce the former type of property into empirical analysis, is a routinely performed task. To introduce the latter type of property not only in a heuristical, but in an explicity measured fashion, requires both a theoretical concept of social structure and a methodology to map this concept in empirical research. Both is available. With regard to the former, we adopt the notion of structure as formulated very clearly by Peter Blau (1981), who straightforwardly states that structural properties are those higher-order properties that cannot be used to classify the component members of the collectivity at hand (e.g., the degree of criss-cross, below); a definition which closely resembles the conceptual base of multi-level analysis as it is developed in the realm of sociological methodology.

Type of delinquent behavior studied

The present analysis is concerned with anomic, socially desintegrative behavior. To be *socially* desintegrative, the behavior must be *outwardly* directed behavior. To be socially *desintegrative*, it should be a type of behaviour that is apt to weaken the 'social bond', i.e. that makes the social relationship less associative or even more dissociative. We regard behavior that either *is* or that *tends to become* 'aggressive' as behavior meeting this criterion of being anomic. As indicators of 'aggressive', outwardly directed behavior, such types of (delinquent) actions are considered relevant that reflect the exercise of power over other individuals or things or that reflect the inclination of being involved in such power-relationships. Analysis will therefore be based on self-reports on special types of usually so-called 'delinquent behavior. In particular, we built an index that records, for every student, whether or not at least one out of the following activities did occur within the last twelve months:

List of indicators used:

1. Things of other people or public things intentionally destroyed or damaged.
2. Someone intentionally trashed.
3. Someone handled roughly in a fight.
4. Someone threatened with a weapon (e.g. knife, brass knuckles) to force him/her to do what is asked.
5. Robbed someone of something.
6. Somewhere broken into a house, car, or automatic vending machine.

Perhaps with few exceptions, these forms of behavior may be relatively harmless in the age-groups under study. They can be regarded, however, as a potential source of more violent forms of aggression taking place under somewhat changed social conditions. Even low-level aggressiveness may be regarded as a weak predecessor of behavior that more pronouncedly reflects the "drive to hurt and harm others because they stand in the way of one's own self assertion" (Galtung 1964:95).

Frame of reference, hypotheses and findings

Table 1 displays the results concerning the estimated *relative risk*, of being involved in the delinquent activities studied, due to the perception of two basic aspects of the social career of juveniles. The relevance of both 'feelings of injustice' and 'unfavourable mobility chances' can be derived from a conception of youth that takes into account the important role youth plays with regard to the basic allocation process in society, that is the process, in the course of which the differently privileged social positions and roles are taken over by the rising generation.

The underlying *ideological* conception of achievement-oriented societies like the FRG implies that it is the formal education completed in youth that gives rise to the social positions later reached in adulthood. This ideology strongly ties youth to the basic societal allocation process in society (Kreutz 1974). The *social organisation of youth* established to assure this distribution of advantages implies therefore both the chance of long-term upward mobility as well as the risk of permanently lowered social position, and it is precisely the very possibility of such career pattern that causes 'status insecurity' (Kreutz 1974) to be a fundamental characteristic of the passage to adulthood. This insecurity will show its effects in particular in cases where the successful mobility out of school is (subjectively) at risk. Thus, mobility chances are defined here in terms of the subjective probability to get in the future the desired school-leaving-certificate.

A second feature of the societal allocation process that affects juvenile behavior is the degree to which the basic criteria governing this process are felt as being unjust. We expect this to be an important condition, because achievement is only the necessary, but not sufficient condition for being allocated to the positions in the social structure. Instead of this, allocation recurs heavily to *cooptation* or *sponsored* mobility. Operationally, the *just-unjust-evaluation* relates to one cooptation indicator: Every student was asked to indicate how fair or unfair he finds the extent to which getting-the-desired-school-leaving-certificate is dependent on whether or not the teachers do like him.

The hypothesis is that the tendency to choose *deviant* means is much more likely in cases where the juvenile subjectively fails to meet the criteria governing the basic allocation process and/or in cases where these very criteria are felt as being unjust (cf. Kreutz 1974).

Table 1: *Delinquent behavior, feelings of injustice, unfavourable mobility chances, and sex*

LOGISTIC MODEL

	Original result	Transformations in terms of probabilities	ratios
	β	a	e^{β}
Basic risk (Constant)	-1.16	.24	0.31
Unfavourable mobility chances	.88	.21	2.4
Feelings of injustice	.24	.06	1.3
Sex (male)	.89	.21	2.4

Coding: Delinquent behavior: 1 if given, 0 otherwise;
Unfavourable mobility chances, feelings of injustice, being male:
1 if condition applies, 0 otherwise (respectively)

GOF: Chi^2: 2.83; df=4; p= .59

As Table 1 shows, both hypotheses are well confirmed: The risk of being involved in delinquent activities is raised in both cases of perceived unfavourable mobility chances and felt injustice.

Basically, Table 1 displays the result of a *logistic* model that serves to estimate, for each set of conditions involved, the natural logarithm *ln* of the ratio of (the cell frequencies of) delinquent to nondelinquent behavior (f_1/f_0), as an *additive* function of the very conditions involved, i.e.:

$$\ln(f_1/f_0) = \beta_0 + \beta_a A + \beta_b B + \beta_c C \qquad (1)$$

(A: Unfavourable mobility chances, B: Feelings of injustice, C: Sex (male), coded as 1 if the condition applies and 0 otherwise, respectively; f_j: *estimated* frequency of individuals in state j (j=0,1)). Since A, B, and C are handled as dichotomous attributes, there are basically 2x2x2=8 configurations of conditions involved, for which the logarithm of the ratio of delinquent to nondelinquent behavior is estimated, and where due to the 0-1 (dummy, not effects) coding used of A, B, and C, respectively, it is the case that only ß-coefficients pertaining to an *existing* condition (i.e., to an attribute variable being in state 1) enter the equation.

Because the equation predicts the natural logarithm of the ratio of corresponding cell frequencies (and not this ratio itself), any attempt to attach empirical meaning to the original result is somewhat complicated. There arises a straightforward interpretability, however, by applying the anti-log function to both sides of the original equation. This mathematical transformation converts the original equation (1) into

$$(f_1/f_0)=e^{\beta 0} \times e^{\beta aA} \times e^{\beta bB} \times e^{\beta cC} \qquad (2)$$

The estimates of effect obtained in this way are displayed in the extreme right coloumn of Table 1. First, we get an estimated risk of 0.31. Since this equals about 0.33, this finding leads us to the expectation of observing delinquent and nondelinquent behavior in a ratio of about 1:3 provided none of the explicit conditions involved in the analysis does apply. Taking this basic risk as the reference point for comparison, it is expected to be raised, for instance, by the factor 2.4 due to unfavourable mobility chances, in this way yielding a risk ratio being about two and a half times the basic risk (i.e., 0.31 x 2.4=0.74). Provided such unfavourable mobility chances, this leads to the expectation to observe occurrences of delinquent and nondelinquent behavior, respectively, in a ratio of about 3:4. In this way, the estimated ratio of delinquent to nondelinquent behavior can be found simply by *multiplying* the basic risk with the risk factors that are actually present (i.e., being in state 1, not 0).

There is another useful way to look at the data and to get an idea of the *relative* risks of delinquency involved. This is provided by a technique of transforming the original ß-coefficients developed by James S. Coleman (1981:30f.). Except for the constant, these *a*-coefficients (with *a* denoting alpha) estimate the effect of the respective independent variable in decreasing or increasing the probability (percentage) of delinquent behavior when this probability is at 0.5. And with regard to the constant, the *a* coefficient amounts to the estimated probability of delinquent behavior when all explicit risk factors are *absent* (i.e. being zero).

To visualize the main findings in Table 1, we have taken the *a*-coefficients pertaining to the constant, unfavourable mobility chances, and to feelings of injustice, respectively. Since they are close to the corresponding coefficients of the *linear* model, we inserted them into the respective linear equation to predict the probability of becoming involved in delinquent activities. Disregarding the additional expected increase, in this probability, due to being male (i.e., the coefficient for males), the impact of unfavourable mobility chances and feelings of injustice, respectively, may be shown through both the location and slope of the plane within the analytical space built-up by these very variables. Figure 1 displays the effects of unfavourable mobility chances ($a_{ch}=0.21$) and feelings of injustice ($a_{i}=.06$), while controlling for the effect of being male. In particular, Figure 1 shows the picture for females. To get the respective picture for males, the expected increase of $a_{m}=.21$ may be added to the constant ($a_{0}=0.24$). This will shift the overall probability from 0.24 up to 0.45 while leaving the slope of the plane unchanged. (Keeping in mind that this holds in an approximate fashion only, since the computations are based on the a-coefficients used here to resemble the original coefficients of the linear model, but not on these linear coefficients themselves, which, strictly speaking, should be the case).

Figure 1 clearly visualises the expected increase due to either poor mobility chances or feelings of injustice regarding the basic allocation process, or due to both conditions, i.e., the overall effect.

Fig. 1: Probability of delinquent behavior, estimated as a function of unfavourable mobility chances and feelings of injustice, while controlling for gender

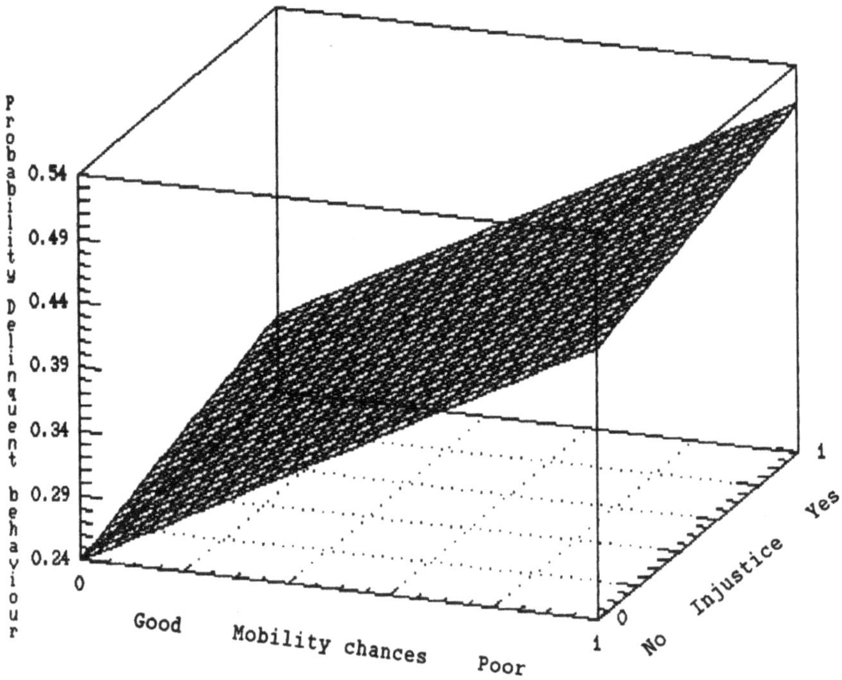

Table 2 displays the findings concerning an important class of social conditions, that is conditions related to the topic of *social rank in society.*

The first condition is the *objective achievement status*: According to the conception outlined above, the risk of (long-term) downward mobility is regarded as one of the more basic social conditions that affect the behavior of juveniles. This risk is highly dependent on the juvenile's achievement status when the latter is being measured in a quasi objective fashion. A *low* achievement status is assumed to be indicative of a *high* risk of downward mobility, and vice versa. The risk of failing to meet the achievement-related role expectations in youth is expected to be given above all in cases of poor school performances (i.e., threatened demotion, repeating a school-class once or more, changing school because of bad marks).

An index was therefore constructed that records, for every student, whether or not at least one of these conditions apply.

As displayed in *table 2*, provided such a low achievement status, the basic probability of $p=.13$ is raised by .16.

In populations of students – like the one with which we are concerned here – *social rankings* on dimensions with high degree of social visibility within the peer-group of class- or school-mates plays an important role. Taking again the achievement dimension, each student was asked to locate him or herself on an achievement-scale having an explicit midpoint indicating school performances on-average when compared with those of the class-mates. This *subjective* achievement is then considered high in cases of performances lying *above* this perceived social average.

Table 2: Probability of delinquent behavior as a function of social and structural characteristics in the peer community at school: Linear model

ß		Effects (additive)
0.13		Constant
0.16	A	Low objective achievement status
0.19	B	Sex (male)
0.06	C	Disequilibrium between objective and subjective achievement status
0.05	D	Low objective achievement status and lack of criss-cross
0.06	E	Lack of criss-cross

$$p(\text{delinquency}) = \beta_0 + \beta_a A + \beta_b B + \beta_c C + \beta_d D + \beta_e E$$

p(delinquency) – *Estimated* probability of delinquency

We then combined the both conditions objective and subjective achievement status in terms of a concept taken out of multidimensional rank theory, that is *rank disequilibrium*. This concept refers to the degree to which the ranks within a given status set deviate from one another, so that the individual occupies high and low ranks at the same time, regardless of *which* of the ranks is high or low (Galtung 1966b:126). In particular, we are concerned here with the case where the objective achievement status as measured by the history of school-performance does not agree with the self-perceived subjective achievement regarding the classroom-community, that is with the effects of a disequilibrium between objective and subjective achievement status; a condition that raises the basic probability by .06.

One topic in theory is the conflict-preventing function of criss-cross. For the purposes at hand, a few remarks may suffice. Criss-cross is a concept that does not refer to individual holders of status-sets, but to social aggregates of such individuals. In the present analysis, this aggregate unit is the community of classmates. Criss-cross, therefore, designates here a certain characteristic of the social structure within these very classroom-communities. To establish the degree of criss-cross, at least two rank dimensions must be taken into account. In the present analysis, this is subjective achievement and social power regarding the class-and schoolmates, respectively, each being considered here as a dichotomy (i.e., as classifying people either as being a T for 'topdog' or an U for 'underdog'). Combined systematically (i.e., crosstabulated), these represent what is termed the social matrix of a community (Galtung 1966a:134). In the present analysis, this matrix has four cells corresponding to the four possible status sets (i.e., TT, TU, UT, UU, for being either a 'topdog' or 'underdog' on the 1st and 2nd rank dimension, respectively). The question then arises of how the members of the community are being allocated to these four possible status sets, and the basic idea, here adopted to classroom-communities, is that lack of criss-cross is perfect when there are no individuals who can serve as bridges between completely disparate conflict groups in the structure. This is the case when *no links* exist between the status sets involved. There *exists* 'a link between two status sets if they have a status in common'. (Galtung, 1966a:137). Thus, between TT and TU, for instance, there is *one* link (holders of these sets would share the first status), but between TT and UU as well as between TU and UT, there are *no* links, and, hence, *no* criss-cross.

If then 'the conditions for very dissociative relations should arise, there will be nothing to impede it, which is the major point about criss-cross' (Galtung 1966a:138).

Table 2 shows, among others, two interesting results. First, lack of criss-cross is a *structural* condition that raises the probability of becoming involved in delinquent activities. Secondly, in cases of lack of criss-cross, a low objective achievement status is coupled with an additionally raised risk of delinquency.

Relations to other studies

Our study supports evidence from other studies that show a low achievement status in school and an unstable position in the peer group as the main predictors for delinquent behavior in adolescence. Many studies have demonstrated that, whether measured by self-report or by official police data, male delinquency is related to academic performance at school (Elliott & Voss 1974; Polk & Schafer 1971; Rutter 1980). While youths from low socioeconomic and minority background are more likely to experience academic failure than middle-class students, the experience of academic failure or success itself appears to be related to delinquency (McPartland & McDill 1977; Stinchcombe 1964). Juvenile delinquents consistently perform more poorly in school than do nondelinquents. Frease (1973) found that officially reported delinquency was highest among boys with low grades who did not like school and lowest among boys with high grades who liked school. Youths who experience success in school are less likely to become delinquent, while those who fail in school are more likely to engage in disruptive classroom behavior and delinquency.

These results suggest that the process of succeeding or failing in school, is related to delinquency. Elliott and Voss (1974) suggest that school failure leads to *alienation from school* and subsequently to drop out and delinquency. They view delinquency as an adaptation to school failure, arguing that those who fail in school become frustrated and are rejected and shunned by others, leading to negative attitudes to school and alternative standards of conduct. Gold (1978) views delinquency as a *defense against feelings of low self-esteem* derived from school failure. He suggests that youths who fail in school seek recognition by engaging in criminal behaviors with delinquent peers. Such students may provide each other with support, rewards, and reinforcements for delinquent behavior that they have not found in a conventional context. There is also evidence that a low degree of commitment to education is related to delinquency. (Elliott & Voss 1974; Brusten & Hurrelmann 1973; Olweus 1983; Apter & Goldstein 1986).

2. Implications for Preventive and Corrective Strategies in School Settings

Exact knowledge of the antecedent conditions, the genesis, and the further development of deviant and delinquent behavior in adolescence is a prerequisite for effective intervention strategies. The efficiency of all intervention measures whose goal is to positively influence the development of adolescents, depends on how precisely they correspond and are related to one of the consecutive stages in the genesis of deviance (Hurrelmann 1987; Hurrelmann, Kaufmann, & Lösel, 1987).

2.1 Classification of Interventions

Intervention strategies can be classified by considering whether they are oriented toward

a) Social demands of the status transition
b) Risk factors leading to delinquent behavior
c) Already existing (manifest) delinquent behavior
d) Consolidation of delinquent behavior and development of a deviant career.

The first two steps characterize preventive interventions, the second two steps postventive (corrective) interventions. Thus, we can take up and modify the concepts known as 'primary, secondary and tertiary prevention' generally used in medicine and psychology (Caplan & Grunebaum, 1967; Cowen, 1983).

We use the term *preventive intervention* to denote all measures that are taken before delinquent behavior becomes manifest. We can distinguish measures of prevention that are a) directed toward an improvement in personal well-being and the social living conditions of a person or group of persons in general, in order to prevent the occurrence of risk constellations leading to delinquent behavior; b) directed toward concrete factors and factor constellations which undisputedly carry a high risk for the occurrence of delinquent behavior.

We use the term *corrective intervention* (in the sense of 'postventive intervention') to designate those measures which

c) focus on already existing delinquent behavior with the aim to contain or to remedy this behavior and
d) which attempt, by remedial actions, to prevent further development, consolidation, or reinforcement of the delinquent behavior and are oriented to the goal of rehabilitation.

In the ideal case, all of the types and forms of intervention mentioned here must be implemented in coordination with one another, if deviance and delinquent behavior is to be fought effectively. Intervention measures must take into consideration all the stages involved in the genesis of problem behavior, because otherwise, they will remain incomplete and unbalanced.

If we want to direct intervention practices towards influencing both *environmental (social)* resources *and personal (individual)* resources, this requires both measures that focus on the individual and are applied directly to the persons concerned, and socially oriented measures that relate to the environment and the social and ecological living conditions.

Measures that focus on the *individual* must essentially aim to encourage the competence of the person in such a way as to enable an appropriate coping with the behavioral demands of the social environment. The general aim of these measures of these intervention must be to reduce the discrepancies between individual action competence and strategies for coping with situations to a level where the situation becomes manageable for the individual person.

Measures focussing on the environment take into account the *social resources* which determine, whether or not adolescents in stressful social constellations can count on support from their social environment. The social network of which adolescents are a part – either through informal groups or formal organizations – decides on the amount of emotional, instrumental, material and practical support given when stressful situations and events arise (Gottlieb 1981).

In figure 2, the main types of intervention mentioned are classified.

Figure 2: Classification of Interventions

	TARGET	
STAGE	personal resources	social resources
preventive	TYPE A – training of scholastic abilities – training of social skills – counceling	TYPE C – clarification of social rules and standards of fairness – improvement of organizational and social climate – strengthening of channels of participation
corrective	Type B – behavior modification – corrective treatment	Type D – reconstructing the social network – strengthening the control system

The majority of crime preventive and corrective intervention measures clearly have personal resources as their target. However, our research results suggest that *contextual* and *situational* rather than dispositional conditions provide a triggering function for a number of crimes. Only few risk factors for delinquency are found that exclusively are bound to *personal* resources. Moreover, the corrective treatment and therapy concepts are very ineffective, very costly, time consuming, and do not effect the overall prevalence rate of delinquency.

We will now shorty assess some of the intervention strategies of all four types that are applied in school settings.

2.2 Strategies of Intervention Focussing on Personal Resources

The most often applied programs of the preventive type in school settings (type A) rely on *ability training programs* which are intended to increase individual's skills in scholastic achievement and avoiding social influences to engage in undesired behavior . These training programs apparently reduce delinquency primarily by improving scholastic achievement, increasing liking for school, success experiences in school and reducing negative peer influence. The strong positive effect on academic learning mainly results from the alternative teaching techniques used. Teacher training can be used to enhance teacher's skills of diagnosing areas of weakness, individualizing learning plans, providing feedback and frequent rewards contingent on individual progress, and grouping students for instructions, according to their achievement levels (Hawkins & Lam 1987).

Social competence training programs are based on curriculum schedules in psychological and sociological training within the classroom. Such programs are dealing with a variety of areas such as effective communicating, identifying and expressing feelings, strengthening self-concept and relations to peers and adults, reflecting social, cultural and legal norms, etc. (Spivack & Shure 1982).

Increasing professional attention has focused on various *consultative* avenues through which to enhance the already existing helping ability of teachers as well as provide them with new. Traditionally, professionals may have been called in to deal directly with problem children confronting a given teacher. Currently, there is beginning to be more of a consultation focus toward teachers and in utilization of teaching personnel in a variety of possible helping roles ranging from direct services to preventive programs. The idea is to increase teachers' understanding of the meaning of pupils' classroom activities as well as effect their responses and reactions to them (McPartland & McDill 1977).

The most often used programs of type B, the corrective stage of interventions targetted to personal resources, are programs of *behavior modification*. These programs involve attempts to enable an individual to gain rewards through desired behavior and to learn to obstain from undesired behavior. These programs can be implemented readily in school settings since here various aspects of adolescents' development can be monitored and manipulated over a period of years. By virtue of their contact with the children the classroom teachers are key figures in the reference system of adolescents. They can have a pervasive influence by their impact on their students' attitudes, emotions, and behaviors (Burchard & Burchard 1987).

All training programs of this type show positive outcomes. This is not to a surprise: Classrooms traditionally have been the place where a good deal of a child's academic and social behavior has been modified. Teachers have always been functioning as behavior modifiers using a variety of contingency sanctions (such as praise, grades, punishment) except they have been generally unaware that these principles can have real impact if used in a more consistent and deliberate fashion.

There are examples of behavioral programs that have been successfully applied in a more preventive intention with educationally handicapped children exhibiting poor self-control and low frustration tolerance as well as self-destructive and emotionally disturbed behavior. The research examining teacher attention effects and use of token reinforcement principles demonstrates that educators can become effective contingency managers in a variety of settings.

2.3 Strategies of Intervention Focussing on Social Resources

There is a growing recognition of the fact that any fixation on measures related to individual resources of children or adolescents "at risk" is bound to be ineffective. As our empirical study shows, the individual capacities and competences for coping with risk constellations cannot be considered to be context-free. Modern socialization theory sees personality development as an active process of appropriation of and interaction with the physical and social environment on the one hand and the person's organism on the other hand and conceives of the individual as a productive processor of internal and external reality (Hurrelmann 1988). Delinquent behavior, in this perspective, is a specific outcome of the processing of reality which demonstrates a form of incompetence to cope with external and internal demands. It must be seen in its developmental and social context and is both a personal and interpersonal response that serves several functions for the individual in his or her specific situation -for example, to solve an interpersonal dilemma, a retaliatory response to a perceived threat, the confirmation of the social position in the power hierarchy of the peer group, a response to a frustrating experience, etc.

Intervention strategies in this tradition have to reduce dysfunctional stress arising from social demands and expectations and to increase the social competences which foster an autonomous and prosocial mastery of environmental demands. Proposed general measures of prevention in this tradition are, for example: reduction of socioeconomic disadvantage; eradication of unemployment; family allowances for poor families; expansion of integration programs for marginal groups; reduction in the presentation of violence in the mass media; eradication of ghetto-type housing conditions; reductions in urban density and restricted living conditions; ecologically adequate design of workplaces and leisure facilities (Lösel 1987).

As research confirms, adolescents who are not committed to the school culture are more likely to engage in delinquent behavior. According to this evidence, efforts of delinquency prevention must focus on changing the *social climate of school settings* in order to develop attachments between the school and the individual student with the aim of replacement of negative social relationships with positive ones. Schools, in this view, have to offer opportunities for meaningful involvement, opportunites to train the necessary skills, and rewards for work well done (Hersov, Berger, & Schafer 1978; Hawkins & Lam 1987).

Thus, there is a growing awareness of the potential effectiveness of measures in school settings affecting the social resources. These concepts of prevention mainly have received support from a study carried out by Rutter, Maughan, Mortimor, and Ouston (1979) on the effectiveness of Inner London secondary schools: In the relatively effective schools, which demostrated a high level of scholastic achievement and attendence and a low level of delinquency and maladaptive behavior, the following social and organizational factors were identified: Academic matters were accentuated, instruction was organized in an active manner, differentiated reward and punishment was implemented, the students were held responsibility for school activities, the staff organization and the social relationships among teachers were relatively stable, and the staff had a relatively homogeneous educational and pedagogical program of activities and daily routines.

How can this be applied to school settings? One of the most comprehensive preventive programs in this area is the project "Positive Action Through Holistic Education" (PATHE) which was implemented in four middle and three high schools for three years as part of the US Office of Juvenile Justice and Delinquency Prevention's Alternative Education Initiative (Gottfredson 1986). The program sought to reduce school disorder by changing three key student attitudes and experiences. It sought to a) decrease academic failure experiences among students in the participating schools, b) to increase social bonding, including attachment to the people in the school, caring about what others think about oneself, involvement in conventional activities, and commitment of time and energy to the enterprise of schooling, and c) to improve student's self-concepts. The program was based on the idea that changes to the general school climate would be instrumental in bringing about the desired changes in student experiences and attitudes. It sought to create a climate of mutual respect and cooperation and a sense of belonging among teachers, administrators, and students; to increase student and faculty involvement in planning and implementing school change efforts, to increase the clarity, fairness, and consistency of school rule enforcement; and to increase teachers' classroom management skills (Gottfredson 1986).

Other innovations were aimed at increasing successful transition to careers and postsecondary education, thus taking account of the perceived unfavorable mobility chances that have been found in empirical studies such as our own. The Career Exploration Programs provided highschool students opportunities to participate in activities designed to introduce them to technical carees such as engineering, computer science, and industrial technology. The Job-Seeking Skills Program provided training in specific skills for finding and keeping a job (for example, interview etiquette) and offered opportunities for broadened career awareness. This intervention was aimed at increasing the educational and occupational attainment of youths by increasing their job readiness, and at increasing students' commitment to conventional goals (Jason, Durlak, & Holton-Walker 1984; Gottfredson 1986).

In the area of corrective interventions, a major set of activities was intended to provide social services to marginal students. These services were intended to increase experiences to academic success, increase self-concept, and strengthen students' bonds to the social order. These programs made use of the fact that the school setting is a complex *social network* which offers many relationships for students involved. Besides direct services for students at risk, these programs suggest indirect services: the provision of assistance to teachers and fellow students as significant others who can strengthen the social support for at-risk students. In school settings, the peer group represents an important and hitherto neglected avenue through which social support is neglected. Cross-age tutoring programs, giving students at risk the role of tutors, can, for example, serve to enhance the tutor's self esteem and self confidence. Troubled students – or: students identified by teachers or peers to be trouble-makers – in these peer-tutoring programs can demonstrate their skills in academic and non-academic areas and can lead these students to experience and to believe that they are valued members of the school community (Antonucci & Depner 1982; Apter 1982).

These programs are designed to engage youths in meaningful activities at improving conditions in the school. Through these activities youths should begin to see the school as an institution of legitimate authority, i.e., that the procedures employed by the institution are fair and that the school and the larger community are places worthy of substancial investment of time and energy, and that they themselves are persons of worth. The projects were designed to test the hypothesis that involvement in decision making would reduce delinquency because it would lead to inreased belief in laws and perceived fairness of laws, and it would increase self-esteem (Gold 1978; Gottfredson 1986).

These programs contain part of activities that can be labeled as *"social network construction/reconstruction"*: Supporting a student to establish satisfactive social interactions with peers and adults and representatives of formal institutions, attempting to cut off those relations that lead to delinquent sub-group activities and strengthening or establishing those relations that support socially desired behavior (Gottlieb 1981).

PATHE Evaluation Results show, for example, that the program was successful in implementing a comprehensive approach to delinquency prevention. The academic and social lives of the students were affected, and the entire school community, parents, and the larger community participated in the effort:

"The PATHE experience implies that altering the school organization can be an effective approach to delinquency prevention. Involving the school staff, students, and community members in planning and implementing change; using information to identify weakness and focusing resources on those weakness; retraining school staff when necessary, making changes in the curriculum and discipline procedures in the school; and creating clear standards for implementing performance is a collection of accomplishments difficult to achieve. But, taken together, these activities reduce the risk of involvement in delinquent activities for the general school population (Gottfredson 1986, p. 798).

3. Caveats and Constraints: Ethical and Methodological Problems

As our paper has shown, there are many arguments available to support a broad spectrum of resources of preventive and corrective intervention in the case of juvenile delinquency. However, research in this area is not yet on safe ground. Delinquency intervention programs have seldom been demonstrated to be effective in terms of strong methodological standards because they rarely have been implemented in ways that allow a careful assessment of the manner in which they are carried out and the features that are responsible for their effectiveness or ineffectiveness. This is not only due to methodical problems of evaluation, but also to the fundamental ethical and political implication of delinquency intervention.

Among the manifold methodical and ethical problems of intervention research one big topic is the problem of risk assessment, diagnosis, and prognosis of delinquent behavior (Farrington, Ohlin, & Wilson 1986; Burchard & Burchard 1987).The appropriate research procedures are not always constructed on a reliable and consensual theoretical and/or political basis. Preventive measures differ from corrective ones by their increased diagnosis of demands and risks. Although longitudial studies and other research have shown some accurate predictions, in general, the persistence of criminal career is difficult to predict (Hirschi 1965; Siegel & Senna 1981; Hirschi & Gottfredson 1983).

Obviously, the assessment of the importance of school in the genesis of delinquent behavior is difficult because the school on the one hand is the source of aggression and delinquency and on the other hand the school is a relevant part of the educational subsystem of society and thus only reflects or mirrors structures and processes of the general society. The school definitely controls major social and psychological forces that provoke delinquent behavior: the school labels students as failures, and by making their scholastic nonsuccess obvious to themselves and to others, can force young people toward aggression and problem behavior as a face-saving response. The school is segregating students according to their scholastic achievement and thus labels youngsters as "losers". This labeling is public and can be observed and perceived by the whole community. The school is the prototype of a social institution which applies the formal criteria of achievement assessment in order to distribute positions in the hierarchy of privileges, which can be considered to be a brutal way of classifying human beings not according to their personal value but according to an abstract standard (Polk & Schafer 1972; Elliot, Huizinga, & Ageton 1985).

Because schools as social institutions and organizations are mediators and transmittors of general social forces, they often are blamed for outcomes that have their origin in other social areas, for example the family, the peer group etc., and they are blamed for manifestly reflecting societal and cultural structures and processes that are characteristic and typical for the society at large. These structures actually cannot be traced back to the school setting because their sources lie outside of the school setting, but the manifestation of these structures and processes is in a form that is typical for this setting (McPartland & McDill 1977; Rutter & Giller 1983).

Schools, for example, can not be made responsible for the economic situation of high rates of unemployment. On the contrary, schools have taken the function to keep young people in the classroom in order to avoid that they are pushed into a labor market that offers too few opportunities for too many school leavers. The school is not responsible for the fact that for many members of the young generation there are hardly any realistic chances to calculate their status transition and to move into the highly valued dimensions of the status called 'adult'. But, the schools are an element of the system that holds young people back. And since criminal acts in some repect represent a response to such frustration, these criminal acts are linked with the school system (Harootunian 1986, p. 122; Goldstein, Apter, & Harootunian 1984).

Thus, we have to face serveral theoretical, methodical, and political problems and implications of research on delinquency intervention. Schools seem to be most effective institutions of intervention when they concentrate on their very business and deliver high-quality instruction which is considered meaningful and worthwile by both teachers and students. All reforms focussing on the improvement of the "quality of school" are the best contribution to delinquency prevention. Schools as institutions should attempt to avoid the enforcement of social control on behalf of social institutions outside. They only should enforce their own social control, which is tied to their education and socialization activities, and should stop all activities that aim at making them part of a general societal control system.

References

Antonucci, T.C., and Depner, C.E. (1982): School support and informal helping relationships. New York: Academic Press.

Apter, S.J. (1982): Troubled children, troubled systems. New York: Pergamon.

Apter, S.J., and Goldstein, C. (Eds.) (1986): Youth violence. New York: Pergamon.

Blau, P.M. (1981): Diverse views of social structure and their common denominator. In: Blau, P.M., and Merton, R.K. (Eds.): Continuities in structural inquiry. London/Beverly Hills: Sage.

Brusten, M., and Hurrelmann, K. (1973): Abweichendes Verhalten in der Schule. Eine Untersuchung zu Prozessen der Stigmatisierung. München: Juventa.

Burchard, J.D., and Burchard, S.N. (Eds.) (1987): Prevention of delinquent behavior. Beverly Hills: Sage.

Caplan, G., and Grunebaum, H. (1967): Perspectives on primary prevention. A review. Archives in Genetic Psychiatry 17, 331-346.

Cowen, E.L. (1983): Primary prevention in mental health: Past, present, and future. In: Felmer, R.D., et al. (Eds.): Preventive psychology. New York: Pergamon, 11-25.

Elliot, D.S., Huizinga, D., and Ageton, S.S. (1985): Explaining delinquency and drug use. Beverly Hills: Sage

Elliot, D.S., and Voss, H. (1974): Delinquency and drop-out. Lexington: Heath.

Engel, U. (1988): Youth, mobility and social integration. In: Hazekamp, J.,Meeus, W., and Y. te Poel (Eds.): European contributions to youth research. Amsterdam: Free University Press, 81-92.

Farrington, D.P., Ohlin, L.E., and Wilson, J.Q. (1986): Understanding and controlling crime. New York: Springer
Frease, D.E. (1973): Schools and delinquency: Some intervening processes. Pacific Sociological Review, 16, 426-448.
Galtung, J. (1964): A Structural Theory of Aggression. Journal of Peace Research 1, 95-119.
Galtung, J. (1966a): Rank and social Integration: A multidimensional approach. In: Berger, J., Zelditch, M., and Anderson, B. (Eds.), Sociological theories in progress, Vol. 1. Boston: Houghton Miffin, 145-98.
Galtung, J. (1966b): International relations and international conflicts: A sociological approach. International Sociological Association, Transactions of the VI. World Congress of Sociology, Vol. 1, 121-61. Geneva.
Gold, M. (1978): Scholastic experiences, self-esteem, and delinquent behavior: A theory for alternative schools. Crime and Delinquency, 24, 290-294.
Goldstein, A.P., Apter, S.J., and Harootunian, B. (1984): School Violence. Englewood Cliffs: Prentice Hall.
Gottfredson, D. (1986): An empirical test of school-based environmental and individual interventions to reduce the risk of delinquent behavior. Criminology 24, 705-729.
Gottlieb, B.H. (1981): Social networks and social support. Beverly Hills, London: Sage.
Harootunian, B. (1986): School violence and vandalism. In: Apter, S.J., and Goldstein, A.P. (Eds.): Youth Violence. NY: Pergamon Press, 120-139.
Hawkins, J.D., and Lam, T. (1987): Teacher practices, social development and delinquency. In: Burchard, J.D., and Burchard, S.N. (Eds.): Prevention of delinquent behavior. Beverly Hills: Sage, 241-274.
Hersov, L.A., Berger, M., and Schafer, (Eds.) (1978): Aggression and antisocial behavior in childhood and adolescence. Oxford: Pergamon Press
Hirschi, T., and Gottfredson, M. (1983): Age and the explanation of crime. American Journal of Sociology, 89, 552-584.
Hirschi, T. (1969): Causes of delinquency. Berkeley: University of California Press.
Hurrelmann, K. (1987): The limits and potential of social intervention in adolescence. In: Hurrelmann, K., Kaufmann, F.X., Lösel, F. (Eds.): Social intervention: Potential and constraints. Berlin: De Gruyter, 219-238.
Hurrelmann, K. (1988): Social structure and personality development. New York: Cambridge University Press.
Hurrelmann, K., Kaufmann, F.X., and Lösel, F. (Eds.): (1987): Social intervention: Potential and constraints. Berlin/New York: De Gruyter.
Jason, L.A., Durlak, J.A., and Holton-Walker, E. (1984): Prevention of child problems in the schools. In: Roberts, M.C., and Peterson, L. (Eds.): Prevention of problems in childhood. New York: John Wiley, 311-341.
Kreutz, H. (1974): Soziologie der Jugend. Munich: Juventa.
Lösel, F. (1987): Psychological crime prevention. In: Hurrelmann, K., Kaufmann, F.X., and Lösel, F. (Eds.): Social intervention: Potential and Constraints. Berlin: De Gruyter, 289-314.
McPartland, J.M., and McDill, E.L. (1977): Violence in schools: Perspectives, programs and positions. Lexington: Lexington Books.
Olweus, D. (1983): Low school achievement and aggressive behavior in adolescent boys. In: Magnusson, D., and Allen, V.L. (Eds.): Human Development. New York: Academic Press, 353-365.
Polk, K., and Schafer, W.E. (1971): Schools and delinquency. Englewood Cliffs, N.J.: Prentice-Hall.
Rutter, M. (1980): Changing youth in a changing society. Cambridge: Harvard University Press
Rutter, M., and Giller, H. (1983): Juvenile delinquency. Harmondsworth: Penguin
Rutter, M., Maugham, B., Mortimor, P., Ouston, J., and Smith, A. (1979). Fifteen thousand hours: Secondary schools and their effects on children. Cambridge, MA: Harvard University Press.
Siegel, L.J., and Senna, J.J. (1981): Juvenile delinquency. Sanct Paul: West Publ.
Spivack, G., and Shure, M.B. (1982): The cognition of social adjustment: Interpersonal cognitive problem solving thinking. In: B.B. Lahey, and A.E. Kazdin (Eds.): Advances in child psychology. New York: Plenum, 323-372.
Stinchcombe, A.L. (1964): Rebellion in a high school. Chicago: Quadrangle Books.

10.
School Delinquency Prevention as Management of Rabble

Ken Polk

Introduction

This paper is concerned with the ways in which emergent school based delinquency prevention programs may become engaged in misdirected forms of social control. Economic transformations have resulted in a breakdown of what used to be reasonably effective transitions from school to work, especially in those links involving preparation for traditional working class occupations. As these connective pathways erode, and result in widespread youth unemployment, inevitably there is generated high levels of youthful alienation. While most analyses have focused on the alienation that results AFTER these individuals leave school and experience the consequent unemployment (e.g., Alder, 1986), there is increasing awareness that alienation will result in the years immediately BEFORE the transition as well (Polk, 1984a; Duster, 1987). When confronted with this alienation schools are likely to call upon their traditional repertory of control procedures (including forms of "delinquency prevention"). Since these control procedures are based in theories of alienation which assume that the problems originate from individual pathology (and thus ignore the structural sources of unemployment and alienation), these are unlikely to provide effective solutions to the youthful troublesome behavior encountered by the school. These may, however, become seen as ways of simply keeping young people "under control" while in the school years, and as such become part of the wider mechanisms for what Irwin has termed the "management of rabble" (Irwin, 1985).

The Economic Transformations

Most of us are familiar with the broad outlines of the economic changes that are part of what some have called the "post- industrial societies" (Jones, 1982). There is, first, the long term and dramatic decline in the need for employment in the essential task of food production. Even a society such as Australia which historically has depended on the export of agricultural commodities as a mainstay of its economy has only just over 5 percent of its labor force involved in agriculture (6.5 % in 1981, down from 7.4 % in 1971). There is, second, the recent sharp decline in manufacturing activity, after some decades of growth, so that in Australia currently less than one in five workers is involved in manufacturing (19.4 % in 1981, down from 24.7 % in 1971). At the same time there is a resultant increase in persons employed in the service sector of the economy (72.6 %

in 1981 in Australia, in contrast with 66.2 % in 1971), such that some prefer the term a "service economy" as being more precise.

What these wider trends mean is that there is a shift taking place in the nature of the attributes that are desired in the work force. Increasingly the corporate and government structures are seeking out workers that are highly skilled, more experienced and better qualified for recruitment into career oriented work, work which is often more capital than labor intensive. There are prices to be paid for this shift to a leaner, better trained, "credentialled" and generally older work force. There is less and less room for the unskilled, inexperienced and unqualified workers.

This can be seen in the trends in teenage employment, especially in the growth sectors of the economy. In Australia between 1971 and 1981 there was a overall growth in the general category of "white collar" work of almost twenty percent (19 % to be precise). In the same period, there was a twenty percent LOSS of jobs for teenagers (aged 15-19) in these same white collar jobs (Polk, 1984b). The reasons for this decline in teenage employment, both in white and blue collar work, are not of central concern to the present discussion. It is perhaps sufficient to note that there is taking place a fundamental alteration in the attributes needed to enter the contemporary labor force, especially in terms of entry into stable, life-long occupations.

Organizations such as government agencies, banks, commercial and business enterprises have been transformed by a wide variety of technological innovations (computers, word processors, new forms of telecommunications, copiers, etc.) so that large staffs of inexperienced and unskilled workers are no longer needed for copy typing, filing, carrying, sorting, copying and similar tasks (Sweet, 1983). There is, thereby, a striking loss of jobs for teenagers in such specific arenas as government (for an analysis of the loss of jobs in the Australian Public Service, see Kalisch and Stretton, 1984). New forms of retailing have evolved which depend less upon large pools of full-time sales and support staffs, and more on discount house forms of selling which call for a core of managers who oversee a large force of part-time, minimum wage, casual employees who have exceptionally limited prospects for career work with the firm (for an analysis of the emergence of these "dual labor markets", see Bluestone and Stevenson, 1981). Even in manufacturing and agriculture, rapid technological developments decrease the need for unskilled workers, and place an increasing dependence upon a much smaller but more highly qualified work force.

For present purposes, a major implication of these changes concerns the issue of how persons gain entry into work careers. In the pre-industrial phases of economic development, persons entered virtually all careers at an early age as inexperienced, unskilled and untrained workers, moving upward in their careers as they gained needed experience and skills (this was just as true for doctors and lawyers as it was for carpenters and weavers).

At the point at which manufacturing reaches its highest peak (in the late 1960s in Australia), patterns of work entry have become more complex. There was still considerable room for entry into work for those entering at age 15 or 16 with relatively little in the way of skills, experience or qualifications, especially in terms of traditional factory labor. A large pool of persons were entering the labor force at a slightly later point (after age 16 but before age 21), with slightly higher levels of qualifications, but still relatively little in the way of either concrete work skills or experience. A smaller group was moving through the elite forms of tertiary education (i.e., university degrees) and entering the work force at age 22 or 23 at relatively high status levels. By this time, in fact, entry into the very highest level of occupations had become limited to those who completed the requisite forms of tertiary education.

The post-industrial phase calls for quite different forms of work entry. The emphasis on capital intensivity requires a more experienced, skilled and qualified work force. Young persons who make their job entry relatively late, who thus are entering into their work careers with relatively high standards of qualifications behind them, and with some apparent claim on requisite work skills, in general can expect to do quite well upon entry into the work force. In fact, if they have appropriate degrees and skills in such high demand fields as computer programming, esoteric fields of engineering, or applied business they may be able to command salaries at work entry that are well above their parents working in traditional service fields such as education, business or government.

Those who attempt their entry into work careers at an early age face quite a different reality. The present work force has a scarcity of places for those who attempt to initiate a career by leaving school at the secondary level with little to offer in the way of skills, experience or qualifications. Further, the high level of unemployment experienced by this group of early school leavers (currently the unemployment rate of the 16- to 19-year-old group in Australia continues to run at just over 20 percent, a level roughly maintained for the past decade), since it is a consequence of the structural changes taking place in the work force, does not easily resolve itself. Many of the early school leavers find themselves, say, at age 26 still lacking the mix of skills, experience and credentials that will make them marketable in the post- industrial work force. There is being created, thereby, a group of "new marginal youth" (Polk, 1984a) in contemporary societies who find themselves locked out of traditional career structures. The actual form this marginality takes may vary from culture to culture. In the United States, for example, recent observers have commented on how young Blacks are becoming part of a "new underclass", and the significance this has for altering the nature of criminal justice (Duster, 1987). Irwin (1985), for one, has described how the criminal justice system can become part of a new pattern of "management of rabble".

The Role of Schooling

Inevitably, this pattern of a new underclass, or new marginality, begins to exert an influence on the educational establishment. As nations moved into the mature industrial phases, complex forms of stratified and differentiated education began to evolve. While the FORM of this stratification varies, each country had to solve the problem of how to provide a system of education that on the one hand recruits "able" students into the growing higher status service (and often credentialled) sector, while at the same time providing a base of minimal literacy and numeracy skills needed for the great variety of lower status , craft, semi-skilled and skilled work that is required in the phase of industrial (and early post-industrial) development.

For the higher occupational status levels, forms of secondary education have evolved which recruit and prepare persons for university level training which will enable entry into a wide range of professional work. The term "recruitment" is used here in a deliberate sense, since expansion of the share of the work in the credentialled sphere of service work is too rapid to be satisfied from the existing pool of privileged persons, nor can it be satisfied under ordinary circumstances by policies of immigration (although there have been particular times in the histories of some nations when there has been concern for "brain drain"). While precise figures on this growth as a relative phenomenon are hard to develop across nations, we know from the United States experience that the total volume of white collar workers (to use a crude measure) doubles every twenty years. The relatively simple solution adopted by most nations to find the new group of privileged workers has been to recruit some number of "able working class" students and prepare them, along with higher status peers, for entry into adult roles within the privileged professions.

Historically, what this has required is the development of highly stratified secondary school systems. These tend to be dominated by the prestigious top layer ("stream" or "track") which is given the task of preparing academically successful young persons for the university education which will follow (at least for those who maintain their eligibility). Since the system has taken on the task of recruiting "able working class" students upward, most will adopt a logic of meritocracy which will dominate the thinking regarding the way students are selected and prepared for these higher status forms of education, a central concept within this being the notion of intelligence.

The actual number of layers or streams will vary from country to country, but one can expect intermediate streams which will provide somewhat lower levels of qualifications which are assumed to be appropriate of middle range white collar occupations, and perhaps the highly skilled, technician component of blue collar work. At the bottom will be those streams which prepare individuals for direct entry to various forms of working class careers, ranging at the very bottom to those being dumped out with relatively low level of skill for direct entry into unskilled work, to those receiving a slightly higher standard (through some mechanism such as apprenticeship) who then are presumed qualified for entry into the skilled sector of the industrial labor force.

Countries have varied in the precise forms adopted to carry out this stratification. Those following the "comprehensive" model, such as the United States, have provided a basically single form of secondary school where virtually all students, regardless of status background, attend the high schol in their neighborhood. In this circumstance, the stratification takes place through the device of a differentiated curriculum, whereby separate "tracks" are provided for students with different career destinations. The major alternative to this comprehensive approach, more common in Europe, has been the so-called "selective" model where quite different schools are provided for those being prepared for university entrance as distinct from those destined for working careers. In its evolution, the schools of Australia (which vary significantly from state to state) tended to adapt some form of the selective system, as in the case of the state of Victoria where 20 years ago the system was clearly divided into independent (private) schools that were the main gateway into university, state supported high schools that would prepare a small number for university and a larger number for intermediate social class destinations upon their departure from secondary school (e.g., commercial institutions and government), and technical schools from which students would enter into various working class occupations.

Many of the studies of a few years ago were concerned with identifying the ways in which the various forms of segregation within schools ("streaming" or "tracking") seemed to result in youth alienation and delinquency because of the stresses such systems exert on those sorted at the bottom of the heap (e.g., Hargreaves, 1967; Polk and Schafer, 1972). Even when times were better in terms of the job prospects for those who left school early, while the students were in their school years the experience of failure seemed to create strong pressures which inclined young persons to respond through the formation of troublesome peer groupings, which in turn provided important supports for involvement in juvenile delinquency.

Schooling and the New Marginality

These pressures operating at the bottom of the educational system of stratification intensify, but also begin to alter their shape in important ways, as the developed economies move into mature stages of post-industrialism. The forms of stratification themselves which appeared to meet the needs of a mature industrial economy begin to experience strain as nations move into the post-industrial phases. This strain, however, is not evenly spread. At the top levels, the system seems to work reasonably well. Thus, the selection of high status students continues, these are prepared for, and enter, universities, and from there they are able to make their way with relative ease into work careers. For this group, in other words, there are few "problems of transition" in the sense that as yet there is still enough career work to accommodate university graduates. Whatever problems they may have, unemployment is not a major one.

Among the bottom streams, the story is quite different. The rapid loss of manufacturing employment, and unskilled work in the white collar sector, creates a major crisis in secondary education. Increasingly, the historic connections between technical education and working class careers become eroded. The exceptionally rapid decline of jobs means an even more rapid decline of jobs at the ENTRY level. Thus, one "solution" to the problem of the decline of work in manufacturing has been to guarantee those already at work either the option of continuing work, or perhaps some form of lucrative superannuation. Such a solution leaves little room for those attempting to enter the labor force as new recruits. It must be underscored, then, that the crisis being experienced by the new marginal youth is a crisis of gaining entry into work, a crisis which tends to be experienced greatest at the lower social class levels.

It would seem inevitable that this will begin to create a crisis in the lower streams of secondary education as well. At the system or policy level, the crisis concerns the question of how to alter and transform what have become clearly inappropriate forms of education. Thus, in Victoria, Australia a major political and policy issue is concerned with what we now should do with technical schools. At the experiential level, the students themselves can be expected to show signs of ANTICIPATED marginality or underclass status. As it becomes clear that the stream they are in is carrying them into a future of marginal or underclass life, and as they come to understand that it is BECAUSE of their stream that they can anticipate such marginality, then various forms of alienation must be anticipated. Further it can be expected that the drift away from school commitment among some will be rapid and extreme, and consist of at time aggressive behavior directed specifically at the school and its agents. Put simply, lower stream schools can anticipate high levels of trouble and delinquency in the coming years.

The School's Response to Troublesome Behavior

What will the response of the schools be to this crisis of new marginality? In some respects, at the system or policy level there will be what appear to be responsible and reasonable attempts to deal effectively with the problem of transforming and modifying the system of education. In Victoria, for example, whole new forms of secondary education are being proposed, new "middle schools" for the early secondary years are emerging, and in many places the older forms of high schools and technical schools are being merged into a single tech-high school format.

At the actual school, and student experience, level, however, there will be the persistent problem of "trouble" since these transformations will be late, and take many years to assume appropriate and adequate new forms. The schools will have to contend with the trouble that is the natural consequence of the new forms of youth marginality. Unfortunately, we can predict with reasonable accuracy the forms that this school response will take.

A first feature of this response will be derived from the fact that the trouble will be understood in INDIVIDUAL terms. School reformers will follow the same path noted by Ignatieff (1981) in his description of prison reformers, where he observed that:

"... at bottom reformers like most of their own class understood deviance in irreducibly individual rather than collective terms, not ultimately as collective disobediance, however much distress and collective alienation influenced individuals, but as a highly personal descent into sin and error" (Ignatieff, 1981, p. 175).

While school personnel may use other terms than "descent into sin and error", they are no less likely to define the problem as an individual one originating in such personal problems as lack of motivation, poor parenting, inadequate personal discipline, and the like, nor are they any more likely to be able to see the collective discontent, let alone respond to it.

Given these individual interpretations of the nature of the problem of trouble, the next feature of the school response becomes one of developing a "classification" of the individuals in terms of the nature of the underlying problem which produces the trouble. A classic formulation of persons in terms of such psychodynamic schemes is the theory of "interpersonal maturity levels" ("I-Levels") which assumes that human development proceeds through seven definable stages from neonatal dependence and nonhuman characteristics to adult maturity. At each of the seven stages there is a basic core structure of the personality around which the individual's behavior is organized. Troublesome adolescents are presumed to be at lower or less developed (but still clearly definable) levels of personality development. The strategy of treatment then consists of providing the appropriate forms of clinical intervention which enable the deviant individual to move upward in terms of personality structure (for a discusion, see Gibbons, 1970).

These clasification schemes then produce the next level of response, which consist of the segregation of particular troublesome students into separate and special units. For example, in the state of Victoria there have been recently established "secondary teaching units" which are designed to:

"... provide a level of help outside of the school situation for children experiencing difficulties at school, especially where it is felt that behavioral problems stem largely from a lack of adequate skills" (Slee, forthcoming).

These units are comparable to the forms of off-site centers for disruptive students that have emerged in recent years in England. These units, which one observer has termed "sin bins" (Newell, 1980) have proliferated rapidly, now number well over three hundred and providing services for several thousands of students. Commenting on the growth of these "annexe" programs in Victoria, Colley and Campbell have observed:

"The establishment of these units is not a conspiracy. It is simply common sense survival by teachers, bosses, inspectors and regional directors. The fact that they are very damaging to the kids is seen as irrelevant, or is unacknowledged. These units are proliferating, encouraged by the expansion of Special Education. If you start an annexe for kids with special needs, you are almost guaranteed to receive approaches from other schools to take their 'uncontrollable' clients" (Colley and Campbell, 1982, p. 3).

There are three particular features of these units which can be argued are responsible for the "damage" commented upon by Colley and Campbell. First, these special units as a consequence of the segregation of the disruptive students STIGMATIZE the young persons involved by imposing upon them visible and public labels which publicly announce their troublesome nature. The assignment into such units makes clear to other students, to teachers and to parents that these individuals are officially defined as trouble-makers. In the language of the labelling perspective, the students now have a public label which conveys to all their defective social status.

Secondly, the language within which the program is cast serves to DENIGRATE these young people. A careful analysis of the language used to describe the program will show that these efforts presume that the persons involved are in some way deficient or defective. Often it is essential that the students come to understand the precise nature of their defects as part of the process of "corection" or "rehabilitation". You can't get "well" until you acknowledge that you "have a problem", but there may be great personal costs to accepting the definition of oneself as "having a problem".

Thirdly, the programs remove individuals from the mainstream sequences of educational development. These developmental sequences often are constructed of subtle, interlocking and cumulative processes which once disrupted, may be virtually impossible to restore. In the first instance it may be difficult to re-enter mainstream education at all. Slee (forthcoming) notes that in one school system in the U.S., only 7 % of students found their way back into regular classrooms after their removal to the segregated units. Even if they are able to go back to regular schools, they may be so out of sequence that they are unable to catch up with their age peers in terms of where they stand in the cumulative processes of schooling. Slee (forthcoming) comments that procedures for returning students are often much less well developed than those for referral to the units.

Special Units, Prevention and Management of Rabble

The present argument presumes that there will be a growing problem of youthful alienation and trouble within the lower status streams of education, that is, those which are likely to lead students into later lives of unemployment and marginality. It is to be expected that schools, when confronted with troublesome behavior, will draw upon their existing theories and methods in order to prevent and control this troublesome behavior. Thus, we can anticipate that the special unit concept will be a preferred organizational approach in the attempt of the school to exert some amount of social control over youthful rebellious behavior. Pratt (1983) is one observer who has expressed concern about the use of these special units to control the new problems arising from marginality and unemployment:

"If we now look...at the pattern of interventions and range of developments related to the activities of young people in the U.K. that are taking place at the present time, then it seems very clear that...a refurbishment of Foucouldian discipline is occuring. I want to suggest that these developments – in education, penal, and social policy – are predicated on the growing crisis of youth unemployment in the U.K. and the threat to social cohesion that this poses ..." (Pratt, 1983, p. 344).

Pratt (1983, pp. 346-347) then goes on to comment on the growth of special education generally, and special units in particular, commenting that these units have become part of strategies for "... managing a specific category of reluctant school children who, on leaving, would almost certainly become unemployed..." (Pratt, 1983, p. 346). Pratt is one who has expressed concern explicitly for the involvement of such strategies and programs in the task of PREVENTION, nothing that such an emphasis is likely to result in a call for regular and earlier referrals in order to, in the actual words on one educator, "save many youngsters who would become completely anti-social and undisciplined..." (Pratt, 1983, p. 347).

When the problem is one of widespread unemployment as a clear destination for some young people (thus serving to cause their alienation), then special units predicated on various forms of individualized theories of intervention, and thus forms of casework and counselling, will be unable to solve the difficulties that confront the youngsters. It should be noted that there are limited gains that might be achieved by such programs. As Colley and Campbell (1982, p. 2) comment, these units at times can help to solve or soften some of the problems of individual children, and they can at times solve some of the problems schools have with individual children. They go on to point out, however that such annexe type units (1) take the pressure off the school to change in fundamental ways, (2) they identify the students as being at fault because they are unable to cope with a school which is failing them, and that ultimately such units (3) "... help to solve the school's problems, not the kids'" (Colley and Campbell, 1982, p. 2).

Further, these special programs, while they may have little positive effect in solving the immediate problems of the young people involved (i.e., since the problem of meaningful employment is not addressed), nonetheless have very wide system appeal. In the U.K., Pratt observed that:

"... it is because of the likelihood that leaving school will result only in unemployment that the M.S.C. is currently proposing a role for itself in the 'education' of 14- to 18-year-olds...this would mean that the M.S.C. need not wait for school-leavers to become unemployed before offering its 'support', but would be able to take out of the education system altogether those of law academic ability (and thus likely to question the value of schooling) and subject them to a four-year programme of training (Pratt, 1983, p. 355).

Pratt has expressed particular concern for the extension of these youthful manpower programs into programs concerned with delinquency and crime. Indeed, the development of various cross-linked youth serving programs aimed at this particular problem population has:

"... generated its own management structure and overlap between various agencies; the scope of these interventions can mean that there is no QUALITATIVE distinction between offenders, the unemployed and all the other sub-divisions of the 'at risk' category, there are merely degrees of 'need'..." (Pratt, 1983, p. 356).

It is here, then, that we begin to see the significant potential for an expansion of formalized forms of social control, especially those which draw upon the coercive, disciplinary frameworks of criminal justice and expand these outward into such community settings such as the school. Such a vision was powerful enough to compel Pratt to conclude that:

"Careful analysis refeals that disciplinary control is more virulent than ever, but that it turns a humane and an apparently caring face to all those trapped in the twilight world of 'training', or 'preparation for work' that never materializes. Their growing numbers are deceived into a voluntary, even a warm acceptance of a discipline of a subtlety and tenacity beyond the scope even of Orwell's fertile and fearful imagination" (Pratt, 1983, p. 357).

Conclusions

So what can we conclude from these observations? It has been argued here that the apparently irreducible problem of youthful unemployment in the contemporary developed economies will place a major structural burden upon schools. One feature of this burden will be rising levels of troublesome behavior in schools, especially in the lower status forms of education where there is a high risk of unemployment awaiting students upon their departure from school. The existing understandings of youthful misbehavior within the school are likely to lead to the development on the part of schools of an expansion of "special units" as a way of coping with the new forms of marginality. Indeed, there is already evidence of a rapid growth of such units.

What are the implications of these trends in terms of delinquency and the criminal justice system? At this time there are two major points which are explicitly conjectural in this argument. One concerns the extent to which the ANTICIPATION of marginality will generate new forms of troublesome behavior in nations such as Australia. There are, certainly, some problems in asserting a link between unemployment and crime, with some arguing that there is little to support the hypothesis of a connection between the two (Wilson and Herrnstein, 1985). There are many other observers, however, who are able to demonstrate persuasively that the experience of unemployment has observable effects in terms of increased criminality (e.g., Duster, 1987; Viscusi, 1986). Further, there is direct evidence of high levels of alienated behavior among the young unemployed (e.g., Alder, 1986).

Only time will tell the extent to which those caught up in the lower streams of education, where there is a high probability of later unemployment, will demonstrate high levels of youthful misbehavior during the later stages of their secondary school years. Such a response seems to be well advanced in countries such as the U.S. and England (Duster, 1987; Pratt, 1983), and the rapid growth of the special education units in Australia (Slee, forthcoming) suggest a similar trend is starting in Australia.

The second point which at this time is only conjecture concerns the role of the school in the management of misbehavior. Given that most contemporary societies seem unable to solve either the problem of high levels of youth unemployment or to provide (at least in the short run) effective new forms of secondary education which offer an alternative to that unemployment for those in the lowest streams in the high school years, then it woul seem virtually inevitable that the scenario sketched by Pratt will be put into place within the school. Special units created for those in the last stages of their educational careers can be anticipated which provide a mix of schooling, training, and forms of formal control derived directly from the criminal justice system.

New forms of delinquency prevention can be expected, in other words, as mechanisms by which the society expands its capacity for engaging in what Irwin (1985) has termed "the management of rabble". It is my expectation that the methods employed by these units will be derived from the traditional approaches taken by the school in its attempt to control disruptive behavior. The theories will be assume fundamentally individualistic causes for the problem behavior, such that clasification and then segregation into special units logically follow, as well stigmatization and denigration as major features of the resultant program activities. Since by definition such individual-centered approaches are incapable of resolving the basic structural sources of the new youth marginality, they will become instead part of an elaborate strategy of control.

Since it is also the case that the structural exclusion of these new underclass or marginal youth is not resolved through maturation (since ageing by itself will not produce the skills, experiences or qualifications needed for career entry), and since the range of problems presented by a singnificant pool of alienated new marginals will not abate, correctional and training programs are likely to emerge for those in the post-school years as well. As suggested by the experience in England (Pratt, 1983), it is further likely that there will be an increasing blurring of the boundaries between the various programs. Wider strategies which are fundamentally about social control are then likely to emerge strategies which call for a linking of the school programs as "first stages" or "preparatory" for those which follow later. Through such devices, the school prevention and control programs would then become explicitly linked to a wider system of management of the new underclass of youth.

While this scenario is clearly pessimistic, it should be emphasized that some alternatives do exist. Nations such as Australia could return to their earlier commitment to a full employment economy. Various "new careers" strategies could be drawn upon to define new career trajectories through stages of education, training and work experience which could vitalize education generally, and transform the lower streams of education specifically (for a discussion see Duster, 1987, or Polk, 1984b). What differentiates such approaches is that these presume that the structural problem of employment is the key matter to be addressed. Economic and youth development become the central features of the approaches to be taken in any attempt at "prevention". Traditional prevention programs focused on individual interpretations of youthful marginality are incapable of addressing these structural issues, and thus will shift their attention to the alternative task of control, and thus will become part of wider strategies of managing the new forms of rabble.

References

Alder, C. (1986): Unemployed women have it heaps worse: Exploring the implications of female youth unemployment. ANZ Journal of Criminology 19, 210-224

Bluestone, B., and Stevenson, M.H. (1981): Industrial transformation and the evolution of the labor market. In: Wilkinson, F. (Ed.): The dynamics of labor market segmentation. New York: Academic Press, 24-46

Colley, R., and Campbell, T. (1982): The annexe. ADVISE (no. 35. November), 1-3

Duster, T. (1987): Crime, youth unemployment and the black urban underclass. In: Crime and Delinquency 33, 300-316

Gibbons, D.C. (1970): Differential treatment of delinquents and interpersonal maturity levels theory: critique. In: Social Service Review 44, 22-33

Hargreaves, D.H. (1967): Social Relation in a Secondary School. London: Routledge and Kegan Paul

Ignatieff, M. (1981): State, civil society, and total institutions: a critique of recent social histories of punishment. In: Tonry, M., and Morris, N. (Eds.): Crime and Justice: An Annual Review of Research, Vol.3. Chicago: University of Chicago Press, 153-192

Irwin, J. (1985): The Jail. Berkeley, California: University of California Press

Jones, B. (1982): Sleepers Wake! Technology and the Future of Work. Melbourne: Oxford University Press

Kalisch, D., and Stretton, A. (1984): Teenage Employment in the Public Sector: Where Have All the Jobs Gone? Canberra: Bureau of Labour Market Research, Working Paper No. 44

Polk, K., and Schafer, W.E. (1972): Schools and Delinquency. Englewood Cliffs, N.J.: Prentice-Hall

Polk, K. (1984a): The New Marginal Youth. In: Crime and Delinquency 30, 462-480

Polk, K. (1984b): Wanted: new careers. In: Australian Society (June), 18-21

Pratt, H. (1983): Reflections on the approach of 1984: recent developments in social control in the U.K. In: International Journal of the Sociology of Law 11, 339-360

Slee, R. (forthcoming): Discipline and the Schools: a Curriculum Perspective. Melbourne: Macmillan

Sweet, R. (1983): Changing patterns of work and education. In: Anderson, D.S., and Blakers, C. (Eds.): Youth, Transition and Social Research. Canberra: ANU Press, 18-38

Viscusi, W.K. (1986): Market incentives for criminal behavior. In: Freeman, R.B. and Holzer, H.J. (Eds.): The Black Youth Unemployment Crisis. Chicago: University of Chicago Press, 301-346
Wilson, J.Q., and Herrnstein, R.J. (1985): Crime and Human Nature. New York: Simon and Schuster

11.
Prevention as a Strategy of Normalizing. An Analytical Approach on Restructuring the Integration Paradigm in Institutional Social Work

Karin Böllert / Hans-Uwe Otto

1. Introduction

The emergence of the social services system in the welfare state was accompanied by a differentiation of distinct patterns of intervention in social work. In spite of all their heterogeneity, the corresponding offers and tasks have their common function in securing and reproducing the state of affairs that is socially constituted as normal. With the change of these states of normality, social work as normalizing work loses its classic frame of reference and has to meet the challenge of renewing the definition of its objectives and responsibilities of its services.

From this point of view, those attempts are becoming more relevant which want to tie a preventive orientation of social work to a re-evaluation of the traditional relation between control and support. The main attention of social work action has shifted from later curing to preventive avoidance of delinquency. The question that remains unanswered is, to what extent these forms of adjusting social norms will be able to supply future social work with starting-points that, on the one hand, refer to processes of social change and, on the other hand, ensure adequate access to the different conditions of the clients' lives.

The requirements of such a preventive orientation of strategies of coping with problems in social work are surveyed by means of an institution- analysis-approach taking youth services as an example. We will, first of all, analyze the consequences for youth services that arise from a change in their social framework conditions. Based on this, we will then state more precisely the theoretical grounds for a corresponding concept of prevention. Finally, we will discuss preliminary estimations of its realizeability.

2. Social Conditions of Normalizing Work

Like all other social services, youth services are also integrated in the function of preventive avoidance and later curing of delinquency (Japp, 1986). Appropriate offers and services are therefore meant to ensure the reproduction of material, social and cultural norms and social framework conditions (Berger/ Offe, 1980). This normalizing work finds its specific expression within the framework of social work in the guarantee of identity structures that can be expected on average (Olk, 1986). In this respect, youth services are primarily orientated towards carrying through a socially accepted development of the adolescents' personalities. Taking this task first of all requires a generalizable idea of how the adolescents' development of personality and their integration into social requirements and interrelations is desired and realizable at the same time. So, the question for youth services is towards which concept of normality to orientate their interventions.

Within a framework of a process of social modernization, with the development of the welfare state tied to the premises of an industrial society, youth services could derive their concept of normal youth from the essential structures of this social conception (cf. Böhnisch, 1982), as well as the desciption of the youth services' functions given above found its justification there (cf. 5. Jugendbericht, 1980). A basic prerequisite for the development, generalization and realization of a binding conception of 'youth' was that, on the one hand, the socially recognized forms of living together are standardized taking the nuclear family as a model and, on the other hand, that forms of profession and work are dominated by the system of employment (cf. Beck, 1986). These facts also help to define the adolescents' central points of reference for future patterns of life.

Family, as the obligatory an publicly accepted form of parents and children living together, constitutes the basis of the individual organization of life of each member of the family. It is the primary place of education and sozialization for children and adolescents. This means that family is part of the social order in a society, which it represents and is meant to reproduce (Karsten/ Otto, 1987). However, the system of employment is supported by the analysis that the private and social situation of the individuals' lives is derived from their position in 'normal conditions of employment' (Teriet, 1980), as they are called. It is said that the role of anybody who is involved in working life is therefore defined in such a way that it provides both an individual and a cultural structure of living and surviving (Mückenberger, 1985). Hence, the integration into the system of employment not only serves as a security for the livelihood of the employees, but also is meant to guarantee the acceptance of appropriate ways of social behavior and attributions of social status.

Consequently, family and employment are existential conditions of the emergence and the continuance of a developed industrial society. In this respect, both the social risks inherent in the employment system and the increasing demands for socialization work resting on the families always also comprise potential dangers for the continuance of this type of society. In this context, the development of a sophisticated social services system in the welfare state, which coincides with the development of the industrial society, is determined by a double objective (Peters, 1984). On the one hand, services of the welfare state are designed to cover correlations in family life and to compensate for social disadvantages; on the other hand, these services also help to carry through or preserve social concepts of normality.

Former offers of youth services have been structured analogously to the function of social services as described above, i.e., against the background of the outlined concept of normality, youth services intervene whenever adolescents are not in a position to meet common and desired concepts or to realize deviant concepts of normality. Hence, the measures of youth services – independent of when they are taken – can be related to the primary aim of integrating adolescents into spheres of life in family and employment. For youth services as well as for all other forms of social services, it is constitutive that they have to achieve some sort of normalizing without being able to set a standard of normality themselves. Starting-point for interventions always is the deviation from a normality that is supposed to be given. Consequently, the problems that youth services are meant to cope with are defined as exclusively negative, especially as there is no socially legitimized conception of what is a successful individual or collective planning of life or prospect for the future of adolescents (Arbeitsgruppe Sozialpolitik, 1986).

The normality that youth services were able to orientate their institutionalization of the concept 'youth' to before, was especially connected with the idea of equal access to the educational system guaranteed by the welfare state. The intended balance between ways of training and chances of employment, however, is fundamentally troubled as a consequence of present day developments on the labor market. The term 'crisis of the working society' (cf. Dahrendorf, 1983; Matthes, 1983; Offe, 1984) describes a change of fundamental forms of socialization. As a consequence of this, more and more people are either excluded from employment or included only on the periphery. In this way, they are expelled from the system of social protection to a large extent (Alheit/ Glass, 1986; Bonss/ Heinze, 1984; Negt, 1985). Extensive rationalization and technological progress in the working world accelerate this process and let phenomena like 'new poverty' or 'two thirds society' become obvious (cf. Balsen et.al., 1984; Chasse, 1988; Leibfried/ Tenstedt, 1985).

At the same time, it is becoming increasingly clear that the programmatic normality of the employment citizen has never been a normal condition empirically, but just a fiction. Non-employed occupations such as housework or educating one's children remain unnoticed as well as the fact that the traditional system of employment is based on the patriarchal relations of the sexes and has always tended to exclude women and other groups (handicapped people etc.) (cf. Werlhof, 1984). These consequences of the system of employment are nowadays decreasingly accepted without contradiction, least of all by female adolescents (cf. Marquardt et.al., 1984; Seidenspinner et.al., 1984).

Especially the changes in the relations of the sexes that are apparent against this background (cf. Hagemann-White, 1984) illustrate that, apart from employment, the model of living in a nuclear family can not be freely taken for granted any longer as well. Particularly the emergence of various alternative ways of living can be interpreted as an indication of the fact that forms of family life multiply at the moment (Graven-Horst et.al., 1984; Karsten/ Otto, 1987). Family, as the central place of reproduction for the adolescents, is ceasing to exist, not only because it has lost its compulsory nature as a means of providing meaning in a lifelong perspective, but also because the increasing unemployment of both the parent and the child generations creates problems which can hardly be coped with by family alone.

Through these essential changes of its normative fundamental beliefs, the programme of the welfare state loses its relevance in a 'new confusion' and what is more, it is not able to develop new and future ways of living (cf. Habermas, 1985). The aim of the welfare state of creating equal chances and establishing egalitarian structures of forms of life and individual scopes of action – which the measures and offers of youth services are also orientated to in the end – has disappeared in administratively distorted and alientated worlds of living (cf. Olk/ Otto, 1985). The relation between the power of definitions of normality and institutional rule, between concepts of normality and needs for intervention is getting less and less determinable by the people concerned (cf. Arbeitsgruppe Sozialpolitik, 1986). The dispossession of self determined courses of life through advanced bureaucracy, growing importance of laws and experts especially in the field of socio-pedagogical work has lead to institutional patterns of courses of life taking the place of traditional relationships and social forms (cf. Kohli, 1986). The separation from contexts of life that had been taken for granted before, has got an individualizing trend under way which replaces collective forms of convictions by individual attitudes and accelerates a far-reaching isolation of individuals. Courses of adolescents' lives are devided into different spheres of life which are connected to institutions so that there is a growing dependence on institutions and the threat of courses of life being politically formed and controlled (cf. Beck, 1986). Taking into account that employment, which has been made a norm, decreasingly corresponds to the actual conditions of life of a growing proportion of the youth services' clients, it is noticeable that the forms of adolescents' lives are increasingly confronted with an institution that works more and more disciplinary in educational respect and which intensifies the contrast between institutionally designed concepts of life and normality as it is experienced by the adolescents.

One possible perspective that emerges in this situation is a conception of practical social work which enables the adolescents to design plans for life and future on their own initiative according to their own needs and interests, which in turn links up to the perspectives of preventive strategies of coping with problems.

3. Prevention as Active Design of 'Patterns of Life'

Prevention is not a new subject neither in youth services nor in other fields of social work. As a rule, prevention characterizes everthing that is generally discussed in this sector as reorientation, change, and innovation. What is still missing inspite of a tradition of the topic prevention is a contextual definition and theoretical explanation of the term prevention which refers to the framework conditions of youth services in the society as a whole and to the changed situation of adolescents' lives. Neither has the question been asked nor answered which adolescents or which concepts of adolescent life youth services should design their offers for. Hence, what is still in the dark above all is which institutionalized objectives and definitions of problems relevant for acting must be developed. Apart from the work by Herriger (1983), there are no studies on problems of prevention at all.

Instead, suggestions have been made mainly on how an adequate access to the problems of the people concerned could be achieved by means of institutional changes (cf. Hottelet, 1984; Müller-Schöll, 1984; Schulz, 1984; Sengling, 1984). The criticism of these approaches refers, on the one hand, to the exclusiveness of administrative rearrangements, which are often accompanied by a technocratic variant of prevention and, on the other hand, to not discussing ambivalent effects of preventive strategies of coping with problems. Such effects have been expressed by several authors in the possible danger of losing the subjective character or of an intensified extension of social control and a 'colonialization of spheres of life' that comes along with it (cf. Otto, 1983; Castel, 1983; Kupffer, 1983; Schulz/ Wambach, 1983).

With the predominant dichotomy of structurally and subjectively related elements of prevention (cf. Herriger, 1983; Vobruba, 1983), people usually start from the assumption that the preference for one of the two levels excludes the choice of the other. It is first of all Herriger, who therefore negates the possibility of structurally related influences and effects of building up structures for socio-pedagogical work in the field of youth services, which means that there is only a marginal inclusion of the clients' conditions of life. However, there have been first attempts to discuss the interrelations of structures and individuals in those preventive approaches that try to theoretically reconstruct the reciprocal character of the relationship between individual and environment (Kommer/ Röhrle, 1981; Fliegel/ Röhrle/ Stark, 1983). In the practical work of projects in community psychology which are similarly orientated, however, the complex structure of the relationship between individual and environment has been resolved again by means of a one sided orientation towards the subjectivly related proportion. Thus, the complexity of the reality of the addressees' lives has been missed to a large extent (cf. Keupp, 1987).

Starting from the socio-ecological tradition of the Chicago school (cf. McKenzie, 1926; Park, 1925; both in Atteslander/ Hamm, 1974), those resesarch projects which are rather more orientated to social spheres examine the urban patterns of the distribution of social problems and the groups of the population who are affected by them. Although socio-ecological research refers to the connection of social problems with surroundings as one of its constituative conditions (cf. Friedrichs, 1977; Göschel et.al., 1977; Hamm, 1980; Meulemann/ Weishaupt, 1981), the respective investigations tend to split up situations of social problems into variables and factors the contribution of which in the causing of complex social problems can hardly be examined theoretically or empirically (cf. Häussermann/ Krämer-Badony, 1980). Results from reseach work in the context of the discussion of a theory of social problems are similarly controversial, since the genesis of social problems or their distribution in spheres have been examined but not the relationship between the structures of spheres and the conditions of the development of social problems (cf. Albrecht, 1980; Rotter/ Steinert, 1981; Savelsberg, 1980; Schneider, 1981; Steinert, 1981; Vascovics, 1982). Moreover, the reception of these approaches had the effect in the field of social work that the consideration of processes of social spheres and social contexts of addressees have almost exclusively been reduced to the decentralization of existing structures of organization (cf. Müller/ Otto, 1980).

The lack of efficiency of social services, on the one hand, and, on the other, the question of how quality of life can be guaranteed in future in view of a 'crisis of the welfare state', have led to an intensified discussion of the concept 'patterns of life' especially in the field of health services during recent years. The starting-point of these discussions is, first of all, the debate of concepts of 'life style' as it is called (cf. Mullis/ Kern/ Curlette, 1987; Taylor/ Ford, 1981; Wiley/ Camacho, 1980) which, however, lack a foundation in social sciences to a large extent. That is why recently more and more of those approaches come to be the center of discussions which try to relate rather more structurally orientated ways of procedure to rather more subjectively orientated interventions with the aid of the concept 'patterns of life'. In this connection, they start from the assumption that 'patterns of life' cover the characteristic process of an individual's life as it is objectively given by social conditions, views and habits on the other (cf. Fehr, 1982; Kühne, 1978; Weidig, 1980). Thus it is not a matter of summarizing structural conditions of life, individual occupations and social connections, but of reflecting social structures of human action. A basic assumption is that 'patterns of life' remains to be connected to social levels and classes, but predominantly refers to social groups and contexts. Hence, the starting point of this approach – and of this investigation as well – is the opinion that human behavior must be traced back to certain economic, ecological, social and cultural conditions under which it developed and manifested itself. As these conditions have a different effect on different groups of people, the fact is implied at the same time that there cannot be a single or dominant 'pattern of life' – analogously to a predominant concept of normality and a correspondingly institutionalized concept of life. In this connection, subjective ways of behavior cannot each be taken for individual decisions, either; they must rather be seen in connection to their overall social and specificly contextual dependencies and functionalities (cf. Franzkowiak, 1987; Wenzel, 1983). On the whole, an integral perspective is therefore pleaded for (cf. Kickbusch, 1983), presenting 'patterns of life' as a 'mediating social sciences conception' (cf. Wenzel, 1983), as an 'imaginary middle between the psychological and the socio-structural' (cf. Horn, 1983).

Distinguishing collective from individual 'patterns of life', the interaction between structural and subjective conditions are also specified and, above all, the significance of patterns of social relations and socio-cultural environment are stressed. Accordingly, the 'patterns of life' of a social group marks all the patterns of meaning and forms of expression that it has built up in the course of collective efforts to cope with the demands and contradictions of social structures and situations common to all its members, while the 'patterns of life' of an individual describes all the normative orientations and structures of action that are built up during one's biography. Connecting individual and collective 'patterns of life', the reference to socio-structural conditions of life are of special importance; i.e., individual behavior becomes understandable to be socially influenced in essence, which means that the change of individual behavior must always be related to social changes (cf. Kahl/ Willsdorf/ Wolf, 1984; Lipphold/ Manz, 1980; Manz, 1981; Wenzel, 1986).

First approaches to transfer the concept of 'patterns of life' into the field of social work start from the prognosis that the 'central scene of social disputes' will shift from closer socio-political to wider socio-cultural subjects in future (cf. Evers, 1985). Thus, a definite evaluation is made in favor of elements mediating new dispositions of behavior and cultural orientations. The basic feature of defining 'patterns of life', however, is the crossing over of socio-economic and socio-cultural levels of life. Embedded in this crossing over, there are material and socio-psychological conditions and chances of life which interactively determine the extent of satisfying 'patterns of life'. In this respect, a culturalistic forming of the concept 'patterns of life' neglects the significance of economic tendencies of development for the design of 'patterns of life' as it has been outlined here within the framework of the employment society. Those attempts are more comprehensive, but also too general, which take the design of 'patterns of life' for a democratic process of building an opinion and for a decision on a framework that is orientated to human needs and within which various froms of living can be freely chosen (cf. Raschke, 1984). Therefore, the main concern of the field of youth services would be to provide options for different 'patterns of life' and the conditions of their development in the social spheres.

Thus, a corresponding preventive conception has been developed which differentiates between structural, subjective and contextual orientations of preventive strategies of coping with problems. The structural orientation refers to conveying conditions of socio-pedagogical action in society as a whole. Accordingly, the structural level of prevention is aimed at the systematic aspect of the emergence of youth problems. Its measures are intended to initiate institutional changes that show themselves as changed opportunities in the lives of the adolescents releasing them from the situation of becoming representatives of social problems. In this respect, the structuring aspects of youth services therefore form a relevant distinctive feature of preventive and interventional patterns of coping with problems. Within this framework, preventive youth services are not only concerned with the punctuality of the detection of possible problematic situation which can as well be achieved by an increased degree of social control. What is of an equally great importance is which subjects the strategies of coping with problems are institutionalized with. While interventional youth services are rather characterized by bringing socio-structural problems into line with pedagogical theories and accepting socio-political services, preventively orientated youth services deal with a constructive analysis and specificly contextual formulation of political regulations. Realizing the structural aspect of preventive youth services therefore requires giving up the orientation to the previously dominant concept of normal adolescence in favor of considering different concepts of normality.

The subjective orientation as another level of preventive youth services is marked by an attempt to consider the totality of adolescent courses of life. Neither a parcelling out and individualizing of situational problems, nor the exclusive appeal to subjective statements of adolescents about themselves are sufficient measures for such a preventive strategy of coping with problems. Prevention concentrating on the subject implies increasing the 'transparency' of action for the acting person (Dewe, 1985). This responds especially to the balance between the individualistic determination of structural conditions of life and a structural determination of subjective identities (Hitzler/ Horner, 1984). This preventive conception has considerable consequences on the interactive process between social workers and adolescents. There certainly is the confrontation with diverging norms and values both in the interventionally and in the preventively orientated process of interaction. The interventional strategies of coping with problems, however, are satisfied with the fiction of a consensus (Weiss, 1983); possibly they even do without any building of consensus referring to a hierarchic difference of power between social workers and their clients. Even in preventive forms of coping with problems, consensus as agreement is only an ideal type of the interactive process. But these forms are characterized by a mutual acceptance of heterogenous conceptions. They take into account the multitude of adolescent forms of identity by means of flexible definitions of problems and are characterized by a sensitization for the respective markedness of different concepts of life. Strategies of coping with problems concentrating on the subject support the adolescents in the process of building up an own identity without fixing term to a previously defined concept of life.

Outlining methods of intervention that are either tendentially concentrated on structures or rather on the individuals does not answer the question of how these two levels can be related to each other in preventive youth services. When on the structural level a general concept of normal adolescents loses some of its importance and on the subject level a trend towards individualization becomes a considerable strain on the adolescents, new resources must be found to make a successful and satisfying development of personality possible for adolescents.

On the level of contextual orientation of preventive youth services, the assumption is that within the social surroundings and its specific lifestyles there already is some revelation of ways to resolve problems which can help to create such strategies of coping with problems that do not deprive the groups or adolescents concerned of ways of resolution they have found themselves. In this context, prevention takes its leave of the conception that its addressees face institutional offers without reservations. With the move towards the social surroundings, the unique problematic situation of the individual case is pushed into the background. Instead the conditions of reproduction and of solving problems set by the social surroundings or rather the people living in it, turn out to be the decisive point of approach and reference for preventive strategies of coping with problems. These differ from interventional forms of coping with problems because of the provision of essential chances of social development by means of an extension of the scope to organize one's social surroundings. The programmatic formula of an active design of lifestyles is meant to express that lifestyles describe the characteristic processes of adolescents' lives as they are objectively conveyed by social conditions on the one hand, and subjectively by individual conditions on the other.

While it is the aim of traditional preventive strategies to align the addressees' concepts of life and aims of action prospectively with the socially predominant and schematized standards of normality, the target groups are enabled to have a constructive and independent look at their spheres of problems. In this respect, prevention strives for a way of dealing with problems that includes the actual interdependences of their specificly biographical constitution and the relations of their social environments.

4. Description of the Project

The project described below investigates the question of which chances of realizing the outlined concept of prevention there are in practical youth services. That is why the professionally and administratively conveyed concepts of normality and an appropriately institutionalized normalizing work are examined. The main emphasis is on the professional and administrative conditions of preventive youth services and on their cooperation in performing social work. It is the aim of the project to systematicly relate to each other the differing approaches of competence in professional action and administrative structures, so that theoretical and practical perspectives adequate for the problems can be developed for a new rationality of preventive strategies in social work.

The youth welfare departments of 29 big cities in North Rhine-Westphalia build the basis of the empirical investigation of the project. Within these departments, the different hierarchic levels were analyzed. On the whole, there were 375 social workers from the field of public educational services that were asked about the administrative framework conditions of their work, the competence in professional action and their respective conception of prevention. The questionnaire was standardized, but also contained some open questions. This survey serves to record varying levels of administrative and professional control as well as to differentiate various forms of competence in action and the corresponding strategies of coping with problems.
In addition to that, another 102 experts were interviewed with the aid of semi-standardized instructions. These were the officials in charge of the social institutions (25), the heads of the youth welfare departments (26), the deputy heads of the youth welfare departments (23), and the heads of other departments concerned (28). The main emphasis of this survey was put on the analysis of concepts of normal youth, the corresponding strategies of action, and the administrative expectations of the social workers' competence in action. Another complex of questions dealt with the socio-political and local integration of practical youth services.
Moreover, 140 social workers altogether have taken part in a standardized study of time budgets, in which they structured their working days in intervals of 30 minutes each over a period of one week. These studies of time budgets facilitate the registration of

interrelation between the administrative and the professional level of control, recording in a contextually qualified way the social workers' performance of action and investigating these quantitatively according to their expenditure of time.

The results of the investigation supply first answers to the question of which institutionalized concepts of normality of adolescents correspond to which forms of normalizing work.

5. Results and Preliminary Tendencies of Preventive Youth Services

With a first analysis of the empirical data at hand, we want to point out possible perspectives which, at the same time, can be taken as evidence for the efficiency of the analytical approach we developed on restructuring the integration paradigm in administrative social work. The social workers' pattern of explaining the present social tendencies of development are of special importance. In this context, it turns out that the classic conceptions of normality of family and work are subjected to a strong change. Especially the changes in the family system are of an important status to the social workers, not least because of the influence of a predominant orientation of the fields of work to family and consequently of a confrontation with changed forms of family life. The social workers also clearly align their evaluation of the specific situation of adolescents with developmental tendencies of society as a whole. This view of the problems primarily considers the increasing individualization of planning one's life and the growing demands on the adolescents' development of the personality. In this respect, those expectations are particularly mentioned which are made of adolescents today and which can hardly be reconciled with each other due to their inconsistency. Moreover, the fact is stressed that adolescents often have to reconsider their future plans and to bring them into line with changed conditions of life. From this point of view, family difficulties increase when the financial dependency on the parents restricts desired freedom.

It is easy to understand that this definition of problems is primarily relevant to the direct context of social workers' actions, since social workers must necessarily take actions when adolescents are unable to develop a satisfying conception of life, when their situation is marked by processes of material and social segregation, and when the social context of spheres of life leads to disadvantages. It is a remarkable fact that the major proportion of all social workers also want to intervene when there is conspicious individual behavior; i.e., the classic procedure of an institutionalized reactive individual help is carried on. Hence, it turns out that the people questioned orientate their actual professional actions to the typical aim of 'boosting the ego-function' of the addressees, which is the basis of individual case attention. Characteristic of this among other things is the individualizing attribution of deficits of behavior as an essential of professional intervention, as well as objectives which are primarily interested in a stabilization of the personality, and the correspondingly labelled reactions to conspiciousness in determining the causes. In contrast to the definitions of problems which are aligned with a variety of norms, normalizing work itself seems to go on following the traditional logics.

Another remarkable fact is that the professionals are allowed a considerable scope of decisions by the adminstration for the practical realization of their definitions of problems which are orientated at the situation of adolescents. Just as little, however, as socio-environmental and socio-cultural definitions of problems, have appropriate forms of work that express themselves in the cooperation with institutions and groups of the districts and in supporting and activating activities in the districts, found their way into administration. Although the social workers talk about the social surroundings and its socio-cultural contents as the essential points of reference for their work, tendencies can also be noticed in this context that only individual case orientated forms of intervention are transferred to the adolescents' social contexts without productively using the special functions of socio-environmental structures. This tendency finds its continuation in the fact that the social workers' abstract, preventively orientated definitions of problems are put in concrete terms along objectives that take up the traditional determination of the functions of social work.

Analogously, the interactive process between social workers and adolescents contains considerable features of a hierarchic structure of relations expressed tendentially in an expertocratic way of proceeding. This refers to a way of looking at the problems that often blocks the entry to communicative processes of negotiation and, what is more, which does not sufficiently consider the situation of the addressees' lives. On the other hand, the institution frequently grants the adolescents competences of definition and decision which increase the probability of being able to set off own conceptions and dispositions, e.g., when the development of alternative chances of solution is discussed with the adolescents or when their perspectives are to be made the starting point for further actions. This, however, is a contradiction to the fact that the administrative control of the interactive structure is based on predominantly individualizing conceptions of help and thus on an antiquated concept of normality.

By means of the differentiation between structural, contextual and subjective points of reference of social work, both in rather more administrative and rather more professional fields, variants of explaining why there is the looming tendency to failure in preventive youth services can be opened up on the one hand. On the other hand, it is possible to check the conditions of realizing a model of prevention that is more differentiated than the given concepts, cnsidering especially the statements of the experts for an evaluation of the results of the standardized interviews. A comparative interpretation of the results on hand now with the postulated assumptions of preventive youth services, first of all, clearly shows that the institutionalization of preventive strategies of coping with problems can not exclusively be tied on the change of administrative framework conditions of socio-pedagogical work. One cannot assume that on the administrative level the prerequisites of preventive youth services are already there. It is, however, exactly the contradictoriness of administrative determinations and regulations finding its expression in a partial loss of control, that offer the social workers chances of showing professional standards in performing their work to advantage. Hence, the structural causes of the adolescents' problematic situations are hardly taken into account on the structural level of administrative prevention, but the social workers are provided with dispositions for deciding on the development of professionally justified definitions of aims.

On the contextual level, the reduction of socio-environmental references to individual causes has such an effect that the intervention potential are predominant even in contrast to the reference to structures and people. The preventive potentials in subjective reference, however, are clearly better developed. This might be an indication that the influence of an individualizing concept of help can be lessened by providing professional and addressee-orientated scopes of deciding and acting.

On the whole, as far as the administrative elements of socio-pedagogical rationality of actions is concerned, we can thus assume an inconsistent institutionalization of both preventive and interventional strategies of coping with problems, as a consequence of which tendentially widened scopes of accomplishing professional standards emerge. The previous analysis for the field of professional elements of socio-pedagogical rationality of actions, however, shows that the social workers to a large extent do not use these scopes of actions fr a preventive design of their coping with problems. On the level of the professional reference to structures, a predominantly reactive objective of the work prevents definitions of problems that are, in contrast, innovatively orientated from thickening into a preventive perspective of problems. On the other hand, preventive strategies of coping with problems that are referred to the social context of the adolescents, seem to be rather more possible – a tendency that does not find its continuation in the subjective orientation because of its rather more expertocraticly controlled structures of interactions. On the grounds of these first results of the investigation at hand, the question must be asked which causes are decisive for the fact that the social workers leave tendentially given scopes out of consideration and that they do not make topical for their performance of actions the social science knowledge that is expressed in their definitions of problems. At the present state of analysis, three variants of explanation can primarily be offered:

(1) The preventively orientated definitions of problems are not applied to the actual field of actions because there is no corresponding repertoire of measures at hand, i.e., the social workers' definitions of problems have no equivalent in local socio-politically and administratively supplied possibilities of coping with problems. This interpretation is primarily based on the statements of the experts most of whom have, on the one hand, developed interventionally characterized definitions of problems and whose ideas of coping with problems, on the other hand, mainly moves within the framework of the traditional understanding of reactive interventions of the practical work of youth services as normalizing work. In contrast to the statements of the social workers, even the lack of success of previous measures to integrate adolescents into fields of training and occupation and

thus the failure of the classic integration paradigm of administrative social work hardly ever is a reason to reflect about alternative offers or about the contents that build the basis of the predominant interventions.

(2) The reversion to traditional forms of individual case handling in the interaction with the clients is an expression of a professional uncertainty and an increasing variety of norms and values. In this perspective, routine actions have the aim of strengthening the certainty of actions. While the social workers' conceptions of prevention have high priority especially on the level of contextual reference, their conceptions of a preventive design of the interactive structure predominantly refer to the claim for a multiplication of existing – often interventional – structures of actions. It is primarily on the level of prevention referring to people that the social workers are faced with the situation that their professional identity is not questioned by administrative regulations anymore, but rather by the addressees or by the alternative concepts of normality they represent. The holding on to conventional forms of coping with problems and thus the missing negotiation with the addressees about innovative concepts of coping with problems is additionally strengthened by the fact that there are hardly any ideas about alternative socio-pedagogical competence of actions on the part of the experts. Their profiles of demand are rather limited primarily to the existence of administrative and bureaucratic knowledge of procedures.

(3) Social science knowledge does in fact lead to adequate definitions of problems, appropriate concepts of aims, however, are located outside of their own context of actions by the social workers. The conceptions of structurally orientated prevention the social workers have developed, are not integrated into the direct performance of actions. In this respect, structurally orientated prevention is – in accordance with most of the experts' statements – not an element of socio–pedagogical actions. A classic concept of social work as exclusively supporting individual cases is therefore maintained, although the social workers' definitions of problems and their evaluation of the adolescents' situations allow to suggest existing and contrary social science knowledge.

The research results now becoming apparent contain some important conditional elements for the explanation of a predominant lack of preventive orientations of youth services. All results of the analysis agree in the conclusion that the professional reference to structures is the decisive factor of prevention. This, on the one hand, confirms the relevance of social science knowledge, on the other hand, however, the fact becomes obvious that the administration does not exert a direct influence on the institutionalization of preventive strategies of coping with problems. It only takes its influence indirectly by providing appropriate structures for the interactive situations and the design of context. This probable result is of special importance since the extent of prevention can in fact be expected to be of the highest grade when all the references to structures, context and people are orientated towards prevention, but the most essential fact is the combination of social science knowledge with preventively orientated processses of negotiation. Thus, on the one hand, the professionalization of the social workers is of a central importance for preventive youth services, on the other hand, there are obviously still no methodical procedures that could make the respective stores of knowledge decisive for actions in the interaction with addressees.

References

Albrecht, G. (1980): Theorien der Raumbezogenheit sozialer Probleme. Referat für die Tagung der Sektion 'Soziale Probleme / Soziale Kontrolle' der Deutschen Gesellschaft für Soziologie in Bamberg. Bamberg

Alheit, P., and Glass, CH. (1986): Beschädigtes Leben. Soziale Biographien arbeitsloser Jugendlicher. Frankfurt/M./ New York

Arbeitsgruppe Sozialpolitik (1986): Sozialpolitische Regulierung und die Normalisierung des Arbeitsbürgers. In: Neue Praxis, 1/2

Atteslander, P., and Hamm, B. (Eds.) (1974): Materialien zur Siedlungssoziologie. Köln

Balsen, W., Nokielski, H., Rössel, K., and Winkel, R. (1984): Die neue Armut: Ausgrenzung von Arbeitslosen aus der Arbeitslosenunterstützung. Köln

Beck, U. (1986): Risikogesellschaft. Auf dem Weg in eine andere Moderne. Frankfurt/M.

Berger, J., and Offe, C. (1980): Die Entwicklungsdynamik des Dienstleistungssektors. In: Leviathan 8: 41-75

Bonss, W., and Heinze, R.G. (Eds.) (1984): Arbeitslosigkeit in der Arbeitsgesellschaft. Frankfurt/M.

Böhnisch, L. (1982): Der Sozialstaat und seine Pädagogik. Darmstadt/ Neuwied

Bundesminister für Jugend, Familie und Gesundheit (1980): 5. Jugendbericht. Bonn

Castel, R. (1983): Von der Gefährlichkeit zum Risiko. In: Wambach, M.M. (Ed.): Der Mensch als Risiko. Frankfurt/M.

Chasse, K.A. (1988): Armut nach dem Wirtschaftswunder. Frankfurt/M./ New York

Dahrendorf, R. (1983): Wenn der Arbeitsgesellschaft die Arbeit ausgeht. In: Matthes, J. (Ed.): Krise der Arbeitsgesellschaft. Verhandlungen des 21. Dt. Soziologentages in Bamberg. Frankfurt/M./ New York

Dewe, B. (1985): Soziologie als "beratende Rekonstruktion". Zur Metapher des "klinischen Soziologen". In: Bonß, W., and Hartmann, H. (Eds.): Entzauberte Wissenschaft. Sonderband 3 der Sozialen Welt. Göttingen

Evers, A. (1985): Sozialpolitik als Gestaltung von Lebensweisen. In: Neue Praxis, Heft 5

Fehr, M. (1982): System und Lebensweise. Probleme in der DDR. In: KZfSS. 34. Jg.: 445-486

Fliegel, St., Röhrle, B., and Stark, W. (Eds.) (1983): Gemeindepsychologische Perspektiven 2, Interventionsprinzipien. München

Franzkowiak, P. (1987): Jugend, Gesundheit und Gesundheitsförderung. In: Neue Praxis, 3/87: 210-225

Friedrichs, J. (1977): Stadtanalyse, soziale und räumliche Organisation der Gesellschaft. Hamburg

Göschel, A., Herlyn, U., Krämer, J., Schardt, Th., and Wendt, G. (1977): Infrastrukturdisparitäten und soziale Segregation. In: Kaufmann, F.X. (Ed.): Bürgernahe Gestaltung der sozialen Umwelt. Meisenheim am Glan

Gravenhorst, L., Cramon-Daiber, B., and Schablow, M. (1984): Lebensort: Familie. Opladen

Habermas, J. (1985): Die neue Unübersichtlichkeit. Frankfurt/M.

Hagemann-White, C. (1984): Sozialisation: Weiblich – männlich?. Opladen

Hamm, B. (1980): Thesen zur Soziologie der Stadt – Ein Ausweg aus der Banalität?. In: Leviathan, 8. Jg. Heft 2: 265-272

Häussermann, H., and Krämer-Badoni, Th. (1980): Ein Beitrag zur Auseinandersetzung mit der Sozialökologie. Stadtsoziologie mit der Meßlatte?. In: Soziale Welt, XXXI. Jg. Heft 2

Herriger, N. (1983): Präventive Jugendkontrolle – eine staatliche Strategie zur Kolonisierung des Alltags. In: Z. f. Päd., 18. Beiheft: 231-236

Hitzler, R., and Horner, A. (1984): Lebenswelt – Milieu – Situation. In: KZfSS, 36. Jg.: 56-74

Horn, K. (1983): Gesundheitserziehung im Verhältnis zu anderen sozialisatorischen Einflüssen. Grenzen individueller Problemlösungsmöglichkeiten. In: Bundeszentrale für gesundheitliche Aufklärung (Ed.): Europäische Monographien zur Forschung in Gesundheitserziehung 5. Köln

Hottelet, H. (1984): Plädoyer für Prävention in der sozialen Arbeit. In: Blätter der Wohlfahrtspflege, Heft 12: 283-286

Japp, K.P. (1986): Wie psycho-soziale Dienstleistungen organisiert werden. Frankfurt/M./ New York

Kahl, A., Wilsdorf, S.H., and Wolf, H.F. (1984): Kollektivbeziehungen und Lebensweise. Berlin

Karsten, M.-E., and Otto, H.-U. (1987): Die sozialpädogogische Ordnung der Familie. Weinheim/ München

Keupp, H. (1987): Psychosoziale Praxis im gesellschaftlichen Umbruch. Bonn

Kickbusch, I. (1983): Lebensweisen und Gesundheit: Einführende Betrachtungen. In: Bundeszentrale für gesundheitliche Aufklärung (Ed.): Europäische Monographien zur Forschung in Gesundheitserziehung 5. Köln

Kohli, M. (1986): Gesellschaftszeit und Lebenszeit. In: Berger, J. (Ed.): Die Moderne – Kontinuitäten und Zäsuren. Soziale Welt Sonderband 4. Göttingen

Kommer, D., and Röhrle, B. (1981): Handlungstheoretische Perspektiven primärer Prävention. In: Minsel, W.-R., and Scheller, R. (Ed.): Brennpunkte der klinischen Psychologie. München

Kupffer, H. (1983): Die Fragwürdigkeit der Prävention in der Sozialarbeit/ Sozialpädagogik. In: Z. f. Päd., 18. Beiheft: 228-230

Kühne, L. (1978): Zum Begriff und zur Methode der Erforschung der Lebensweise. In: Weimarer Beiträge. 24. Jg. Heft 8: 27-56

Leibfried, S., and Tennstedt, F. (1985): Politik der Armut und die Spaltung des Sozialstaats. Frankfurt/M.

Lippold, G., and Manz, G. (1980): Zur Anwendung der Zeitkategorien für die Darstellung der Lebensweise. In: Akademie der Wissenschaften der DDR. Berlin

Manz, G. (1981): Aspekte der Bestimmung und der planmäßigen Gestaltung der sozialistischen Lebensweise. In: Wirtschaftswissenschaft 8: 936-948

Marquardt, R., Diezinger, A., Schildmann, U., and Westphal-Georgi, U. (1984): Am Rande der Arbeitsgesellschaft: Weibliche Behinderte und Erwerbslose. Opladen

Matthes, J. (Ed.) (1983): Krise der Arbeitsgesellschaft? Verhandlungen des 21. Deutschen Soziologentages in Bamberg. Frankfurt/M./ New York

McKenzie, R.D. (1926): Konzepte der Sozialökologie. In: Atteslander, P., and Hamm, B. (Eds.) (1974): Materialien zur Siedlungssoziologie. Köln

Meulemann, H., and Weishaupt, H. (1981): Örtliche und soziale Milieus als Konzept für Sozialisations- und Entwicklungsprozesse. In: Walter, H. (Ed.): Region und Sozialisation. Beiträge zur sozialökologischen Präzisierung menschlicher Entwicklungsvoraussetzungen, Bd.1 und 2. Stuttgart

Mullis, F.Y., Kern, R.M., and Curlette, W.L. (1987): Life-Style Themes and Social Interest: A Further Factor Analytic Study. In: Individual Psychology, Vol.43 (3), September: Austin/ Texas

Mückenberger, U. (1985): Die Krise des Normalarbeitsverhältnisses. Teil 1 und 2. In: Zeitschrift für Sozialreform: 415-434 und 457-475

Müller-Schöll, A. (1984): Heimerziehung und Prävention. In: Blätter der Wohlfahrtspflege, Heft 12: 289-291

Müller, S., and Otto, H.-U. (1980): Gesellschaftliche Bedingungen und Funktionsprobleme der Organisation sozialer Arbeit im Kontext staatlichen Handelns. In: Neue Praxis, Sonderheft 5: 5-28

Negt, O. (1985): Lebendige Arbeit, enteignete Zeit. Politische und kulturelle Dimensionen des Kampfes um die Arbeitszeit. Frankfurt/M./ New York

Offe, C. (1984): "Arbeitsgesellschaft". Strukturprobleme und Zukunftsperspektiven. Frankfurt/M.

Olk, Th. (1986): Abschied vom Experten. Weinheim/ München

Olk, Th., and Otto, H.-U. (Eds.) (1985): Der Wohlfahrtsstaat in der Wende. Umrisse einer zukünftigen Sozialarbeit. Weinheim/ München

Otto, H.-U. (1983): Prävention – Zauberwort für gesellschaftliche Veränderung oder eine Form der Sozialkontrolle?. In: Z. f. Päd., 18. Beiheft: 219-220

Park, E.R. (1925): Die Stadt als räumliche Struktur und als sittliche Ordnung. In: Atteslander, P., and Hamm, B. (Eds.) (1974): Materialien zur Siedlungssoziologie, Köln.

Peters, H. (1984): Sozialarbeit: Systemintegrative Reserve mit sozialintegrativem Sachverständnis?. In: Neue Praxis, Heft 1: 21-26

Raschke, J. (1984): Politik und Wertewandel in den westlichen Demokratien. In: Aus Politik und Zeitgeschichte. B 36: 23-44

Rotter, M., and Steinert, H. (1981): Stadtstruktur und Kriminalität. In: Walter, H. (Ed.): Region und Sozialisation. Beiträge zur sozialökologischen Präzisierung menschlicher Entwicklungsvoraussetzungen. Bd. 1 und 2. Stuttgart

Savelsberg, J.J. (1980): Sozialräumliche Prozesse: Übersehene Determinanten der 'Konstitution sozialer Probleme'? Das Beispiel Jugendkriminalität. In: Verhandlungen des 20. Deutschen Soziologentages zu Bremen: Lebenswelt und soziale Probleme. Bremen

Schneider, H.R. (1981): Anforderungen an eine Theorie sozialer Probleme und kritischer Anmerkungen zum Forschungsstand in der BRD (1). In: Kriminalsoziologische Bibliographie, 8. Jg. Heft 32/33: 21-45

Schulz, Chr., and Wambach, M.M. (1983): Vorbemerkungen. Oberfläche und Dunkelfeld. In: Wambach, M.M. (Ed.): Der Mensch als Risiko. Frankfurt/M.

Schulz, H. (1984): Prävention und Einflußnahme im kommunalpolitischen Raum. Entwicklung der ambulanten und teilstationären Erziehungshilfen als Ausbau der offensiven Jugendhilfe in Kassel. In: Blätter der Wohlfahrtspflege, Heft 12: 293-295

Seidenspinner, G., Burer, A., Rettke, U., Reinhardt, M., Jenkins, E., Bednarz-Braun, E., and Brüning-Regenbogen, A. (1984): Vom Nutzen weiblicher Lohnarbeit. Opladen

Sengling, D. (1984): Offensive Jugendhilfe im Stadtteil. Erziehungsberatung zwischen Prävention und Intervention. In: Blätter der Wohlfahrtspflege, Heft 12: 287-289

Steinert, H. (1981): Widersprüche, Kapitalstrategien und Widerstand oder: warum ich den Begriff "sozialer Probleme" nicht mehr hören kann. Versuch eines theoretischen Rahmens für die Analyse der politischen Ökonomie sozialer Bewegungen und "soziale Probleme". In: Kriminalsoziologische Bibliographie, 8. Jg. Heft 32/33: 56-88

Taylor, R., and Ford, G. (1981): Lifestyle and ageing: three traditions in lifestyle research. In: Ageing and Society, 1. Jg. (3): 329-345 Cambridge

Teriet, B. (1980): Mit Zeitsouveränität zu neuen Ansätzen für die Arbeitszeit, das Erwerbseinkommen und die Freizeit. In: liberal, Heft 12: 890- 903

Vascovics, L.A. (1982): Raumbezogenheit sozialer Probleme. Opladen

Vobruba, G. (1983): Prävention und Selbstkontrolle. In: Wambach, M.M. (Ed.): Der Mensch als Risiko. Frankfurt/M.

Weidig, R. (1980): Zur Dialektik der Entwicklung von Sozialstruktur und sozialistischer Lebensweise in der DDR. In: Deutsche Zeitschrift für Philosophie. Heft 8: 5-18

Weiss, J. (1983): Verständigungsorientierung und Kritik. Zur Theorie des kommunikativen Handelns von Jürgen Habermas. In: ZfS, 35. Jg.: 108-120

Wenzel, E. (1983): Die Auswirkungen von Lebensbedingungen und Lebensweisen auf die Gesundheit – Synthese des Seminars. In: Bundeszentrale für gesundheitliche Aufklärung (Ed.): Europäische Monographien zur Forschung in Gesundheitserziehung 5. Köln

Wenzel, E. (1986): Die Ökologie des Körpers. Frankfurt/M.

Werlhof, C. von (1984): Der Proletarier ist tot. Es lebe die Hausfrau. In: Werlhof, C. von, u.a. (Eds.): Frauen, die letzte Kolonie. Reinbek

Wiley, J.A., and Camacho, T.C. (1980): Life-Style and Future Health: Evidence from the Alameda County Study. In: Preventive Medicine, 9. Jg. (1): 1-21 New York

Part III
Inquiry into the Ethical Aspects of Prevention

12.

Problems of Access to Data and of the Right to Privacy in Criminological Research

Karl F. Schumann

Recently German criminological research faces increasing hesitation of state agencies to grant access to files on criminal cases or to police records. To protect personality rights, that is personal data, administrative laws have been put into action which tighten the control on information transfer. Scientists are barred from getting access to such data. Statements of consent by the persons on file are required before the files are opended to the researchers. While the scientific community of German criminologists becomes more and more embarrassed about that development, a calm analysis of the situation seems to be useful to be able to get at an appropriate balance between research interests on the one hand, and the necessity to protect privacy on the other.

This paper starts with a general overview on the situation of data access in German criminological research. Thereafter a brief description is provided on the main argument between criminologists and state authorities who are in charge to protect the informational self-determination of the people (Datenschützer). Then follows a methodological note on errors in research to estimate the scope of error which might be caused if research were to be restricted only to persons consenting with the researchers' access to their files. Finally, I will argue the case for a double-standard regulation which implies that research on control agencies should be privileged in granting access to court files without consent, while etiological research should not.

1. Access: discriminatory practices

Problems of access to data on file with police or courts have been discussed in recent years in a controversial manner. Research agencies funded by the state have been accused to monopolize research access with the effect that university researchers tend to be more often denied accesss to data necessary for their criminological studies. Brusten has summarized this position as follows:

State agencies make sure that criminological research will produce useful results for their political goals by using two strategies:

"a) the strategy of *offensive social control* by establishing state research units, by initiating research grants and by funding selectively research projects;

b) strategies of *defensive social control* e.g., through generating obstacles to academic research; that is by turning down requests for cooperation and data access, by censoring research instruments or publications, by rejecting research proposals etc." (1986, p. 194).

Examples of the offensive type are according to Brusten the research units of the police (Polizeiakademie Hiltrup), of the ministries of justice (e.g., in the State of Baden-Württemberg, Lower Saxonia, etc.) or of prison systems (so called Kriminologischer Dienst). Those units and research grants funded by ministries of interior, of justice as well as of the Federal Police Agency (BKA) tend to push aside university based research in terms of funding and access to data. This tendency is even more increased by defensive social control like rejection of access to research fields where the criminal justice systems function as gate-keepers to data (e.g., the prison system). Other defensive strategies include the delay of decisions on requested access to data or grant access depending on changes in research design or instruments.

In a recent study on conflict situations in social research we found that in criminological research is a substantial danger to suffer from a rejection of data-access if
a) the results might be used within the antagonistic structure of the criminal justice system e.g., by offenders or prisoners, or if
b) the results might destroy or contradict the legitimation of agencies of social control, or if
c) there is no guarantee that the expectation of confidentiality about unlawful practices of the staff will be honored, or if
d) results might prove lacking efficiency, or if
e) results are not predictable thus leaving little chances to calculate their risks or usefulness for the criminological justice system (see Brusten et al., 1981, p. 72).

To calculate the risks involved with a given research proposal the agencies of social control who are gatekeepers to data look, consistent with their tendency to judge the guilt of persons, at the person of the researcher and his former research, rather than at the research proposal in question. "Dangerousness" of research will be predicted if the researcher works within the framework of the labeling approach or if he tended not to be loyal to the criminal justice system before.

If researchers working in state research units or in universities apply for data access at the same time, the chances of the university researcher are poorer to get it. There is a mechanism of suppression going on which selects from all applications those of the most loyal researchers while the rest is being turned down for lacking capacity to cooperate with all. A Ph. D. candidate of mine recently asked prison authorities of the state of Hesse to be allowed to interview the heads of some 10 prisons on matters of participation of prisoners. The ministry of justice replied:

"In the prisons currently some research projects are carried out which are attended by the heads of prisons or their assistants. The compliance with your request for an interview in a way sufficient for scientific standards would demand a substantial amount of time. The workload of the heads of prison and their assistants is however so high that additional work – like especially the job to answer your questionnaire – cannot be done" (letter of 17/9/1987).

The story is that the Ph. D. candidate had some years ago helped to establish the first prisoners' union in the state of Hesse. He also used to be a critic of the prison authorities for years. Of course the ministry of justice might have left the decision to the prison-heads themselves who might have agreed with or rejected the request for an interview according to their factual work load, rather than paternalistically turning down the request in toto. This case is just another incident in a long list of discriminations against scholars who are known as not being uncritical in respect to the criminal justice system.

Whenever that discrimination is at issue the criminologists who work for state research units react nervously. For example, F. Berckhauer, working at the ministry of justice in Lower Saxonia, accuses Brusten to over-exaggerate the situation. State researchers would get very little funding; moreover their access to data would be complicated by the fact, that "many 'free'colleagues have generated an image of criminology as a sience which observes the practice in a critical, disturbing, and unfavorable manner" (1985, p. 133). R. Blath, junior criminological researcher in the Federal ministry of justice in Bonn, strongly denied the danger that state research might push aside the university research, but stressed at the same time the importance of the usefulness of research for political decision-making: "A criminology which is based on a critique of the existing social and penal order (does not) fit for a rational communication between criminology and criminal policy, because it tends to mix empirical results with value judgments". (1985, p. 91). Only criminologists who criticize in a constructive way and accept the existing legal order as legitimate fit for cooperation with politicians. Such researcher leave value judgments to politicians and restrict their competency to empirical research. To do just that they should be assisted – seems to be the logical conclusion.

Those statements suggest a quite vivid hostility between university and state researchers in Germany. Most recently however that hostility seems to fade away. Three observations indicate this trend:

1) The discriminatory pratices are applicable only where agencies of social control are in the position of gate-keepers to data, that is to records and files of the criminal justice system. Research on deviant persons or the social and psychological context of deviancy is beyond their influence and that type of field-research becomes more and more relevant even for criminal policy;
2) Critical criminological research becomes rare itself. Critical criminologists stop doing research. Is that already the result of the discriminatory pratices in providing data

access? I doubt it. Rather I think critical thinkers leave criminology to enter other fields with a more satisfactory level of thinking.

3) There seems to emerge a new confrontation between criminologists of all political orientation (liberals, conservatives, socialists) on one side, and the "ombudsmen" for the protection of individual data on the other. The reason for this development is the supreme court decision on the unconstitutionality of the Federal Census of 1983 (BVerfGE 65, 1) which stressed the principle of "informational self- determination". It has been implemented also into regulations important to criminological research. In fact there emerged new "gate-keepers", quite influential ones, namely the data-protecting state-authorities, who try to restrict research in general, irrespective of their financial or organizational basis. The monopoly of the criminal justice system to grant or deny access to its files and records is endangered. University researcher however face now twice a high barrier to their protected research, because the criminal justice system learned quickly to block outside research by pointing at the necessity to protect the data of their clients. The next paragraph will be concerned with the question if it would be a good idea for critical criminology to join forces with the conservatives and state researchers against the protection of private data by authorized agencies.

2. Controversy about protection of data

In July 1987 the director of the Federal Criminological Research Unit in Wiesbaden (Zentralstelle), Dr. Jehle, sent letters to all professors of criminology to sign a statement on data protection. The professional criminological societies as well as the Chairman of the Advisory Board of the (rather critical) journal "Kriminologisches Journal" had accepted this statement before; signatures of scholars were collected. I know of very few professors who did not sign this statement.

My decision eventually not to sign it, was based mainly on the fact that research interests were weighted much stronger than the protection of privacy of offenders; moreover, the statement was extremely and unduly soft when it came to the demand for a researchers privilege in criminal cases to refuse testimony in courts on research data (or to protect research data from being subpoenaed). I was however ambivalent about my decision; as a researcher I felt bad about my lack of loyality to the fellow-researchers who fought for the freedom of scientific work. It may be helpful to clarify the ambivalence by looking closely at the focal sentences of that statement. It reads like this:

"The transfer of data on file at state authorities to a researcher is always justified if the data are necessary to carry through a given project, if misuse of the data is precluded, if the administrative work implied by the data-transfer is fungible, and if the invasion into privacy of the subjects caused by the data-transfer is not unproportional in relation to the results to be expected from the research.

Under the specified conditions any transfer of personal data from state authorities to researchers does not affect personality rights of the subjects whose data are transferred. Therefore it is not necessary to request a statement of consent by the subject as a condition for the transfer of data." (No.7 and 8 of the statement; see Jehle, 1988, pp. 407 et seq.).

Apparently criminologists demand the privilege to get access to data without consent of the clients of the criminal justice system. Constitutional law says: the principle of informational self-determination constitutes a guarantee that data are used only for the purpose they are collected for in administrations. Thus personal data in court files may be used only for decision-making in criminal procedure. To transfer such data to a researcher transcends the purpose which legitimized the data collection; therefore, a statement of consent by the subject whose data are on file will be necessary. Of course, to obey this constitutional principle implies for criminological research a substantial handicap; it demands to write to everybody whose records or files may be of interest for a statement of consent, including offenders and staff personal. Letters will get lost because addresses are wrong, letters will be left unanswered, requests will be turned down. The more hostile a person is toward the criminal justice system, the smaller the chance for consent. Criminologists realistically predict that under such circumstances "representative research is no longer possible" (see Jehle, 1988, ibid.).

Such restrictions would affect not only etiological research which uses records and files for the collection of data on the causes of crime. It would also affect research related to the social reaction approach, maybe even more. Persons who felt being unfairly treated by criminal justice would tend to reject the request for consent more often than properly treated persons. Also middle class and upper class offenders might withold consent more often than lower class people lacking knowledge about their rights. Such tendencies would distort the sample in a way that research on class justice, on unequality in judicial decision-making and on discrimination of poor people might become senseless because cases of extreme misjudgements will be no longer available due to lacking consent of the respective offenders. Thus even a critical criminologist may have some problems with simply subscribing to the principle of informational self-determination. How can this dilemma be solved?

3. Fetish representativeness

The wrong way seems to be to choose between the two alternatives to request always or never consent as a prerequisite for data access. Such dualism would neglect the difficulty of the issues involved. Rather it seems necessary to consider two lines of thought before any decision is being made.

The first issue has to do with one of the main standards of empirical research: its representativeness. To be sure criminological research cannot simply suspend that standard for the benefit of protection of privacy of subjects. If research based on consent to the transmission of filed data is not possible in a representative manner, the state of the art is strongly endangered. Looking back to the last decades German criminological research fought a successful fight against the empirical "methodology" of forensic psychiatrists who drew far-reaching conclusions on the causes of crime based on a few pathological cases. Such highly selective samples were criticized as being distorted by the decision-making process of the criminal justice system itself, thus reflecting the selective criteria of decision-making rather than "causes" of crime. It was argued that only probability samples would allow meaningful criminological research. Especially the followers of the labeling approach insisted that non-representative samples might imply the danger of reification of the selectivity of the agents of social control.

In fact it was the representativeness of results which made criminology a science in the eyes of penal lawyers as well. To speculate from knowledge of a few cases is something every lawyer is able to do himself. Large populations however, may only be studied be a real, positivist researcher. Lacking representativeness is in their eyes an error restricting the usefulness of the results for criminal policy. To build political decisions on the ground of an unrepresentative study causes the danger that the behavior of important parts of the populations (those who have been ignored) cannot be influenced by that policy.

There are however good reasons not to overexaggerate the insistence in representativeness. To give priority to that standard of research seems to be quite dishonest in view of the many types of errors in research which are taken as unavoidable. In my opinion representativeness has become a fetish rather than a rational principle of research design. In fact there are many strategies quite common in criminological research which ignore that principle quite strongly. Cooperative persons are substituted for persons who refuse to be interviewed to make sure that a quorum of interviews can be arrived at. Studies based on files of court cases tend to ignore the fact that many files are unavailable due to pending court cases so that the files are "somewhere", that is: lost for research purposes. Those problems are however minor.

More important is the fact that generally the population which is to be represented by a given sample, is never specified in any exact manner (Philips, 1974). For example, a study which is based on files of the year A in jurisdiction B is representative exactly for files in the year A in jurisdiction B. Any statement which extends that scope of representativeness is erroneous; despite that fact it is common use to draw conclusions from such a sample in a rather general manner, such as generalizing for all jurisdictions of a region or even country and of course to generalize for a longer time period.

If researchers accept such far-reaching erroneous generalizations, that is if such a deceit about the scope of cases represented by the sample is silently accepted, why not accepting an error caused by the selectivity of a consent- requesting procedure? In fact, if one follows the ideas of Glaser and Strauss on theoretical sampling, the question becomes if a probability sample is indeed such a superior research strategy compared to a stepwise procedure to select cases which maximalize the variance according to theoretical expectations (1968, chap. 2).

In addition one may ask, if the principle of representativeness deserves such a priority in regard to the principle of informational self-determination, if on the other side, the scientific community readily accepts the fact that studies based on records produce results about personal behavior which are most probably without much validity. Records contain only that information about persons which is relevant either to arrive at decisions or to dress them up in a lawful manner. As descriptions of persons they are highly distorted. Such well known criticism about lacking validity of data may be neglected if the research is aimed at decision patterns of agencies of social control, who produce the records for their own activities. This distinction between persons who are subjects of the files and persons/agencies who produce the files is important.

While researchers who use court records for the study of persons, accept or even ignore the lack of validity the same persons however insist in strict compliance with the standard of representativeness even if this implies an infliction of the right of informational self-determination. How come? Do those researchers nurse a professional view on persons which considers important only the crime-related features of their existence? One is tempted to believe, that due to a professional distortion people are indeed perceived no longer as human beeings with very complex characters and biographies but rather as items reducable to their criminal biography which is seen as a public matter anyway. To realize the fact that their crime history is only a small, even a neglectable, part of their life, does not come to the mind of those scholars. It is this lack of a comprehensive understanding of the human existence of criminals which seems to be the reason for neglectance of lacking validity of the files on offenders as well as of their rights to privacy.

4. The case for a double-standard

This ignorant attitude towards human beings leads me to suggest a double-standard for granting access to data. Two additional aspects may justify this double-standard. I mentioned already the fact that files and records say a lot about the persons who produce the files, but little on the persons covered by the files. A similar distinction can be made according to how constitutional law protects the right to privacy.

During a congress on data protection in criminological research in March 1987 it was pointed out by a constitutional lawyer, Professor Berg, that Article 5 of the German constitution guarantees the freedom of research from being controlled by the state. Thus a researcher who demands access to files of state agencies has a right to get those files if the research is concerned with the practices of the agencies. They have to accept public scrutiny of their work, including a possible control by research (Berg, 1988). This right to get access exists however only regarding authorities not regarding third parties (e.g., persons covered by the files). That is: research on offenders is impossible without their consent, while research on agencies of control does not depend of consent. Neither the record-keeping persons have to aggree because they have to accept public control nor the offenders have to give their consent because the research is not at all interested in them as persons. Thus a far reaching, almost perfect strategy of anonymization is possible without any risk of damage to the research aiming at behavior patterns of the agency staff. Therefore the problem of access is, according to Berg, rather uncomplicated for research on the criminal justice system itself (Jehle, 1988). While constitutional law seems to justify the double standard which privileges research on agencies of control, it may however be quite impractical. Research aiming at the study of persons may be camouflaged as research aiming at the decision patters of agencies. How such a double standard could be protected against circumvention is not at issue here. The practically is a different matter. At the moment I want to point only at the congruence of justifiability of a double-standard in data access to arguments formulated 15 years ago when Sagarin (1973) demanded the right of deviant groups not to be researched.

Sagarin argued that certain deviant groups are in danger to be more closely controlled if research data on them are available. They should be protected from being subjected to research if they decide so. Covert research on them should be considered unethical. In contrast organizations serving the public should be granted such a right not to be researched. Galliher (1973) explicitly suggested this double-standard to be included in the code of ethics of the American Sociological Association. I used to definitely defend that double-standard of ethics of research as a justification of covert research on power elites and as a preclusion of covert research among deviants: The more powerful an organization, that is the more it can protect itself from being subjected to research, the more it will be justified on ethical grounds to do clandestine research on it (see Schumann, 1974).

In the USA where generally any research presupposes informed consent of the research subjects, the San Diego-School of investigative research, founded by Jack Douglas, advances the same posititon. Research on organizations which notoriously provide incomplete informations on their practices or even lie to the public or manipulate the media deliberately for a favorable image, deserve to be decepted by covert research which aims at telling the truth. Many other authors who do not share the critical stance of the San-Diego-School join however that argument (Bulmer, 1982). Without any other option to prove discriminations of groups or the ignorance of the rights of powerless persons (Punch, 1985, p. 42) covert research is concidered acceptable by many scholars. They agree for example that Rosenhans study "on being sane on insane places" was justified because stigmatization of insanity was demonstrable only by using sane persons in a covert experiment. The argument is that different ethics may be necessary for research upward or downward the status pyramid. While elites may protect themselves from being researchers, vulnerable groups like children, prisoners, handicapped persons etc. will need a comprehensive protection. They may not understand all dangers involved with being subjected to research and are less experienced and effective in the rejection of research requests. Being used to be controlled by state agencies they wave their right to privacy more easily than elites. The latter are effective in shielding themselves from the curiosity of people with lesser status (like sociologists).

Actually such a standard seems to be partly accepted by German "ombudsmen" for the protection of personal data ("Datenschützer"). They stopped a research project using the files of prisoners after they became aware of the fact that the prisoners had not been asked for informed consent. A study of persons not guilty because of insanity who lived in psychiatric institutions was stopped and partly terminated in respect to those persons who did not retrospectively consent with their files being analysed and their interviews having been taped and used for research purposes (Leuze, 1986, p. 54).

Both research projects did not have sinister goals. Rather they aimed at improvements of the sociotherapeutic assistance to those subjects under study. The authorities in charge of protection of informational self-determination however reasoned that as long as the benevolent aims of research are not communicated to the subjects in a way which convinces them to give their informed consent, access to their files should be blocked. The essence of all this is: offenders are no longer the handy research material for criminologists.

5. Conclusion

This paper attempted to clarify some problems involved in access to data on file at various agencies of the criminal justice system. There are many other issues to be raised on that topic which have been left aside. Currently criminologists who have for a long time been used to free availability of data on offenders and prisoners have to revise their negligent attitude toward offenders' rights to privacy. In a strange way criminologists are currently being resocialized themselves. They can no longer consider the files of prisoners as their research property. Critical criminologists who see now a better chance to get access to data on everyday routines of the criminal justice system, must be aware of the danger that without any legal regulation or with a very general one the old battle-array will be restored. That is: court files will be open to researchers looking for causes of crime while scholars with a less affirmative attitude toward law enforcement agencies will find closed doors again. We experience only a short period of irritation. It is essential therefore to arrive at specific regulations of accesss to data which make a distinction between research interested in organization practices without interest in individuals on one side, which should have unlimited access to files, and research of the etiological type which should be obliged to request informed consent from the subjects whose files are to be used as research material. The distinctions in analysis should be open to the control by the authorities who protect the right to informational self-determination.

References

Berckhauer, F. (1985): Zur Auseinandersetzung um die "Staatskriminologie". In: Kury, H. (Ed.), Kriminologische Forschung in der Diskussion: Berichte, Standpunkte, Analysen, Köln: Heymanns

Berg, W. (1988): Informelle Selbstbestimmung und Forschungsfreiheit: Zum Spannungsverhältnis zwischen zwei in der Verfassung verankerten Rechten. In: Jehle (Ed.) 1988

Blath, R. (1985): Kriminologische Forschung aus strafrechtspolitischer Sicht. In: Kury, H. (Ed.): Kriminologische Forschung in der Diskussion: Berichte, Standpunkte, Analysen. Köln: Heymanns

Brusten, M. (1986): Probleme kriminologischer Forschung. In: Brusten/Häußling/Malinowski (Eds.): Kriminologie im Spannungsfeld von Kriminalpolitik und Kriminalpraxis. Opladen: Westdt. Verlag

Brusten, M., Eberwein, W.D., Feltes, T., Gollner, G., and Schumann, K.F. (1981): Freiheit der Wissenschaft – Mythos oder Realität? Frankfurt: Campus

Bulmer, M. (Ed.) (1982): Social Research Ethics. London: MacMillan

Galliher, J.F. (1973): The Protection of Human Subjects. In: American Sociologist, 93-100

Glaser, B., and Strauss, A. (1968): The Discovery of Grounded Theory. Chicago: Aldine

Jehle, J.M. (Ed.) (1988): Datenzugang und Datenschutz in der kriminologischen Forschung. Wiesbaden: Kriminologische Zentralstelle

Leuze, R. (1986): Datenschutz für unsere Bürger. 7. Tätigkeitsbericht. Stuttgart

Phillips, D. (1974): Abandoning Methods. London/San Francisco: Jossey Bass

Punch, M. (1986): The Politics and Ethics of Fieldwork. Beverly Hills: Sage

Sagarin, E. (1973): The Research Setting and the Right Not to be Researched. In: Social Problems, 52-64

Schumann, K.F. (1975): Ethische und rechtliche Probleme bei der Erforschung von Macht. In: Eser, A., and Schumann, K.F. (Eds.): Forschung im Konflikt mit Recht und Ethik, Stuttgart: Enke

13.
Data Protection and Prevention

Alfred Büllesbach

I. Are data protection and scientific freedom conflicting goals?

The starting point for the discussion on sector-specific data protection in science and research[1] is the relationship of tension between scientific freedom and the right to informational self-determination. Science's claim to information is fundamental and extensive. Modern information technology is seen by science as an opportunity and a challenge to test and to practice new forms of obtaining, analyzing and storing information. The perpetual deepening and broadening of its possibilities of knowledge is a matter of course for the claim of science. In this striving of science and research for more extensive – also more person-related – information on the one hand and the aim of data protection to safeguard the personal rights on the other, lies the reason for the relationship of tension between scientific freedom and data protection. In many fields of practical, scientific research it is a matter of information which, in its quality and quantity, could cause serious disadvantages for those concerned upon becoming known. This risk can not be countered in such a way that one argues that research is not interested in knowledge about individual persons but is rather pursuing general statements. Then in data surveys the individual would only be important as a holder of certain characteristics[2]. Such an attitude is, of course, significant for the concrete assessment of risks but can not alone support the demand for the granting of a privilege, however conceived, to research over data protection. It is indeed predominantly the case that research can work with anonymously held data, but it is in no way uncommon to maintain individual personal references for certain research projects, as, e.g., in the research on individual criminal careers or in the publications, that can occasionally be observed, of case studies which in no way are completely anonymous. Data stores are only anonymous when it in fact is no longer possible to establish a reference to the person to whom they relate. Such an actual process of keeping anonymous exists when the researcher or other persons who have access to the data material can only establish the personal reference with a completely inappropriate and therefore not to be expected expenditure, whereby it doesn't matter whether this is actually intended; it suffices when this remains objectively possible[3].

Legal Solution of the Field of Conflict

In practice, legal questions of data protection occur in research projects especially in the obtaining and safeguarding of data:

- in the obtaining of names and addresses of persons who are to be questioned or through whom further information is to be obtained (address material)
- in the obtaining of other person-related data and
- in the safeguarding of person-related data against unauthorized access and the later destruction of data material in conformance with data protection.

The problematical nature that arises when researchers would like to have access to existent administrative file material in the obtaining of information must be especially emphasized. In the surrendering of file material for the purpose of inspection, a transmission of person-related data can be seen for which there is presently a legal basis only in the lands of Hesse, Bremen and North Rhine-Westphalia. The problems that result therefrom have been set up in the constitution itself. The inspection of files for scientific purposes without the consent of the person concerned is only admissible when a legal basis exists which corresponds to the requirements of the Federal Constitutional Court in the so-called Census Decision[4)]. According to this constitutionally anchored right to informational self-determination, the individual is protected against unlimited collecting, storing, application and transmission of his personal data. This right is derived from Art. 2. paragraph 1 Constitution in connection with Art. 1, paragraph 1 Constitution (GG). The right to informational self-determination guarantees the authority of the individual to decide fundamentally by himself on the disclosure and application of his personal data[5)]. Restrictions are only admissible in the predominant general interest and require a constitutional, legal foundation that must be in accordance with the constitutional principle of the clarity of norms[6)]. The legislator has to attend to the principle of commensurability and to take organizational and procedural precautions which counteract the danger of an infringement of personal rights. Put concisely and precisely, the individual must know who knows what about him when.

Up to the decision in December, 1983, the prevailing opinion in adjudication and literature took the view that the granting of file inspection to third parties, who are not or were not involved in the administrative process, should be left up to the due discretion of the agency in charge of the files. According to this the inspection of files without legal basis was admissible according to the principle of commensurability, which required a weighing up of the public interest and the protection of the private sphere in the individual case[7)].

On the basis of the demand of the Federal Constitutional Court the question arises of how long one can go on waiting to pass sector-specific norms for research and what applies to the transitional period. Can the previous legal situation be further applied here or – with respect to the more recent adjudication – should certain research projects that involve the processing of person-related data be restricted in terms of data protection law? In the scientific discussion this problem is debated under the designation "transition bonus". The adjudication has repeatedly decided in cases of altered constitutional interpretation that interventions in civil rights, which still have no legal basis, must be tolerated for a certain transitional period[8]. Yet this only applies under the condition that an otherwise occurring functional inefficiency of state institutions must be avoided which would be even more foreign to constitutional order than the previous condition[9]. The guaranteeing of the constitutionally anchored right to the free development of science and research according to Art. 5, paragraph 3 Constitution, also belongs to the ordered fulfillment of state functions. It is recognized that civil rights do not exhaust themselves in the mere function of defense, but also positively oblige the state to make an effective exercise of civil rights possible[10]. However, the civil right to scientific freedom imparts no directly constitutional claim to the inspection of files for research purposes[11]. It is true that this constitutional value decision obliges the state, according to the adjudication of the Federal Constitutional Court, also to carry out those measures that are imperative for the protection of a free exercise of science, nevertheless, for the maintenance of a free operation of science, the surrendering of file material with personal references from public agencies for the purpose of inspection is not imperative. Regardless of that, the derivation of individual, positive performance duties of the state from a value-deciding principle norm is only possible on the basis of a weighing up of this constitutional value with other, equally constitutionally guaranteed rights of freedom and value decisions[12]. In this critical development, the relationship of tension – occasionally referred to as a conflict of goals – between data protection and research appears on the level of constitutional law. Art. 5, paragraph 3 Constitution and the right to informational self-determination of Art. 2, paragraph 1 in connection with Art. 1, paragraph 1 Constitution stand in opposition to each other.

These conflicting civil rights are to be construed according to the principle of the greatest possible concordance and related to one another[13]. A general or even only a fundamental priority of the scientist's claim to information over the citizen's claim to data protection is therefore ruled out.

The possibility of circumventing this conflict, in that the consent of the person concerned is previously obtained by the authorities or the data (files) are made actually anonymous before inspection, comes up in practice against the limitations of the capacities of the administration as a higher administrative expenditure and is not seldom connected with this procedure. For the transitional period, therefore, from the aspect of the weighing up of goods and of commensurability, only for each concrete individual case will one be able to answer the question of whether the desired inspection of the files is absolutely necessary and therefore admissible. Also important in this connection is the consideration of whether it is a matter of especially sensitive and thus especially protection-worthy data that are coming into question here and whether from this aspect likewise certain portions of the files should be excluded from inspection as they, for example, are subject to a special professional secrecy.

In weighing up one must also take into account whether it has been made certain that the research authority has assured the data against alienation of purpose and unauthorized use and that the data will only be used for the stated purpose of the research project and nowhere else. Here it must be pointed out that the deciding factor is the purpose of the research project and not the purpose of research in general. In the decision it is ultimately significant whether the researcher has arranged that the data stay anonymous and which guarantees exist so far. Likewise appropriate conditions will be able to be connected with the positive decision on the inspection of the files. It is also of significance whether data protection agreements have been concluded with the researchers involved. Whereby it must be made clear that data protection agreements are only possible on the basis of legal regulations. The ethical self-commitments of scientific associations are, of course, significant and important, but can not replace legal bases.

It is evident that presently the planning and execution of research projects, due to the requirements of data protection law that arise out of the right to informational self-determination, thus involves a certain measure of imponderability for the researcher if he doesn't inform himself sufficiently about questions of data protection and data security. Only the legislator can redress this legal uncertainty – whereby the urgently necessary regulation in the Federal Data Protection Law must be especially pointed out due to its nation-wide influence. As already mentioned, the lands Hesse, Bremen and North Rhine-Westphalia, which have adopted research clauses into their new data protection laws, have taken on a pioneering role. The regulation on the researcher's right to refuse to give evidence seems to be especially significant precisely from the aspect of criminological research; this however, is only possible on the basis of federal law.

New Research Regulations

According to section 21 BrDSG (Bremen Data Protection Law) (Law Gazette 1. of October, 29, 1987, No. 3, pp. 263 et seq.), person-related data may fundamentally only be processed to carry out certain research projects if the person concerned has given his consent to this. If this is the case there is no conflict between the personal rights of the individual and the research interests because the person entitled to protection has placed his own data at the disposal of scientific research. The deadlines for explanation and instruction, revised and expanded in section 3, are to be observed in obtaining the consent of the person concerned. The special regulation in paragraph 2 of section 27 BrDSG applies to the phase of transmission. Hereby the law proceeds conceptionally from the idea that the consent of the person concerned with the processing of his person-related data should receive priority. Without the consent of the person concerned, the data may only be processed in so far as his interests that are worthy of protection are not encroached upon, especially with regard to the type of data, their obviousness or the type of processing. The transmission of data without the consent of the person concerned is only possible if public interest in the research project being carried out considerably outweighs the interests worthy of protection of the person concerned, and if the project can not be carried out in any other way or only with an inappropriate expenditure.

Finally, paragraph 3 stipulates the immediate separation of the criteria of the survey from the auxiliary criteria with personal references and obliges the research authority to erase the auxiliary criteria data, with which the personal reference could be established, as soon as the aim of the research has been achieved. Special attention is given to 4 of section 21, whereby the collected data may not be processed for other than research purposes. A transmission of the collected or transmitted data may only take place with the consent of the person concerned. Finally, should those authorities that are not subject to the Land law be transmitted data according to section 21, they have to submit to these regulations of data protection and the control of the Land agents for data protection. This regulation should ensure in particular that independent, private research institutions which obtain data from the public sector are subject to the same requirements of data protection law.

In addition to these regulations in the Bremen Data Protection Law, section 33 of the Data Protection Law of Hesse of November 11, 1986 (GVBl. 1, 1986, p. 309) contains a similar regulation on data processing for scientific purposes. One is also referred in the end to section 28 of the Law for Further Development of Data Protection in the Land North Rhine-Westphalia of March 10th, 1988. The draft for the amending of the Federal Data Protection Law of November 5, 1987 similarly includes after all in section 36 a regulation on the admissibility of the processing and utilizing of person-related data for scientific research.

II. The Special Relationship of Tension Between Data Protection and Prevention Research

When, according to the Federal Constitutional Court, personal rights comprise the power fundamentally to decide for oneself when and within which limits personal living circumstances are to be disclosed, then this statement must be regarded against the background of the present and future conditions of modern data processing in as much as this right requires protection to a special degree. For today, with the help of automatic data processing, individual information about personal or material circumstances of a specific or specifiable person may, from a technical point of view, be stored unlimitedly and be called up at any time within seconds without consideration of distances. They can further – especially with the expansion of integrated information systems – be consolidated with other data collections into a partially or considerably complete picture of a personality without the person concerned being sufficiently able to control its accuracy or application. Thus the possibilities of inspection and influence have expanded in a previously unknown way that is capable of effecting an individual's behavior merely by virtue of the psychological pressure of public sympathy. In the view of the Federal Constitutional Court, whoever has no adequately certain, clear view of which information that pertains to him is known in certain areas of his social environment, and whoever is not relatively able to appraise the knowledge of potential partners in communication can be essentiallly hindered in his freedom to plan and decide based on self-determination. Whoever is accordingly uncertain whether deviant modes of behavior are at any time being noted and permanently stored, used and transmitted as data information will try not to be conspicuous through such modes of behavior. He may possibly renounce an exercise of his civil rights. This would impair not only the individual chances of development but also the common weal, for self-determination is an elementary functional condition of a freedom-loving, democratic community founded upon its citizens' ability for action and cooperation[14)]. Behind all this is the consideration that at the center of the constitutional order are the worth and the dignity of the person who becomes a member of a free society in free self-determination. The dangers indicated by the Federal Constitutional Court comprise precisely preventive strategies as well since they tend to subject societal processes to an uncontrollable surveillance. A threshold could also be reached here beyond which the freedom of research and univeral personal rights could no longer be brought to the greatest possible development by means of practical concordance.

I would like to illustrate this thesis with the shift of emphasis in the combatting of criminality, recently noticeable in pracice, from repression to prevention and there specifically to prevention by means of security[15)]. The talk is of prevention by means of security, and the term 'security state' has been introduced. This functional change of the state into a state in which security has priority produces a special demand for fact-finding knowledge of deviations, disturbances, crises and conflicts of individual or collective, current or potential nature[16)]. The introduction of the computer and of the information network have made this possible. This technological leap is at the same time a social-technical one because from now on the fact can be used that every contact a person has with an institution leads to information which makes it possible to increase the knowledge about the persons concerned. Information systems are designed in such a way so that data may be compiled according to optional, formal rules. This applies in particular to the area of deviance. Yet these risk groups represent only abstract constructions that can no longer be subsumed under the classic sociological group concept. Consequently, the term 'risk group' was replaced by the term 'risk population'. This is based on the suspicion that the gestation of risks can arise out of all social areas and zones. The source of danger is accordingly no longer only a small minority but rather an object of observation because the source of danger can also be the majority.

But thanks to the new information and communication techniques, the suspecting glance can also be cast on every man, who is "somehow and somewhere" gestating risks. It follows therefrom that the tendency to include the whole of society in its observation is inherent to prevention strategy. Statements of the former president of the Federal Bureau of Investigation also fit into this context, i.e., when he says: "But I place my hope in the computer as an instrument for diagnosing an entire society. That is a new kind of prevention that in the end neutralizes also the causes of terror, shifts this state, designs it differently, creates equality and equal standing in the process and in the economy. With the help of this means I can see where the trouble is: classes, social differences and unequal importances, injustice, poverty and discrimination – I can read off all that."[17] A prevention project, in which societal change were only necessary in order to organize comprehensive compulsions to make the subjects adapt, marks the extreme value of repressive prevention. That its realization amounts to the immobilization of society has been thoroughly analyzed in the meantime[18]. Such a conception of preventive criminological policy is also completely contrary to the statements of the Federal Constitutional Court in its census decision.

The quoted observations are not simply to be rejected as the vision of an outsider but rather are the result of a consistent and logical follow up of preventive criminological political approaches to their final conclusion. It is justified by the fact that with preventive combatting of crime, undesirable developments are identified as early as possible and nipped in the bud. For police law this means that potential danger takes the place of traditional danger as a reality that may be statistically virtually prognosticated and possibly avoided. In so far it calls to mind the duty to prevent dangers contained in the new model drafts for police law. The decisive premises of this development are the generalization of suspicion and the generalization of risks, which are to be understood as complementary conditions. A current discussion about the so-called mass data processing shows that data adjustments within the existent data stores throw up fundamental constitutional questions. Data are adjusted, separated from concrete suspicion and separated from concrete proceedings[19]. When such analyses are implemented as so-called "instruments of suspicion"[20], this occurs partially also on the basis of prevention strategies and their fundamental assumptions. Prevention strategies are employed for social control and thus also for social management without the citizen or person concerned being aware of it. Whether this is in conformity with the image of man and the guaranteed freedoms of our Constitution is doubtful. Data protection is protection of the citizens as well as protection of democracy, for the right to informational self-determination implies that the individual must be able to know who knows what about him when and that it is possible, free from anxiety, to safeguard democratic rights.

Here it is also no further help to cast certain preventive strategies into a legal form in order to get a grip on the deviant behavior of individuals or certain groups as at this stage no danger yet exists and the persons concerned have not yet appeared to act criminally or unlawfully. Proven findings that every incident of deviant behavior changes to the liability to punishment or when deviant behavior necessarily changes to the liability to punishment do not exist. Thus it would be a violation of the principle of commensurability if person-related data were to be stored for this reason.

Due to the indicated risks and dangers, and especially in the sphere of prevention research, one must ask how these risks are to be dealt with on the basis of new societal and technological developments and which traditions will be linked up with in this connection. Thus critical prevention research and data protection do not oppose, but rather give rise to each other.

III. On the Relationship of Data Protection and Criminological Research

In summary and at the same time as a reply to the statement of several criminologists on the relationship of data protection and criminological research of September 21, 1987, I would like to state that out of the right to informational self-determination arises the duty of every researcher to obtain the consent to the data survey from the person concerned, whether from him directly or from a third party. A written form is provided for the declaration of one's consent, and the person concerned is to be informed about the object and objectives of the research project as well as about the intended application of the data upon the obtaining of his consent. But when it is conceded in the statement of September 21, 1987 that under certain conditions certain details of the research project may at first be withheld from the person concerned, one must ask how this type of research can be reconciled with the order to safeguard human dignity. Let me point out that, e.g., the National Institute of Mental Health (NIMH) in America holds the deception of test subjects to be fundamentally inadmissible and rejects the support of corresponding projects.

If the obtaining of consent can not reasonably be expected of the researcher, then the admissibility of data surveys without the consent of the person concerned must be precisely legally defined. General clauses should be avoided. Should these requirements for admissibility be fulfilled, one must nevertheless not dispense with making a legal provision that one must first attempt to obtain the consent, as some criminologists demand. For the person concerned should not be excluded from the very beginning from the process of decision on the transmission of his data. The requirements for admissibility should be oriented to section 75 of the Social Security Code X in terms of content. In the consideration which ensues one must also examine whether it is possible to transmit the data in an anonymous form. A transmission in anonymous form also does not violate Art. 5, paragraph 3 Constitution. If this civil right guarantees no claim to the inspection of files, then it also guarantees no claim to which data in which form the researcher should obtain from public agencies.

It also lies in the researcher's power of definition when certain deviant behavior is picked up and the person thereby becomes a carrier of risks; first he is observed out of research considerations and later, for preventive reasons, observed and possibly handled by the police and in the final conclusion discriminated against.

The famous reformer of criminal law, Franz von Liszt, referred to the close connection of crime prevention and socio-political function when he stated that criminological policy may only be the ultima ratio of social policy[21]. These trains of thought show how closely the connection of prevention and the guaranteeing of the right to informational self-determination is bound up with a certain prevention strategy in the societal-political sphere. A specific prevention strategy, which focuses its range of vision particularly on individually oriented intervention of potential offenders and victims, fails to recognize this social structural connection where, following the example of preventive medicine, it is absolutely a matter of eliminating the factors that cause disease. For criminality this means that it can be most effectively combatted – already in its formation – when its social origins are prevented. This reasoning hopefully suffices to show that forcing data protection back to the approach oriented to individuality is in no way sufficient, but rather that data protection, as the protection of democracy, definitely must also take up the entire connection of social structural and societal-political information processing. The right to informational self-determination is not only misused in individual cases but can be channeled by entire societal prevention strategies into a wrong direction that impairs the beneficial development of this right. Recognizing this process is one part of the task; the scientific and political discussion about the correct solution is the other.

Notes

1 Cf. esp. the publication of the conference, Kaase, M. et al. (Eds.): Datenzugang und Datenschutz, Konsequenzen für die Forschung; Büllesbach, A. (1981): Datenschutz versus Wissenschaftsfreiheit? In: ÖVD, No. 3, pp. 9 et seq.; Bull/Dammann (1982): Wissenschaftliche Forschung und Datenschutz. In: ÖVD, No. 6, pp. 213-223; Eberle, C.-E. (1981): Implikationen des Datenschutzes für die empirische Forschung. In: Zeitschrift für Soziologie, pp. 196 et seq.; Borchert, G. (1981): Datenzugang für die Forschung. In: ÖVD, No. 7/8, pp. 18 et seq.

2 Erklärung zum Verhältnis von Datenschutz und kriminologischer Forschung. In: Jehle, J.-M. (Ed.) (1987): Datenzugang und Datenschutz in der kriminologischen Forschung. Wiesbaden, pp. 405 et seq.

3 Büllesbach, A.: Ausgewählte Datenschutzprobleme im Bereich der medizinischen und medizinsoziologischen Forschung. In: Reichertz, P.L. and Kilian, W. (Eds.): Arztgeheimnis-Datenbanken-Datenschutz. pp. 176, 182-184.

4 BVerfGE 65, pp. 1 et seq.

5 BVerfGE 65, p. 1, head note 1.

6 BVerfGE 65, p. 2, head note 2.

7 BVerfGE 27, 344, p. 352.

8 BVerfGE 33, 1, p. 12, p. 13; 41, 251, p. 267.

9 BVerfGE 41, 251, p. 267.

10 BVerfGE 43, 242, pp. 267 et seq.; 47, 327, p. 367; 35, 79, p. 114.

11 BVerwG BayVBl. 1986, p. 121; OVG Rheinland Pfalz, DVBl. 1983, pp. 600 et seq.

12 OVG Rheinland Pfalz a.a.O.

13 Cf. the statement on data protection and the application of person-related data for research purposes of the European Science Foundation of November 12, 1980. In: 9. Tätigkeitsbericht des Hessischen Datenschutzbeauftragten, No. 6, pp. 75 et seq., or In: Datenschutz und Datensicherung. No. 1/1982, pp. 50-53; with respect to data protection practice, see 3. Jahresbericht des Landesbeauftragten für den Datenschutz Bremen (Drucksache der Bremischen Bürgerschaft – Landtag – 10/483), Point 5.2.5.1., pp. 32-34; on respecting the professional secrecy of physicians in medical research, see Deneke, J.F. Volrad, in: Deutsches Ärzteblatt und ärztliche Mitteilungen. 78th year of publication, No. 30, pp. 1441-1442, 1444; see also the report of the scientific advisory board of the Federal General Medical Council: Empfehlung zur Beachtung der ärztlichen Schweigepflicht bei der Verarbeitung personenbezogener Daten in der medizinischen Forschung. In: Deutsches Ärzteblatt und ärztliche Mitteilungen. 78th year of publication, No. 30, p. 1443.

14 BVerfGE 65, 1, pp. 41 et seq.; Gallwas, H.-U. (1986): Datenschutz und historische Forschung in verfassungsrechtlicher Sicht. In: Der Archivar, p. 314, pp. 317 et seq.

15 Riehle (1983): Sicherheit im Vorfeld des Rechtes. In: Wambach (1983) (Ed.): p. 274

16 Schulz/Wambach (1983): Das gesellschaftssanitäre Projekt. In: Wambach (1983) (Ed.): 75, p. 82

17 Herold, H. (1983): Herold gegen alle, 1980, quoted in Vobruba, G.: Prävention durch Selbstkontrolle. In: Wambach (1983) (Ed.): p. 35

18 Vobruba (1983): Prävention durch Sozialkontrolle. In: Wambach (1983) (Ed.): 29, p. 35

19 Büllesbach, A. (1985): Datenschutz: Hoffnung oder Hemmnis? In: Die Polizei, No. 4, 104, p. 106.

20 Schreiber, M. (1985): DV-Technik – Gewinn oder Schaden? Ein Beitrag zur Bürgernähe? In: Die Polizei, No. 4, pp. 111 et seq., p. 115

21 Liszt, F. von: Das Verbrechen als sozial-pathologische Erscheinung. In: Strafrechtliche Aufsätze und Vorträge, Vol. II, Berlin, 1905, reissued in Berlin, 1970, pp. 230 et seq.

Selected Reference List

Büllesbach, A. (1985): Informationstechnologie und Datenschutz. Munich

Hohmann, H. (Ed.) (1987): Freiheitssicherung durch Datenschutz. Frankfurt

Jehle, J.-M. (Ed.) (1987): Datenzugang und Datenschutz in der kriminologischen Forschung. Wiesbaden

Kunz, K.-L. (1987): Vorbeugen statt verfolgen. Bern, Stuttgart

Wambach, M.M. (Ed.) (1983): Der Mensch als Risiko. Frankfurt

14. The Ethics of Informed Consent in Adolescent Research

R. John Kinkel and Norma C. Josef

Introduction

Research in the United States and other Western countries has identified several major problems confronting young people today: drug abuse, teen pregnancy, suicide, interpersonal violence. Numerous programs have been developed in order to reduce the likelihood of these events occurring. Invariably, before such programs are initiated, investigators must examine the prevalence of specific youth problems as well as factors that may be associated with the "distressed adolescent". In the last decade a significant number of social surveys and epidemiological studies have been undertaken in order to understand youth problems and to offer suggestions on how to develop effective intervention programs.

Several ethical and legal problems have arisen for investiators seeking to conduct these studies. The purpose of this paper is to explore the difficulties investigators encounter in dealing within formed consent requirements for adolescent research in the United States. Several solutions are proposed in studies using social surveys and epidemiological models, which may be useful in the United States and other countries as well.

1. Informed Consent in Recent Research

The first attempt to formulate the ethical guidelines for those who participate in medical research is found in the Nuremberg Code (U.S. Department of Defense, 1949, p. 181) which states: "The voluntary consent of a human subject is absolutely essential." This document does not distinguish between minors and adults but clearly indicates that voluntary consent means the "person involved should have legal capacity to give consent; should be so situated as to be able to exercise free power of choice, without the intervention of any element of force, fraud, deceit, over-reaching, or other ulterior form of constraint of coercion".

The World Medical Association Declaration of Helsinki in 1964, and amended in 1975, addressed the issue of human subjects and research on children when consent is received from "the responsible relative" (Declaration of Helsinki, 1975). Since then, the United States government in consultation with professional organizations has been attempting to clarify the precise ethical standards to be followed when children are involved as subjects in research. The most recent statement governing research with children in the United States that investigators must obtain the "assent of the children and the permission of their parents or guardians..." (Federal Register, 1983, p. 9816). The recently announced "Model Federal Policy" for the protection of human subjects (Federal Register, 1986, pp. 20204 et seq.) offers no new directives regarding informed consent. These regulations require that both the assent of the minor and permission of the parents or guardian be documented in writing. Although these official regulations permit waivers under certain circumstances, university and hospital review boards have been reluctant to allow such options, fearing no doubt, possible law suits and loss of government funds. Nevertheless, there is a growing body of evidence which indicates that studies following the current federal regulations on informed consent produce inferior results; this research may not be valid, reliable or useful.

2. Research in the Field: A Call for Change

The terms "unanticipated consequences" and "social dysfunctions" (Aram, 1986; Merton, 1968) have taken on new meaning today as we apply them to research regulations rather than to traditional targets of analysis, namely, government intervention into business. In the last decade business leaders in the United States have been rather pleased with the deregulation emphasis of the Reagan administration. "Government works best that govern least" represents the dominant private sector viewpoint. Unlike the private business sector, the professionals during the 1980's, viz., medicine, law, research, have experienced higher levels of regulation. Some have called this a movement toward "deprofessionalization". Many feel we need greater refinement and clarification among professionals, especially in the area of research on human subjects. Unfortunately the regulations and public policy generated this far have not always been sensitive to the professional research community and the needs which have been articulated by those laboring in research settings.

The negative consequences of the present regulations and the local organization policies based on them have been particularly detrimental to those conducting social surveys and epidemiological studies. Singer (1978, p. 144) notes in her study using personal interviews that certain groups champion the new regulations on informed consent whereas others opposed them in the belief that they will destroy the possibility of conducting needed research. Singer's data (n=2, 084) revealed that required informed consent procedures significantly reduced subject response. Response rates for those *not* asked to sign consent forms were 71 percent compared to 64 percent for those asked to sign a consent form before and 65 percent for those asked to sign forms after an interview.

The ethical principles which are at the core of the informed consent doctrine (Veatch, 1981, pp. 7-8) are, first, the desire to protect human subjects from harm; secondly, the goal to elicit from participants a legal and adequate consent. How can these values be preserved and at the same time allow professionals to conduct quality research? Singer is right in identifying the problem, but the points she makes represent only the tip of the iceberg. Severson and Avy (1983, p. 433) reported considerable bias in the dependent measure (drug use) when positive consent of the parents was required in a survey of smoking and marihuana use among youth. Only 59 percent of the student sample were allowed by parents/guardians to participate in the youth survey. Singer and Frankel (1982, p. 416) report that quality of response to their questionnaire was adversely affected by informed consent procedures, namely, the disclosure of the study's purpose. Kearney et al. (1983, p. 101) document the problem of sample bias which resulted from having to obtain written parental permission for youth participation in a social survey. The school-age population studied was grades 4 through 12. Employing the required consent procedure Kearney and associates obtained a sample which was only 51 percent of the eligible population (n=1618); the sample was biased in terms of racial composition as well. Using implied consent procedures (parents must state child may *not* be involved, otherwise he/she is included in the survey), has improved response rates somewhat but self-selection still remains a problem. Although Thompson's research (1984, p. 783) suggests that there are means available to increase parental consent rates, her study reveals several weaknesses. The small sample (n=50) makes interpretation difficult and the method used to increase response – communication with parents – is time consuming and costly. Here, again, self-selection is not addressed. Thus, the proposed solution may not be a viable option for most investigators. In summary, social surveys, particularly those involving children, are seriously compromised by a rigid adherence to current U.S. regulations on informed consent.

Before turning to epidemiological surveys, it is important to articulate in more detail the basic elements of informed consent (Federal Register, 1983, p. 9818). They are:

1. Investigators are required to explain the purpose of the research, time involved, procedures to be used.
2. The subject must be informed about foreseeable risks as well as potential benefits to the subject and others.
3. One must disclose alternative procedures, if any, and indicate provisions for confidentiality.
4. Investigators must disclose what compensation is provided subjects if research involves more than minimal risk; medical care should be available in the event of injury.
5. A statement regarding the voluntary nature of the subject's participation ought to be made; subjects should know they are free to terminate their participation in the research project at any time without penalty.

Although the core ideas of informed consent focus on the two principles of (1) no harm to subjects, (2) and the importance of a legally adequate consent, the details concerning these concepts are somewhat more complicated. Despite the fact that most scientists adhere to the values behind the regulations described (free choice, privacy, safety, etc.), these same government provisions exempt certain research activities (Federal Register,

1983, p. 9815) from the regulations, namely, surveys and interview procedures, *unless* children are involved in the study. Some Institutional Review Boards (IRBs) may develop policies so that surveys are reviewed even though the regulations do not require such procedures (Cann and Rothman, 1984, p. 5). Epidemiological studies may be particularly hard hit.

In theory, most epidemiology studies call for exemption under current regulations because subjects are considered at no more than minimal risk by participating. Minimal risk as defined by the regulations is "the probability and magnitude of harm or discomfort anticipated in the research are no greater in and of themselves than those ordinarily encountered in daily life or during the performance of routine physical or psychological examinations or tests" (Federal Register, 1983, p. 9817). Typical epidemiological studies of youth have focused on demographic measures, drug and alcohol measures, mental health indicators (suicide and depression scales), child abuse indices. Because many of these studies use self-report instruments with assurances of absolute anonymity, there is no way the subjects' answers can be connected with them. Since the issue of confidentiality cannot be considered a problem, therefore, many feel this type of research should be exempt (Cann and Rothman, 1984). What is often overlooked by Institutional Review Boards and regulatory agencies is that high response rates are crucial to social research. Subject participation below 80 percent in case control studies could seriously jeopardize the interpretation. Perhaps one inherent problem in the process of policy formation has been a failure to distinguish between clinical studies and epidemiological surveys. The former can employ randomization to prevent bias, but high rates of participation are the only sure and effective way to avoid self-selection bias in social surveys and epidemiology studies. Moreover, nonparticipation has been shown to correlate with the prevalence of risk or disease (Criqui, 1978). Cann and Rothman (1984, p. 6) summarize the problem by stating that complying with regulations and IRB policies "consumes substantial research funds and staff effort and decreases subject participation unnecessarily, from an ethical or legal perspective, by imposing unnecessary barriers." Several alternatives have been proposed to deal with the above problems.

3. Toward a Tentative Solution: Quality Research, Reasonable Ethical Norms

The general outline responding to the above problem rests on two observations: 1) social surveys and the type of epidemiological studies we discuss involve only minimal risks, thus they qualify for exemption under current regulations or at least an expedited review by the IRB. 2) Current practice which calls for parental permission so that minors may participate in research may not be necessary. As in any controversy, the answer to the problem outlined lies in balancing the rights of one group with those of another. In this controversy the public interest cannot be ignored. Some authors (Veatch, 1981) assert society's obligation to preserve individual rights at all costs. This involves the rights of privacy, freedom of choice and so on. When minors are involved, the argument centers on the principle that children cannot make a legally binding agreement; moreover, their lack of experience limits their capacity to weigh all relevant issues in making a decision. Hence, parents or guardians must decide for children on whether to allow them to participate in research.

The argument emphasizing individual rights seems to overlook a number of central features in social life today. First, the studies we need to conduct regarding youth today are not frivolous or optimal. Youth siucide in the United States, for example, has reached alarming proportions. Completed suiced rates have doubled for adolescents in the last two decades and there is no decline in sight (Kinkel et al., 1986). Increasingly, parents are attending the funerals of their teenagers rather than graduation ceremonies.

Drug abuse, youth violence and murder in urban settings reveal a pattern of destruction unheard of this century. These problems, which the United States and other Western societies face, require effectively executed social surveys and epidemiological studies as an absolute prerequisite for meaningful intervention and prevention programs. There is a growing awareness among those concerned with public health that psychopathology among youth has not been studied effectively in the past and thus needs greater understanding and research today to identify the factors related to youth problems as well as to formulate public policy directions for the future.

Secondly, the individual rights argument which asserts the necessity of parental permission for minors to participate in research fails to take into account many practices today that do not require absolute adherence to informed concent procedures. Veatch (1981, p. 7) points out that numerous state statutes exist today which permit minors to assent to certain treatment for venereal disease, contraception and abortion services, alcohol and drug therapy. The U.S. Supreme Court, in a one-sentence decision (4-4 vote), upheld a lower court ruling that struck down an Illinois law restricting the right of teenage girls to obtain abortions (Congressional Quarterly, 1987, p. 3132). The Illinois law at issue in *Hartigan v. Zbaraz* required young women under 18 to notify their parents before obtaining an abortion. It also required that these women then wait 24 hours before undergoing the procedure. Although this ruling does not set any national precedent, it does alert us to a growing consensus about a minor's rights and society's interest in fair treatment to minors. Minors can assent, that is, make an affirmative agreement to participate in such medical procedures (Federal Register, 1983, p. 9819) but they do not truly *consent* to them. Parental permission can be bypassed because it is in the State's interest that minors obtain treatment and not avoid it; the onus of obtaining parental permission could deter the minor from receiving needed health care. The argument rests on social utilitarian grounds (society's interests); these values are asserted over and against individual rights of parents to govern. The child is viewed as incapable of consent but only able to assent (i.e., assuming mature minor). Veatch (1981, p. 7) claims that what is really going on in this social interaction process is that parents are waiving their rights in order to choose a higher good, i.e., the treatment of a problem that the child is suffering versus nontreatment. Unwilling to grant that the child is competent to consent, Veatch (1981, p.

7) states this is a classic case of "physician paternalism" which justifiably replaces parental consent with the professional's nod. In summary, court decisions as well as some ethical theory offers us a window to view the doctrine of informed consent. In some circumstances it is legitimate to waive some aspects of informed consent for a higher good. The interesting conclusion Veatch comes to is that such a waiver does not apply to research. Holder, on the other hand, (1981; 1983) presents just the opposite view. Veatch asserts that it is unreasonable to assume that parents would permit the child's participation in research because no direct benefits probably would accrue to the minor subject and some risk would be incurred. It is unclear what position Veatch would take if the subject's risk was minor. Moreover, others (Furlow, 1980) have stated that parents may not permit children to be involved in research since the minor is exposed to at least some risk with little chance of direct benefit from the results. The discussion with regard to minors' participation in research seems to conclude that the risk benefit ratio must be tilted in favor of the minor before participation in medical research could be sanctioned. It is unclear how these authors would argue if only social surveys and epidemiological studies were at issue.

Not only have treatment experiences with adolescents called into question the doctrine of informed consent under certain conditions, but the process of formulating informed consent regulations has revealed that not all actors in the process play by the same rules. For example, school administrators recommended to the National Commission for the Protection of Human Subjects (Federal Register, 1978, p. 31791) that the research which they have a direct interest in concluding be exempt from parental consent requirements, that is, virtually all educational research, even on primary-grade students, conducted in the schools. The current regulations obliged this group's request with the following:
Research activities in which the only involvement of human subjects will be in one more of the following categories are exempt from these regulations unless the research is covered by other subparts of this part: Research conducted in established or commonly accepted educational settings, involving normal educational practices, such as (i) research on regular and special educational instructional strategies, or (ii) research on the effectiveness of or the comparison among instructional techniques, curricula, or classroom management methods (Federal Register, 1983, p. 9819).

Research involving survey or interview procedures is not exempt when children are involved as subjects. We must now examine what options are available to those who wish to conduct social research with minors. The first source for guidance is the informed consent document; secondly, we examine the ethical principles from which the regulations emerge.

4. Parental Consent: Absolute Requirement for Adolescent Research?

We have already reviewed two possible responses to this question. The first answer asserts that parents must give written consent before minors can be subjects in research studies. Such a requirement seriously threatens the quality of the research product so that the results may not be usable for planning and intervention. A second response claims that parents should *not* consent to have their children involved in research because there may be no prospect of direct benefit to the child and the minor will incur some risk even though minimal (Furlow, 1980; Veatch, 1981). The latter response would result in almost no research on teenagers, and this seems totally unacceptable, given the problems this population is encountering today. Are we faced with the prospect of conducting marginal research, given the restrictions of informed consent documents?

Nachmias and Nachmias (1981, p. 490) help us in answering this question:
The principle of informed consent should not...be made an absolute requirement for all social science research. Although usually desirable, it is not absolutely necessary in studies where no danger or risk is involved. The more serious the risk to research participants, the greater the obligation to obtain informed consent.

Although the above authors point out that special provisions must be taken when studying children, the general principle regarding the nonabsolute nature of informed consent is a valid insight in this ethical dilemma.

These sentiments are echoed in the current regulations if the IRB determines that a research protocol is designed for conditions or for a subject population for which parental or guardian permission is not a reasonable requirement to protect the subjects (for example, neglected to abused children), it may waive the consent requirements in Sub Part A of this part and paragraph (b) of this section, provided an appropriate mechanism for protecting the children who will participate as subjects in research is substituted, and provided further that the waiver is not inconsistent with federal, state or local law. The choice of an appropriate mechanism should depend upon the nature and purpose of the activities described in the protocol, the risk and anticipated benefit to the research subjects, and their age, maturity, status and condition (Federal Register, 1983, p. 9819, par. 46.408).

These regulatory provisions clearly reflect the sentiment of the antional Commission's Report and Recommendations for Research on Children (Federal Register, 1978, pp. 2084–2114):
If the Institutional Review Board determines that a research protocol is designed for conditions or a subject population for which parental or guardian permission is not a reasonable requirement to protect the subjects, it may waive such a requirement provided an appropriate mechanism for protecting the children who will participate as subjects in the research is substituted.

The reasonable conclusion one must draw from these documents is that there is considerable consensus in the research community that there are circumstances in which parental consent may not be required when conducting research on children. Levine (1983, p. 2) suggests that the types of research for which parental or guardian permission might not be a reasonable requirement may be difficult to determine. Nonetheless, in Levine's view, the "neglected and abused children" category mentioned in the regulations is meant to be illustrative, and not exhaustive. Holder (1983) takes a similar view. The National Commission for the protection of Human Subjects (1977, pp. 17-18) lists additional examples which quality for a waiver.

Research designed to identify factors related to the incidence or treatment of certain conditions in adolescents, for which, in certain jurisdictions, they may legally receive treatment without parental consent; research in which the subjects are 'mature minors' and the procedures involved entail essentially no more than minimal risk that such individuals might reasonably assume on their own; research designed to meet the needs of...children designated by their parents as 'in need of supervion'; and research involving children whose parents are legally or functionally incompetent.

In summary, it would appear that the following conditions would qualify a research protocol from the informed consent requirement of parental/guardian permission.

1. The research involves no danger to subjects, less than minimal danger, or no more than minimal danger.
2. The research method involves social surveys or epidemiological studies.
3. Research is conducted in schools, or other educational settings.
4. Data is collected so that responses are recorded in such a manner that the human subjects cannot be identified, directly, or through identifiers linked to the subjects.

The regulations consider this latter point crucial for exemption and it seems relevant here since the studies we are concerned with (drug abuse, suicidal behavior, child abuse) would employ self-report instruments with assurances of absolute anonymity (Kinkel and Bailey, 1985). Several studies have shown that self-reports are reliable methods for measuring deviant behavior (Akers et al., 1983; Bauman, Koch, Bryan, 1982) and thus would provide useful information for prevention and intervention.

Even with these factors in place, the regulations suggest other considerations to protect vulnerable human subjects such as children. The general requirement to obtain parental permission may be waived provided an appropriate mechanism for protecting children is substituted. This could involve an appointment by the IRB of a "surrogate parent" or "advocate" for the children who is not a member of the research team. The task of this person would be act on behalf of the children and safeguard the interests of the minors. This mechanism seems to resolve the inherent problem of exploitation (Marshall, 1986), p. 6) that could emerge in research settings.

The role of the surrogate parent or advocate would be to monitor the research setting, verify minimal risk, and ensure the IRB that the "assent" of minors was voluntary. Investigators would do well to remind themselves that the fundamental responsibility of the IRB is to protect the welfare of subjects and to provide reasonable assurance that studies are conducted ethically. The role of the research scientist within the university setting is to seek the truth and expand our knowledge about reality. These roles will conflict at times and this is to be expected. Cann and Rothman (1984, p. 7) remind investigators, and rightly so, that they have a professional responsibility to make sure legitimate research goals are not impeded by easy acceptance of unjustifiable demands by IRB's. We are in a fluid period in the development of informed consent principles with some consensus and considerable diversity of opinion.

The U.S. regulations employ the term "reasonable" several times in the rules of informed consent. A sense of rational accomodation is needed in this time of conflicting viewpoints.

5. Philosophical Roots of the Informed Consent Controversity

This discussion would fall short of its goal by limiting its focus to current regulations, commission recommendations, and the fundamental thought systems that underlie this controversy?

On the one hand we encounter the Kantian assertion of individual autonomy and the notion of duty (Kant, 1953) clashing with the views of the utilitarians and Jeremy Bentham (1823). The latter views took root in the teleological school of ethical theory, asserting that the morality of an act is determined by the good or evil it produced. Accordingly, the purpose of morality is to promote human welfare by minimizing harm and maximizing benefits (Buchholz, 1986). The Kantian view, on the other hand, asserts categorically that the concept of duty is independent of the concept of good. Morality consists of doing one's duty and, of course, satisfying the legitimate claims of others. This general notion espouses the concept of autonomy and the "self-legislating will" as Kant described it (Faden and Beauchamp, 1986). The autonomous agent is one who is selfdirected rather than one who obeys the commands of others. Ethics for the Kantian asserts that we have a duty to respect one's life plans, preferences, and wishes. These views dominate the deontological school of ethical theory. For Kant and deontological theory an act is good or bad depending on how it satisfies some overriding principle, e.g., doing one's duty to tell the truth. In the informed consent debate, the direction is clear: respect the self-legislating will of the individual; do not expose the individual to harm if there are no direct benefits. Taken to an extreme, these views would require that we obtain the consent of parents to conduct research on their children. The parents should not give permission, unless the child receives a direct benefit (unlikely) since some risk is involved. Parents have a duty to protect children from harm and the risk of harm. The utilitarians object to this conception of reality because it lacks insight into social and historical reality; it is extremely individualistic, in that social factors are ignored; it would lead us to inaction or to a response of poor quality when just the opposite is needed in our contemporary society.

In the first place, Kantian ethics abstract from the sociohistorical context to arrive at generalized principles that can be applied to all mankind. Hence, the approach is called universalism. Today we need to understand a particular social context (youth problems) and determine what response is needed at this unique time in history. Secondly, an individualistic approach that asserts one's rights must be balanced by the notion of social obligation. The Belmont Report (1979, p. 7) rightly points this out in referring to the beneficence principle (maximize benefits and minimize harms). "Beneficence thus requires that we be concerned about the loss of the substantial benefits that might be gained from research." This is particularly crucial when the research subject is being exposed to less than minimal risk and alternative approaches are not viable. Thirdly, the utilitarians argue that it is unethical to withhold a response or respond in an inferior way to grave social problems, e.g., teen suicide, violence, substance abuse. Thus, from a philosophical standpoint, it is controversy, and that there are underlying value conflicts to what may appear on the surface as mere quibbling over the modus operandi of research. The differences we have articulated will remain with us; consensus is not at hand. "Reasonable" approaches to this conflict ought to prevail.

6. Conclusion

There is no doubt that the issue of informed consent occupies a great deal of attention in both the United States and Western Europe. Informed consent involves not only professional ethical practice, but public policy and legal doctrine as well. In recent years those who have asserted the importance of informed consent, proclaim the importance of self-determination and autonomy, in matters of personal choice and health care. For some it has become a symbolic ideal for modern professional-client relations. Shultz (1986, p. 24) summed up current thinking on informed consent this way:

Due to extended discussion of informed consent we have now attained a level of discource which can rightly be called 'ideology', which in some instances may be perceived as preaching, rather than scholarship.

This attitude may be particularly tempting when dealing with research on children. Many studies have rightly pointed out how crucial it is to regulate research, especially when it deals with the most vulnerable of subjects. Nevertheless, the U.S. regulations suggest that all procedures be cognizant of the "rule of reason".

References

Akers, R.L., Massey, J., Clark, W., and Lauer, R. (1983): "Are self-reports of adolescent deviance valid? Biochemical measures, randomized response, and the bogus pipeline in smoking behavior." In: Social Forces 62, 234–251

Aram, J. (1986): Managing Business and Public Policy. New York: Longman (2nd Edition) Baumann, K., Koch, G., and Bryan, E. (1982): "Validity of self-reports of adolescent cigarette smoking." In: International Journal of the Addictions 17, 1131-1136

Bentham, J. (1823): An Introduction to the Principles of Morals and Legislation. London: Pickering

Bochholz, R. (1986): Business Environment and Public Policy. Englewood Cliffs, NJ: Prentice-Hall (2nd Edition) Cann, C., and Rothman, K. (1984): "IRBs and Epidemiologic research: How Inappropriate Restrictions Hamper Studies." IRB: A Review od Human Subjects Research 6 (July/August), 5-6

Congressional Quarterly (1987) 45 (51): 3132

Criqui, M., Barrett-Connor, E., and Austin, M. (1978): Differences between respondents and non-respondents in a cardio vascular disease study. In: American Journal of Epidemiology 108, 367-372

Declaration of Helsinki (1975): The 18th World Medical Assembly Statement at Helsinki, Finland. Revised 1965 Declaration in Tokyo, Japan

Faden, R.R., and Beauchamp, T.L. (1986): A History and Theory of Informed Consent. New York: Oxford University Press

Federal Register (1983): "Protection of Human Subjects." 48 (46), March 8, 9814-9820

"Model Federal Policy for Protecting Human Subjects" (1986): Federal Register 51 (106), June 3, 20204-20217

Furlow, T.G. (1980): "Consent for Minors to Participate in Nontherapeutic Research." In: Wecht, C. (Ed.): Legal Medicine. 1980, 261-273

Holder, A. (1983): "Teenagers and Questionnaire Research." IRB: A Review of Human Subjects Research 5 (3) 1983, 4-6

Holder, A.R. (1981): "Can Teenagers Participate in Research without Parent Consent?" IRB: A Review of Human Subjects Research 3 (2), 5-7

Kant, I. (1953): Critique of Pure Reason. Trans. by N. Kemp Smith. New York: Macmillan

Kearney, K., Hopkins, R., Mauss, A., and Weisheit, R. (1983): "Sample Bias Resulting from a Requirement for Written Parental Consent." In: Public Opinion QUARTERLY 47, 96-102

Kinkel, R., and Bailey, C. (1985): "Substance Abuse among Youth in Genesee County." Flint, Mich: University of Michigan

Kinkel, R., Josef, N., and Bailey, C. (1986): "Suicide attempts by school-age adolescents" New Research Proceedings, 139th annual meeting of the American Psychiatric Association, Washington, D.C., May, 1986

Levine, R.J. (1983): "Research involving children: an interpretation of the new regulations," IRB: A Review of Human Subjects Research 5 (4), 5-6

Marshall, E. (1986): "Does the Moral Philosophy of the Belmont Report Rest on a Mistake." IRB: A Review of Human Subjects Research 8 (6), 5-6

Merton, R.K. (1968): Social Theory and Social Structure. New York: Free Press

National Commission for the Protection of Human Subjects of Biomedical and Behavioral Research (1977): Research Involving Children: Report and Recommendations. Washington, D.C.: U.S. Government Printing Office

National Commission for the Protection of Human Subjects (1979): The Belmont Report. Washington, D.C.: U.S. Government Printing Office

Nachmias, D., and Nachmias, C. (1981): Research Methods in the Social Sciences. New York: St. Martin's Press (2nd Edition)

Severson, H., and Ary, D. (1983): "Sampling Bias due to Consent Procedures with Adolescents." In: Addictive Behaviors 8, 433-437

Shultz, M. (1987): "Informed Consent, A Symbol Analyzed." Hastings Center Report (June), 24-25

Singer, E. (1978): "Informed Consent: Consequences for Response Rate and Response Quality in Social Surveys." In: American Sociological Review, 43, 144-162

Singer, E., and Frankel, M. (1982): "Informed Consent Procedures in Telephone Interviews." In: American Sociological Review, 47, 416-427

U.S. Department of Defense. "Nuremberg Code". U.S. v. Karl Brandt. Trials of War Criminals Before Nuremberg Military Tribunals Under Control Law No. 10. Washington, D.C.: Government Printing Office, 1949, Vol.2, pp. 181-183

Veatch, R.M. (1981): "Beyond Consent to Treatment." IRB: A Review of Human Research, 3 (2), 7-8

15.

Ethical Problems of Survey Research on Delinquency: An Empirical Analysis of Accessing and Interviewing Young Offenders

Günter Albrecht, Susanne Karstedt-Henke

1. Colonizing Life Worlds: A New Ethical Problem for Social Scientists?

The concept of "life world" is central to a recent debate about empirical social research which has flared up in the course of the reception of the latest works of Habermas (1981). Empirical social research is accused of "colonizing" the life world of the subjects who are the objects of social research. This debate is not centering on the often inadequate methods of social research and its frequently discussed methodological problems; its essential point is rather an ethical and moral problem concerning the core of the ethical standards of social research. It can be stated in the following way: Is the social researcher allowed to "invade" the life world of his subjects by the use of quantitative methods of sampling and data analysis; is he allowed to analyse these data according to his own scientific objectives and will he contribute by such a "scientification" (Verwissenschaftlichung) to the final destruction and decay of life worlds in modern societies by means of "colonizing" them through social engineering (Habermas, 1979)? This discussion includes problems of the theory of social sciences (phenomenology vs. positivism) as well as problems of applied social research, mainly concerning the responsibility of the social researcher for his results, their application in political action or the application of his instruments for practical purposes (e.g., the application of psychological tests for screening and assessment).

Within such a broad range of problems discussed on the basis of a single concept it seems to be appropriate to start midway between the extreme positions mentioned above: basic research is as well accused as applied research. Therefore, our inquiry will concentrate on basic research, its ethical and moral problems and standards[1]. This requires a precise definition of the concept of life world as a first step.
Every ethical and moral evaluation and standard requires an exact definition of those actions or realm of actions which are the subject of the respective code of ethics. The social researcher himself as well as those who judge his actions and methods should define exactly the course of action they are referring to in their moral judgements. Otherwise, there would be such an insecurity and diffusion concerning the foundations of

moral judgements, that the purpose of ethical and legal codes – to enforce the universal validity of a set of moral judgements – could not be obtained.
After having obtained a precisely defined concept of life world, our next step will be to investigate, if social research is in fact an invasion of the life world of subjects, and which actions and methods applied by the social researcher actually consitute such an invasion. Finally, we can examine which of these actions and methods are not in accordance with basic ethical standards of everyday life and especially of social research. Schuler (1982) has pointed out, that the prevailing everyday moral standards of a society – being the foundation of its legal order – apply to scientific research just as well. Exceptions from these standards must be justified and wellfounded as for example in the case of legal and moral judgements of self-defence. The moral judgements concerning scientific social research are based on the evaluation of the consequences to its subjects. Therefore, an exact examination of whether the scientific research has in fact caused damaging consequences which are not in accordance with moral standards, is necessary. Consequently, such judgements of scientific research have to be based on an empirical inquiry into its factual consequences with regard to the subjects.

Similarly, a moral judgement about the invasion into the life world of the subjects by a social scientist for reasons of scientific research relies on the examination under which conditions and in which cases such an invasion and its effects are ethically and morally objectionable. This empirical foundation of a moral judgement requires – besides a precise definition – the operationalization of the concept of life world.

2. The Concept of "Life World"

One of the most vague and diffuse concepts of modern sociology is the concept of life world. Having its roots in the phenomenological philosophy of E. Husserl, it has made its way into the phenomenological sociology by Schütz, Luckmann and Berger without having been sufficiently clarified for the purposes of empirical social research[2)]. Its different meanings – Bergmann counts eight variants of meanings (1981, p. 69) – have characteristics in common: all sociological concepts of life world refer to the material, social and cultural environment, unquestioningly taken for granted in a naive way by the individual. "The life world (of individuals) is constituted by more or less diffuse, though never problematic basic ("background") convictions. Thus, the life world as a background is the source of definitions of situations which are assumed to be unproblematic by those concerned." (Habermas, 1981, p. 107).

As such, the concept of life world refers to the non-scientific experiences of everyday life and Husserl has explicitly pointed out, that scientific research on life worlds is part of the field of descriptive cultural sciences, a "mundane empiriography" (Welter, 1986, p. 87), including qualitative as well as quantitative research. Thus, it is one of the principal tasks of the social scientist to describe and analyze the life world of his subjects. On the other hand, it is not evident, in which way basic social research may violate and destroy the naive perspectives and "background convictions" (Habermas, 1981, p. 107) which constitute the life world of the subjects, e.g., by sampling, by systematicly analyzing and by developing typologies. Furthermore, if participation in social research initiated some reflection on these background convictions destroying their naivety and making them problematic, would that be an acting that had to be objected in terms of moral standards[3)]?

Thus, it is more reasonable to look for a concept rather similar to that of life world, a micro-sociological paradigm based on the analysis of interactions and the constitution of meanings and definitions of situational settings. We therefore will refer to Goffman's analysis of face-to-face interactions and the concept of the "territory" of individuals. It seems to be more appropiate for our task of laying the empirical foundations of moral judgements about basic social research.

3. Goffman's Micro-Sociological Paradigm: Interaction Rituals and the "Territories of the Self"

Goffman's purpose is to study the "face-to-face interaction as a naturally coherent field – a sub-area of sociology" (1969, IX). His analyses focus on the development and preservation of the identity of the individual – the "self" – in social encounters. The "countless patterns" and "natural sequences of behavior" (Goffman, 1967, p. 2) occuring whenever people meet are in no way determined by structurally defined role sets; the social order of situational settings is analyzed in terms of "interaction rituals" and "games" people play interchanging with one another[4)]. Goffman uses a "double definition of the self: The self as an image pieced together from the expressive implications of the full flow of events in an undertaking; and the self as a kind of player in a ritual game who copes ... with the judgmental contingencies of the situation" (1967, p. 31). Thus, the individual has to manage a double task in the exchange with others: preserving the image of the "self" he has made up as well as reaching his goals. The individual has to make "claims" (1972, p. 51) concerning the image of the self and the goals of his strategic interactions. A crucial type of claim is "a claim exerted in regard to territory" (1972, p. 51). This term from ethology is assigned to the spatial, situational and spiritual and mental – as I would like to add – realm the individual claims control of. Goffman names eight territories: personal space, the stall, use space, the turn, the sheath, possessional territory, information preserve and conversational preserve, the latter being the most important concepts for our study[5)]. The boundaries of the territories are "ordinarily controlled and defended" by individuals (1972, p. 52), the invasion of the thus more or less distinctly marked realm requires the explicit allowance of the claimant. By controlling and protecting his territories, the individual protects the self against injuries with regard to the body and mind, as well as to the social status the individual claims to have in social encounters with others. To be brief, the preservation of the several territories is a necessary condition of the physical and mental health of the individual, and thus, of the basic skills and requirements of social interaction and integration. On the other hand, the violation of the boundaries of individual territories may cause physical, mental or social destablization. Thus, Goffman has analyzed the process of stigmatization as a series of repeated violations of the different territories of the individual (1963) and has shown that the social order of total institutions is based on the continuous ignorance of the territories of the inmates (1961).

By the concept of "individual territories" the interactions between the researcher and his subjects can be analyzed with regard to violations of these territories caused by the process of social research and the subsequent consequences of such violations. Two territories or "preserves" will be of special interest. The first is the "information preserve", defined by Goffman as "the set of facts about himself to which an individual expects to control access while in the presence of others" (1972, p. 63). The information preserve contains facts about the individual about which to ask someone is judged as inquisitive and indiscrete, biographical facts over the divulgence of which he claims to maintain control, and furthermore, the observation of specific actions of the individual which are normally private ones. Goffman links this concept to the more traditional and legally defined concept of privacy (1972, p. 63, fn. 15). The second is the "conversational preserve" defined by Goffman as the "right of an individual to exert some control over who can summon him into talk and when he can be summoned" (1972, p. 64).

It is obvious that the techniques of interviewing – oral techniques as well as paper-and-pencil techniques – and techniques of observation are invasions into the information preserve, and that every interview as a whole and with regard to special parts must be admitted and tolerated within the "conservational preserve". One general feature of the several forms of territoriality is their socially determined variability with regard to power and position. The territories of children, patients in mental hospitals, and prisoners are far more restricted than those of the populace in general. As such, access to them will be more easily obtained, and social scientists have often derived benefit from this. But one should be aware of the cumulative effects of intruding on preserves already restricted by institutional arrangements.

4. The Violation of Territorial Integrity by Strategies of Social Research

The inquiry into the ethical, as well as the methodological problems of the invasion into the information preserve, the privacy and the conversational preserve of the subjects by means of social research, has a long and well-established tradition, the methodological perspective dominating the discussion[6]. The efforts of methodological inquiry are concentrated on three main tasks: first, the analysis of the willingness of the subjects to participate in the research especially with regard to the resulting systematic biases of response rates; second, the problem of the refusal to answer embarrassing questions, and third, the problem of dishonest answers to questions invading the information preserve by asking for facts a person is not willing to divulge to strangers. The development of a broad range of different techniques shows, that social scientists respect the boundaries and claims of the informational preserve as far as possible with regard to their scientific purpose to improve the validity of their data. There are techniques of randomization (Greenberg et al. 1969) and other techniques guaranteeing the anonymity of the subjects' answers, e.g., by paper-and-pencil methods and techniques concealing the response to the answer from the interviewer as e.g., by lists and sorting cards. By this, the scientific and instrumental goals of the research contribute to the compliance with ethical standards of social research.

The dominance of methodological issues in this discussion and the neglection of ethical issues seems to be caused by the principle of voluntary participation in social research. This seems to solve the ethical problems of the invasion into the information and conversational preserves. Analyzing his research strategies according to ethical principles, the social scientist will find that they become crucial in the course of his research with regard to five problems: (a) the amount of information given to subjects about the purpose of the research, (b) sampling on the basis of a preselected group (e.g., patients of mental health centers, former prisoners), (c) indirect and covered strategies of research (e.g., covered participant observation), (d) intrusive and embarrassing questions, and (e) repeated contact with and interviewing and testing of subjects in the course of longitudinal studies.

a.) Amount of information given on the purpose of the research and the content of questionnaires

Controlling the conversational preserve requires information about the contents and the partner(s) of the conversation as well as about other persons receiving information on this conversation ("overhearing"). The access to the conversational preserve by the social scientist is based on the "informed consent" of the subjects implying the disclosure of purpose and content of the questionnaire as a whole and its special parts to the subjects as well as the giving of information on subsequent data processing. Having obtained this information from the social scientist, the subjects can decide, if and with regard to which topics they will grant access to their conversational preserve[7].

In the case of interviews concerning topics like deviant behavior, personal problems, mental and physical health, these requirements of informed consent may seriously and systematically reduce the willingness to grant access to the conversational preserve and to participate in the research resulting in a sample of doubtful quality. The decision on the amount of information sufficient for informed consent by the subjects has to take into account methodological standards on the one hand, and ethical standards on the other hand, balancing the opposing requirements of the two. The decision should be based on the different capabilities of the subjects of giving "informed consent" (e.g., in the case of children and adolescents) and on their demand for information which will vary according to their social setting. Basicly, the social scientist will start from minimal requirements of

information which fulfill the ethical as well as the methodological standards and will increase the amount of information on demand.
The problems of compliance with ethical standards are more serious in the case of research designs which require giving an intentionally biased information to the subjects or which require the application of covered techniques (covered tapes, covered observation). In this case, the social scientist will have to examine if the physical and mental well-being of his subjects will be affected and if – in the case of disclosure – these will be disturbed or deprived with regard to their social relationships.

b.) Sampling techniques requiring special information about the subjects

Surveys on special groups – minorities, members of total institutions and special organizations, former patients, offenders and prisoners, drug-users – imply difficult problems with regard to the integrity of the information and the conversational preserve of the subjects. This is due to the selection of the subjects which is based on information accessible to the scientist *before* he has contacted his subjects to ask for their participation. This information necessarily includes facts the individual normally claims to maintain control of and which are usually not disclosed to others. Besides this violation of the information preserve, an invasion into the conversational preserve is caused by the disclosure of this information to the subject to assure his informed consent which implies to make these facts (e.g., being a former patient of a mental hospital) the topic of a conversation between the interviewer and the subjects. Being selected for the sample means loosing control of the preserves, causing feelings of fear and stigmatization which may seriously hurt the subjects. On the other hand, various protective and defensive maneuvers against the invasion of their preserves are available to the members of these groups. This is shown by the difficulties to gain access to these groups social scientists are so often complaining about. Villmow and Stephan (1983, p. 248) show that the rate of participation in a self-report study on delinquency decreases significantly for persons having become known to the institutions of social control. The results of our study show the same tendency. In a survey of a representative sample of 13- to 17-year-old adolescents in two cities in the western part of the Federal Republic of Germany we obtained a response rate of 54,7%, while among adolescents who were asked for an interview after having been prosecuted by the public prosecutor the rate of refusals was much higher. For the mode of directly mailing their *consent* to being interviewed to the research project, the return rate was 24%. For the mode of mailing their *dissent* to the prosecutor, the return rate, i.e., the rate of refusals, increased to 40%. If the interviewers directly contacted the subjects and asked them for their participation, the response rate (consent) was 40%, totalling much less than the response rate of the representative sample[8].
Besides the instruction and training of the interviewers and sufficient and helpful information for the adolescents and their parents, technical solutions for the ethical problems seem to be appropriate. These solutions comprise the establishment of "mixed files", which conceal the special groups in a larger file of simple random samples of the

whole population making the identification of the members of the special group impossible[9]. Still, the social scientist should be aware that accessing these special groups may result in additional damage for an already injured self.

c.) Covered techniques of survey

Covered research strategies are mainly used in experimental designs and participant observation. Concerning survey research – interviews as well as mailed questionnaires – these techniques are applied to obtain informations the subjects normally would refuse to divulge to others. It is the crucial point of these covered techniques that the subjects cannot control and judge the factual extent of information they allow access to. As such, covered techniques include those instruments of survey research which imply an embarrassing information on the subject by summing up more or less "innocent" single items. Consequently, all kinds of tests measuring mental health or personal traits the subjects would judge to be embarrassing information to somebody else have to be examined with regard to violations of the information preserve and the resulting violation of ethical standards. The observation of the boundaries of the information and conversational preserves requires some kind of "informed consent" of the subjects in these cases, and consequently, the social scientist will have to consider effects on the validity of his data.

d.) Embarrassing questions

Goffman defines the information preserve as the realm "control over which is threatened when queries are made that (the individual) sees as intrusive, nosy, untactful" (1972, p. 63) Even the most harmless questionnaire usually contains one of these questions: the question for the income of the subjects. Generally, questions concerning deviations from norms seem to be experienced as embarrassing. The "image of the self" the individual presents in situations of public encounters is an image of "normality", deviations from norms being concealed from the public view. In this way, possible consequences of the visibility of deviance like degradation and stigmatization are avoided as well as resulting destabilizing effects on the "self" (Goffman, 1963). Koolwijk (1969) found out, that subjects experience questions as embarrassing, when they actually deviate from the established norms (normality) of behavior the question concerns[10]. Our own results confirm this: adolescents who have committed several different offenses rate self-report questions about deviance as more embarrassing; the more intense and varied the deviation of legal norms is, the more embarrassing this issue seems to be.

The most popular techniques of solving the problems of embarrassing questions are randomization, paper-and-pencil-methods, card-sorting etc., which conceal the information from the interviewer in the situational setting of the interview. These techniques help the social scientist to comply to high standards of ethical conduct and they discharge him from the reproach of having invaded the privacy of his subjects in an unreasonable and hurtful way.

e.) Repeated access to subjects in the course of longitudinal (panel-) studies

Usually, a social scientist contacts his subjects only once. Though this unique access to the information and conversational preserves of the subjects may result in negative effects, it seems to be appropriate to suppose them to be short-termed. On the contrary, the repeated participation of subjects in a study and the corresponding access to the "territories of the self" may result in lasting changes of the "self", especially with regard to the perception of stigmatization and, consequently, a decrease of self-esteem. Being repeatedly the subject of social research can have effects of stigmatization, mainly for minority or deviant groups[11)]. Goffman has pointed out, that a continuous violation of the boundaries of the territories of the self is crucial to the process of stigmatization. The social researcher cannot ignore the problems of ethics he has to tackle in the course of panel studies of such groups, and it must be admitted that solutions of these problems are difficult to be obtained. It seems to be appropriate to offer some sort of guidance or therapy to the subjects as far as requirements of validity give way to such measures.

Generally, we can state that the concept of the "territories of the self" lays the foundations for a more empirical analysis of the problems of ethical standards of social research, and that it is well-fitted for our task. Furthermore, the concept corresponds well to the positive-legal definitions of privacy and its protection laid down in the constitution. Thus, the actions of the social scientist can be judged according to moral as well as to legal standards.

In the course of our study on the effects of diversion on young offenders we were confronted with several of the problems outlined above: the problems of access to special groups and repeated measurement in the course of a panel study, as well as the problems of embarrassing questions. Besides looking for adequate solutions to these problems, we started an empirical analysis of the access to the subjects by the interviewers and obtained ratings of the interviews, by both the interviewers and the young offenders. Our purpose was to obtain systematic information on the scope of the problem. Our preliminary results, based on a small sample of subjects, will be presented in the following sections.

5. Quantitative and Qualitative Analysis of the Access to the Subjects and of Participation in the Research

The question of how to obtain cooperation of the persons selected for the research is a main topic of textbooks as well as the subject of a vast amount of empirical investigations. Scientific standards and economic considerations require high efforts to maximize response and participation rates. The broadest spectrum of information and, in conclusion, the smallest systematic bias is obtained by maximizing these rates. Will this access be obtained by way of mailed notes and information in advance of the personal contact; which information should the interviewers provide on the telephone, on personal visits and toward other persons (e.g., the parents of adolescents); which sort of reward or amount of financial incentive will substantially increase the participation rate: the validity of the data and the success of the research crucially depend on the correct answers given to these questions in advance, the diffculties increasing in the case of sampling from the special groups outlined above. This requires the access to the files of institutions of social control and in this way, embarrassing information on the subjects is obtained by the social scientist.

In the course of our study of young offenders, we obtained access to them by way of the files of the public prosecutor with three modes of access being applied in succession.
First mode: The young offenders received a letter from the prosecutor containing a letter from the research group and a participation form. They were asked to mail this form – including their address – directly to the research group. By means of this procedure, their participation would not become known to any institution of social control. Within a period of four weeks, we obtained a response rate of 24% resp. 33% in the two regions where the research was carried out, a result unacceptable according to the standards of survey research. Furthermore, we had reason to assume that this procedure of access resulted in a considerable and systematic bias of the sample, eliciting a response mainly from those young offenders who were more reliable and skilled concerning the managing of the affairs of everyday life and who got sufficient support from their parental homes. In a word, a large group of the sample consisted of more or less untypical offenders.
Second mode: As a result, the mode of access was changed. In a similar letter from the public prosecutor the subjects were requested to mail a form to the prosecutor including their *refusal* of participation only. Otherwise, the adress was given to the research group. This mode resulted in a response rate of 33% resp. 40% within a period of two months. Considering that the effort was exactly the same for the adolescents, the comparatively increased rate of refusals was an unexpected result. It can be explained by the incentive given to the young offenders by the chance of refusing a request toward an institution of social control, thereby compensating for feelings of powerlessness during the course of the prosecution. We assume that this group consists mainly of adolescents unwilling to participate in any way. The remaining group of ca. 60% of the subjects were personally contacted by the interviewers. Within this group, a participation rate of 60% was obtained resulting in a total participation rate of 40%.

Third mode: The permission to practise the second mode of access was withdrawn by the Ministery of Justice after a complaint by a social worker and a campaign in the local press. Thereupon, the research group was allowed to obtain each adress from the prosecutor and to contact the young offenders directly. Shortly before the initial contact by the interviewer, a letter is mailed to the adolescents, including a letter to their parents or legal guardians and an offer of guidance for the parents. With considerable efforts by the interviewers, a particip iation rate of ca. 40% is obtained.

Starting with the second mode of access, we held an inquiry into the attributes of the process of accessing and contacting the young offenders. Subjects of the inquiry were: the problems of obtaining access to the adolescents, their maneuvers of defense against unwanted invasions into their information and conversational preserve, their arguments concerning their willingness and their refusal to participate. Because of the requirement of obtaining the permisson of the parents for interviewing their children, the corresponding contacts with parents were examined in the same way. The interviewers had to record the course of the contact in a semi-standardized "contact sheet". The recording of quantitative attributes contained – besides the dates – the frequency of telephone calls and personal visits, the frequency of missed appointments, and the person contacted. Qualitative attributes of the course of contacts were reported by the interviewers according to the following categories: arguments supporting and rejecting participation, arguments concerning deviance and the problems of protection of personal data and information mainly concerning the access to the name and adress. Furthermore, the interviewer had to report his personal impression of the situation, the adolescents and their parents. The results presented below are based on 63 "contact sheets". 51 (81%) of the subjects were males, 12 (19%) females; 28 (44%) of the subjects contacted participated, 43% of the boys and 58% of the girls, resulting in an over-representation of girls in the sample. A high proportion (14%) of the subjects could not be accessed by telephone calls and had to be paid personal visits to. The adolescents often live in families whose name they do not bear (with their grandparents, their step-father, other persons taking care of them). Generally, more than one call was necessary (mean = 1.33) to fix an appointment or to obtain a refusal, sometimes up to 6 calls. The interval in which the calls took place, ranged from 1 day to 13 days, the mean being just under 3 days. 23 personal visits were made by the interviewers, up to three visits, the mean distance being 6 km. The index of "contact intensity", i.e., the frequency of contacts during the interval from the initial contact up to the realization of the interview, shows that the interviewer contacted the subjects every other day (mean contact intensity of realized interviews: 0.5)[12]. Summing up these results, it seems to be the difficulties of accessing this special group of young offenders, which accounts for the lack of participation of this group in the study of Villmow and Stephan (1983). A high proportion of young offenders belongs to special groups with respect to various attributes (e.g., broken homes), a fact which accounts for the cumulation of difficulties in accessing them. This requires a level of activities by interviewers far above the routine level, and substantially increases their workload.

Our qualitative data analysis is based on 32 recorded conversations; 25% were conversations with a female offender; 9 conversations with the fathers were recorded and 18 with the mothers of the young offenders. The structure of the family manifested itself on contacts with its environment: all conversations with fathers concerned male offenders only.

The recordings by the interviewers were rated and coded according to 90 categories belonging to 12 main subjects of the research, most important of which were maneuvers of defense and protection, demand for information on several topics, stress resulting from this event, the young offenders' attitudes toward their deviant behavior and such behavior in general, affective reactions like aggressive expressions and actions. Furthermore, the notes of the interviewers concerning the situation of the family and special characteristics of the situational setting were analyzed in order to describe a wide spectrum of problems concerning the access to the subjects of our research.

Spontaneous consent was obtained by *all* female offenders participating in our study. They gave their consent without further requests. With regard to the arguments refusing a participation, girls are proportionally represented with the popular arguments of refusal such as "not interested", "no time", "don't feel like it". Arguments supporting consent mainly imply curiosity to meet students and scientists from the local universities and an interest taken in the subject and the purpose of the project. The young offenders are apt to generalize their cases and want to contribute with their interviews to an overall improvement of the situation of young offenders ("P. thinks that it is important"; "P. wants to improve the situation of adolescents"). The financial incentive (15,-DM) is hardly ever mentioned during these conversations by the young offenders.

Analyzing those rejections of participation, the reasons for which are not frankly given as "not interested, no time" or by a strictly rejective answer ("on no account"), we find concealed maneuvers of defense and false pretences. The young offenders put the interviewers off from day to day with empty promises, they ask for time to think it over, they deny to have received the letter in advance or they pretend that name and address are wrong and that they never had dealings with any institution of social control.

Rarely is the fact of having been prosecuted for an offense a topic of the conversation between the adolescents and the interviewers. Two strategies and types of arguments are discernible: on the one hand, negative and worrying experiences with the institutions of social control are mentioned; the adolescents want to be left alone and to "suppress everything related to the event". On the other hand, participation is rejected on reasons resulting from minimizing the importance of the event (offense and prosecution). "P. thinks, that she has no problems concerning this event" (female offender, interview rejected). Both types of arguments are equally distributed in the groups of rejecting and participating offenders. The perception and experience of high or low stress by the event thus results in increasing as well as decreasing motivation to participate.

Concerning the personal impressions recorded by the interviewers, the young offenders are described as "confident", "open-minded" and "well-considered" mainly independently of participation and rejection. The same result holds true concerning the opposite impressions of "insecurity", "depressiveness" and "shyness". Consequently, we assume that adolescents decide on their conversational preserve in a rather assured and confident way, and in most cases are not asked too much of by the conversation and the decision. Rarely do they request further information on the study and they are not interested in information on reliable measures of protecting their individual data by procedures of anonymity. This is the predominant topic of the conversations with their parents.

If they allow their children to participate, most parents (66%) consent spontaneously, they are sometimes ready to convince the adolescents themselves to participate, and – at this first opportunity – start talking about psychological and educational problems as well as problems of the family to the interviewer, who is totally unknown to them. On the other hand, the parents are disinterested, leaving the decision to the 14- to 17-year-old adolescents, or take a sceptical attitude and sometimes reject the request aggressively, including verbal injuries and threats of injuries. "Leave us alone! Get moving on!" was the reaction of a mother towards the request of a female interviewer. The parents are interested in protecting their children from further embarrassing and stressful events: "he (the adolescent) has had enough to chew on"; "the father thinks that it is advisable not to expose his son once more to stressful experiences related to the offense and the prosecution". The readiness of the parents to protect their children against further stressful events is clearly shown by their way of raising the issue of deviance. They back their children and diminish or extenuate the accusations: "he was dragged into it by another guy"; "he wanted to prevent the offense and has been falsely accused of participation in the offense".

The fear of neighbors and the anxiousness of saving face toward the interviewer who knows about the cause for interviewing the adolescent, is substantially increased for the parents, while for the adolescents no such remarks are recorded. Even here, we have not found any relation with the final consent to participate. The fear of further stigmatization by the interview itself is recorded for two parents, though in both cases the interviewer could dispel these reservations and realize the interview. A general consent to the purposes of the project – especially concerning diversion of young offenders – is rarely expressed. The demand of the parents for information is centered on the protection of the data and on procedures guaranteeing anonymity. This is the most frequent topic, being brought up in almost half the conversations, fathers being slightly over-represented. The reactions of the parents include the request for further information, doubts concerning the legality of the access to the files to obtain the adress, and aggressive remarks. Nevertheless, these doubts do not necessarily result in a rejection of the interview: while in four cases such disputes resulted in a refusal to allow the participation, for 7 others consent was obtained despite "considerable doubts" or "with bad feelings only".

In four cases, parents seized the opportunity of this first contact to raise the issue of educational and family problems, both parents equally being interested in such topics. These initiatives of extending and opening the information and conversational preserves include statements concerning a general apprehension of the adolescent up to completely divulging the situation of the family: "His step-father is in jail, too". But in general, the parents or legal guardians are more distanced and reluctant to allow an invasion into the information and conversational preserves of their children than the young offenders themselves. "Open-mindedness" and "interest" as a personal impression were recorded only twice by the interviewers, "irresoluteness", "scepticism", "disinterest", "aggressiveness" being predominant in their recordings of conversations with parents. Even in cases of a considerably reserved attitude, the interviews were realized to some extent. Many of the young offenders and their families live in areas which are the focus of social problems; a relation between social class (as far as it has been rated and recorded by the interviewers) and participation could not be established.

6. The Risk of Being Stigmatized by Social Research

One of the often heard objections to panel studies is the supposition that the data collection activities by the social reseacher could result in a stigmatization of the subjects under certain circumstances. Brought to a point, the thesis could be: That "dramatization of evil" which is meant to be avoided by diversion if possible and perhaps may be avoided, will in fact be produced by a panel study with repeated, intensive and rather long lasting interviews. This will be the more probable the less serious the offence and the more numerous the repetitions of the interviews and the greater the length of the research period are.

Formulated very polemically one may ask: Is it ethically acceptable to expose subjects to an apparently unpredictable risk of stigmatization by research activities in the context of a research project whose main objective it is to identify unnecessary and detrimental stigmatization[13)]?

This risk might consist in the fact that by repeated contacts and appointments with the former delinquent and visits by the interviewer such persons might get knowledge about the deviant behavior of the interviewee who originally didn't know anything about it (grandparents, brothers and sisters, friends, neighbors). Furthermore, it might be possible that those persons in the social network of the subjects (probably just those persons that function as significant others) that almost had forgotten about the deviant behavior and had managed to "normalize" the relationship with the our subjects, will be reminded of the deviant act by repeated interviewing. That may lead to the consequence that the reconstitution of intact and trustfull network relations that increase the probability of conformity will be interrupted if not blocked for ever. Finally, it may be true that the renewed topicality of the deviant act and the possible traumatizing experience of being discovered, convicted and interrogated will produce or harden a deviant self concept.

Without doubt every responsible social researcher has to face himself with these possible problems. He has to make sure theoretically and empirically how serious the mentioned risk will be and whether he can run it. We will collect and discuss some relevant arguments and show why we believe the risk to be a very small one.

Let us start with a purely formal but nevertheless important argument. If it is true that juvenile delinquents have to suffer negative identity transformations in the course of the traditional criminal justice procedures by the usual degradation ceremonies, and if it is true that these identity transformations increase the risk of a criminal career then a research project whose objective is the avoidance of just these processes of stigmatization, will be legitimate because all subjects and all future delinquents will gain by a change of the traditional criminal justice procedure. An ethical problem could only arise when the stigmatizing effects by the research procedure are nearly as serious as those produced by the traditional criminal justice procedure. Should it be the case that the stigma effects in fact are very small and irrelevant for the future development of the adolescent then it would be extraordinarily improbable if the effects caused by the research interview were notable and negative[14)]. Brought to the point: If the central premises of the labeling approach are correct, social research undertaken to further the application of this approach is justified; if the central assumptions of this approach are inaccurate, we must not take into account that research activities of the above mentioned type will do harm to the subjects concerned.

We will not leave it at that formal argument, but add some short theoretical considerations. Let us start with the propositions Harold Garfinkel (1956) formulated about the conditions of successful degradation ceremonies by which the whole identity of a person may be altered into a negative one. The first central condition thus demands that the moral indignation is expressed by public denunciation of the deviant actor by means of which a different, socially constructed and validated motivational scheme is ascribed to him that makes his actions easy to be explained. Secondly, the action and the actor have to be removed from their everyday context; they have to be defined as out of "normality". Thirdly, actions and actors have to be related to each other in such a manner that the acts will not be seen as unique events that will not reoccur but as part of a stable pattern. Any accidental nature of the deviant act has to be denied as absolutely unthinkable. The act has to be conceived as a choice out of several alternatives lead by a deviant motivation. The denunciator or accuser must present himself to witnesses of the ceremony in such a way that he seems to be no private person but a representative of the public, a deputy of experiences and evaluations of the public, and of the witnesses, too, who has the right and the authority to speak for all the other people. The accuser must not only emphasize the distance to the accused but the public has to recognize the distance, too. The accused has to be separated ritually from the legitimate order; he has to be placed "outside" the legitimate order.

Let us now take a closer look at our interviews with respect to the question whether the situation during our research interviews has any traits of the above mentioned conditions of successful degradation ceremonies[15]. The main criterion, the publicity of the attack on the former social identity, is not given without any doubt. The situation of the research interview is characterized by an intimate relationship (high confidentiality), not to mention the fact that all subjects participate on a completely voluntary basis and would be able to protect themselves against any "attacks" and any "unreasonable demands" by the interviewer and break off the interview immediately. Furthermore, the presence of third persons during the interview is not the normal case and shall be avoided by the interviewer as far as possible. Therefore, the risk of a proliferation of unpleasant information to the interviewer or third persons can be minimized. This is especially so as the most compromising questions must not be answered verbally but the answers are to be written in a small questionnaire that is shut up before the interviewer or any other person who can have a look at it.

The interview should be designed in such a manner[16] that the deviant act will not be removed from its everyday context; on the contrary: The kind of interview and the questions themselves make it clearer to the interviewee than any earlier treatment of the problem that there is a strong relation between everyday life and the deviant behavior. The subject may recognize for the first time that his deviant act is no expression of extremely unusual and pathological individual traits. In some respects and at some points of the interview, the interviewer functions and communicates with the former deviant adolescent as a representative of society. He is neither comparable with the accuser nor with the witness in Garfinkel's scenario. Dramaturgy and role behavior in the social research interview do not allow the interviewer any verbal or nonverbal criticism of the statements made by the interviewee. The role obligations call for the interviewer to show friendly indifference and understanding even when the interviewee's answers strongly contradict his own values and evaluations. The formulation of questions or their introduction emphasizes quite expressively that it is possible to look at the problems from very different points of view, to see them in different ways[17]. The main principle of the scientific research interview is not to encounter the interviewee from the standpo-int of the higher authority of popular sentiment or all upright people. Thus, the subject will not get the impression that his former deviant behavior draws a line between him and all other people. Finally, the preparation and the conduct of the interview do not result in a ritual symbolical demarcation of the former deviant. Quite the reverse: Representatives of the concurring societal groups with a relatively high social prestige ask the interviewee emphatically and almost submissively for his cooperation, offer some money for the interview, accept dates for the interview just as they are convenient to the interviewee and come to his home. All events take place on a territory that is under the authoritative control of the interviewee, and the interviewer apparently is very glad, when the subjects act cooperatively[18].

Because of limitations of space we cannot discuss the results of research about methodological problems of survey methods and the question of which effects we have to expect for our subjects. On the other hand, we must see that this research looks at different aspects of the problem. These studies explore how the subject reacts, expecially with respect to his tendency to answer certain questions according to social desirability, for instance. They discuss the complex interplay of attributions and dispositions of the interviewee, the interviewer, the content of questions, the form of questions and the setting of the interview in order to create the basis for a critical evaluation and an appropriate interpretation of the resulting data. They are seeking for an answer to the question how to ask embarrassing and threatening questions in such a way that the researcher receives reliable and valid answers[19)]. The problem of which immediate and/or long lasting effects are produced on the side of the interviewee by the interview, is no objective for this type of research insofar as these studies do not need this information to evaluate the methodological quality of the answers. This type of research tries to come to terms with the "reactivity problem" in social research and has produced such a lot of publications that it is nearly impossible to manage it (Belson, 1986; Sudman and Bradburn, 1982; Magione et al., 1981). There is no doubt that "reactivity" in the research interview is an indisputable phenomenon with a rather complex system of rules. The researchers can handle and control this complex processes only by applying a system of checks and crosschecks in order to determine specific effects of variables that produce reactivity. One of the central assumptions is that reactivity is a situative and specificly ephemeral phenomenon without any long lasting consequences for the subjects. It is threatening the reliability and validity of the data but not the identity of the interacting and communicating individuals. Till now, it is an open question whether this perspective is correct and appropriate, even after many decades of empirical social research.

Against any suspicion that, under certain circumstances, interviews have serious and therefore problematic ethical consequences for the subjects, there are many objections, especially all principles of designing an ideal interview: Orientation to the paradigm of everyday routine communication between strangers that had no contact before and will have no contact in the future; exclusion of any influences on the interviewee by behavior of the interviewer outside the rules that are cogently imposed on him; acceptance of all opinions, statements and behavioral acts of the interviewee as long as he follows the rules of the interview; silent, friendly but consequent denial to take a position even when the interviewee asks for it. Even if the normal, real processes of interviewing do not follow exactly this line of conduct (and maybe cannot follow this line in most cases) the deviations should be small ones without serious consequences for the subjects because there are some further regulative mechanisms to be discussed a little later.

We did not want to be dependent on mere suppositions with respect to the actual effects of some parts or some questions of our interview. Therefore, we have directed some questions at the interviewers and at the subjects. We wanted to know how our interviewers thought about cooperativeness, trustfulness and emotional stress on the side of the subjects in general and with respect to some questions that might be embarrassing in particular. On the other hand, we have asked our subjects to classify the interviewer and his behavior, the interview itself and the stress by special questions. The research procedure guaranteed that both partners could not get information about the classifications they received by the other ones.

Till now we have data for 43 cases only because our field work started with a delay of several months. Therefore, we can only report about tendencies in our data that have to be checked at a later stage. One of the most important limits of our results is the fact that we do not know the effects of repeated interviewing because all subjects have been interviewed only once by our project.

In 80% of all cases the interviews were conducted with the subjects alone, only in a few cases parents or brothers or sisters were present during the interview. Interventions from outside were rare events (below 10%). Our interviewers classified the statements by the subjects in more than 90% as reliable. The fact that in about 25% of all cases the subjects initiated a conversation after the interview that lasted up to 30 minutes in one quarter of the cases, shows that our interviewers were not percepted as intruders who were to be refused or avoided. In 20% of our interviews a conversation about the young offenders took place between interviewers and parents after the interview. About 60% to 70% of these conversations did not last longer than 15 minutes. They were concentrated almost ecxlusively on pedagogical and psychological questions. About 44% of the subjects were classified as "open and open- minded" on a scale from "open and open-minded" to "highly distrustful" and about 37% were classified on the stage next to the category "open and open-minded". Only 2% were rated as "more distrustful".

Our interviewers reported that 28% of the subjects experienced the interview as "not stressing", while 47% of the interviews were classified as "nearly without stress" and 25% as "a little bit stressing". On a five stage continuum from "cheerful" to "depressed" about 50% of the subjects lay on the neutral center and about 33% were classified as "more cheerful". Only about 12% of the subjects were said to be "more depressed" ("a little bit depressed"). With respect to the criterion "light-hearted" vs. "stressed" nearly 50% lay one step from the neutral center toward "light-hearted". Not more than 19% of the interviewees were classified as below the center toward "stressed".

Our interviews were also meant to evaluate the reactions of the subjects to certain questions in order to determine at what points of the interview the subjects got into trouble. We cannot go into further details, but at a first glance we see that most questions were classified as neutral by the great majority of the subjects. The other subjects in nearly equal parts chose a classification of these questions that was one point more positive or one point more negative respectively – with some exceptions. First of all, the reactions to the question about the self-evaluation of the subjects were shifted a little to the positive end while the opposite was true for the question about the climate within their families. A very important result is that the reactions to questions about delinquency were not shifted to the negative side. Apparently, the subjects did not experience this seemingly delicate question to be very embarrassing.

The overall evaluation of interviewee behavior by the interviewers with respect to the stressfullness of the interview was very positive. More than 55% of the subjects did not show negative reactions in any of the parts of the interview that were presumed to be embarrassing. For only 30% of the subjects our interviewers reported a maximum of one negative reaction.

The manifest statements by the subjects on their personal interpretation of the interview yielded some interesting results. Nearly 50% of the subjects classified the interview with respect to the dimension "excitement" as neutral. The other subjects in equal parts chose the two categories "a little exciting" and "less exciting". About 50% of the subjects judged the interview as neutral with respect to the "importance" for themselves, but more subjects evaluated the interview as "important" than "unimportant" (39% and 12% respectively). A very important fact is that about 79% of the subjects described the interviews as not stressing. Only 5% judged the interview to be "very stressing" and about 7% "a little stressing". Most subjects evaluated the interview as neutral with respect to the category "supporting", in general a positive evaluation. More than 72% of the subjects experienced the interview as "not difficult". Almost all other subjects chose the neutral category.

56% of our interviewers were said to be "very helpful" and 40% "helpful". Thus, only a very small minority of the subjects had a negative impression with respect to the helpfulness of the interviewers. The same holds true for the dimension of "friendliness": 100% of our interviewers were categorized as "very friendly". A similar result is to be reported about regarding "trustfulness":

30% of our interviewers were said to be "strongly inspiring confidence" and 58% to be "inspiring confidence". All the remaining evaluations lay on the neutral point. So, no reaction of distrustfulness did appear. The subjects emphasized the patience and the cheerfulness of the interviewers (about 23% "very cheerful" and about 62% "cheerful") and their willingness to accept the desire to have a talk after the interview.

Analyzing which questions were experienced as embarrassing by the subjects we find that questions about pocket money, dwelling situation, marital relations of parents, school and occupation, parent's and friends' opinions of oneself, sources of advice and help, and leisure time activities were absolutely *not* embarrassing. Apparently, the subjects felt the questions about deviance (about 5% "very embarrassing" and about 19% "embarrassing"), opinions of oneself and police rather more embarrassing.

We cannot go into further details but should finally report that our first analysis demonstrates that the classification of questions as embarrassing or not is only loosely coupled with the fact whether the subject belongs to a special problem group. To say it with an example: The experience of the question about delinquency is only weakly related to the factual experience of delinquency.

All these results – as preliminary as they are – support the thesis that our surveys are accepted and voluntarily admitted interferences that are experienced as relatively normal and non-stressing by the subjects. Interviewers have competences and skills of mastering situations that wait for further exploration by survey research methodologists.

What about the consequences of these results for our general question of identity transformations by repeated interviewing. In the last few years the "rediscovery of the self" (Hales, 1985; Epstein, 1985; Pratkanis and Greenwald, 1985; Swanson, 1985; Covington 1985; Miller and Turnbull 1986; Markus and Wurf, 1987; Pittman and Heller, 1987; Singer and Kolligian, 1987) has created such a lot of new theoretical ideas that we have to revise many older sociological theories about identity. In particular, we have to emphasize that we ought to start from the idea of a multi-dimensionality of the self-concept or the identity so that it is not useful to speak about *the* self- concept. Instead, it is necessary to speak of a "working- self-concept", "on-line" or "accessible" self-concept (Schlenker, 1985; Markus and Nurius, 1986; Markus and Wurf, 1987). That does not mean any thing else than that not all representations of the self or all "identities" that are part of the whole self-concept, are ready to respond or accessible at the same time. The working-self-concept or the "on-line self concept" is to be seen as a constantly active, changeable arrangement of the accessible and available knowledge of the self. As Markus and Wurf (1987, p. 306) have shown such a conception of the self-concept is able to account for the empirical results that individuals are highly influenced in all aspects of their judgements, their memories and their actual behavior by the currently accessible stock of ideas, attitudes and beliefs. Furthermore, it is compatible with the position of symbolic interactionism that there is no static self but only a current self-concept built out of individual social experiences.

After all, from this point of view the self-concept las to be conceived as stable and workable at the same time. Central aspects of the self (self-schemata) can be relatively invariant with regard to changes in the specific social environment. Because of the great importance of the specific environmental conditions for the definition of the self and because of the variety of their forms they can be supposed to be continuonsly available and accessible. "Many other self-conceptions in the individual's system, however, will vary in their accessibility depending on the individual's motivational state or on the prevailing social conditions. The working self-concept thus consists of the core self-conceptions embedded in a context of more tentative self-conceptions that are tied to the prevailing circumstances" (Markus and Wurf 1987, p. 306).

Such a conception indicates different types of identity transformations that should be distinguished. Two of them shall be sketced: First, it is possible that a temporary change of the self-concept results from activating a special set of potential self-concepts and ignoring some other potential self-concepts that are not accessible at the moment, and secondly, a lasting change may take place when new self-concepts are added to the old ones, when they change their meaning or when the relations between the various self-concepts change. From such a perspective, it becomes clear that during and by a social science research interview completely different working-self- concepts are made topical than during a trial. Treating the same problem (delinquency for instance) will therefore have completely different consequences for the identity developement depending on the conditions of interaction and communication.

7. Summary and Conclusions

Though our results are based on a small sample and caution has to prevail concerning the subjectivity of the ratings of the interviewers, we can preliminarily sum up our results to the fact, that our study does not have any effects on the young offenders which could be judged as morally objectionable even by the most stringent standards.

1) With regard to the interview, our results show that the interview itself – especially its parts of self-report – does not have any consequences which would be morally objectionable.
2) Additional stress by being interviewed cannot be supposed, because those who are anxious of that, reject the request.
3) The adolescents who decide for or against participation, are sufficiently confident and competent to control their information and conversational preserve.
4) The adolescents have at their disposal overt as well as covered maneuvers of defending an unwanted invasion into their preserves.
5) The fear of being additionally stigmatized by the interview is rare, and even then, it does not result in a rejection of the request.

With regard to methodical standards, our results are encouraging. A general scepticism toward survey research and concerning the protection and anonymity of the data files, fears with regard to contacts with institutions of social control do not inevitably result in a rejection of the request. Consequently, we can assume that our sample will not be systematically biased – at least with regard to these variables. Still, results concerning the effects of repeated access and interviewing are lacking, though our first results show, that we can enter this subsequent task in compliance with rigorous standards of ethical conduct for social scientists.

These are the reasons why we answer everyone who claims that our research activities were ethically problematic interferences and interventions into the life world of our subjects, with a verse from Goethe's Xenia: "I know it!. If they have nothing reasonable left to answer, they quickly make it a matter of your conscience."

Notes

1 Cf. for a general inquiry Schuler, H. (1982a), and with regard to the ethical problems of applied research and applied psychology Kruse, L. and Kumpf, M. (1981); Steere, J. (1984).

2 Welter (1986, pp. 117, 185) points out, that the very concept of life world, which the phenomenological sociology has developed with reference to Husserl, more exactly corresponds to the term "environment" in Husserl's work; he proposes to use the term "environment" for

sociological inquiries only, leaving the term "life world" to philosophy. Further he critcizes Schütz and Luckmann because of unnecessarily adding the terms "everyday" and "social" to the concept of life world. The term life world should be substituted by the terms "life" and "environment" in the works of these authors (p. 168).

3 It should be noted by those who attack social research with arguments based on the concept of life world, that these arguments can easily contribute to a growing movement of "counter-enlightenment" within the scientific community as well as the public without being intended to do so.

4 One of Goffman's early masterpieces "The Presentation of Self in Everyday Life" (1959), demonstrates that his methods yield vivacious descriptions of everyday life, especially of the spatial and social territories of the individuals.

5 The concept of "personal space" has made its way into the social sciences though its meaning has been extended to include other territories named by Goffman; cf. Ashcroft, N. and Scheflen, A.E. (1976), and Malmberg, T. (1980). This concept is most narrowly related to the concepts of ethology, defining the imaginary boundaries around the body, the transgression of which is an aggressive action (Goffman, E., 1972, p. 52). Goffman himself explicitly refers to ethology and acclaims "its value for us as a model" (1972, p. 22).

6 Many of these studies are by-products of social research, though meanwhile the social scientist can rely on a growing stock of systematic analyses of response and participation rates, of reactions to embarrassing questions etc.; cf. Esser, H. (1975) for an overview.

7 Cf. Kinkel and Josef in this volume.

8 For a detailed analysis, see section 5.

9 The scientist should be aware that the subjects not belonging to the special group might feel discriminated; further, the costs of the survey increase.

10 Therefore, questions about the educational, occupational and family situation may elicit severe negative reactions from subjects who have problems in the respective fields (low educational level; unemployment; divorce).

11 On the other hand, panel studies can have positive effects resulting from repeated contact with social scientists, e.g., a panel study of children of outstanding intelligence.

12 The index of contact intensity was calculated by dividing the frequency of contacts by the number of days from the first contact up to the realization of the interview; the value of "1" indicates that the interviewer realized (tried) a contact every day.

13 Cf. for example, Goffman, E. (1963). Meanwhile the development has overcome this rather proto-scientific stage. Compare for example, the contribution to Ainly, St. C.; Coleman, L.M. and Becker, G. (Eds.) (1986)

14 Cf. for instance, as an introduction to the theoretical background of this project: Albrecht, G. and Karstedt-Henke, S. (1987)

15 Cf. with respect to the special properties of sociological fieldwork Gachowetz, H. (1984); Bortz, J. (1984, pp. 163 et seq.)

16 Cf. as a still remarkable contribution to the research interview Cannell, Ch.F. and Kahn, R.L. (1968); Koolwijk, J. van (1974, pp. 9-23); Kreutz, H. and Titscher, St. (1974, pp. 24-82)

17 Cf. Erbslöh, E. and Weindieck, G. (1974)

18 Cf. with respect to the importance of the above mentioned properties of the social situation of our research interviews Schuler, H. (1982b, pp. 341-364, espec. 355 et seq.)

19 Cf. with respect to this problem Barton, A.H. (1958); Koolwijk, J. van (1968); Koolwijk, J. van (1969)

References

Ainly, St.C., Coleman, L.M., and Becker, G. (Eds.) (1986): The Dilemma of Difference. A Multidisciplinary View of Stigma: New York – London Plunim Press

Albrecht, G., and Karstedt-Henke, S. (1987): Alternative Methods of Conflict-Settling and Sanctioning: Their Impact on Young Offenders. In: Hurrelmann, K., Kaufmann, F.-X., and Lösel, F. (Eds.): Social Intervention: Potential and Constraints, Berlin – New York: de Gruyter, 315-332

Ashcroft, N., and Scheflen, A.E. (1976): People Space, New York: Anchor Press

Barton, A.H. (1958): Asking the Embarrassing Question. In: Public Opinion Quarterly, Vol. 22, 67-68

Belson, W.A. (1986): Validity in Survey Research, Cambridge: University Press

Bergmann, W. (1981): Lebenswelt, Lebenswelt des Alltags oder Alltagswelt? In: Kölner Zeitschrift für Soziologie, Vol. 33, 50-72

Bortz, J. (1984): Lehrbuch der empirischen Sozialforschung für Sozialwissenschaftler. Berlin, New York: Springer

Canell, C.F., and Kahn, R.L. (1968): Interviewing. In: Lindzey, G., and Aronson, E. (Eds.): Handbook of Social Psychology. Vol. 2, Research Methods, Reading Massachusetts: Addison-Wesley

Covington, M.V. (1985): The Role of Self-Processes in Applied Social Psychology. In: Journal of the Theory of Social Behavior, Vol. 15, 355-389

Epstein, S. (1985): The Implication of Cognitive-Experiental Self-Theory for Research in Social Psychology and Personality. In: Journal of the Theory of Social Behavior, Vol. 15, 283-310

Erbslöh, E., and Wiendieck, G. (1974): Der Interviewer. In: Koolwijk, J. van, and Wieken-Mayser, M. (Eds.): Techniken der empirischen Sozialforschung. Vol. 4, Erhebungsmethoden: Die Befragung, München – Wien: Oldenbourg, 83-106

Esser, H. (1975): Soziale Regelmäßigkeiten des Befragtenverhaltens. Meisenheim am Glan

Gachowetz, H. (1984): Feldforschung. In: Roth, E. (Ed.): Sozialwissenschaftliche Methoden. Lehr- und Handbuch für Forschung und Praxis, München – Wien: Oldenbourg, 255-276

Garfinkel, H. (1956): Conditions of Successful Degradation Ceremonies. In: The American Journal of Sociology, Vol. 61, 420-424

Goffman, E. (1959): The Presentation of Self in Everyday Life. Garden City, New York, Doubleday Anchor

Goffman, E. (1961): Asylums. Essays on the Social Situation of Mental Patients and Other Inmates. Chicago: Aldine

Goffman, E. (1963): Stigma. Notes on the Management of Spoiled Identity. Englewood Cliffs N.J.: Prentice Hall

Goffman, E. (1967): Interaction Ritual. Essays in Face- to-Face Behavior. Chicago: Aldine

Goffman, E. (1969): Strategic Interaction. Philadelphia: University of Pennsylvania Press

Goffman, E. (1972): Relations in Public. Microstudies of the Public Order. London: Penguin

Greenberg, B., Abul-Ela, A.-L., Simmons, W.R., and Horvitz, D.G. (1969): The Unrelated Question Randomized Response Model: Theoretical Framework. In: Journal of the American Statistical Association 64, 520-539

Habermas, J. (1979): Einleitung zu: Stichworte zur "Geistigen Situation der Zeit". Vol. 1, Frankfurt/M.: Suhrkamp Verlag, 7-35.

Habermas, J. (1981): Theorie des kommunikativen Handelns. Vol. 1, 2, Frankfurt/ M.: Suhrkamp

Hales, S. (1985): The Rediscovering of Self in Social Psychology: Theoretical and Methodological Implications. In: Journal of the Theory of Social Behavior, Vol. 15, 227-282

Holm, K. (Eds.) (1982): Die Befragung. Vol.1, München: A.Franke Verlag

Kinkel, R.J., and Josef, N.C. (1987): The Ethics of Informed Consent in Adolescent Research. (in this volume) Koolwijk, J. van (1968): Fragebogenprofile. In: Kölner Zeitschrift für Soziologie und Sozialpsychologie, Vol. 20, 780-791

Koolwijk, J. van (1969): Unangenehme Fragen. Paradigmen für die Reaktion des Befragten im Interview. In: Kölner Zeit- schrift für Soziologie und Sozialposychologie, Vol. 21, 864-875

Koolwijk, J. van (1974): Die Befragungsmethode. In: Koolwijk, J. van, and Wieken-Mayser, M. (Eds.): Techniken der empirischen Sozialforschung. Vol. 4, Erhebungsmethoden: Die Befragung. München: Oldenbourg, 9-23

Kreutz, H., and Titscher, S. (1974): Die Konstruktion von Fragebogen. In: Koolwijk, J. van, and Wieken-Mayser, M. (Eds.): Techniken der empirischen Sozialforschung. Vol. 4, Erhebungsmethoden: Die Befragung. München-Wien: Oldenbourg , 24-82

Kruse, L., and Kumpf, M. (1981): Psychologische Grundlagenforschung: Ethik und Recht. Bern, Stuttgart, Wien: Huber

Malmberg, T. (1980): Human Territoriality. The Hague, Paris, New York: Mouton Publishers

Mangione, T.W., Hingson, R., and Barret, J. (1981): Collecting Sensitive Data, A Comparison of Three Survey Strategies. In: Heise, D.R. (Ed.): Sociological Methods and Research. Vol.10, No. 1, Beverly Hills: Sage Publication

Markus, H., and Nurius, P. (1986): Possible Selves. In: American Psychologist, Vol. 41, 954–969

Markus, H., and Wurf, E. (1987): The Dynamic Self-Concept: A Social Psychological Perspective. In: Annual Review of Psychology, Vol. 38, 299–337

Miller, D.T., and Turnbull, W. (1986): Expectancies and Interpersonal Processes. In: Annual Review of Psychology, Vol. 37, 233–256

Pittmann, Th.S., and Heller, J.F. (1987): Social Motivation. In: Annual Review of Psychology, Vol. 38, 461–489

Pratkanis, A.R., and Greenwald, A.G. (1985): How Shall the Self be Conceived? In: Journal of the Theory of Social Behavior, Vol. 15, 311–329

Singer, J.R., and Kolligian, J. (1987): Personality: Development in the Study of Private Experience. In: Annual Review of Psychology, Vol. 38, 533–574

Schlenker, B.R. (Ed.) (1985): The Self and Social Life. New York: McGraw-Hill

Schuler, H. (1982a): Ethical Problems in Psychological Research. New York, London: Academic Press

Schuler, H. (1982b): Ethische Probleme der Feldforschung. In: Patry, J.-L. (Ed.): Feldforschung. Bern, Stuttgart, Wien: H. Huber, 341–364

Steere, J. (1984): Ethics in Clinical Psychology. Oxford: University Press

Sudman, S., and Bradburn, N.M. (1982): Asking Questions. London: Jossey-Bass Publishers

Swanson, G.E. (1985): The Powers and Capabilities of Selves: Social and Collective Approaches. In: Journal of the Theory of Social Behavior, Vol. 15, 331–354

Villmow, B., and Stephan, E. (1983): Jugendkriminalität in einer Gemeinde. Freiburg i.Br.: Eigenverlag, Max-Planck-Institut für ausländisches und internationales Strafrecht

Welter, R. (1986): Der Begriff der Lebenswelt. München: Fink

16.

On Dangerous Research: The Fate of a Study of the Police in Norway

Thomas Mathiesen

1. Introduction

The concepts of prevention and intervention, which are key concepts at this conference, are generally used in connection with various forms of traditional crime. In that context, both concepts imply policies which in my mind easily become very problematical: By being future-oriented and oriented toward the control of whole categories of people, the policies easily involve changes to new and subtler forms of control as well as the waivering of basic principles of due process.

But the concepts of prevention and intervention also have another aspect. I am thinking of prevention of and intervention with crimes performed by *the State*. In orther words, rather than implying policies geared "downward" toward the general population, the concepts may imply policies geared "upward" toward those in power and authority. It is interesting, but not surprising, to see that the concepts are used much more rarely in the latter context. While prevention and intervention are politically very popular concepts in connection with traditional crime, they are far less popular – indeed, they are met by a number of strategies and tactics – when used in connection with the crimes of the state.

In this paper, I shall discuss some questions related to the problems of preventing and intervening with *the crimes of the state*. My point of departure is police crime, more specifically police violence, defined in the traditional sense of illegal or unlawful physical assault on the part of the police against members of a given population. Concretely, the main questions which I wish to address today, are the following:
What happens when research into police crime, as an aspect of state crime, becomes so incisive or intensive that it threatens the basic legitimacy of that branch of the state? What counter-measures are then used by that branch of the state? How is the research dealt with, how is it counteracted and neutralized? These are crucial questions for us as social researchers, but, as I have indicated, they are also important questions from the point of view of prevention of and intervention with state crime.

My presentation will follow the following main steps:
First I will relate a story. It is a true story, about what happened to an important research

project dealing i.a. with police violence in Norway. As I hope to be able to convey, the story is dramatic in itself, and I relate the details of the story partly to make a qualified international audience of criminologists and sociologists of law aware of it: International awareness of national issues such as this is one way of gaining strength and support in the conflict over the issue; the widening of the national public sphere or "Öffentlichkeit" to an international public sphere is in itself an aspect of political struggle.
Then, after I have related the story, I will provide some interpretations concerning counteracting strategies and tactics used by the state.
But before actually starting my presentation, I have to say a few words about Norway as a country, because the Norwegian context is important for an understanding of the story I have to tell.

Keeping in mind the dangers inherent in facile generalizations about whole countries or the cultures of whole countries, I wish to emphasize five major features of Norwegian social structure and culture:
Firstly, Norway is a *small* society. For this reason, news defined by news agents or political leaders as important or sensational, easily reach the far corners of the society, in a sense unifying the society around given issues. This tendency is enhanced by the fact that Norway, because it is a small society, has only one television channel (though we are now increasingly getting satellites from the sky above us), and two radio channels (though we are now also getting some local private radio stations). The national broadcasting media effectively communicate news which are defined as important or sensational by the news agents and/or by the political leadership to the very outskirts of the society.

Secondly, Norway has a *long and strong social-democratic tradition*. The Norwegian Labour Party was early, in the 1920s, one of the most radical socialists parties of Scandinavia. As the party seized power in the mid-thirties, it became less radical, and during its long regime after World War II the de-radicalization continued. But the party for a long time maintained a strong image of being the only or the main party thinking systematically of the welfare of the people. Because of this, and because the party, as I have said, has been in power for so long (excepting World War II, almost without any break from 1935 to 1965, as well as during most of the 1970s and recent years in the 1980s), the Norwegian state itself has received a strong image of being a kind, benevolent state, always doing what is best for the people. While this is an impression which most states try to give of themselves, the Norwegian state has, through the social-democratic tradition, been particularly successful.

Thirdly, Norway has a *tradition of an impeccable state bureaucracy*. In terms of causation, this tradition is probably partly rooted in the social-democratic tradition mentioned already, but in part it also has independent sources. It will lead us too far afield to go into these sources. Suffice it here to say that the state bureaucrat is a man (or, in more recent times, a woman) with a *calling* or vocation in a Weberian sense. Note that I am not saying that the Norwegian state in fact has an impeccable bureaucratic machinery, I am only saying that it has a tradition which emphasizes it.

Fourthly, especially during the years following World War II, Norway has witnessed an increasing *interweaving of the organizations of the various social classes.* The organizations of the working- and property-owning classes have increasingly become linked to each other, in intricate networks of cooperation, exchange and integration.

Fifthly and finally – and here I am frankly speculative – I believe it is correct to say that Norway is a society which in a certain sense *defines conflict as a bad thing.* Let me immediately qualify this. To be sure, conflicts are not foreign to Norwegian farmers, fishermen, or local communities. When I say that conflict is defined as a bad thing, I am thinking of conflicts within the state. The state is concidered as a set of institutions or a machinery which should be integrated and if possible "conflictless". And when conflicts nevertheless occur, they should be spelled out and take place within highly institutionalized frameworks. "Wild" conflicts within the state, or in the wake of state policies, which might be considered a sign of a living and active democratic tradition, are – I postulate – not considered as such in the Norwegian context.

As I have said, these five features – Norway's smallness with the concurrent even spread of given news, the social democratic tradition of the Norwegian state, the tradition of an impeccable state, the organizational interweaving of classes, and the definition of state conflicts as a bad thing – constitute an important context for an understanding of the story about police research which I have to tell: Within this context, the demasking of important state crimes, such as widespread police violence, has a particularly "explosive" effect, and becomes particularly threatening to state legitimacy. By the same token, such demasking also leads to particularly strong state counter measures, counter measures of a character suggesting indeed that the very honour of the state is at stake.

I am not saying that countries ranking lower on the five dimensions I have outlined, are lacking in state counter measures to the demasking of state crimes. I am only suggesting that the context which I have sketched may make the counter measures and defensive reactions in general on the part of the state particularly vociferous. Thus, the context is supplied as an interpretative framework for the state which I am going to describe below. Now, after this introduction, let us move on to the story itself.

2. The Story

The point of departure is a research study of violence in the Norwegian city of Bergen, located on the west coast of Norway. The study in question investigated reports concerning physical violence identified in doctors' and dentists' offices as well as local hospitals during a given period of time in the 1970s. The study also included interviews with samples of victims. Edvard *Vogt*, at the time a senior lecturer at one of the colleges in Bergen, and Gunnar *Nordhus*, a law student, conducted the study. Initially, the study was directed by a professor of medicine who died during the research. Two other professors succeeded him, but played a less important role, and when the study was published the two researchers were alone held responsible for it.

At first, the two researchers did not think of police violence when gathering their data. They "stumbled" on it: An increasing number of reports, and subsequent interviews, showed a large number of violent assaults etc. performed by the police in the city of Bergen. In 1981 a book, called *Violence and its Victims*, was published by the two researchers, based on about 10.000 pages of written material. The book reported on family violence, street violence, violence against children, etc. – and police violence.

No debate whatsoever followed concerning family violence etc. – only debate about police violence. The Bergen police vociferously criticized the study, but as I see it without damaging in any critical way the validity of the study. One of the major claims was that the other party, the police man, had not been heard. The researchers replied to this that they had tried to get interviews with the police side, but they had refused, which was true. The researchers gave detailed information on how they had conducted their interviews, and argued that though the interviews might contain memory slips, skewed statements about reality, and even falsehoods, *the general tendency* in the material as a whole was correct. No really good arguments were presented against this defence.

But during this debate, the Bergen mass media, especially the newspapers, entered the scene, clearly on the side of the police. A few words should be said about the city of Bergen: Bergen is an old Hanseatic city with a commerce base, deep class divisions, and a wealthy business class in control of major political institutions. It is a rather special city, with a distinct dialect invested with great local pride. The study of widespread police violence landed as a major shock in this socio-political context. The newspapers, dominated by a large conservative paper (the labour party paper is small and not exactly radical) came out, as I have said, strongly on the police side. The researchers were classified as liers and cheaters.

The debate consequently reached the national level. The national papers were more inclined to listen to research claims, but – since major national papers in Norway are also conservative – they too were to a considerable extent critical. In short, the structure and culture of the city of Bergen created a context which enhanced local reactions. In turn, these reactions were further escallated on the background of the contextual features of Norway in general which I mentioned above. Put differently, within a double set of contexts, the violence study functioned as two step missile.

As the debate reached the national level, the Ministry of Justice also became involved, as the major relevant political institution. If there was something in the claims of the researchers, the Minister of Justice – the channel to the (at that time conservative) Government itself – was ultimately responsible. While standard criminological research often does not reach the newspapers at all, and certainly almost never shakes the government, this study, and the spiralling effect of the debate emanating from the class-divided, bourgeois Hanseatic city on the west coast, clearly did.

Before I go on to tell you what the Minister of Justice did, let us consider for a moment another possible outcome of the conflict as it developed up to the point I have dealt with so far. The police and the press could have *silenced* the study. The press in a sense "had" to pick it up for a period, but – knowing how modern newspapers function in the context of the modern concept of what is "news" – the topic could soon have been left for other sensations, and thereby forgotten. Why did this not happen?

The reason why silence did not become the road, becomes understandable in the light of the socio-political context of Bergen and Norway, which I just mentioned: Silence was impossible *on the basis of the honour of the old city as well as of the benign, presumably impeccable state machinery of the country.*

So, what did the Minister of Justice do? She used the age old tactic of setting up a committee.

In the Fall of 1981 an "investigative committee" consisting of two members was appointed by the Ministry of Justice. The committee's task was to investigate and evaluate the police study from Bergen, along with some other studies of aspects of police violence which had appeared earlier. Interestingly, two *lawyers* were appointed to evaluate sociological research. One of them was a well known attorney, the other an established professor of law at the University of Oslo. The professor of law became a very important actor in the subsequent events: Anders *Bratholm*, who has recently written two books on the topic of police violence and the events following the Bergen study (Bratholm, 1986 and 1987).

I should make explicit that prior to the events I relate here, the professor of law in question had written two articles which maintained that police violence in fact constituted a problem. The other committee member had never publicly engaged himself in the issue, and was skeptical to the existence of police violence as a problem. We do not know what the Minister of Justice (and the government?) expected and hoped from the investigative committee. But we can guess: On my part, I believe that by appointing the two lawyers in question to serve on the committee, the expectation and hope was to get a "balanced" conclusion which, though it might concede that police violence did exist as a problem, also gave considerable concessions to the police side in the controversy, thus silencing of some police violence would only increase the credibility of the absence of violence as the major trend. This would be the normal, expected "*puncturing effect*" of a committee like this.

But this did not become the effect. The report of the committee was unusually meticulous and detailed. The two lawyers had gone very carefully through the research results, personally interviewed a number of victims, and consulted research methodologists to evaluate research methods. While individual cases of violence could have been exaggerated etc., the committee concluded that the major trend in the material was valid and reliable – and this was precisely the view of the researchers.

This, however, did not end police activity and criticism. While a negative conclusion would have had a "puncturing effect" and silenced the issue, a positive conclusion did not. This is sociologically important and says something about how mechanisms of neutralization function selectively, depending on which side is to be neutralized. The Bergen Police, and the National Police Association, asserted that the report of the committee was a concious attempt to damage the reputation of the police. Parts of the local and national press followed suit, so that the conflict continued. The issue of honour, or reputation, was placed more squarely than ever on the agenda of the debate. Sociologically, we would say that the whole question of *legitimacy* of a major state institution with a monopoly on physical force was now pushed to an extreme in Norwegian society. The courts also became involved. The Bergen researchers took out a libel suit against a newspaper in town for having accused them of lies and fraud. They lost the case, the newspaper won, and the Supreme Court refused to review an appeal. Legally, this was very surprising, because legally, the case was strong. Sociologically, from what we know about how legal institutions function during state crises, it was less than unexpected. In general, "legalization" of political conflicts is a dangerous tactic – a major point to which I will return later on.

The loss of the libel suit made the professor of law whom I mentioned, Anders Bratholm, look closely at the case – which he critized severely on legal grounds – and at the debate in general which followed in the wake of the committee report. At the same time, Bratholm collected more material substantiating the existence of police violence. All of this was reported in his book *Police Violence* (1986), which I mentioned above.

Once again, the Bergen police and the National Police Association reacted vociferously. A basic point made by them was that the victims in the original study as well as in the new book were *anonymous*. There were obvious reasons for the anonymity: Anonymity must be guaranteed to get the information, to protect the informants, etc., and as everyone knows, it is a standard procedure in social research. But in the context of the police crisis in Norway (which I think it is fair to call it), it was used against the research: Because of anonymity, the police presumbly could not defend themselves concretely.

At this debate on the validity and reliability of the material, and the anonymity of the victims, escallated during the Summer of 1986, the two Bergen researchers had already gathered considerable new material from victims or witnessess concerning violence or other types of infringement in the Bergen police, pertaining especially to the years 1980–1983. A number of these victims or witnessess had waived anonymity. In view of the debate, and the frustration they felt over not being believed, they were willing to witness in full name. Professor Bratholm also participated in recording a number of these cases, and in november 1986 about 220 witness statements from about 140 individuals were presented at a large press conference in Oslo. Only a few of the victims/witnessess had reservations about going public with their statements. At the press conference names were deleted, but the names were made available to the authorities, including the Attorney General. In his book *Police Transgressions and Persecution of Individuals*, Bratholm reports these statements in detail. In addition to regular police violence, they include infringements such as refusals to receive reports of police violence, offers of alcohol or pills to suspects, illegal acquisition of property belonging to victims, and, last but not least, harassments of the researchers.

Before relating the finale of this story, which involved still further escallation, a few details should be added concerning the latter harassments – those directed toward the researchers. I have so far emphasized the *argumentative* basis of police counter attacks, in other words, police activity in the public sphere. But it should be added that police activity also had a very *physical* basis, especially in that the Bergen police increasingly persecuted and harassed the researchers physically. Anders Bratholm has recorded 27 cases of driving controls performed by the police of one of the researchers, Gunnar Nordhus. About half of these were witnessed by third parties, most of them established people in Bergen. Some of them were early in the sequence of events related here: After the publication of the original study in 1981. But many of them came late, in 1986, during the period I am telling about now. A number of the controls were extremely frightening and anxiety provoking. Let me mention one case which became important in the subsequent events: One day Gunnar Nordhus found a match box containing cannabis in the bottom of his car. It should be added that Mr. Nordhus is a teetotaler, a passionate jogger, and in terms of values at an extreme distance from anything resembling drugs. In fact, he did not know what the match box actually contained, and after having sought the advice of the other researcher, he destroyed it (the possession of cannabis is illegal in Norway). According to his own statement he was subject to an extremely thorough traffic control soon after having discovered the match box. I shall return to this particular incident later. In general, rumours have been circulated in Bergen to the effect that the researchers actually were involved in drug dealing. The police in Bergen were clearly behind these rumours. In connection with interrogations or arrests, a number of people were asked by the police whether they had information about criminal activities on the part of Gunnar Nordhus (sometimes also of Edvard Vogt). Anders Bratholm has recorded 19 reported cases of this type of questioning (1987, chap. 3). According to the reports, the type of questioning varied, from casual questions to promises of rewards in the form of alcohol, cash or lenient treatment in return for information. In part, the questioning concerned participation in narcotics trade. On several occasions, the interrogators were interested in information about the sources of Gunnar Nordhus' money – where did he get his support from? (most of it was paid by the other researcher, Edvard Vogt, who, it might be mentioned, was a Catholic priest until the age of 50, whereupon he left his church vocation and married). The 19 reported cases of this type of police questioning most likely hide significant dark figures.

Returning now to the press conference and the presentation of concrete names of about 140 victims and witnesses, I want to tell you what finally happened – up to now.

As an anticipatory reaction to the pending press conference, the Attorney General of Norway on the day before decided to implement a full scale police investigation of the Bergen police. Presumably in order to prevent the Bergen police from destroying information, a branch of the Oslo police secretely flew to Bergen. The whole affair was very secretive: The Oslo police officers did not know what their mission was before they came to the airport. During the night the Oslo branch in question, led by a specially appointed state attorney, abruptly entered the Bergen Police headquarters, confiscated materials, sealed archives etc. and undertook a major investigation of the issue of police violence in Bergen.

I assure you, it was very dramatic. Something similar to this had never happened in Norway before. A few details should be emphasized:
Firstly, the police of course knew of what the pending press conference would provide – non-anonymous statements about police violence. Seizing control of the Bergen headquarters, which the Oslo police in fact did, was therefore wise from a police point of view: It took the blunt edges of the critique at the press conference away. Also, something was now being done to the question of police violence by the police itself.

Secondly, the police by this tactic received considerable sympathy in the mass media. Bergen police officers called for psychiatric help against the shock, and local psychiatrists offered such help. When the police abruptly enter houses inhabited by vagrants and youthful occupants, shock treatment is hardly provided, but here the claim was taken very seriously. In all, then, the decision of the Attorney General had crucial functions for the police – whatever his motives might have been.

What were the results of this grand scale police initiative and investigation? Half a year passed, with, incidentally, further public debate. In june, 1987 at a large press conference, the state Attorney in charge and representatives of the Oslo police presented the results: Nothing at all. It was admitted that one victim had once been pulled by the hair. Excepting that particular case, no charges were made against any of the Bergen police officers, and the police man who was indicted for having pulled a victim by the hair was later acquitted by the court. No criticism of the police was presented. A number of victims and witnesses had presumably withdrawn their statements (I shall return later to the actual numbers involved), or moderated them. Those who had upheld their statements had not presented material which convinced the police that any crimes had been committed.

From the point of view of the police, the presentation functioned very well in the mass media. As I have said, the question of police honour or reputation, to use their words, or legitimacy, to use the sociological word, and by now come to a critical point in the public sphere. The "puncturing effect" which might have followed from the investigative committee a few years earlier, came now instead – after a police investigation. In large head lines the major newspapers presented what they consider "the facts": *No criminal indictment means no police violence.* This now in a sense became public opinion. The large conservative Bergen newspapers carried the head line "The Violence Researchers 'Executed'", and the smaller social-democratic paper in Bergen stated "Nordhus, Vogt and Bratholm: 'Publicly Executed'".

In the wake of this, the question of honour has been further pressed by the police: On june 25, 1987 the Head of the Police in Bergen said to the large conservative Bergen newspapers: "It is up to the Ministry of Justice to evaluate whether a public criminal case should be launched against Bratholm, Nordhus and Vogt for conciously attempting to undermine the Bergen Police Headquarters... He believes that the Ministry may employ sec. 130 of the Criminal Code". Sec. 130 of the Norwegian Criminal Code criminalizes those who in spite of their knowledge to the contrary publicly attribute acts to state powers or other public authorities, which they have not committed, or provide a misleading presentation of the circumstances under which, or the way in which, they have acted. The state Attorney responsible for the police investigation said to the same newspaper that "We have not decoded the question of public indictment of Anders Bratholm, Gunnar Nordhus and Edvard Vogt". These are only two examples of threats of criminalization being used to characterize the researchers, not the police, as the guilty party. The Norwegian Police Association has engaged a well-known attorney to evaluate libel actions against the researchers, and the researchers have been reported to the police (by police officers) for false charges and are currently under investigation for this.

As a climax to these events up to now, one of the researchers, Gunnar Nordhus, was arrested under dramatic circumstances on board the Oslo-Bergen plane, and kept over night in prison. You will remember the case of the match box containing cannabis, which I mentioned a minute ago. A witness appeared who said he had in fact *seen* the police investigate Gunnar Nordhus' car during the subsequent police control, a police control which the police claimed had not occured. Now this witness mysteriously – because of the pressure? – withdrew his testimony. (The witness was later, in April 1988, found guilty of false testimony by the Bergen City Court, and sentenced to 21 days conditional imprisonment and a fine of 5000 Norwegian crowns – 1366 DM. The guilty verdict and sentence was given despite the fact that he a few weeks before the trial had stated to a Norwegian author that his first testimony had been correct, and that he had withdrawn it because of pressure. The statement was taped by the author in question.) Mr. Nordhus – still a law student not protected by any academic titles – was arrested and charged as a contributory to a false witness statement! He was subject to very intensiv interrogation and at the time of writing the case is still being investigated by the police.

I take it you by now understand why I have called this paper "On Dangerous Research". So much of what we researchers do is not dangerous, while these men have engaged in something which is extremely dangerous, and have elicited responses from the Norwegian state which are reminiscent of conditions in countries with very different political systems. The arrest of Gunnar Nordhus is, as far as I know, the first arrest of a social researcher in Norway undertaken because of the research. Before I wind up by presenting some interpretations and conclusions, let me add the following – which adds to the feeling that this is dangerous research:

- A number of victims/witnesses have been severely harassed during the Oslo police investigation of the Bergen police. Some of the witnesses are articulate people who have given concrete evidence concerning this, among others the former wife of Gunnar Nordhus, a senior lecturer in psychology at the University Bergen, who was very severely harassed. About 30 witnesses have to a greater or lesser degree complained about the way in which they were interrogated, and many of them have felt the situation as threatening and that they were pressed to give a particular kind of statement. Many have clearly felt threatened by the fact that they are regular clients of the police, and many therefore meet the police again later. And the threat is real: About 40 witnesses/victims are currently under police investigation for false witness statements. A special task force has been established to conduct this investigation. What began as a study of the police has ended as an investigation of the victims and the researchers.
- Only 12 % of the witnesses fully renounced their statements. A larger number softened their statements, but maintained the core point that infringements had taken place. The fact that only 12 % actually renounced their original statements was, interestingly, not mentioned at the police press conference. The percentage is small when seen in the context of the police methods which were used.
- A portion of the material presented by the researchers was kept which were used.
- Many previous Bergen police officers have stated that police violence takes place, but their statements are considered irrelevant by the police. Present officers who are critical do not dare to say anything. Two radio reporters from the Norwegian Broadcasting Company have been investigated by the police for libel against a state attorney in Bergen, in connection with their criticism of his handling of some cases of police violence. The case was dropped only after a long-drawn process.

The state Attorney of Bergen has initiated investigations of Nordhus/Vogt and representatives of Anmesty International, London, in connection with a visit in Bergen. Amnesty wished to interview some of the police violence witnesses, and in order to facilitate the interviewing, the two researchers found lodgings for the witnesses in various hotels in Bergen. In a newspaper article the state Attorney claimed that Amnesty had interviewed witnesses who were intoxicated, also insinuating that witnesses had been bribed. The head of Amnesty's European section, who was one of the two Amnesty representative conducting the interviews, said that she had never experienced anything similar in any other country where she had conducted investigations. Countries such as Turkey and Iran were mentioned as examples. Amnesty demanded an official excuse from the state Attorney. At the time of writing, no excuse has been produced. These are only a few aspects of the large scale police investigation which are important to keep in mind. I do not think it is an overstatement to say that the investigation has in fact been a major cover-up action. Before investigation, Anders Bratholm used the term "disinformation" to characterize the way in which the police handled criticism for police violence. By "disinformation" he meant concious or negligent spreading of erroneous information (Bratholm, 1986, pp. 255-259). The term is equally applicable for the large scale police investigation.

3. Some Conclusions

By way of conclusion, I want to emphasize a few salient features.

3.1 Legalization

The first thing which I wish to emphasize, is the dangers inherent in what may be called the "legalization" of political conflicts involving the state as one major party. By "legalization" I mean the employment of state organized legal institutions such as the police, the courts etc. to evaluate the conflict. Legalization implies not only that a state branch investigates and evaluates the state, which is bad enough. It also implies that the conflict is transformed into something else, into a legal issue which involves different criteria and is on a different level, than the original conflict.

The basic point became very apparent in the Norwegian police case. When the police finally was called in to investigate the issue, the issue was transformed – in addition to the fact that police power was used during interrogations.

In a research project the major tendencies, or trends, in the material are the important points. The total configuration of facts is the crux of the matter; individual cases are far less important.

In a police investigation, on the other hand,

- cases prescribed by time limitations are taken out,
- cases with no identifiable performer are taken out (this of course happens when the performer simply is unknown, but also when members of a given group protect each other so that the individual who has committed the illegal act is unidentifiable),
- the benefit of the doubt is given to the performer (in cases of police violence to an extreme degree),
- the police are the "interpreters" of reality, making "truth" systematically skewed in the direction of a police understanding of it.

These are only some of the criteria making a police investigation different from a research investigation, and making a police investigation a poor instrument of finding truth in a sociological sense.

My point can be refrased as follows: Even under the best of circumstances, without police brutality etc. – which are extremely unlikely conditions – police investigation constitutes a transformation of the issue.

Frequently, legalization through criminalization and police investigation is demanded by those who criticize state affairs. It is as if we, as critics, do not understand and see the full important of what we are criticizing, thus calling on page 2 upon the control institution whose limitations as a truth finding instrument we have criticized on page 1. To some extent we are also "sluiced" into this channel because there are so few other options and because the "system" therefore challenges us to demand criminalization and police investigation, a challenge which rings bells and demands an "answer" in the public sphere, the mass media. In any case, it is an unfortunate road.

In the Norwegian police case described here, the legalization through police intervention of the issue in question was embarked on by the state itself, including the police.

But legalization, the transformation of the political conflict into a legal issue involving a different set of criteria, does not stop with criminalization and police investigation. *If* the quieting function of this legalizing step for some reason does not occur, there is still another step: the courts. In the courts, the transformation is carried even further. Several court cases involving police violence testify to this: No guilt on the part of the police. Again, the "not guilty" verdict is taken to mean that no violence has taken place. Other cases, not involving the police as such, testify to the same (Mathiesen, 1983).

Generally, then: Various state institutions may be used incessantly, depending on what is necessary and expedient.

3.2 Prevention

The process of legalization has a further importance in our context here.

As I said at the outset, the notion of prevention of crime is willingly used – by state authorities – in relation to traditional crime. It is increasingly a popular notion, and the dangers of the concept are to a large extent ignored. Where it might be appropriate – in relation to state crime – the concept is viewed differently, and if "preventive" measures are instituted by critics, major defensive weapons are being used in the state's counter attack. Legalization is one of the most important weapons against measures intended to prevent state crime. Legalization in this context implies a narrowing of the issue which is highly functional from the point of view of the state.

In the concrete case described earlier, the narrowing of the issue also involves a dangerous attack on the freedom of expression and freedom of research in Norway. Who will now dare to criticize police infringements and violence?

3.3. The Oslo Development

I wish to end, however, on a more optimistic note.
Firstly, the debate is not over. A number of us are engaged in it, and there is an increasing grassroot's understanding of the actual existence of police violence.
Secondly, and as a further substantiation of this understanding, let me briefly recapitulate some recent developments in Oslo, the capital city of Norway.

During the past year we have seen some demonstrations in Oslo against Norway's NATO politics, concretely demonstrations against a visit of the British Prime Minister Thatcher and of the then US Defence Minister Weinberger. During the latter demonstration, brutality on a wide scale on the part of the Oslo police was documented concretely. During a climax in may of this year, the police entered a restaurant – with helmets, batons and dogs – to arrest a particular demonstrator, and in the course of the arrest they beat a number of people, including old ladies who were drinking their afternoon tea. The restaurant happened to be a hang out of attorneys and journalists, some of whom also were attacked, and the police action received widespread and very negative press coverage. This is in itself interesting: the police "landed", so to speak, in the middle of the bourgeois public sphere, and the press reacted accordingly. Had they "landed" elsewhere, for example, in the Cafe for Unemployed People, the reactions would probably have been close to nil.

In any case, a number of people were arrested and interrogated, and a number of fines were imposed. The press again reacted negatively, and a demonstration took place through the streets of Oslo in which 7-10.000 people participate – a very large number by Oslo standards today. The demonstration, actually a march, was illegal (this time, the police begged the demonstrators to ask for permission, but the organizers refused to ask for it), and punkers and other demonstrators on motorcycles directed the traffic. A number of demonstrators brought charges against the police, and a new police investigation of police brutality – headed by the police chief of a neighboring district – was conducted. The police once again found no one guilty of police violence, though in this case they did criticize their colleagues, largely for bad planning. This time, however, the weapon of legalization through police investigation was clearly less effective: When repeated, and especially when repeated in the context of a situation where attorneys, journalists and old ladies had seen what happened, its edge was blunted. The ensuing press conference of the police several months later did not appear to have the same neutralizing effect in the public sphere, although it did receive more media attention than a subsequent press conference conducted by the demonstrators.

So, the struggle goes on, especially the struggle over the criteria and definition of thruth in the matter of police violence as a form of state crime. And, again: International attention to, and support of, a struggle as the one taking place with a background in the Bergen case, is highly important.

References

Bratholm, A. (1986): Politivold – omfang, årsaker, forebyggelse (Police Violence – Extent, Causes, Prevention, A Study in Disinformation), Oslo

Bratholm, A. (1987) (Ed.): Politiovergrep og personforfølgelse (Police Transgressions and Persecution of Individuals), Oslo

Mathiesen, T. (1983): "Civil Disobdience at 70° North". In: Contemporary Crises

Nordhus, G. & Vogt, E. (1981): Volden og dens ofre (Violence and Its Victims), Oslo

Politivoldrapporten. Rapport om politivold fra utvalget til å undersøke forekomsten og arten av politivold m.v., Oslo 1982, oppnevnt av Justisdepartementet 27. oktober 1981 (The Police Violence Report. Report on Police Violence from the Committee to Investigate the Incidence and Types of Police Violence Etc., Oslo 1982, appointed by the Ministry of Justice October 27, 1981)

Bei Fragen zur Produktsicherheit wenden Sie sich bitte an:
If you have any questions regarding product safety,
please contact:

Walter de Gruyter GmbH
Genthiner Straße 13
10785 Berlin
productsafety@degruyterbrill.com